One Big Ha

RICK DETORIE

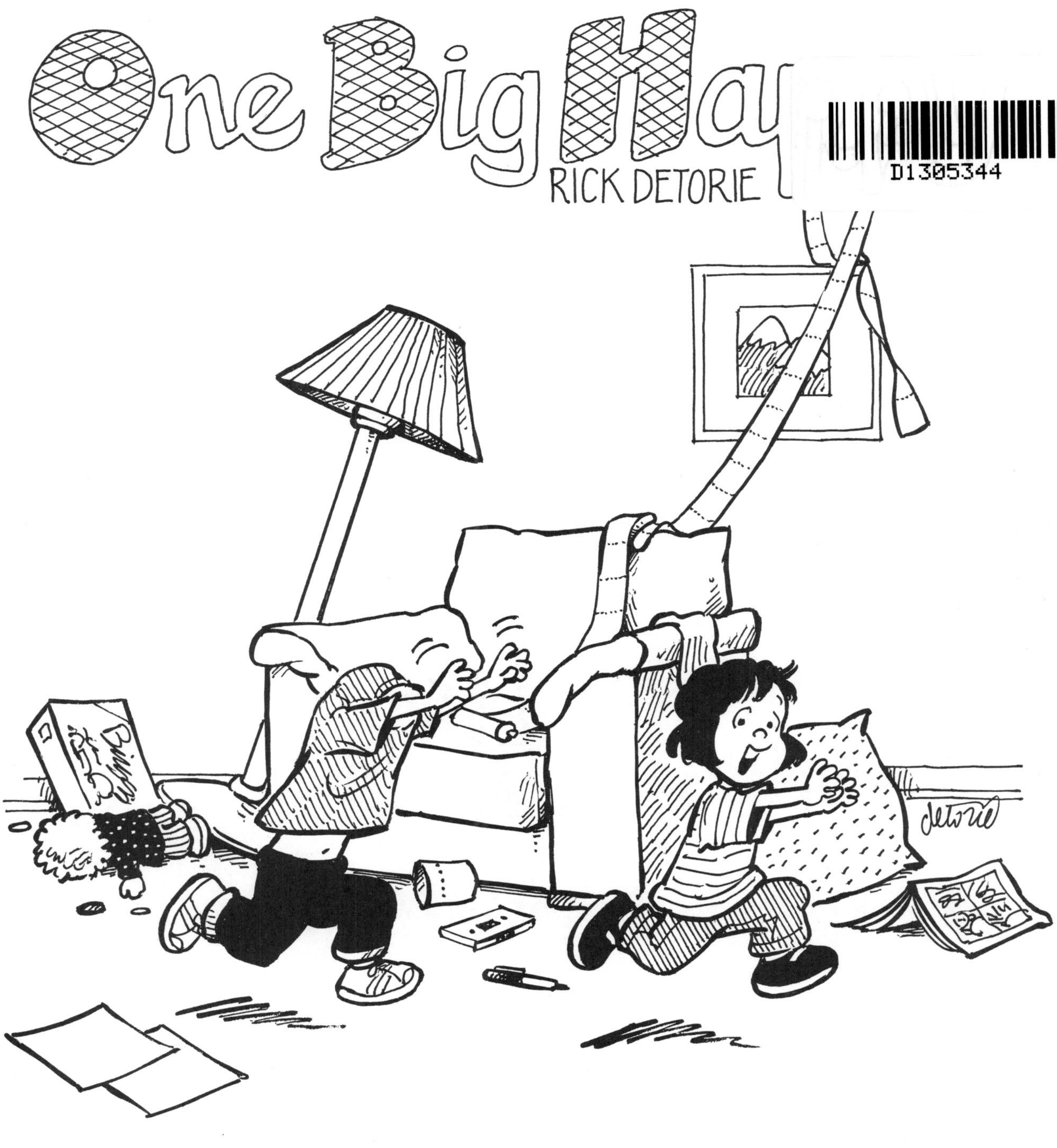
detorie

For Hannah,
Matthew, Jessica,
Tricia, and
Little Lilly

One Big Happy

NONE OF THIS FUN IS MY FAULT!

Rick Detorie

NANTIER · BEALL · MINOUSTCHINE
Publishing inc.
new york

Also Available:
One Big Happy: "Should I Spit On Him?", $9.95
Son of Drabble: $9.95
Drabble: "MallCops, Ducks, & Fenderheads", $9.95
(Add $3 P&H 1st item, $1 each addt'l)

NBM has over 150 graphic novels available
Please write for a free color catalog to:
NBM -Dept. S
185 Madison Ave. Ste. 1504
New York, N.Y. 10016

ISBN 1-56163-217-1
©1998 Creators Syndicate
Printed in Canada

5   4   3   2   1

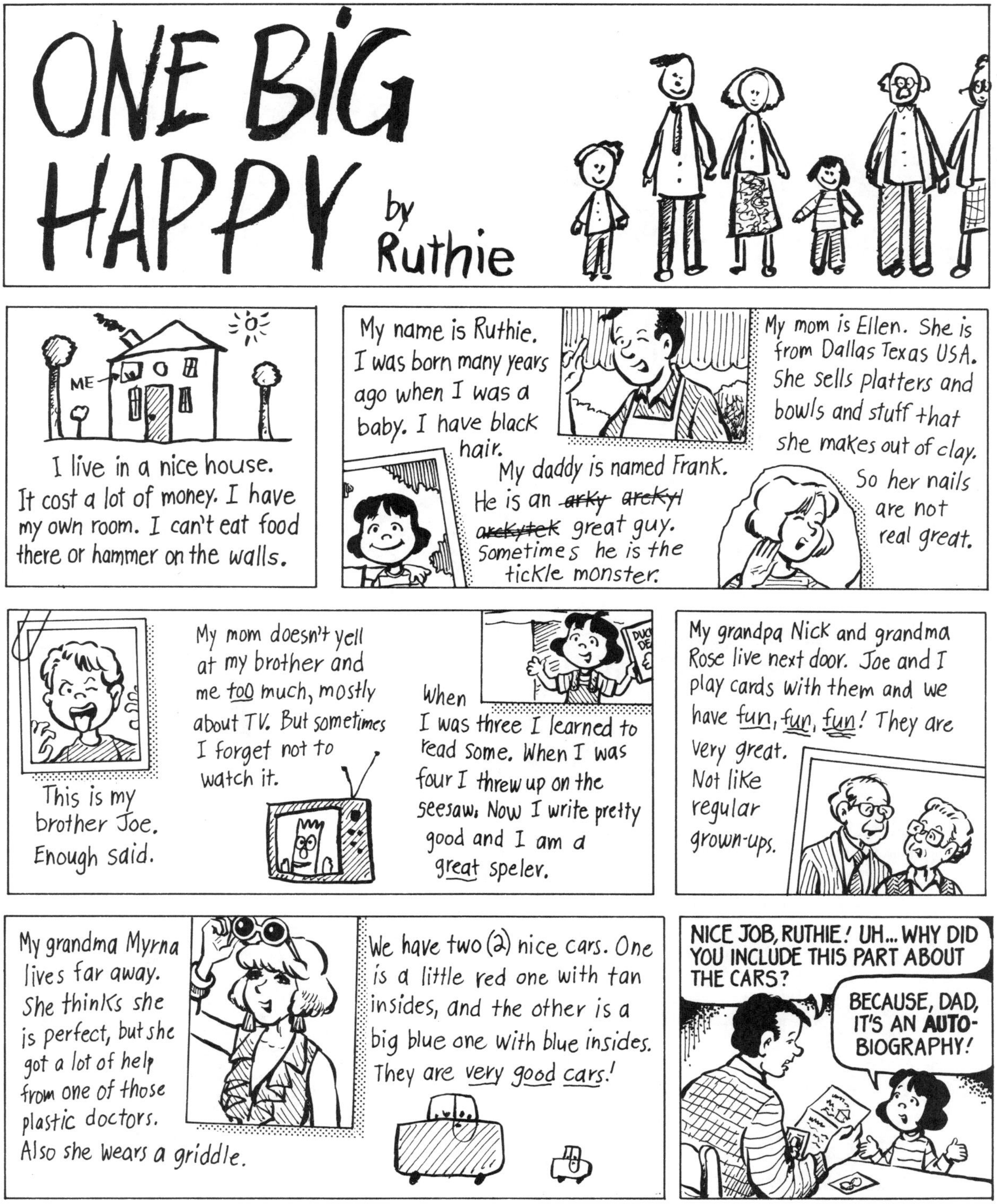
ONE BIG HAPPY by Ruthie
ME
I live in a nice house. It cost a lot of money. I have my own room. I can't eat food there or hammer on the walls.
My name is Ruthie. I was born many years ago when I was a baby. I have black hair.
My daddy is named Frank. He is an ~~arky~~ ~~arekyl~~ ~~arekytek~~ great guy. Sometimes he is the tickle monster.
My mom is Ellen. She is from Dallas Texas USA. She sells platters and bowls and stuff that she makes out of clay. So her nails are not real great.
This is my brother Joe. Enough said.
My mom doesn't yell at my brother and me too much, mostly about TV. But sometimes I forget not to watch it.
When I was three I learned to read some. When I was four I threw up on the seesaw. Now I write pretty good and I am a great speler.
My grandpa Nick and grandma Rose live next door. Joe and I play cards with them and we have fun, fun, fun! They are very great. Not like regular grown-ups.
My grandma Myrna lives far away. She thinks she is perfect, but she got a lot of help from one of those plastic doctors. Also she wears a griddle.
We have two (2) nice cars. One is a little red one with tan insides, and the other is a big blue one with blue insides. They are very good cars!
NICE JOB, RUTHIE! UH... WHY DID YOU INCLUDE THIS PART ABOUT THE CARS?
BECAUSE, DAD, IT'S AN AUTO-BIOGRAPHY!

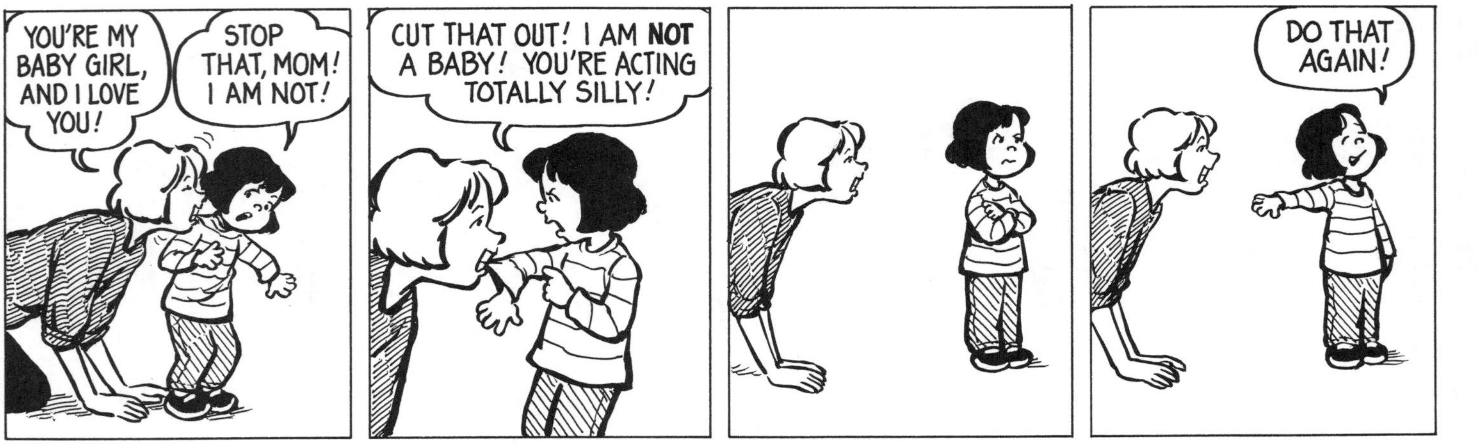
YOU'RE MY BABY GIRL, AND I LOVE YOU!
STOP THAT, MOM! I AM NOT!
CUT THAT OUT! I AM **NOT** A BABY! YOU'RE ACTING TOTALLY SILLY!
DO THAT AGAIN!

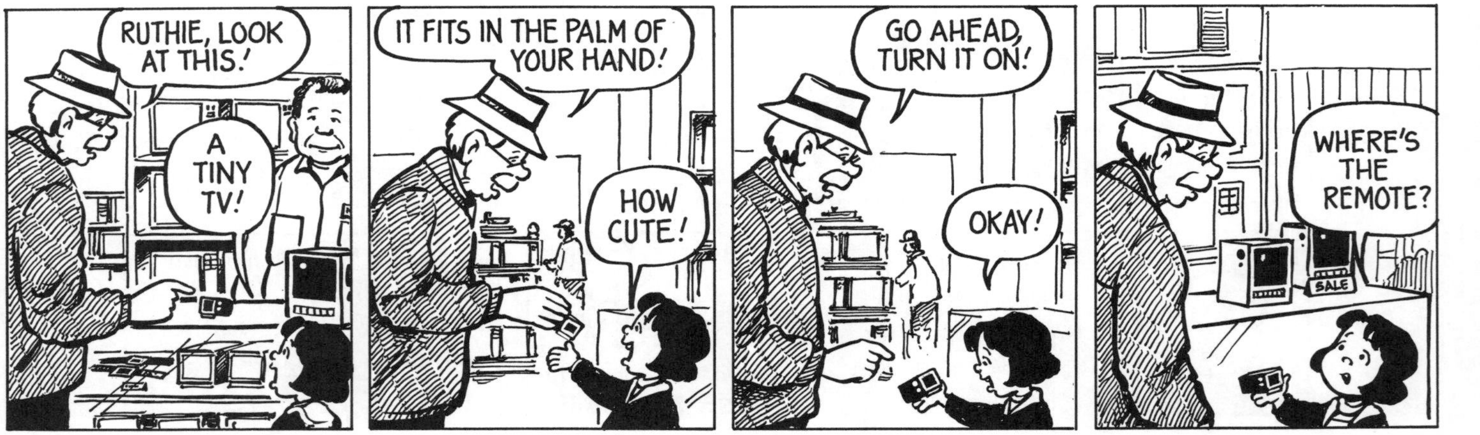
RUTHIE, LOOK AT THIS!
A TINY TV!
IT FITS IN THE PALM OF YOUR HAND!
HOW CUTE!
GO AHEAD, TURN IT ON!
OKAY!
WHERE'S THE REMOTE?
SALE

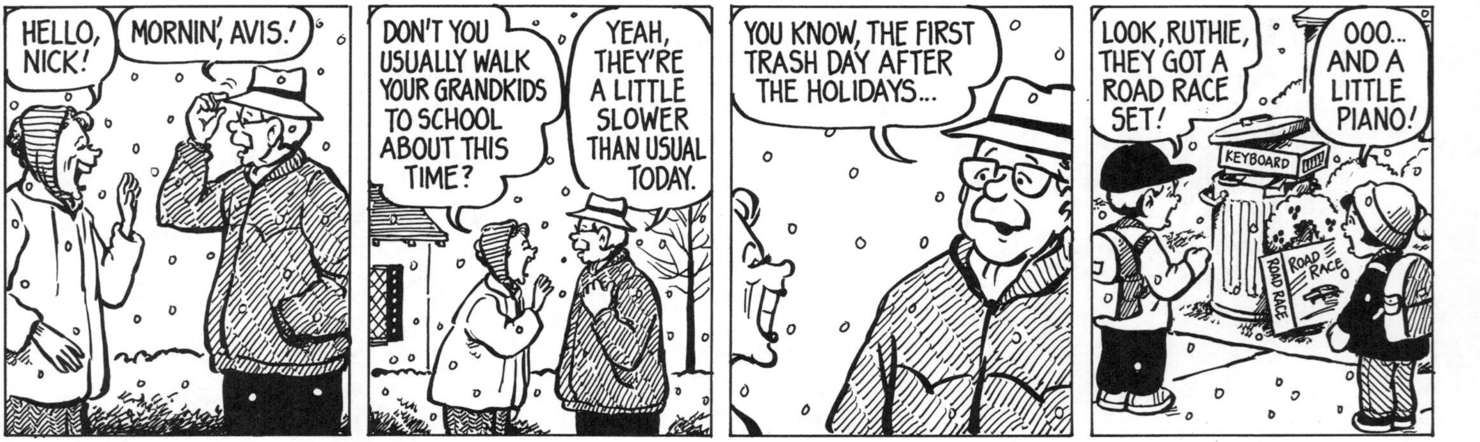
HELLO, NICK!
MORNIN', AVIS!
DON'T YOU USUALLY WALK YOUR GRANDKIDS TO SCHOOL ABOUT THIS TIME?
YEAH, THEY'RE A LITTLE SLOWER THAN USUAL TODAY.
YOU KNOW, THE FIRST TRASH DAY AFTER THE HOLIDAYS...
LOOK, RUTHIE, THEY GOT A ROAD RACE SET!
OOO... AND A LITTLE PIANO!
KEYBOARD
ROAD RACE
ROAD RACE

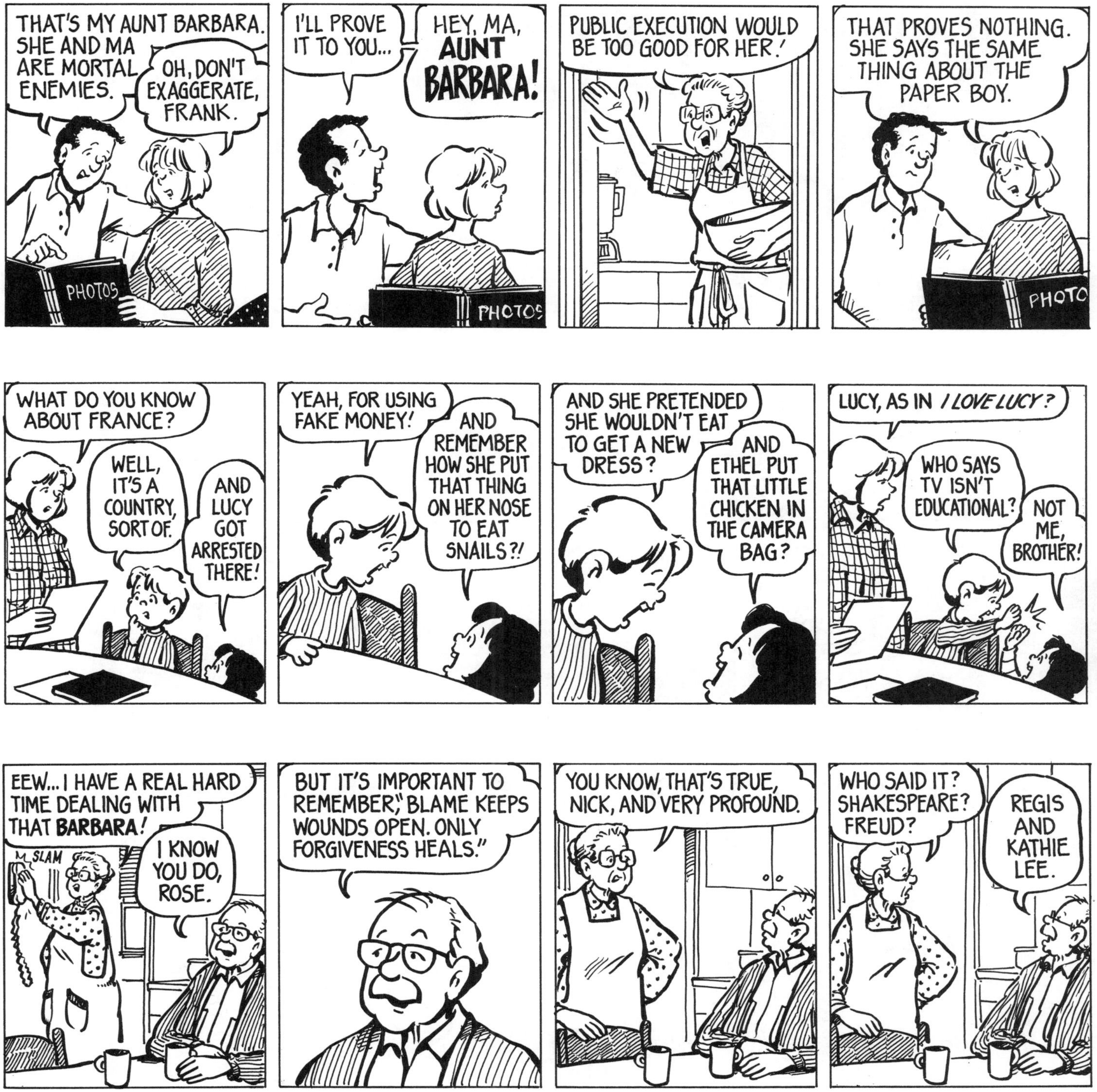
THAT'S MY AUNT BARBARA. SHE AND MA ARE MORTAL ENEMIES.
OH, DON'T EXAGGERATE, FRANK.
PHOTOS
I'LL PROVE IT TO YOU...
HEY, MA, AUNT BARBARA!
PHOTOS
PUBLIC EXECUTION WOULD BE TOO GOOD FOR HER!
THAT PROVES NOTHING. SHE SAYS THE SAME THING ABOUT THE PAPER BOY.
PHOTO
WHAT DO YOU KNOW ABOUT FRANCE?
WELL, IT'S A COUNTRY, SORT OF.
AND LUCY GOT ARRESTED THERE!
YEAH, FOR USING FAKE MONEY!
AND REMEMBER HOW SHE PUT THAT THING ON HER NOSE TO EAT SNAILS?!
AND SHE PRETENDED SHE WOULDN'T EAT TO GET A NEW DRESS?
AND ETHEL PUT THAT LITTLE CHICKEN IN THE CAMERA BAG?
LUCY, AS IN *I LOVE LUCY*?
WHO SAYS TV ISN'T EDUCATIONAL?
NOT ME, BROTHER!
EEW... I HAVE A REAL HARD TIME DEALING WITH THAT BARBARA!
SLAM
I KNOW YOU DO, ROSE.
BUT IT'S IMPORTANT TO REMEMBER, "BLAME KEEPS WOUNDS OPEN. ONLY FORGIVENESS HEALS."
YOU KNOW, THAT'S TRUE, NICK, AND VERY PROFOUND.
WHO SAID IT? SHAKESPEARE? FREUD?
REGIS AND KATHIE LEE.

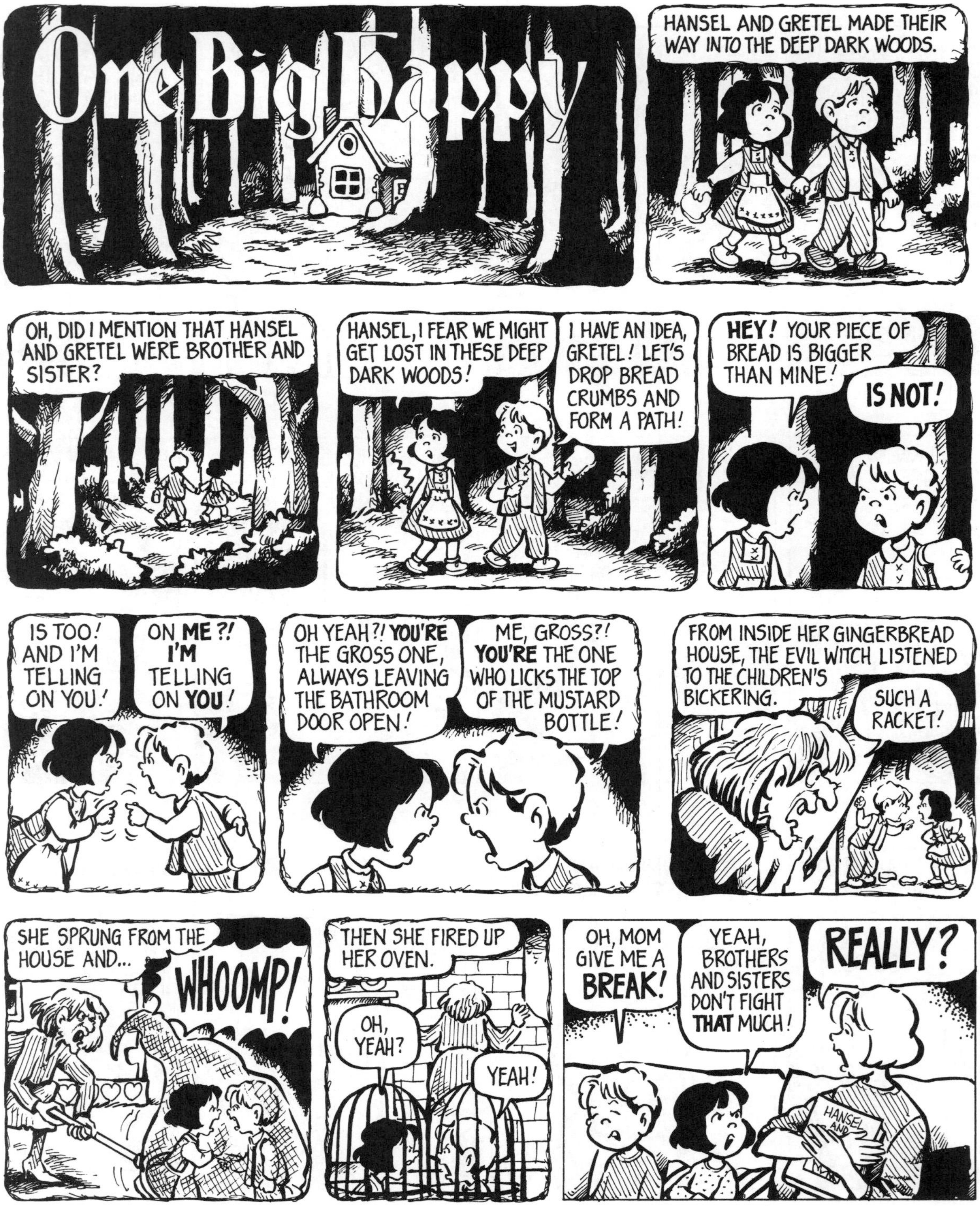
One Big Happy
HANSEL AND GRETEL MADE THEIR WAY INTO THE DEEP DARK WOODS.
OH, DID I MENTION THAT HANSEL AND GRETEL WERE BROTHER AND SISTER?
HANSEL, I FEAR WE MIGHT GET LOST IN THESE DEEP DARK WOODS!
I HAVE AN IDEA, GRETEL! LET'S DROP BREAD CRUMBS AND FORM A PATH!
HEY! YOUR PIECE OF BREAD IS BIGGER THAN MINE!
IS NOT!
IS TOO! AND I'M TELLING ON YOU!
ON ME?! I'M TELLING ON YOU!
OH YEAH?! YOU'RE THE GROSS ONE, ALWAYS LEAVING THE BATHROOM DOOR OPEN!
ME, GROSS?! YOU'RE THE ONE WHO LICKS THE TOP OF THE MUSTARD BOTTLE!
FROM INSIDE HER GINGERBREAD HOUSE, THE EVIL WITCH LISTENED TO THE CHILDREN'S BICKERING.
SUCH A RACKET!
SHE SPRUNG FROM THE HOUSE AND...
WHOOMP!
THEN SHE FIRED UP HER OVEN.
OH, YEAH?
YEAH!
OH, MOM GIVE ME A BREAK!
YEAH, BROTHERS AND SISTERS DON'T FIGHT THAT MUCH!
REALLY?
HANSEL AND

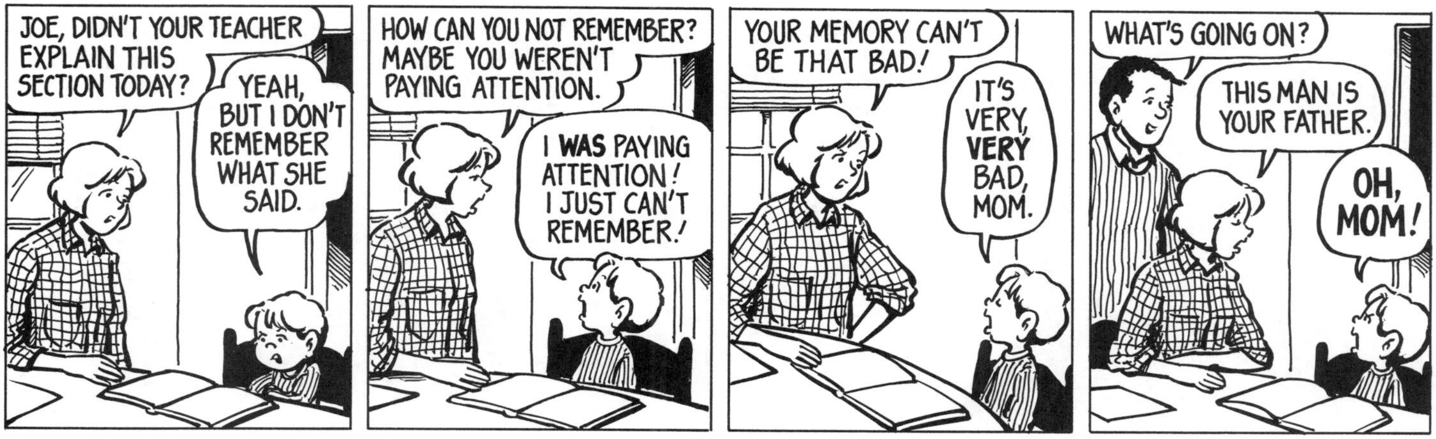
JOE, DIDN'T YOUR TEACHER EXPLAIN THIS SECTION TODAY?
YEAH, BUT I DON'T REMEMBER WHAT SHE SAID.
HOW CAN YOU NOT REMEMBER? MAYBE YOU WEREN'T PAYING ATTENTION.
I **WAS** PAYING ATTENTION! I JUST CAN'T REMEMBER!
YOUR MEMORY CAN'T BE THAT BAD!
IT'S VERY, **VERY** BAD, MOM.
WHAT'S GOING ON?
THIS MAN IS YOUR FATHER.
OH, MOM!

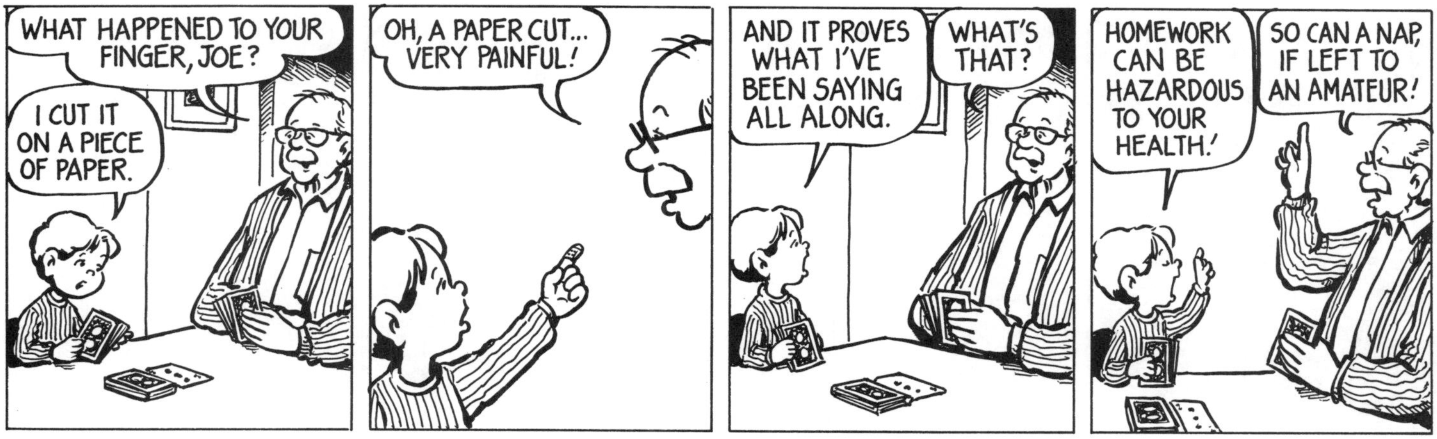
WHAT HAPPENED TO YOUR FINGER, JOE?
I CUT IT ON A PIECE OF PAPER.
OH, A PAPER CUT... VERY PAINFUL!
AND IT PROVES WHAT I'VE BEEN SAYING ALL ALONG.
WHAT'S THAT?
HOMEWORK CAN BE HAZARDOUS TO YOUR HEALTH!
SO CAN A NAP, IF LEFT TO AN AMATEUR!

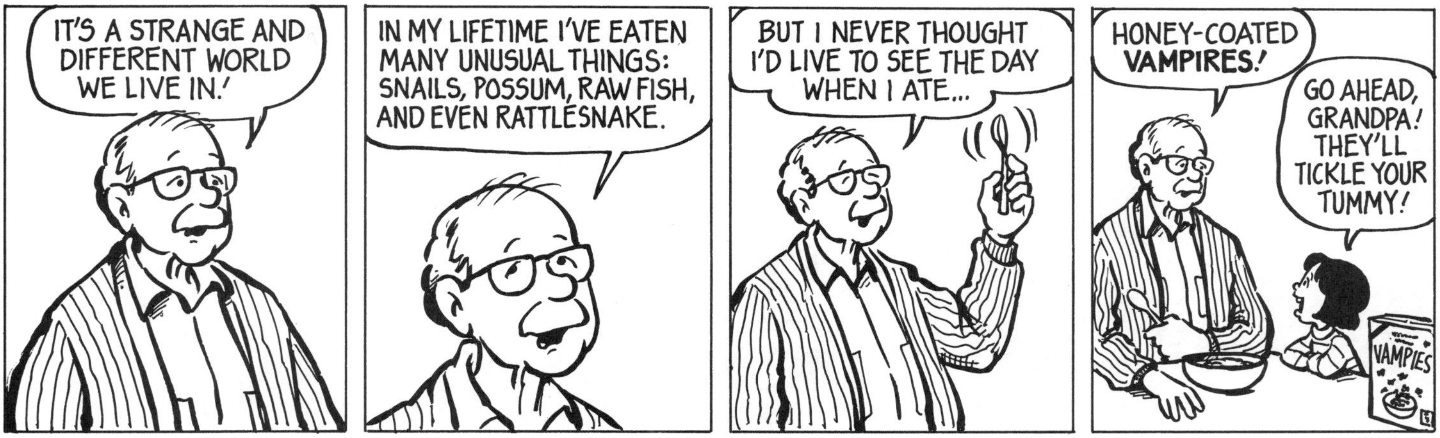
IT'S A STRANGE AND DIFFERENT WORLD WE LIVE IN!
IN MY LIFETIME I'VE EATEN MANY UNUSUAL THINGS: SNAILS, POSSUM, RAW FISH, AND EVEN RATTLESNAKE.
BUT I NEVER THOUGHT I'D LIVE TO SEE THE DAY WHEN I ATE...
HONEY-COATED **VAMPIRES!**
GO AHEAD, GRANDPA! THEY'LL TICKLE YOUR TUMMY!
VAMPIES

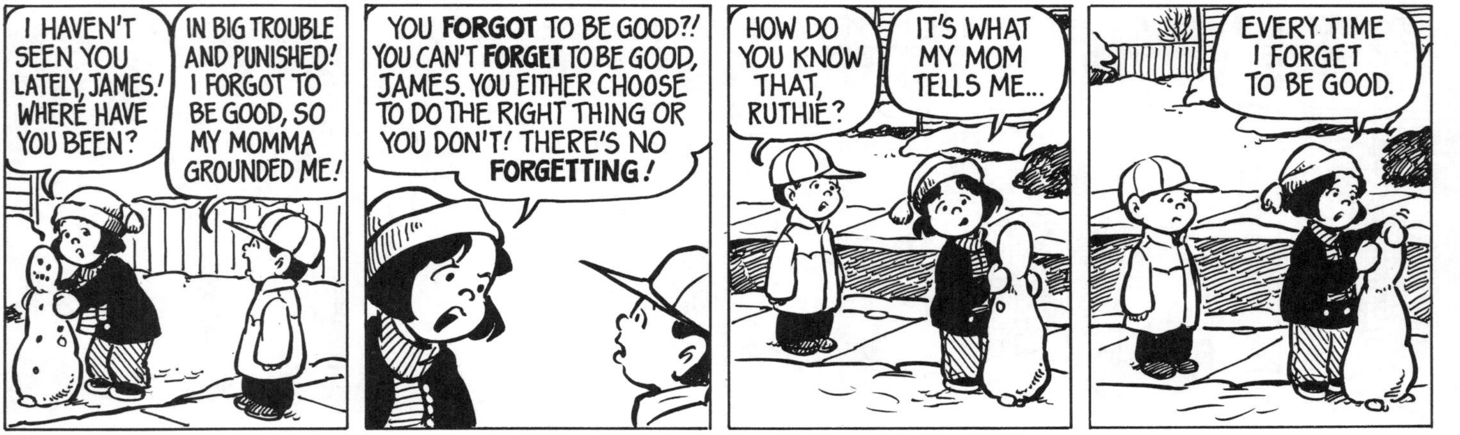
I HAVEN'T SEEN YOU LATELY, JAMES! WHERE HAVE YOU BEEN?
IN BIG TROUBLE AND PUNISHED! I FORGOT TO BE GOOD, SO MY MOMMA GROUNDED ME!
YOU FORGOT TO BE GOOD?! YOU CAN'T FORGET TO BE GOOD, JAMES. YOU EITHER CHOOSE TO DO THE RIGHT THING OR YOU DON'T! THERE'S NO FORGETTING!
HOW DO YOU KNOW THAT, RUTHIE?
IT'S WHAT MY MOM TELLS ME...
EVERY TIME I FORGET TO BE GOOD.

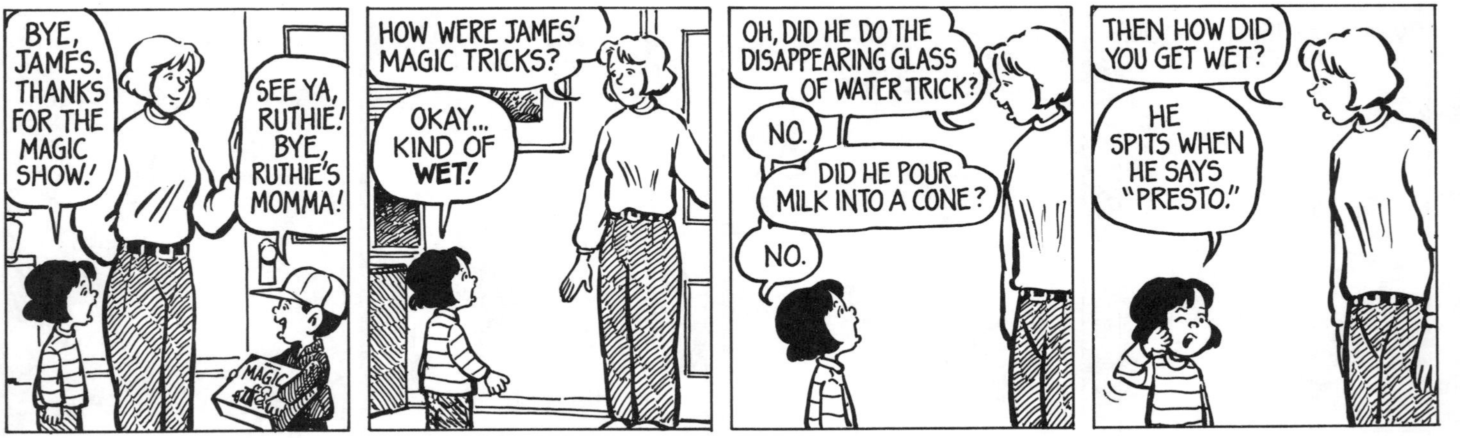
BYE, JAMES. THANKS FOR THE MAGIC SHOW!
SEE YA, RUTHIE! BYE, RUTHIE'S MOMMA!
MAGIC
HOW WERE JAMES' MAGIC TRICKS?
OKAY... KIND OF WET!
OH, DID HE DO THE DISAPPEARING GLASS OF WATER TRICK?
NO.
DID HE POUR MILK INTO A CONE?
NO.
THEN HOW DID YOU GET WET?
HE SPITS WHEN HE SAYS "PRESTO."

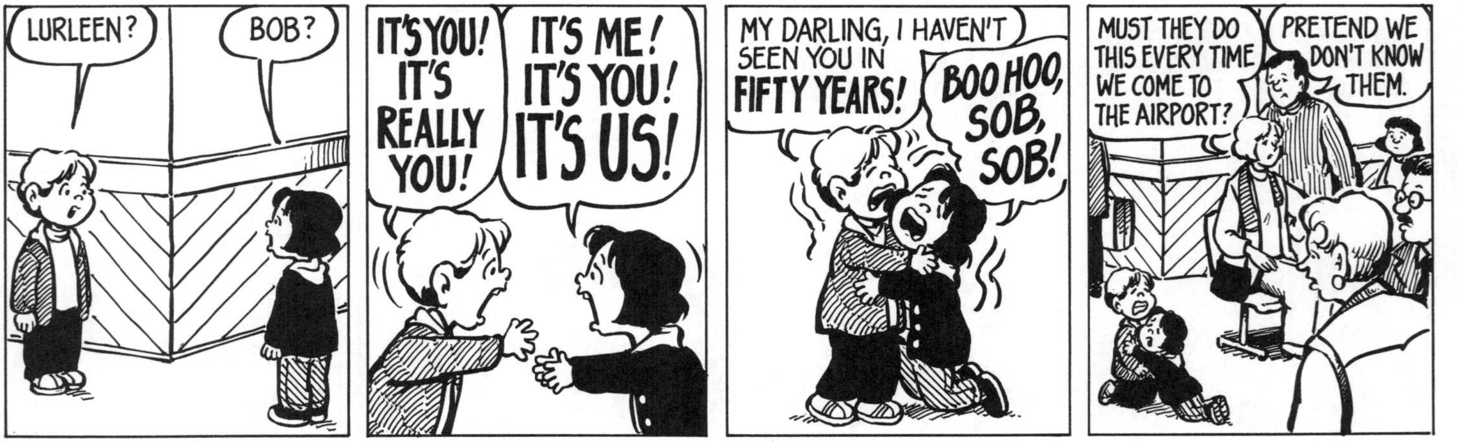
LURLEEN?
BOB?
IT'S YOU! IT'S REALLY YOU!
IT'S ME! IT'S YOU! IT'S US!
MY DARLING, I HAVEN'T SEEN YOU IN FIFTY YEARS!
BOO HOO, SOB, SOB!
MUST THEY DO THIS EVERY TIME WE COME TO THE AIRPORT?
PRETEND WE DON'T KNOW THEM.

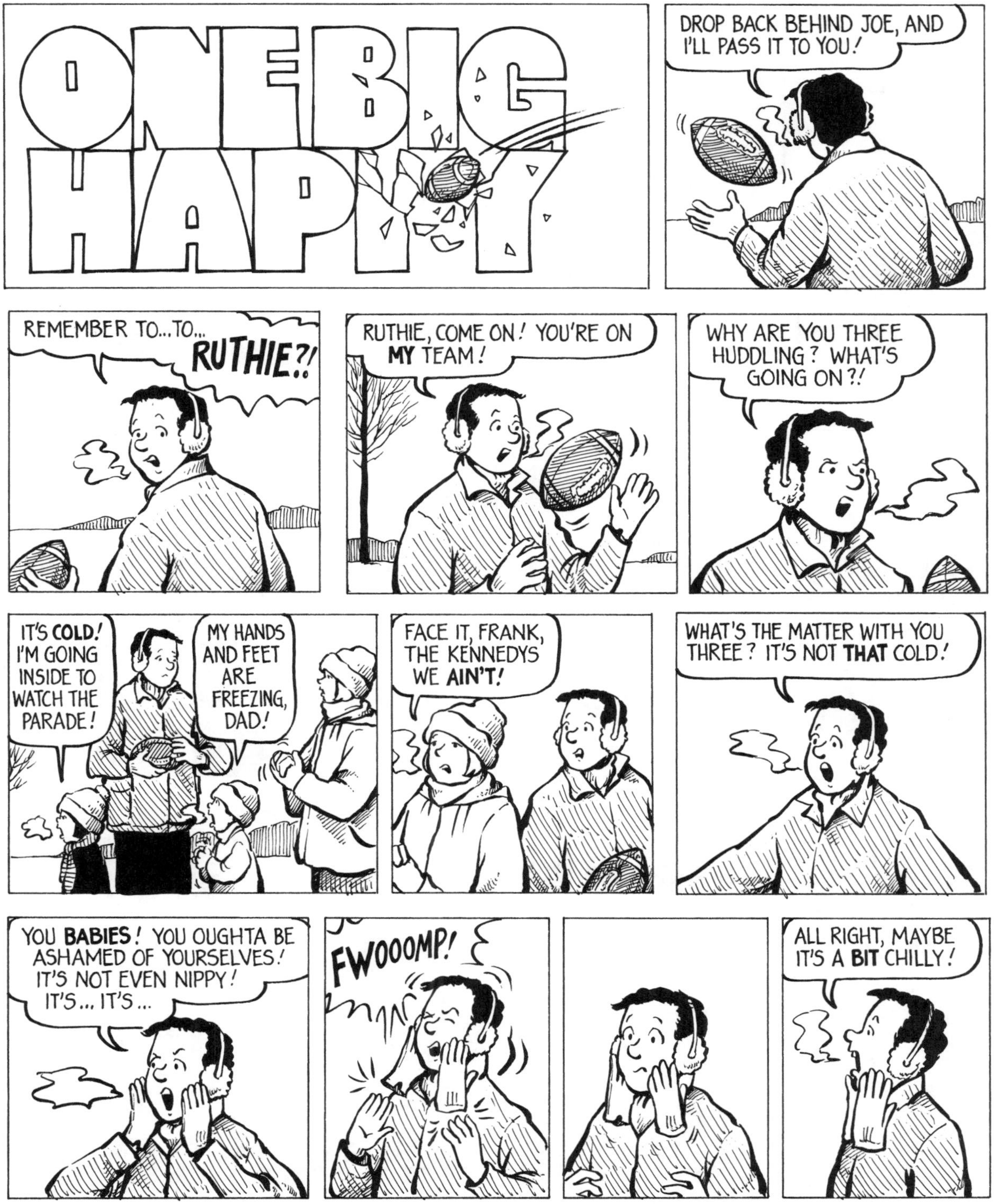
ONE BIG HAPPY
DROP BACK BEHIND JOE, AND I'LL PASS IT TO YOU!
REMEMBER TO...TO... RUTHIE?!
RUTHIE, COME ON! YOU'RE ON MY TEAM!
WHY ARE YOU THREE HUDDLING? WHAT'S GOING ON?!
IT'S COLD! I'M GOING INSIDE TO WATCH THE PARADE!
MY HANDS AND FEET ARE FREEZING, DAD!
FACE IT, FRANK, THE KENNEDYS WE AIN'T!
WHAT'S THE MATTER WITH YOU THREE? IT'S NOT THAT COLD!
YOU BABIES! YOU OUGHTA BE ASHAMED OF YOURSELVES! IT'S NOT EVEN NIPPY! IT'S... IT'S...
FWOOOMP!
ALL RIGHT, MAYBE IT'S A BIT CHILLY!

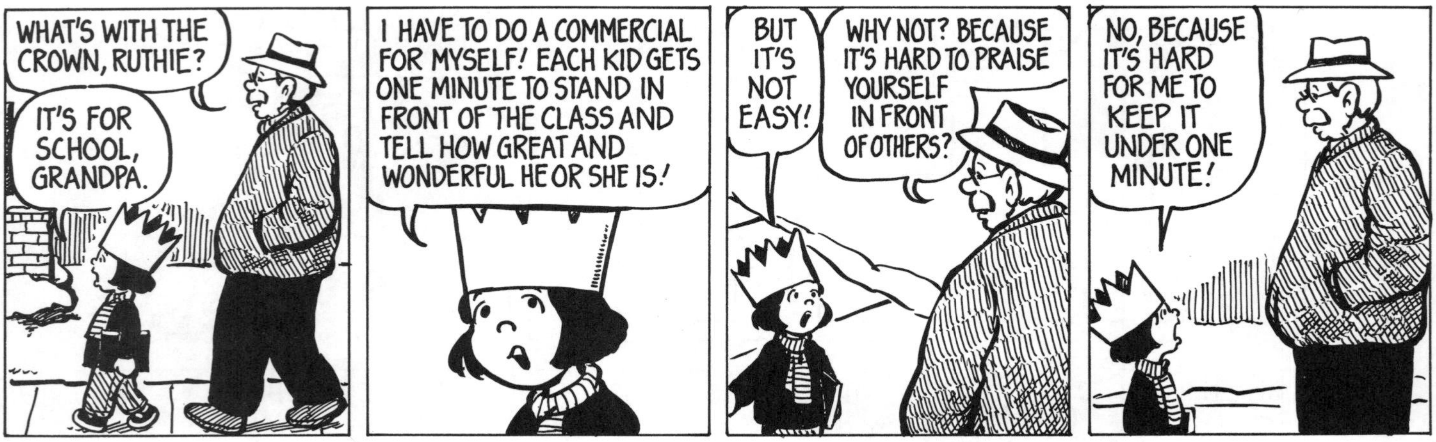
WHAT'S WITH THE CROWN, RUTHIE?
IT'S FOR SCHOOL, GRANDPA.
I HAVE TO DO A COMMERCIAL FOR MYSELF! EACH KID GETS ONE MINUTE TO STAND IN FRONT OF THE CLASS AND TELL HOW GREAT AND WONDERFUL HE OR SHE IS!
BUT IT'S NOT EASY!
WHY NOT? BECAUSE IT'S HARD TO PRAISE YOURSELF IN FRONT OF OTHERS?
NO, BECAUSE IT'S HARD FOR ME TO KEEP IT UNDER ONE MINUTE!

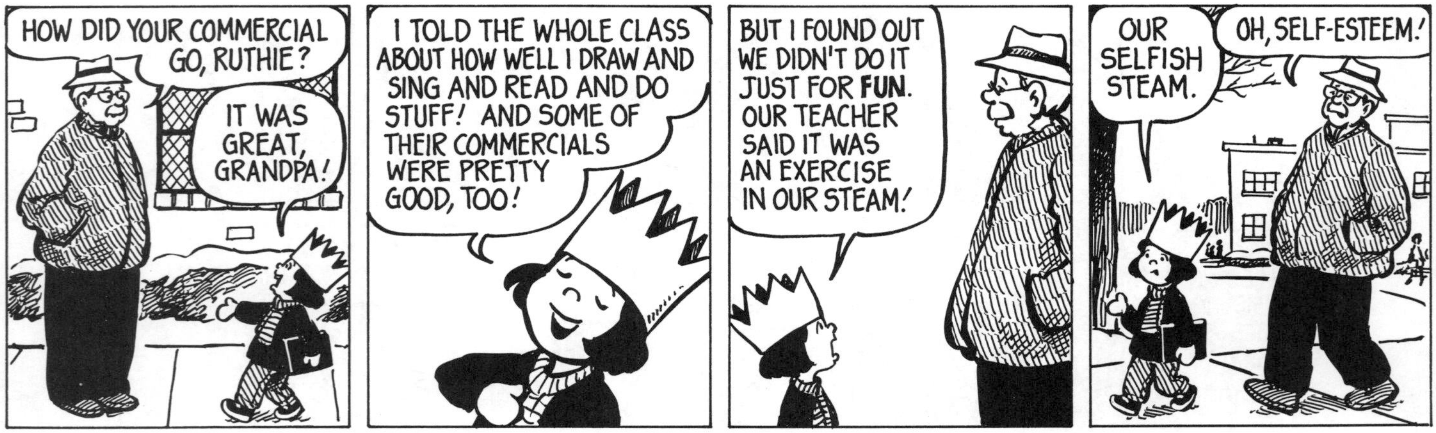
HOW DID YOUR COMMERCIAL GO, RUTHIE?
IT WAS GREAT, GRANDPA!
I TOLD THE WHOLE CLASS ABOUT HOW WELL I DRAW AND SING AND READ AND DO STUFF! AND SOME OF THEIR COMMERCIALS WERE PRETTY GOOD, TOO!
BUT I FOUND OUT WE DIDN'T DO IT JUST FOR **FUN**. OUR TEACHER SAID IT WAS AN EXERCISE IN OUR STEAM!
OUR SELFISH STEAM.
OH, SELF-ESTEEM!

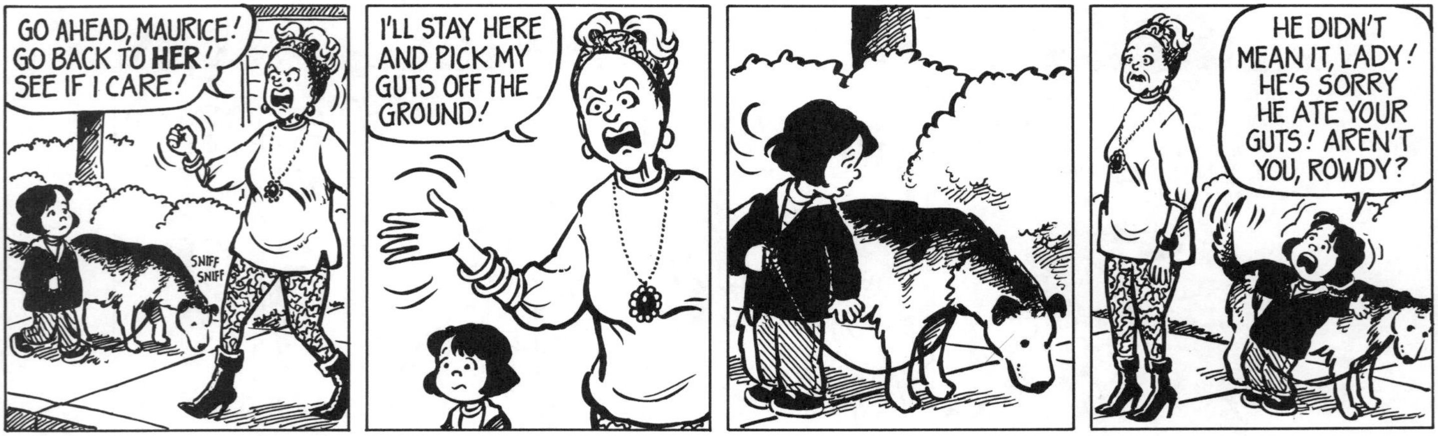
GO AHEAD, MAURICE! GO BACK TO **HER**! SEE IF I CARE!
SNIFF SNIFF
I'LL STAY HERE AND PICK MY GUTS OFF THE GROUND!
HE DIDN'T MEAN IT, LADY! HE'S SORRY HE ATE YOUR GUTS! AREN'T YOU, ROWDY?

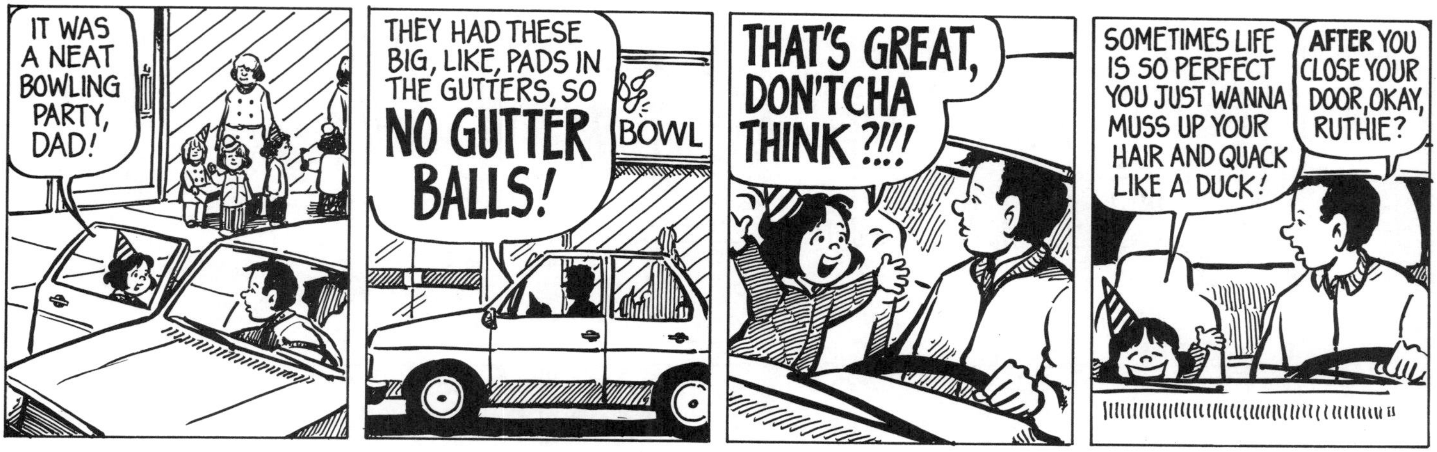
IT WAS A NEAT BOWLING PARTY, DAD!
THEY HAD THESE BIG, LIKE, PADS IN THE GUTTERS, SO NO GUTTER BALLS!
BOWL
THAT'S GREAT, DON'TCHA THINK ?!!!
SOMETIMES LIFE IS SO PERFECT YOU JUST WANNA MUSS UP YOUR HAIR AND QUACK LIKE A DUCK!
AFTER YOU CLOSE YOUR DOOR, OKAY, RUTHIE?

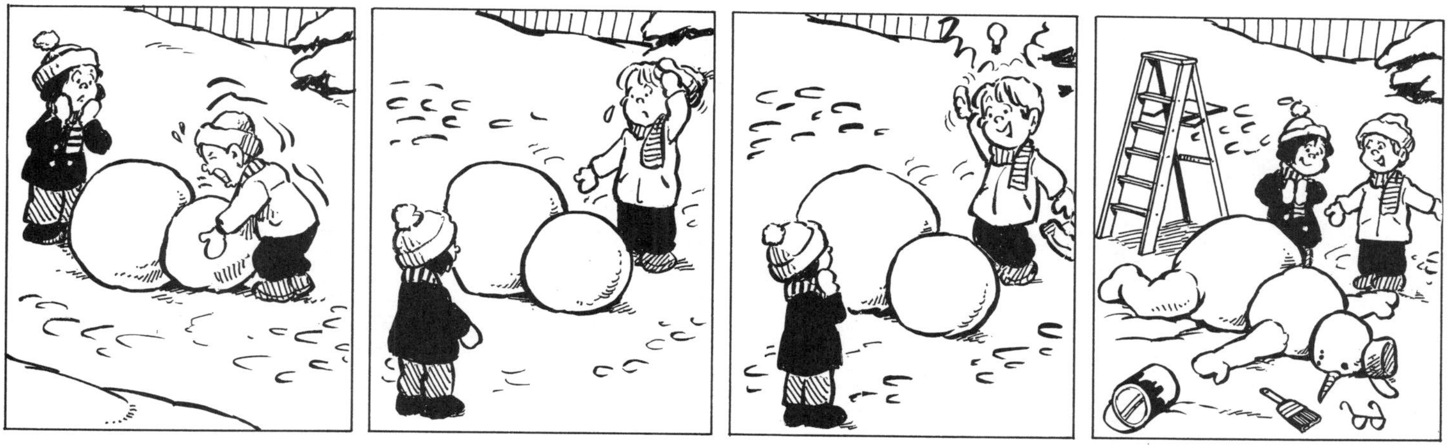

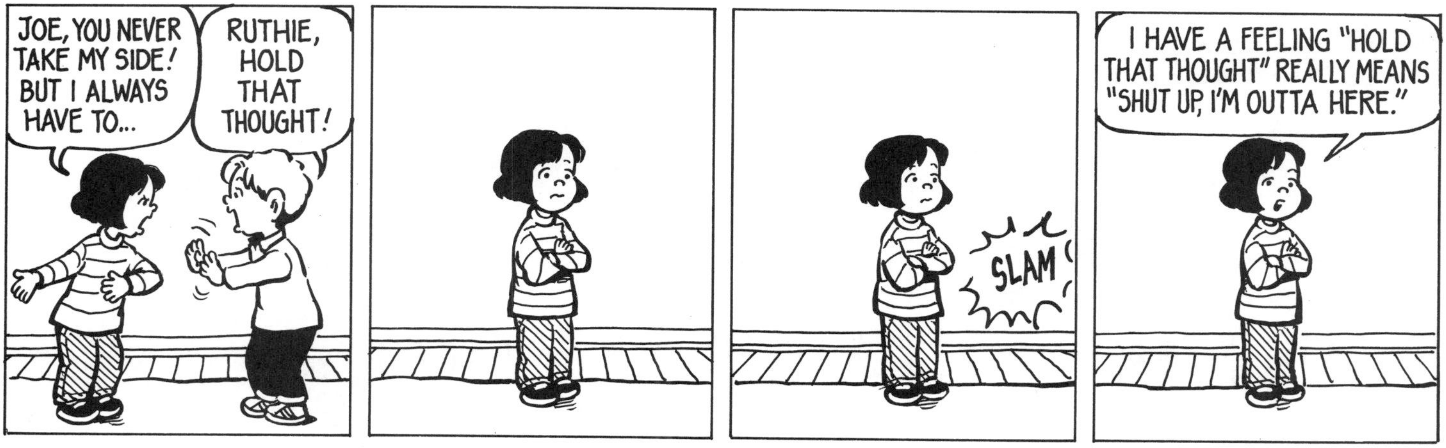
JOE, YOU NEVER TAKE MY SIDE! BUT I ALWAYS HAVE TO...
RUTHIE, HOLD THAT THOUGHT!
SLAM
I HAVE A FEELING "HOLD THAT THOUGHT" REALLY MEANS "SHUT UP, I'M OUTTA HERE."

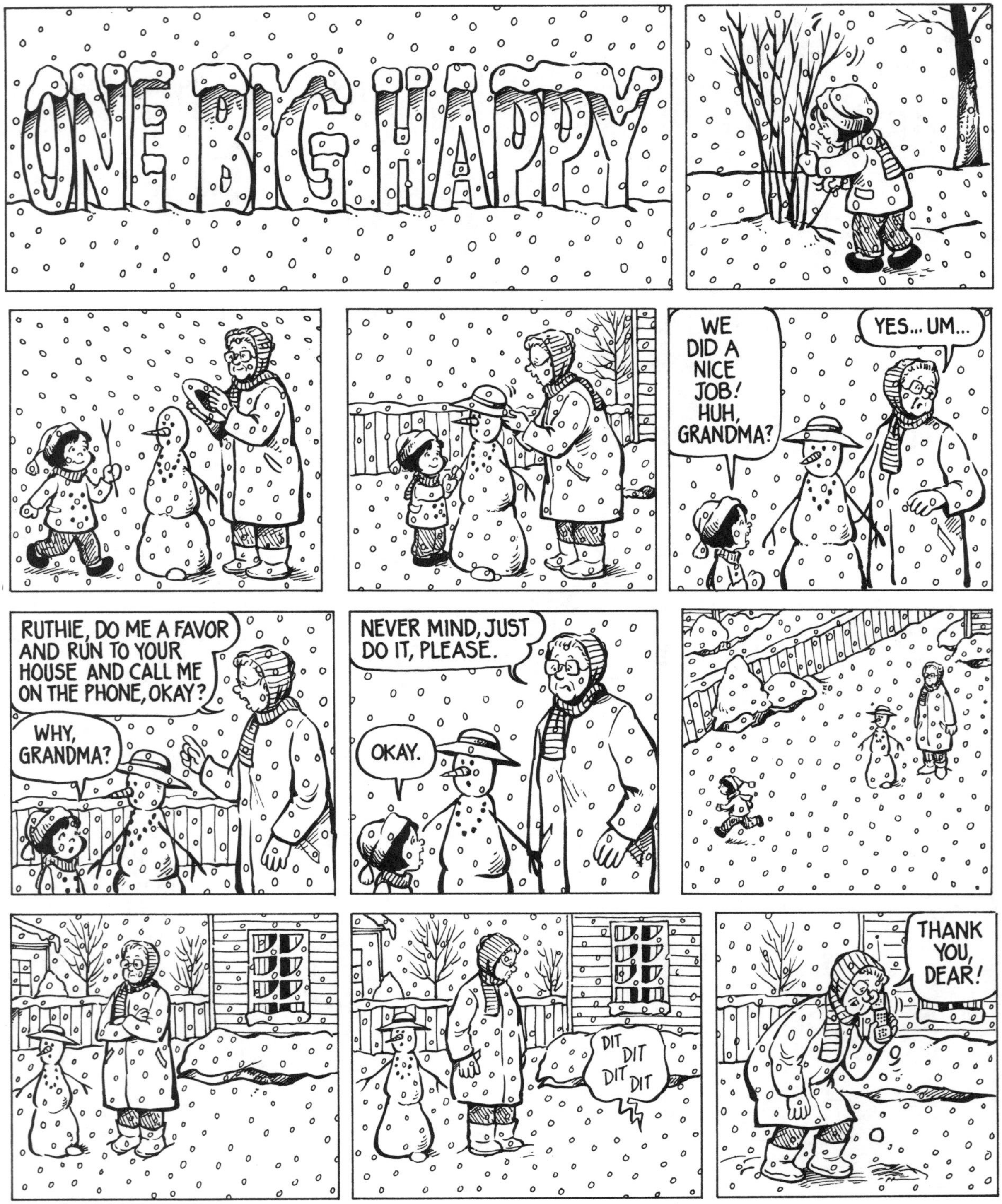
ONE BIG HAPPY
WE DID A NICE JOB! HUH, GRANDMA?
YES... UM...
RUTHIE, DO ME A FAVOR AND RUN TO YOUR HOUSE AND CALL ME ON THE PHONE, OKAY?
WHY, GRANDMA?
NEVER MIND, JUST DO IT, PLEASE.
OKAY.
DIT DIT DIT DIT
THANK YOU, DEAR!

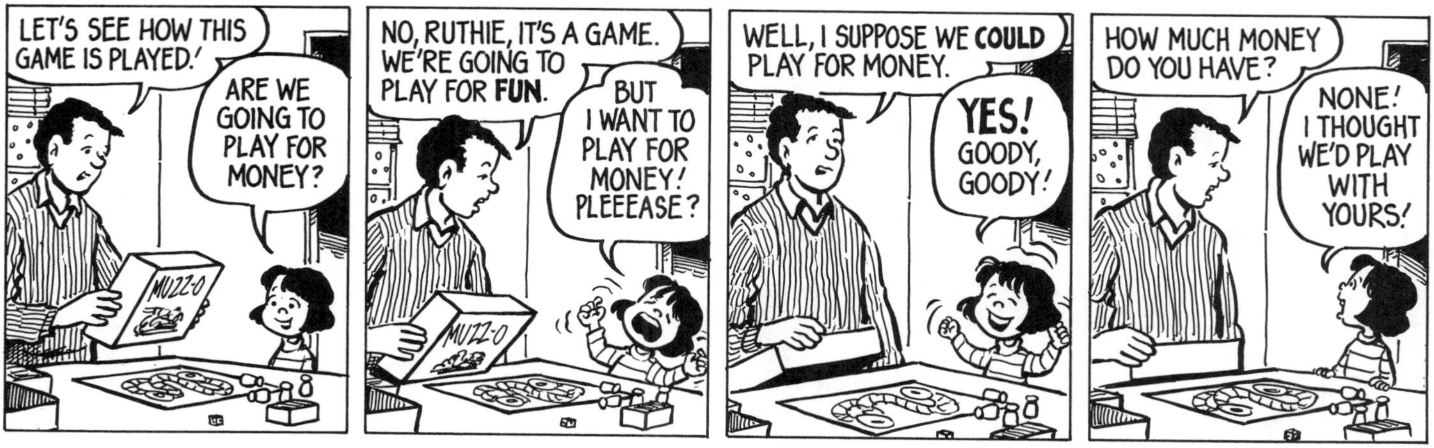
LET'S SEE HOW THIS GAME IS PLAYED!
ARE WE GOING TO PLAY FOR MONEY?
MUZZ-O
NO, RUTHIE, IT'S A GAME. WE'RE GOING TO PLAY FOR **FUN**.
BUT I WANT TO PLAY FOR MONEY! PLEEEASE?
MUZZ-O
WELL, I SUPPOSE WE **COULD** PLAY FOR MONEY.
YES! GOODY, GOODY!
HOW MUCH MONEY DO YOU HAVE?
NONE! I THOUGHT WE'D PLAY WITH YOURS!

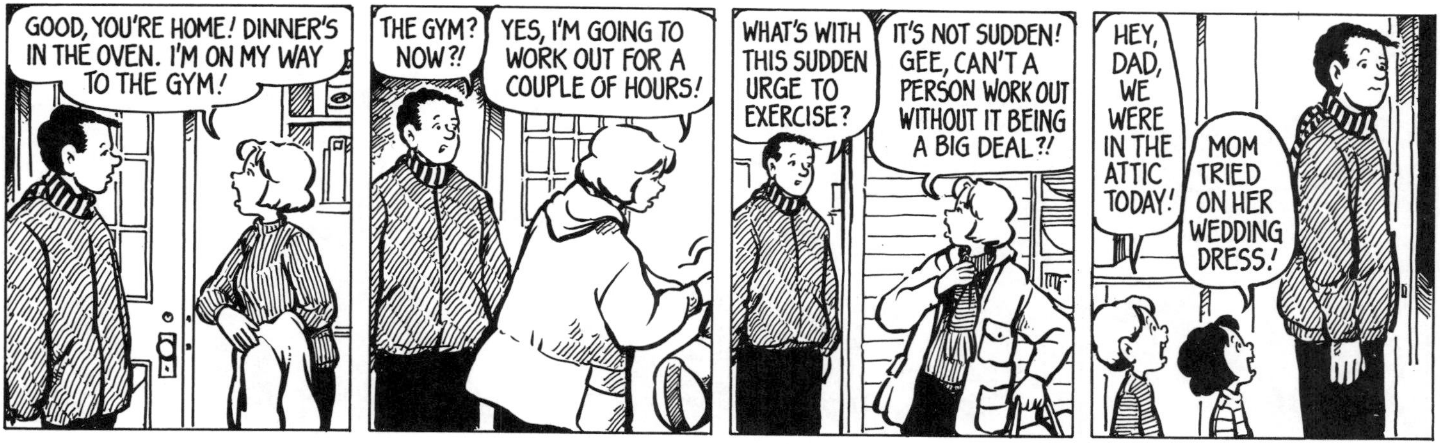
GOOD, YOU'RE HOME! DINNER'S IN THE OVEN. I'M ON MY WAY TO THE GYM!
THE GYM? NOW?!
YES, I'M GOING TO WORK OUT FOR A COUPLE OF HOURS!
WHAT'S WITH THIS SUDDEN URGE TO EXERCISE?
IT'S NOT SUDDEN! GEE, CAN'T A PERSON WORK OUT WITHOUT IT BEING A BIG DEAL?!
HEY, DAD, WE WERE IN THE ATTIC TODAY!
MOM TRIED ON HER WEDDING DRESS!

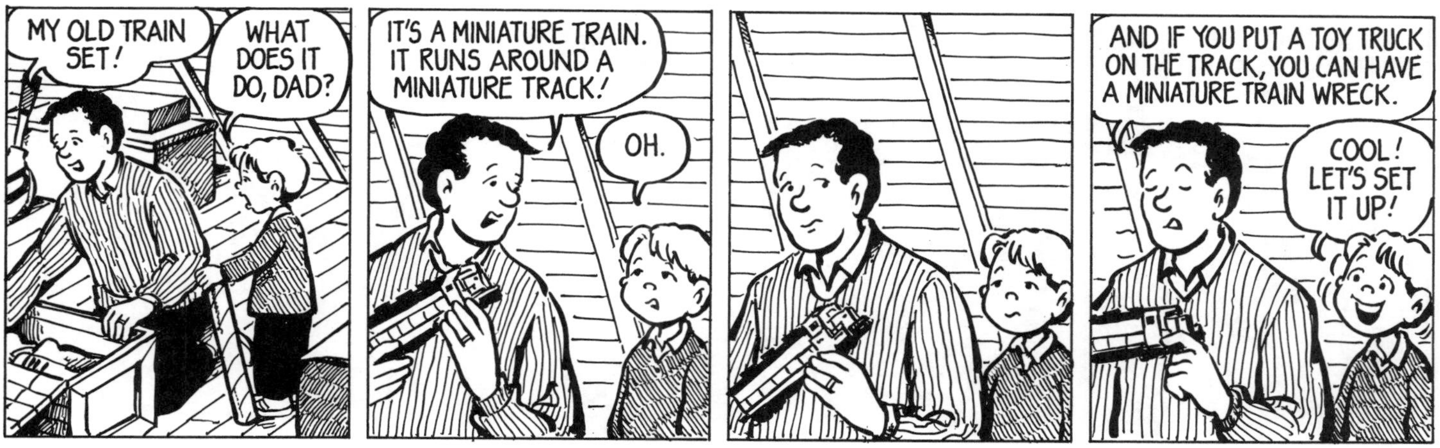
MY OLD TRAIN SET!
WHAT DOES IT DO, DAD?
IT'S A MINIATURE TRAIN. IT RUNS AROUND A MINIATURE TRACK!
OH.
AND IF YOU PUT A TOY TRUCK ON THE TRACK, YOU CAN HAVE A MINIATURE TRAIN WRECK.
COOL! LET'S SET IT UP!

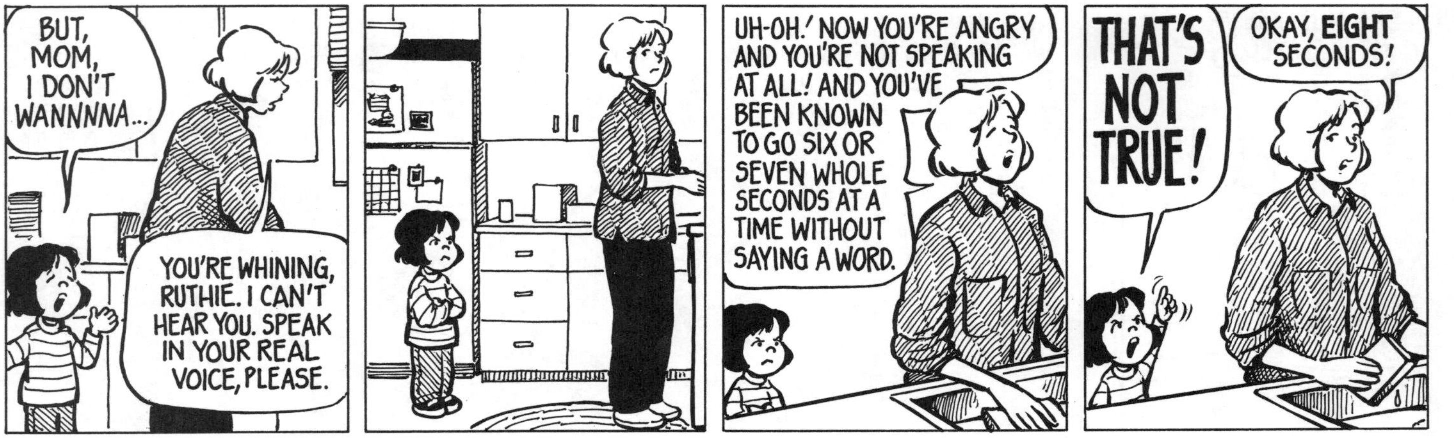

BUT, MOM, I DON'T WANNNNA...
YOU'RE WHINING, RUTHIE. I CAN'T HEAR YOU. SPEAK IN YOUR REAL VOICE, PLEASE.
UH-OH! NOW YOU'RE ANGRY AND YOU'RE NOT SPEAKING AT ALL! AND YOU'VE BEEN KNOWN TO GO SIX OR SEVEN WHOLE SECONDS AT A TIME WITHOUT SAYING A WORD.
THAT'S NOT TRUE!
OKAY, EIGHT SECONDS!

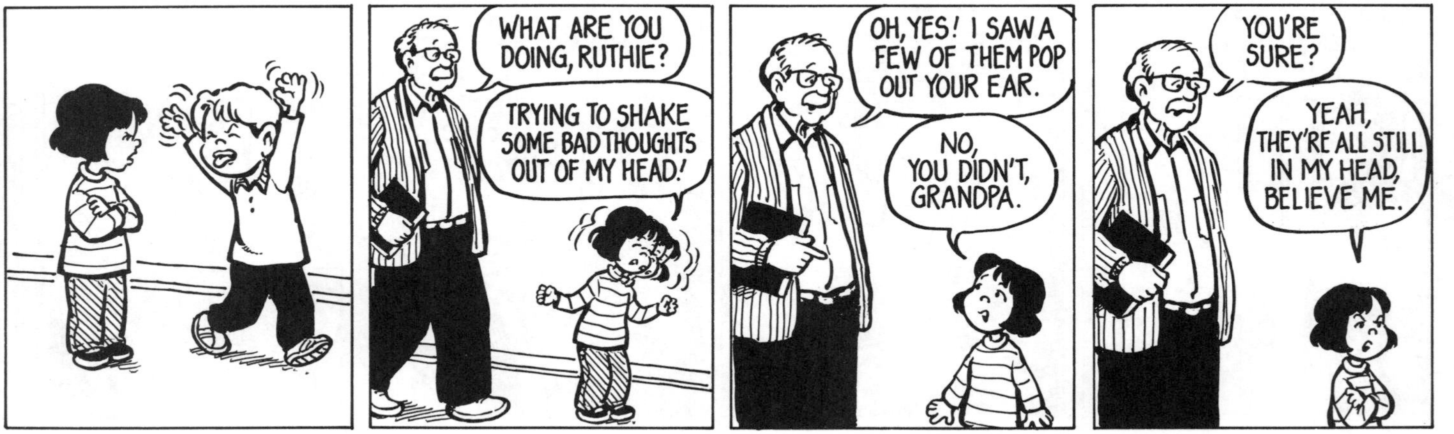

WHAT ARE YOU DOING, RUTHIE?
TRYING TO SHAKE SOME BAD THOUGHTS OUT OF MY HEAD!
OH, YES! I SAW A FEW OF THEM POP OUT YOUR EAR.
NO, YOU DIDN'T, GRANDPA.
YOU'RE SURE?
YEAH, THEY'RE ALL STILL IN MY HEAD, BELIEVE ME.

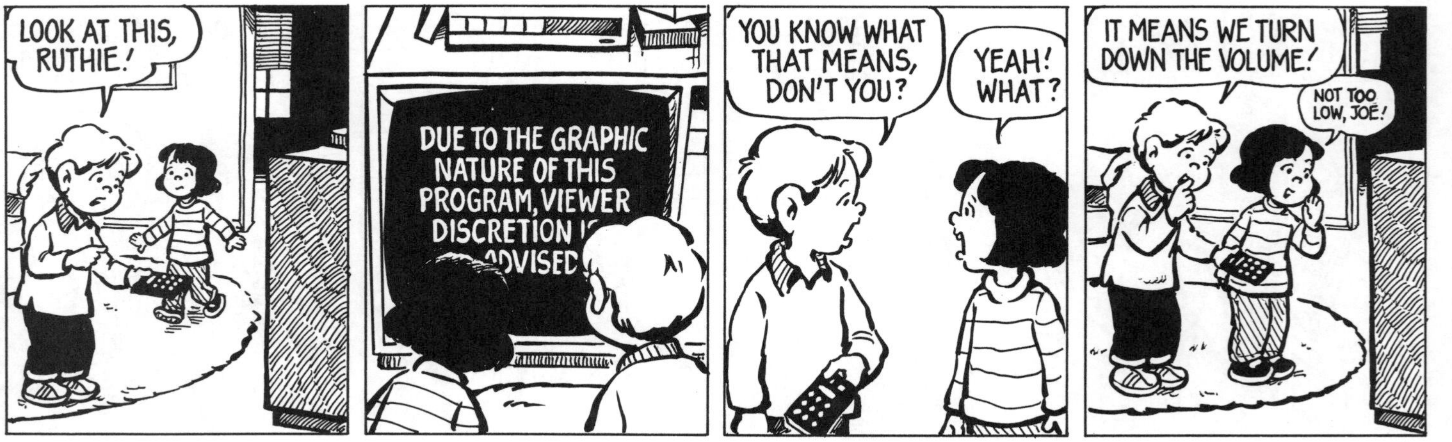

LOOK AT THIS, RUTHIE!
DUE TO THE GRAPHIC NATURE OF THIS PROGRAM, VIEWER DISCRETION I
ADVISED
YOU KNOW WHAT THAT MEANS, DON'T YOU?
YEAH! WHAT?
IT MEANS WE TURN DOWN THE VOLUME!
NOT TOO LOW, JOE!

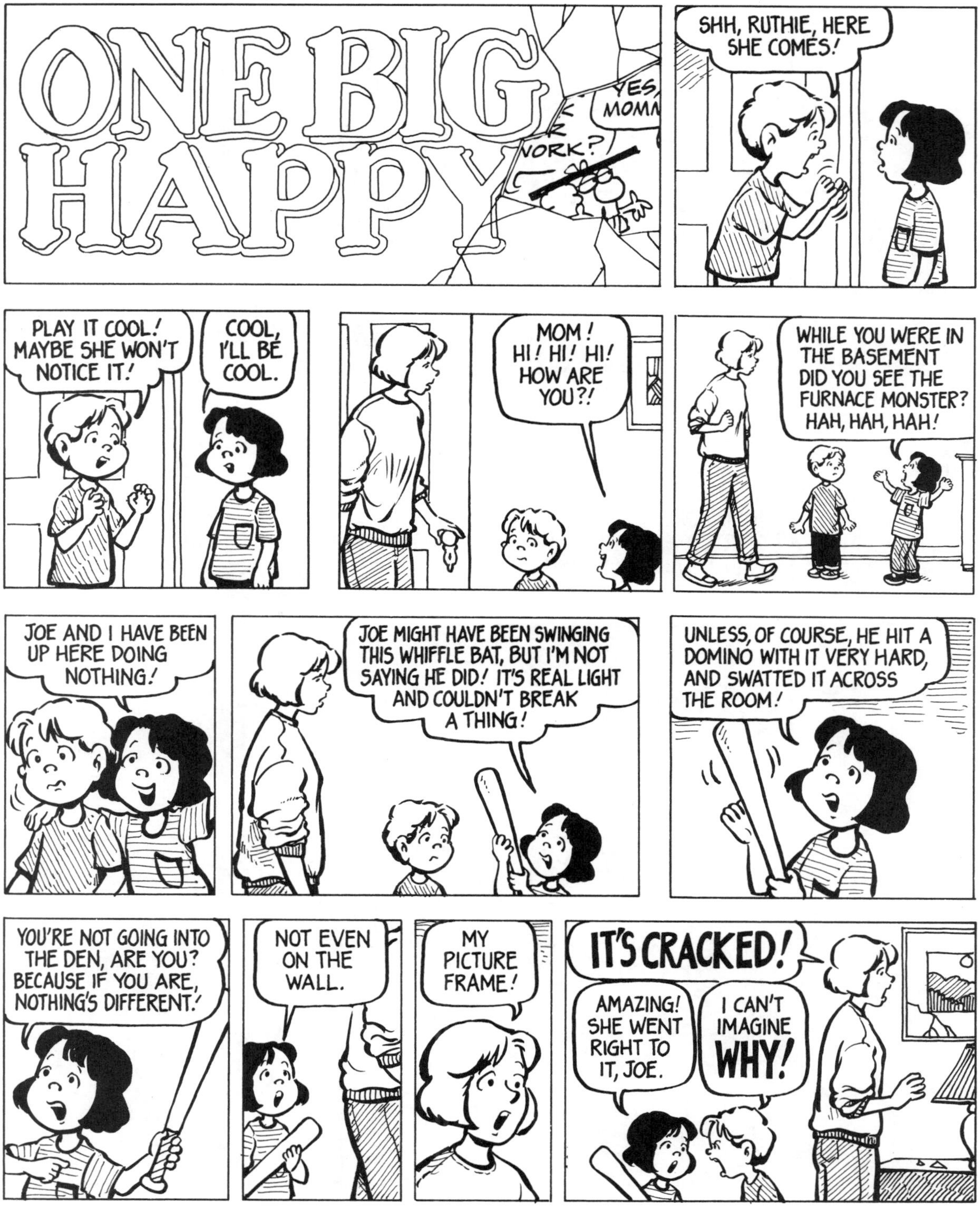
ONE BIG HAPPY
SHH, RUTHIE, HERE SHE COMES!
PLAY IT COOL! MAYBE SHE WON'T NOTICE IT!
COOL, I'LL BE COOL.
MOM! HI! HI! HI! HOW ARE YOU?!
WHILE YOU WERE IN THE BASEMENT DID YOU SEE THE FURNACE MONSTER? HAH, HAH, HAH!
JOE AND I HAVE BEEN UP HERE DOING NOTHING!
JOE MIGHT HAVE BEEN SWINGING THIS WHIFFLE BAT, BUT I'M NOT SAYING HE DID! IT'S REAL LIGHT AND COULDN'T BREAK A THING!
UNLESS, OF COURSE, HE HIT A DOMINO WITH IT VERY HARD, AND SWATTED IT ACROSS THE ROOM!
YOU'RE NOT GOING INTO THE DEN, ARE YOU? BECAUSE IF YOU ARE, NOTHING'S DIFFERENT!
NOT EVEN ON THE WALL.
MY PICTURE FRAME!
IT'S CRACKED!
AMAZING! SHE WENT RIGHT TO IT, JOE.
I CAN'T IMAGINE WHY!

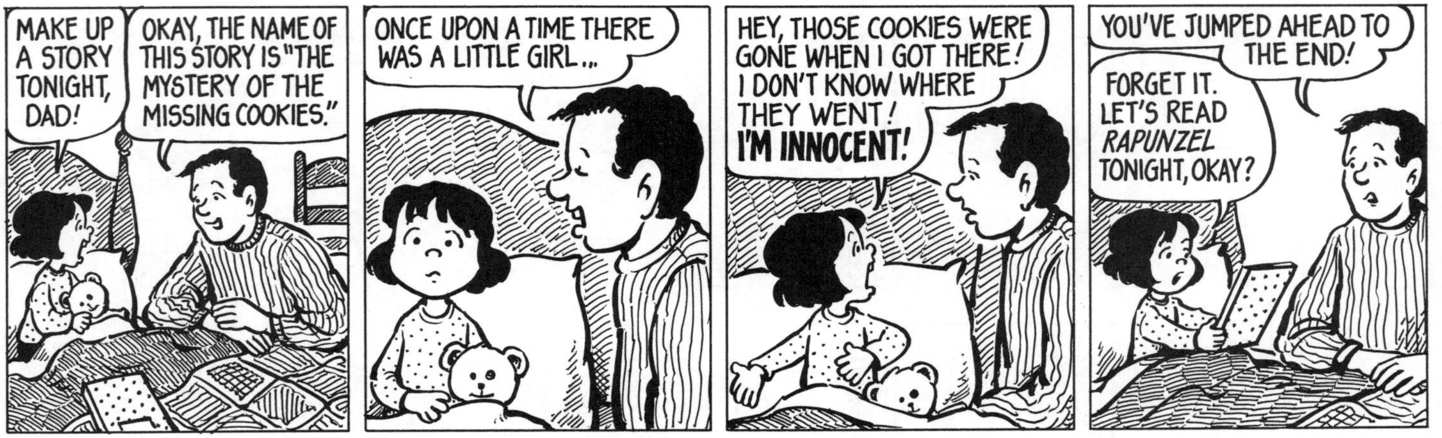
MAKE UP A STORY TONIGHT, DAD!
OKAY, THE NAME OF THIS STORY IS "THE MYSTERY OF THE MISSING COOKIES."
ONCE UPON A TIME THERE WAS A LITTLE GIRL...
HEY, THOSE COOKIES WERE GONE WHEN I GOT THERE! I DON'T KNOW WHERE THEY WENT! **I'M INNOCENT!**
YOU'VE JUMPED AHEAD TO THE END!
FORGET IT. LET'S READ *RAPUNZEL* TONIGHT, OKAY?

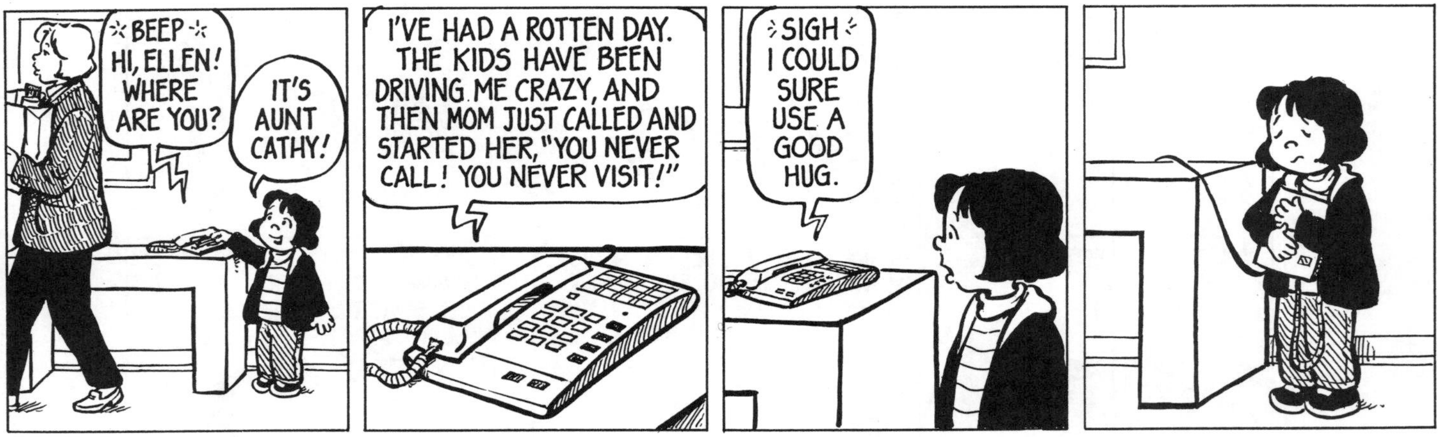
✲BEEP✲ HI, ELLEN! WHERE ARE YOU?
IT'S AUNT CATHY!
I'VE HAD A ROTTEN DAY. THE KIDS HAVE BEEN DRIVING ME CRAZY, AND THEN MOM JUST CALLED AND STARTED HER, "YOU NEVER CALL! YOU NEVER VISIT!"
SIGH I COULD SURE USE A GOOD HUG.

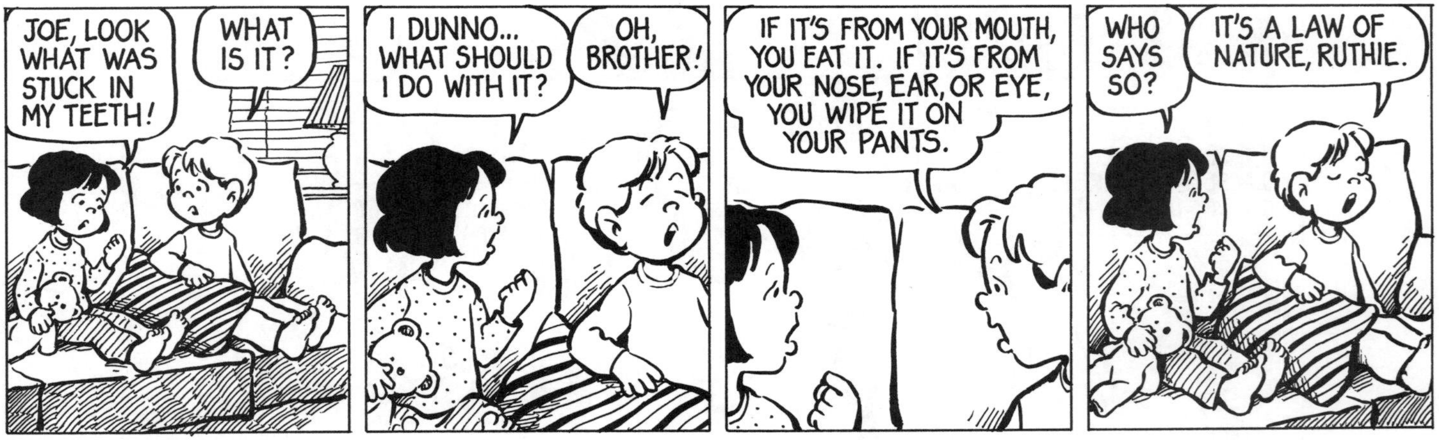
JOE, LOOK WHAT WAS STUCK IN MY TEETH!
WHAT IS IT?
I DUNNO... WHAT SHOULD I DO WITH IT?
OH, BROTHER!
IF IT'S FROM YOUR MOUTH, YOU EAT IT. IF IT'S FROM YOUR NOSE, EAR, OR EYE, YOU WIPE IT ON YOUR PANTS.
WHO SAYS SO?
IT'S A LAW OF NATURE, RUTHIE.

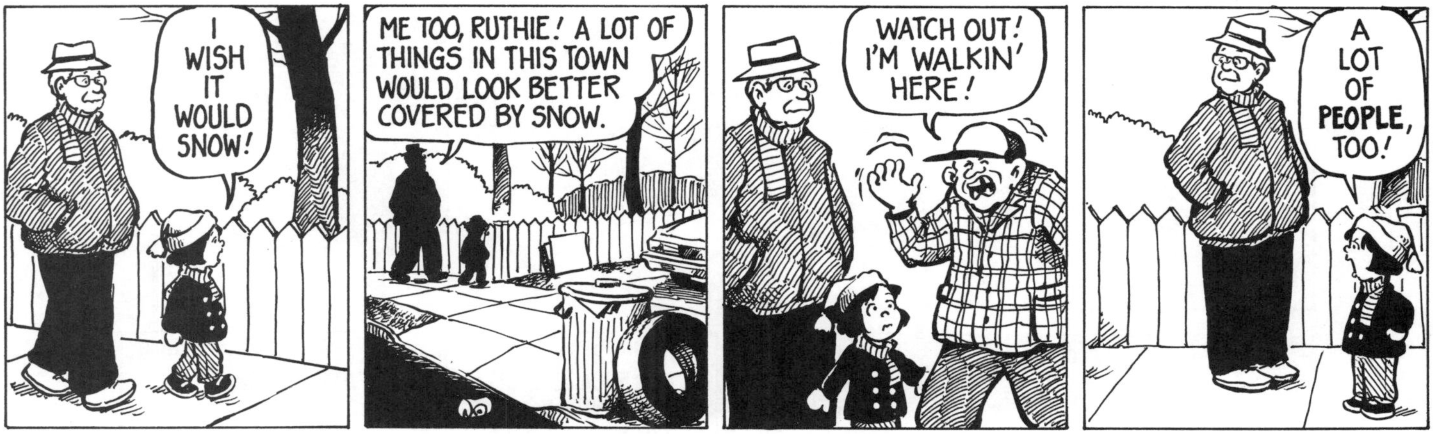
I WISH IT WOULD SNOW!
ME TOO, RUTHIE! A LOT OF THINGS IN THIS TOWN WOULD LOOK BETTER COVERED BY SNOW.
WATCH OUT! I'M WALKIN' HERE!
A LOT OF **PEOPLE**, TOO!

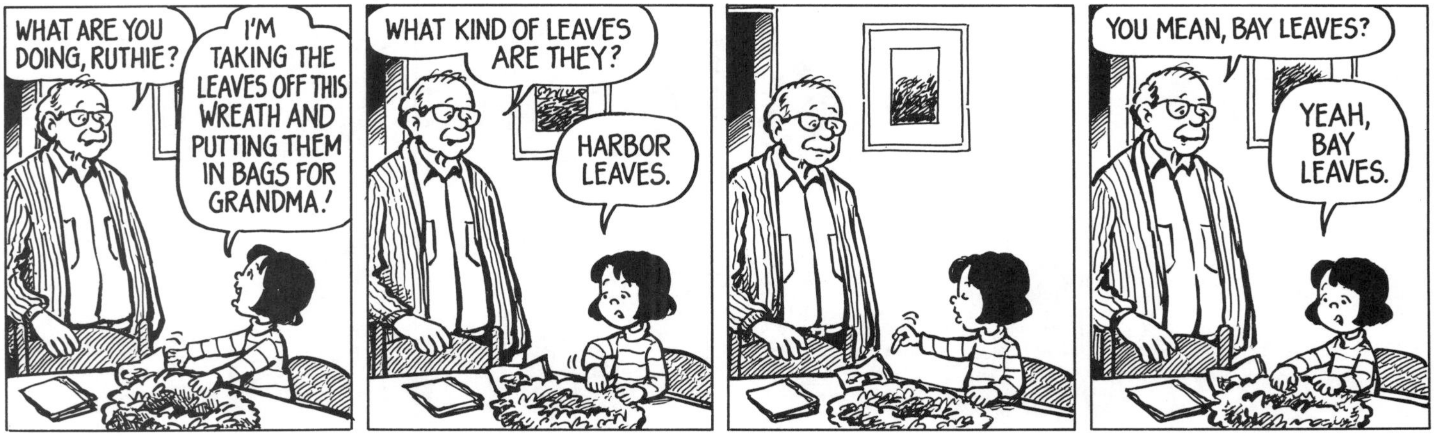
WHAT ARE YOU DOING, RUTHIE?
I'M TAKING THE LEAVES OFF THIS WREATH AND PUTTING THEM IN BAGS FOR GRANDMA!
WHAT KIND OF LEAVES ARE THEY?
HARBOR LEAVES.
YOU MEAN, BAY LEAVES?
YEAH, BAY LEAVES.

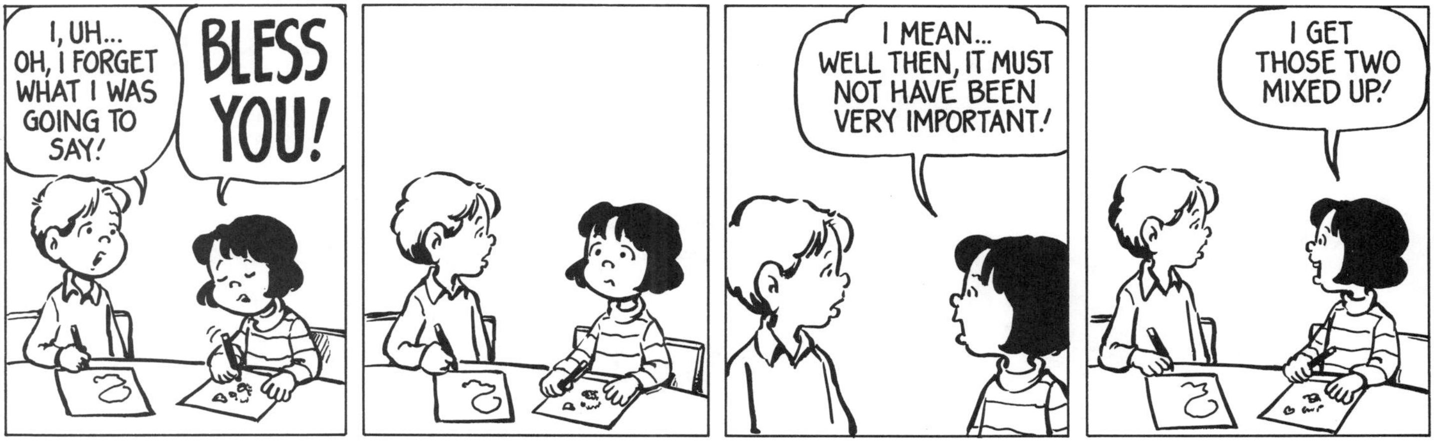
I, UH... OH, I FORGET WHAT I WAS GOING TO SAY!
BLESS YOU!
I MEAN... WELL THEN, IT MUST NOT HAVE BEEN VERY IMPORTANT!
I GET THOSE TWO MIXED UP!

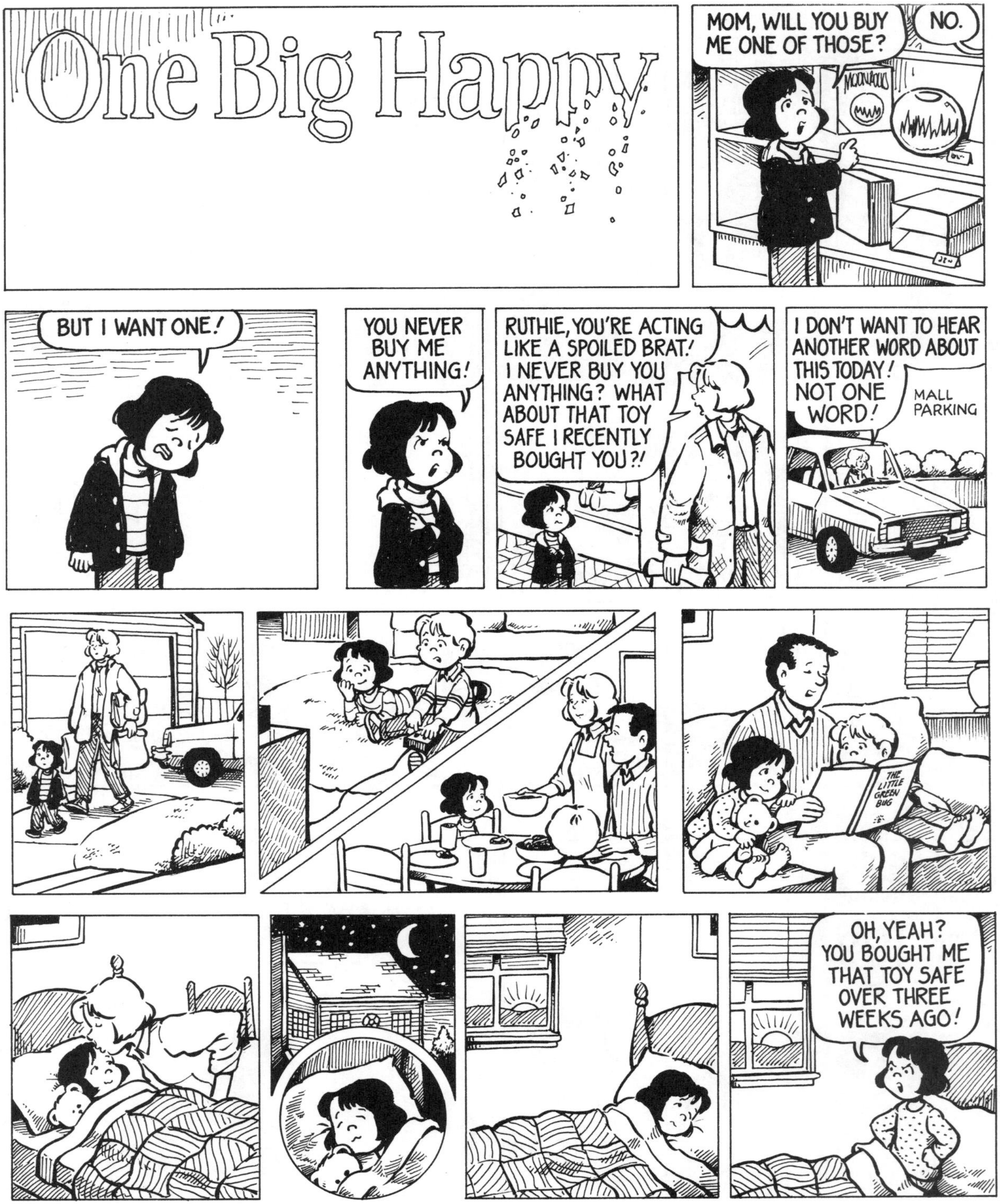
One Big Happy
MOM, WILL YOU BUY ME ONE OF THOSE?
NO.
BUT I WANT ONE!
YOU NEVER BUY ME ANYTHING!
RUTHIE, YOU'RE ACTING LIKE A SPOILED BRAT! I NEVER BUY YOU ANYTHING? WHAT ABOUT THAT TOY SAFE I RECENTLY BOUGHT YOU?!
I DON'T WANT TO HEAR ANOTHER WORD ABOUT THIS TODAY! NOT ONE WORD!
MALL PARKING
THE LITTLE GREEN BUG
OH, YEAH? YOU BOUGHT ME THAT TOY SAFE OVER THREE WEEKS AGO!

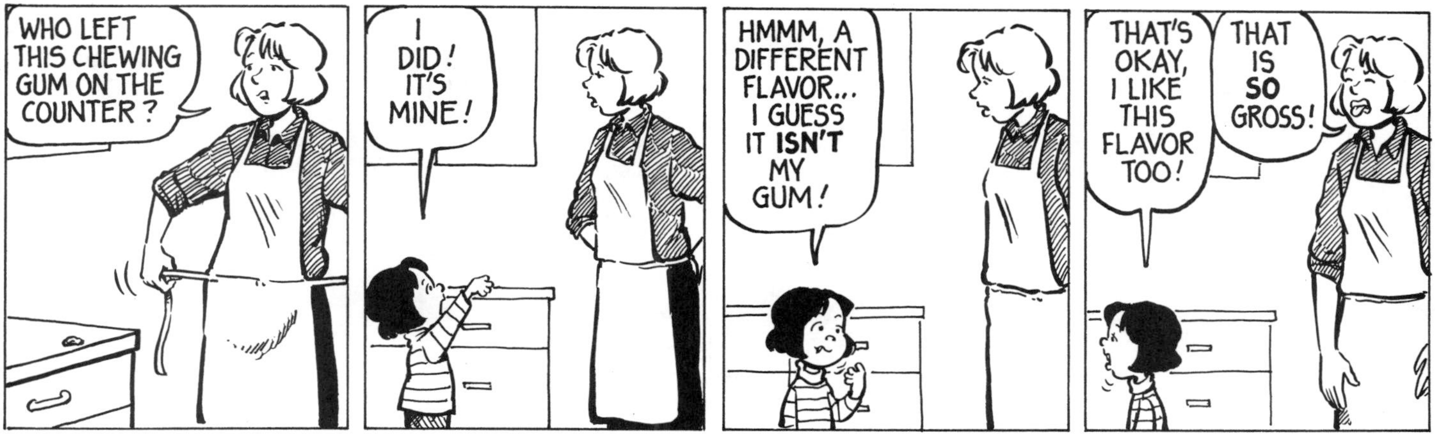
WHO LEFT THIS CHEWING GUM ON THE COUNTER?
I DID! IT'S MINE!
HMMM, A DIFFERENT FLAVOR... I GUESS IT **ISN'T** MY GUM!
THAT'S OKAY, I LIKE THIS FLAVOR TOO!
THAT IS **SO** GROSS!

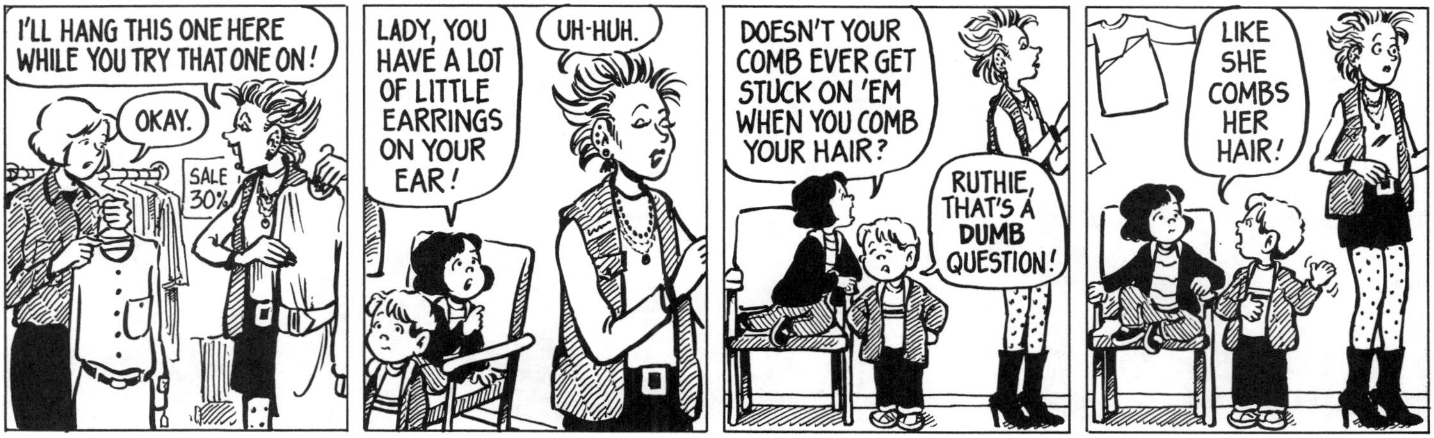
I'LL HANG THIS ONE HERE WHILE YOU TRY THAT ONE ON!
OKAY.
SALE 30%
LADY, YOU HAVE A LOT OF LITTLE EARRINGS ON YOUR EAR!
UH-HUH.
DOESN'T YOUR COMB EVER GET STUCK ON 'EM WHEN YOU COMB YOUR HAIR?
RUTHIE, THAT'S A **DUMB** QUESTION!
LIKE SHE COMBS HER HAIR!

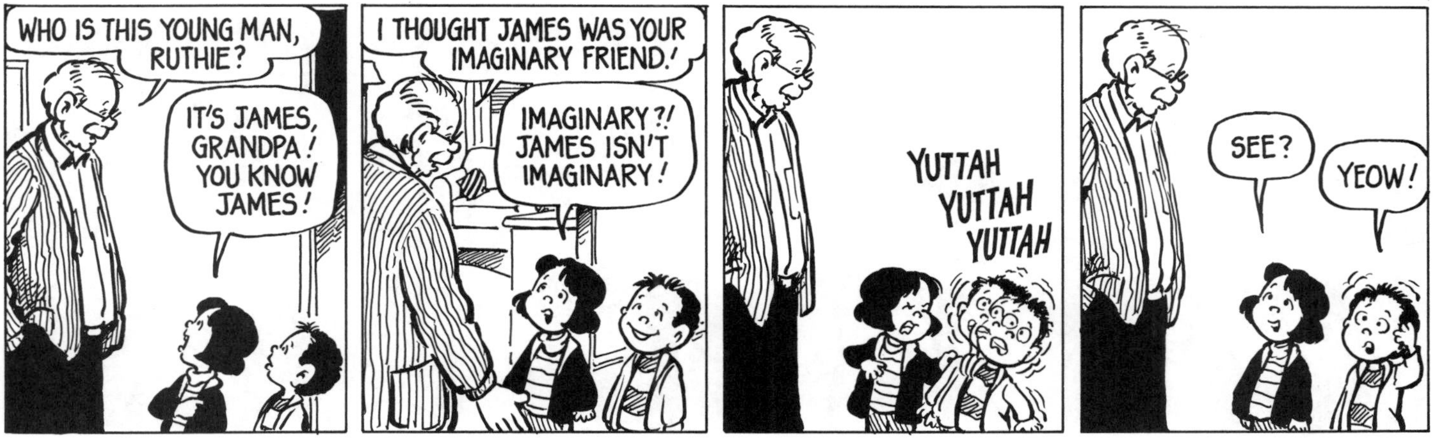
WHO IS THIS YOUNG MAN, RUTHIE?
IT'S JAMES, GRANDPA! YOU KNOW JAMES!
I THOUGHT JAMES WAS YOUR IMAGINARY FRIEND!
IMAGINARY?! JAMES ISN'T IMAGINARY!
YUTTAH YUTTAH YUTTAH
SEE?
YEOW!

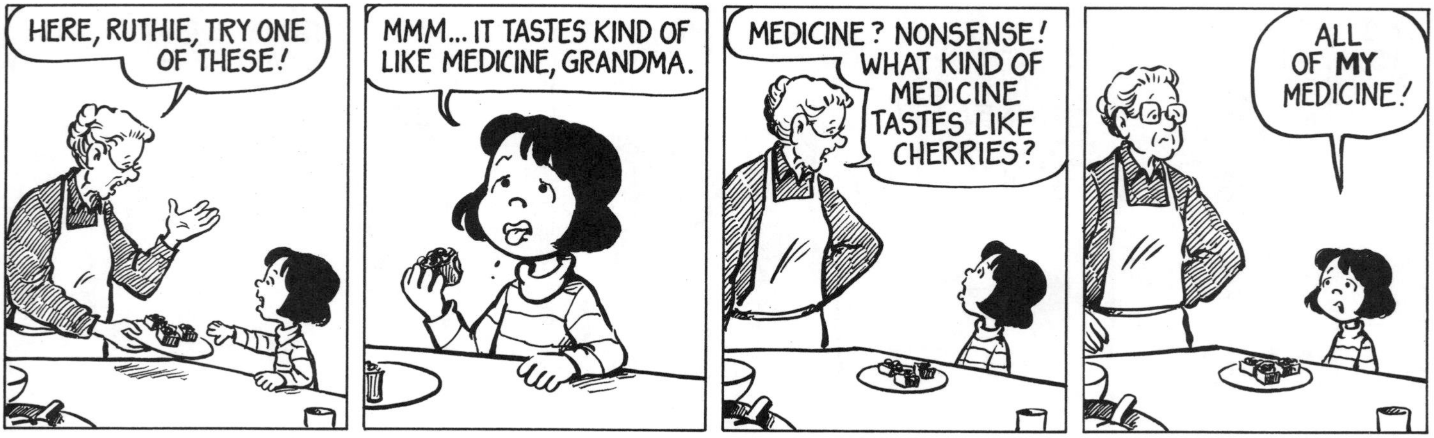
HERE, RUTHIE, TRY ONE OF THESE!
MMM... IT TASTES KIND OF LIKE MEDICINE, GRANDMA.
MEDICINE? NONSENSE! WHAT KIND OF MEDICINE TASTES LIKE CHERRIES?
ALL OF **MY** MEDICINE!

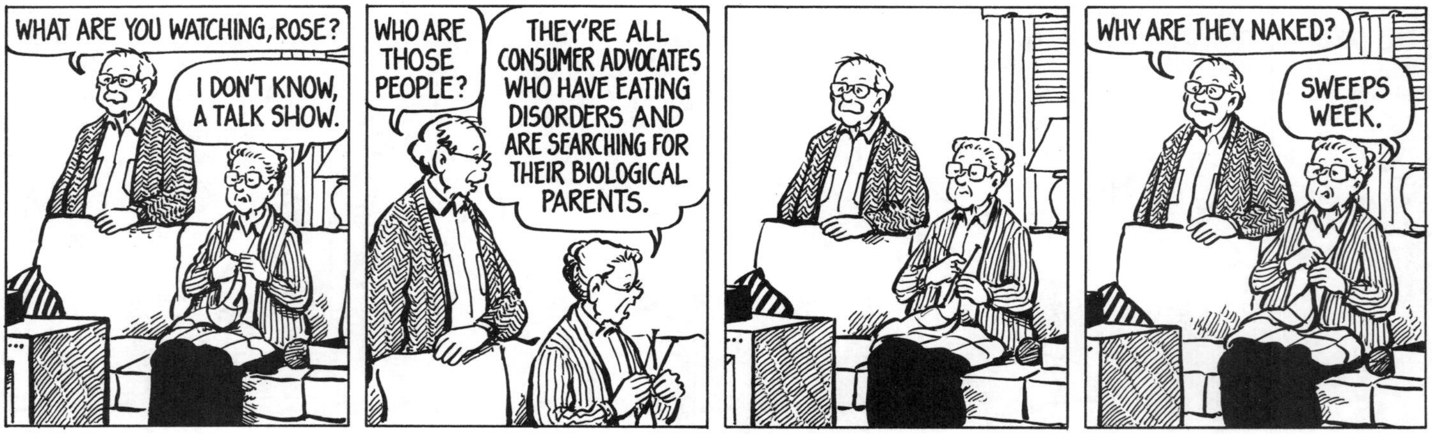
WHAT ARE YOU WATCHING, ROSE?
I DON'T KNOW, A TALK SHOW.
WHO ARE THOSE PEOPLE?
THEY'RE ALL CONSUMER ADVOCATES WHO HAVE EATING DISORDERS AND ARE SEARCHING FOR THEIR BIOLOGICAL PARENTS.
WHY ARE THEY NAKED?
SWEEPS WEEK.

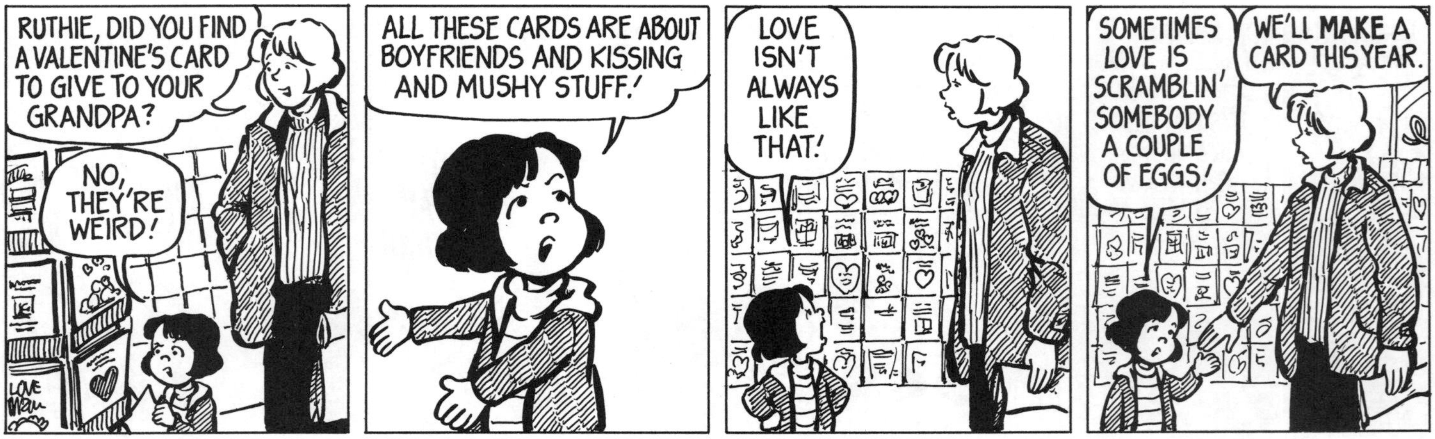
RUTHIE, DID YOU FIND A VALENTINE'S CARD TO GIVE TO YOUR GRANDPA?
NO, THEY'RE WEIRD!
ALL THESE CARDS ARE ABOUT BOYFRIENDS AND KISSING AND MUSHY STUFF!
LOVE ISN'T ALWAYS LIKE THAT!
SOMETIMES LOVE IS SCRAMBLIN' SOMEBODY A COUPLE OF EGGS!
WE'LL **MAKE** A CARD THIS YEAR.

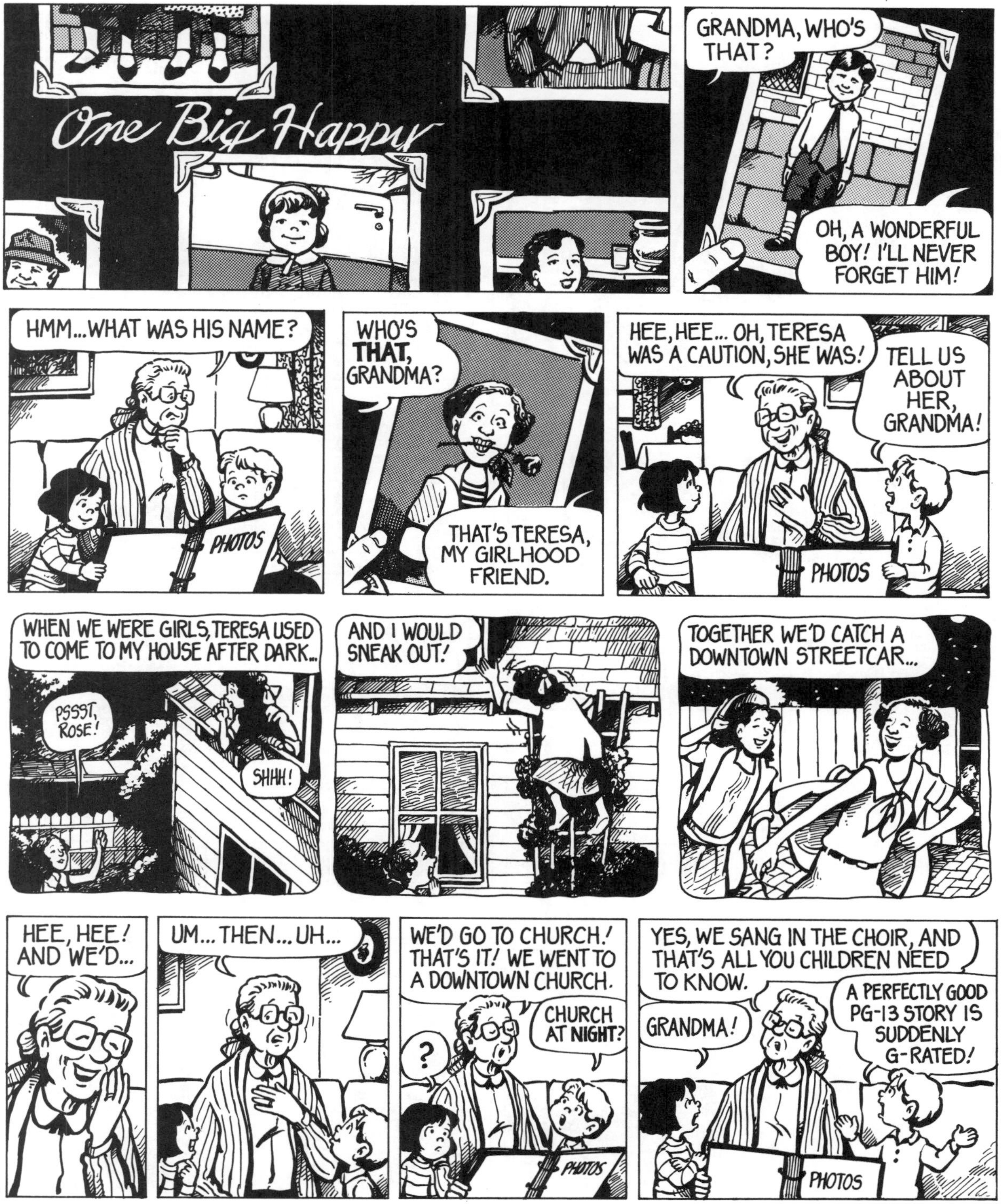
One Big Happy
GRANDMA, WHO'S THAT?
OH, A WONDERFUL BOY! I'LL NEVER FORGET HIM!
HMM... WHAT WAS HIS NAME?
PHOTOS
WHO'S **THAT,** GRANDMA?
THAT'S TERESA, MY GIRLHOOD FRIEND.
HEE, HEE... OH, TERESA WAS A CAUTION, SHE WAS!
TELL US ABOUT HER, GRANDMA!
PHOTOS
WHEN WE WERE GIRLS, TERESA USED TO COME TO MY HOUSE AFTER DARK...
PSSST, ROSE!
SHHH!
AND I WOULD SNEAK OUT!
TOGETHER WE'D CATCH A DOWNTOWN STREETCAR...
HEE, HEE! AND WE'D...
UM... THEN... UH...
WE'D GO TO CHURCH! THAT'S IT! WE WENT TO A DOWNTOWN CHURCH.
?
CHURCH AT **NIGHT**?
PHOTOS
YES, WE SANG IN THE CHOIR, AND THAT'S ALL YOU CHILDREN NEED TO KNOW.
GRANDMA!
A PERFECTLY GOOD PG-13 STORY IS SUDDENLY G-RATED!
PHOTOS

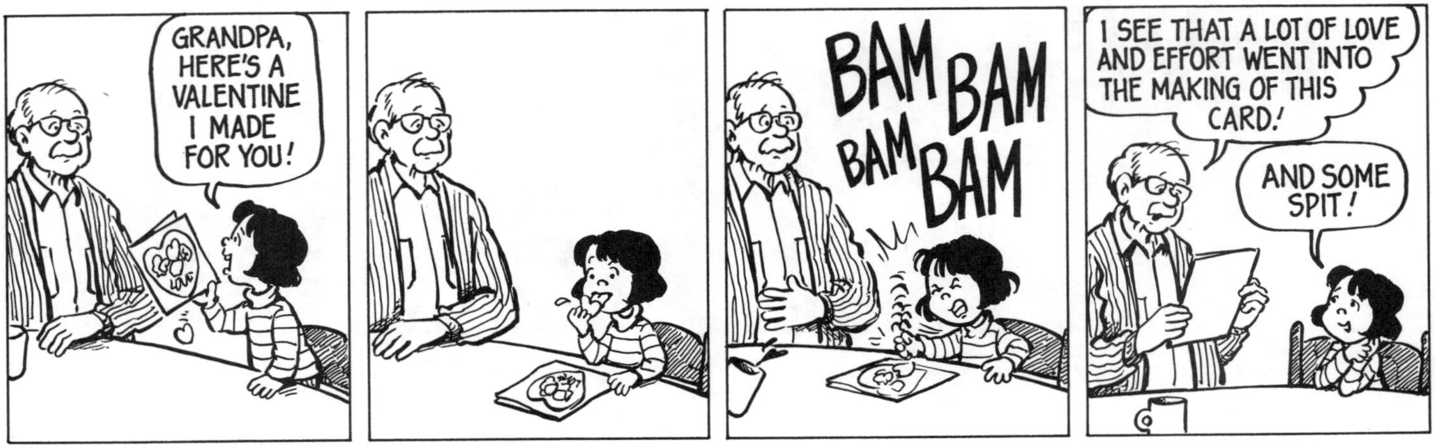
GRANDPA, HERE'S A VALENTINE I MADE FOR YOU!
BAM BAM BAM BAM
I SEE THAT A LOT OF LOVE AND EFFORT WENT INTO THE MAKING OF THIS CARD!
AND SOME SPIT!

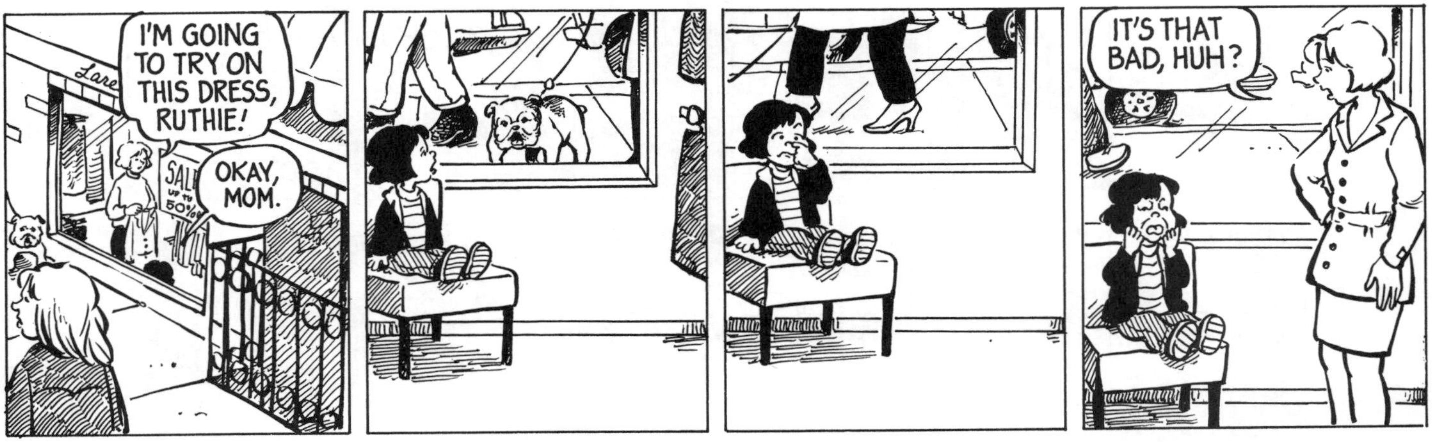
I'M GOING TO TRY ON THIS DRESS, RUTHIE!
OKAY, MOM.
IT'S THAT BAD, HUH?

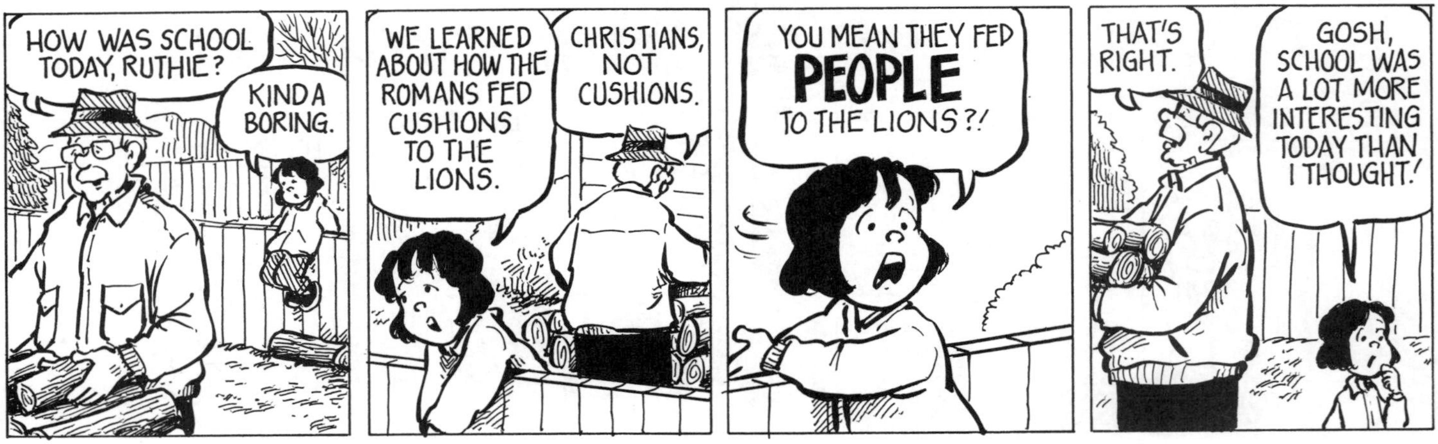
HOW WAS SCHOOL TODAY, RUTHIE?
KINDA BORING.
WE LEARNED ABOUT HOW THE ROMANS FED CUSHIONS TO THE LIONS.
CHRISTIANS, NOT CUSHIONS.
YOU MEAN THEY FED **PEOPLE** TO THE LIONS?!
THAT'S RIGHT.
GOSH, SCHOOL WAS A LOT MORE INTERESTING TODAY THAN I THOUGHT!

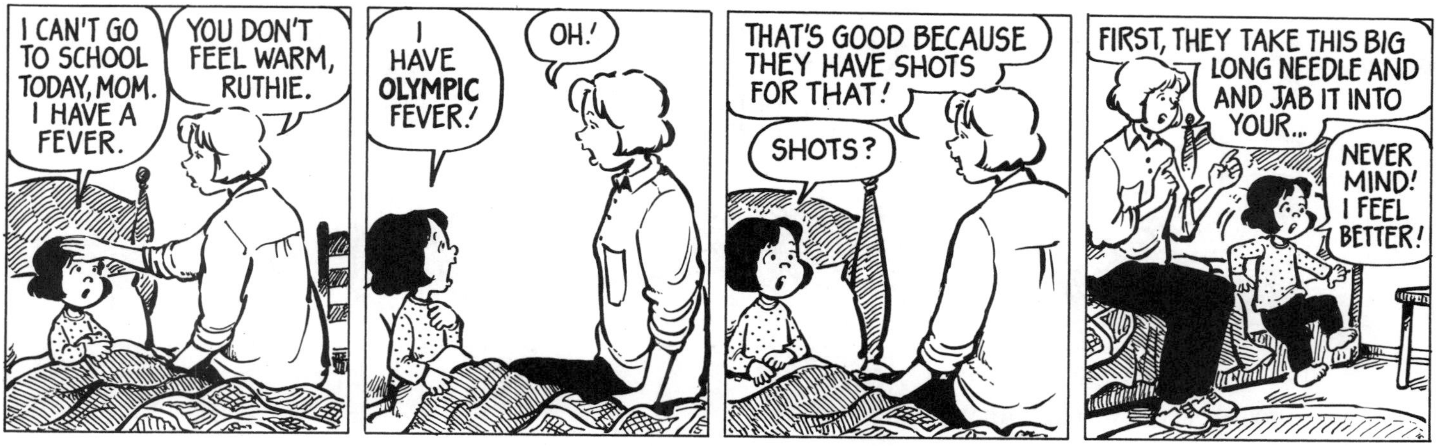
I CAN'T GO TO SCHOOL TODAY, MOM. I HAVE A FEVER.
YOU DON'T FEEL WARM, RUTHIE.
I HAVE **OLYMPIC** FEVER!
OH!
THAT'S GOOD BECAUSE THEY HAVE SHOTS FOR THAT!
SHOTS?
FIRST, THEY TAKE THIS BIG LONG NEEDLE AND AND JAB IT INTO YOUR...
NEVER MIND! I FEEL BETTER!

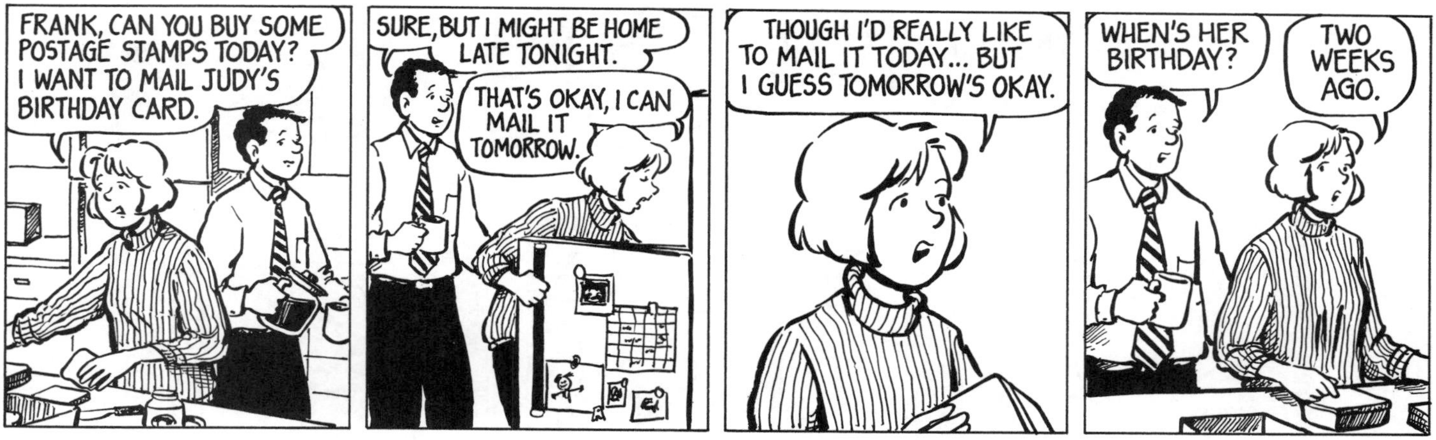
FRANK, CAN YOU BUY SOME POSTAGE STAMPS TODAY? I WANT TO MAIL JUDY'S BIRTHDAY CARD.
SURE, BUT I MIGHT BE HOME LATE TONIGHT.
THAT'S OKAY, I CAN MAIL IT TOMORROW.
THOUGH I'D REALLY LIKE TO MAIL IT TODAY... BUT I GUESS TOMORROW'S OKAY.
WHEN'S HER BIRTHDAY?
TWO WEEKS AGO.

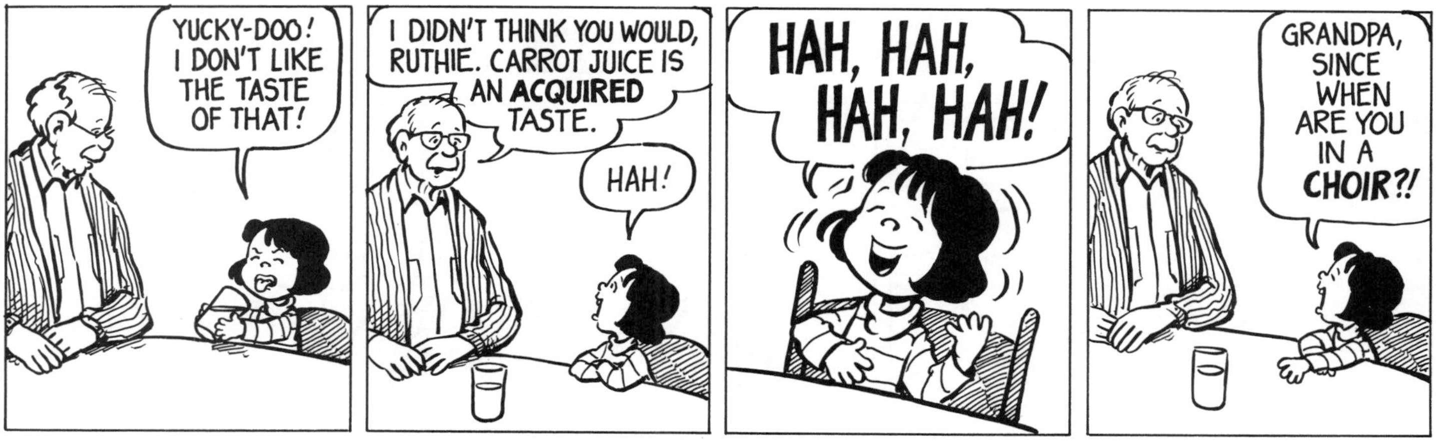
YUCKY-DOO! I DON'T LIKE THE TASTE OF THAT!
I DIDN'T THINK YOU WOULD, RUTHIE. CARROT JUICE IS AN **ACQUIRED** TASTE.
HAH!
HAH, HAH, HAH, HAH!
GRANDPA, SINCE WHEN ARE YOU IN A **CHOIR**?!

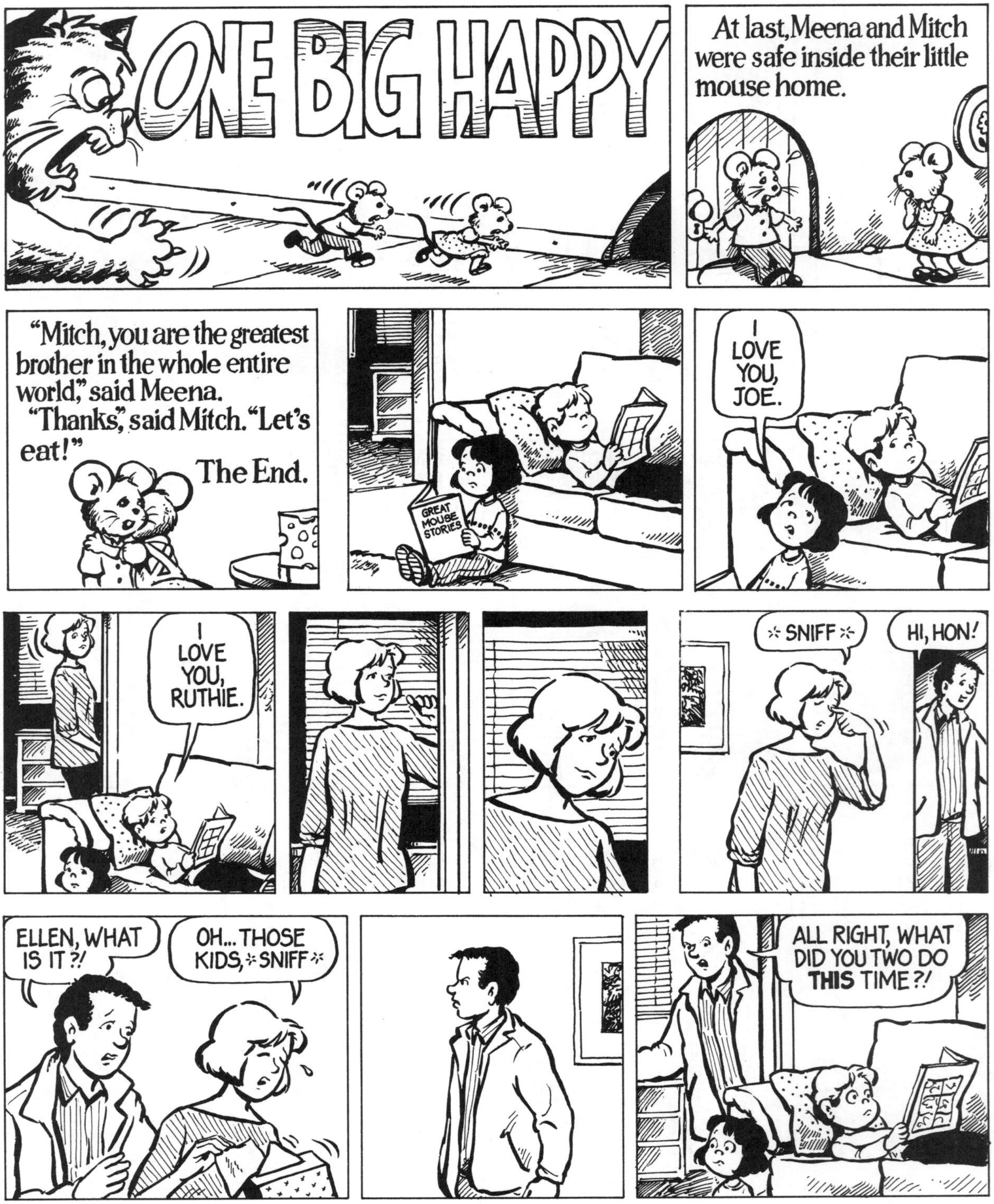
ONE BIG HAPPY
At last, Meena and Mitch were safe inside their little mouse home.
"Mitch, you are the greatest brother in the whole entire world," said Meena.
"Thanks," said Mitch. "Let's eat!"
The End.
GREAT MOUSE STORIES
I LOVE YOU, JOE.
I LOVE YOU, RUTHIE.
* SNIFF *
HI, HON!
ELLEN, WHAT IS IT?!
OH... THOSE KIDS, * SNIFF *
ALL RIGHT, WHAT DID YOU TWO DO THIS TIME?!

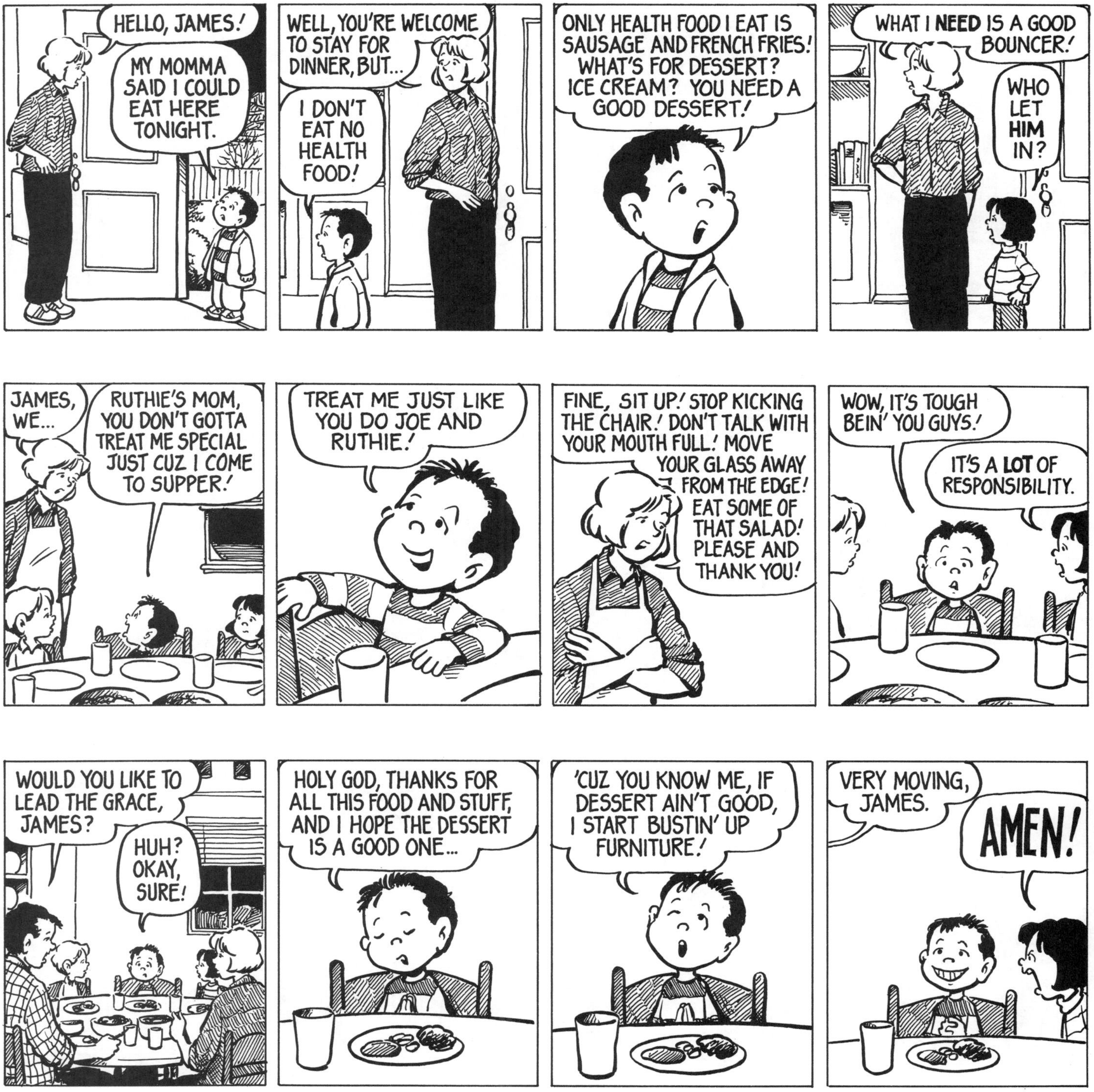
HELLO, JAMES!
MY MOMMA SAID I COULD EAT HERE TONIGHT.
WELL, YOU'RE WELCOME TO STAY FOR DINNER, BUT...
I DON'T EAT NO HEALTH FOOD!
ONLY HEALTH FOOD I EAT IS SAUSAGE AND FRENCH FRIES! WHAT'S FOR DESSERT? ICE CREAM? YOU NEED A GOOD DESSERT!
WHAT I NEED IS A GOOD BOUNCER!
WHO LET HIM IN?
JAMES, WE...
RUTHIE'S MOM, YOU DON'T GOTTA TREAT ME SPECIAL JUST CUZ I COME TO SUPPER!
TREAT ME JUST LIKE YOU DO JOE AND RUTHIE!
FINE, SIT UP! STOP KICKING THE CHAIR! DON'T TALK WITH YOUR MOUTH FULL! MOVE YOUR GLASS AWAY FROM THE EDGE! EAT SOME OF THAT SALAD! PLEASE AND THANK YOU!
WOW, IT'S TOUGH BEIN' YOU GUYS!
IT'S A LOT OF RESPONSIBILITY.
WOULD YOU LIKE TO LEAD THE GRACE, JAMES?
HUH? OKAY, SURE!
HOLY GOD, THANKS FOR ALL THIS FOOD AND STUFF, AND I HOPE THE DESSERT IS A GOOD ONE...
'CUZ YOU KNOW ME, IF DESSERT AIN'T GOOD, I START BUSTIN' UP FURNITURE!
VERY MOVING, JAMES.
AMEN!

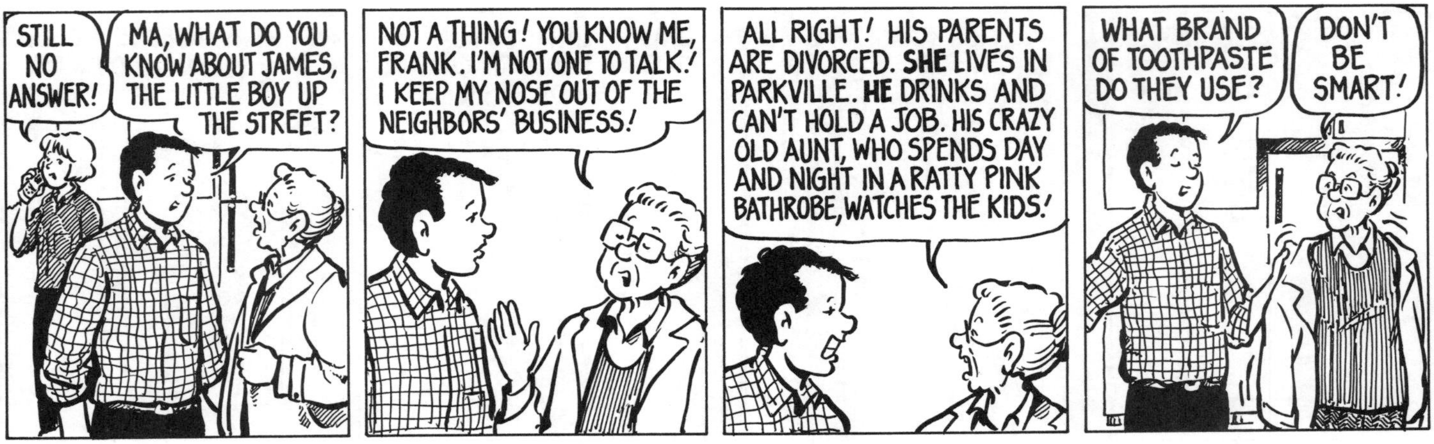
STILL NO ANSWER!
MA, WHAT DO YOU KNOW ABOUT JAMES, THE LITTLE BOY UP THE STREET?
NOT A THING! YOU KNOW ME, FRANK. I'M NOT ONE TO TALK! I KEEP MY NOSE OUT OF THE NEIGHBORS' BUSINESS!
ALL RIGHT! HIS PARENTS ARE DIVORCED. SHE LIVES IN PARKVILLE. HE DRINKS AND CAN'T HOLD A JOB. HIS CRAZY OLD AUNT, WHO SPENDS DAY AND NIGHT IN A RATTY PINK BATHROBE, WATCHES THE KIDS!
WHAT BRAND OF TOOTHPASTE DO THEY USE?
DON'T BE SMART!

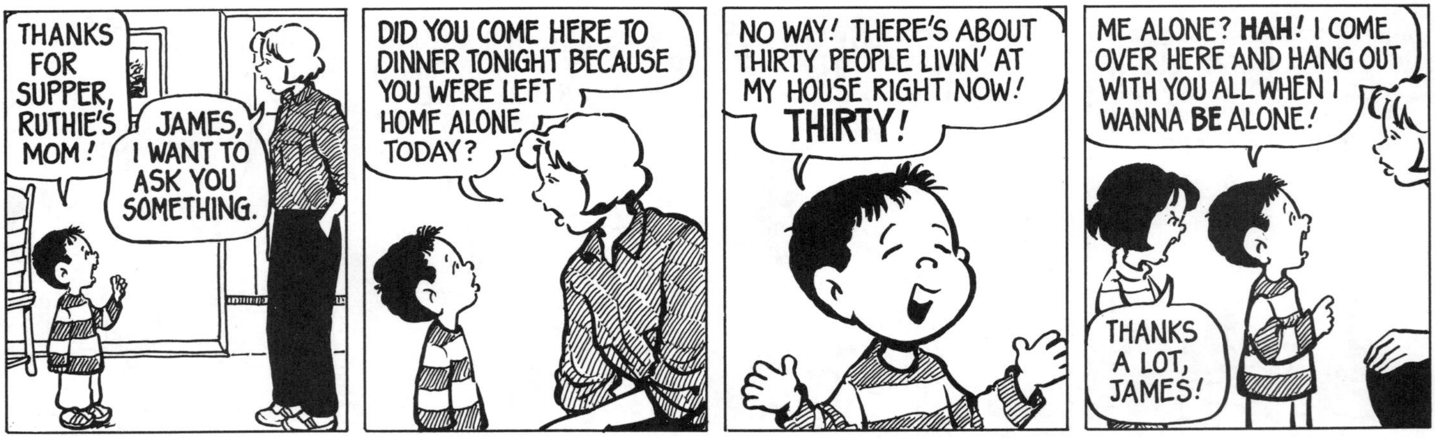
THANKS FOR SUPPER, RUTHIE'S MOM!
JAMES, I WANT TO ASK YOU SOMETHING.
DID YOU COME HERE TO DINNER TONIGHT BECAUSE YOU WERE LEFT HOME ALONE TODAY?
NO WAY! THERE'S ABOUT THIRTY PEOPLE LIVIN' AT MY HOUSE RIGHT NOW! THIRTY!
ME ALONE? HAH! I COME OVER HERE AND HANG OUT WITH YOU ALL WHEN I WANNA BE ALONE!
THANKS A LOT, JAMES!

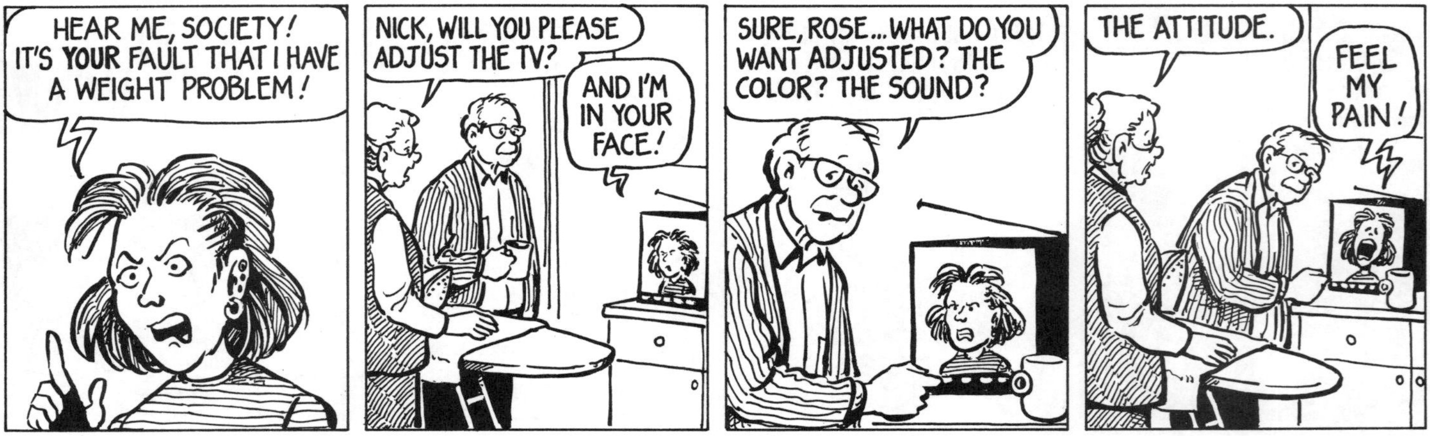
HEAR ME, SOCIETY! IT'S YOUR FAULT THAT I HAVE A WEIGHT PROBLEM!
NICK, WILL YOU PLEASE ADJUST THE TV?
AND I'M IN YOUR FACE!
SURE, ROSE... WHAT DO YOU WANT ADJUSTED? THE COLOR? THE SOUND?
THE ATTITUDE.
FEEL MY PAIN!

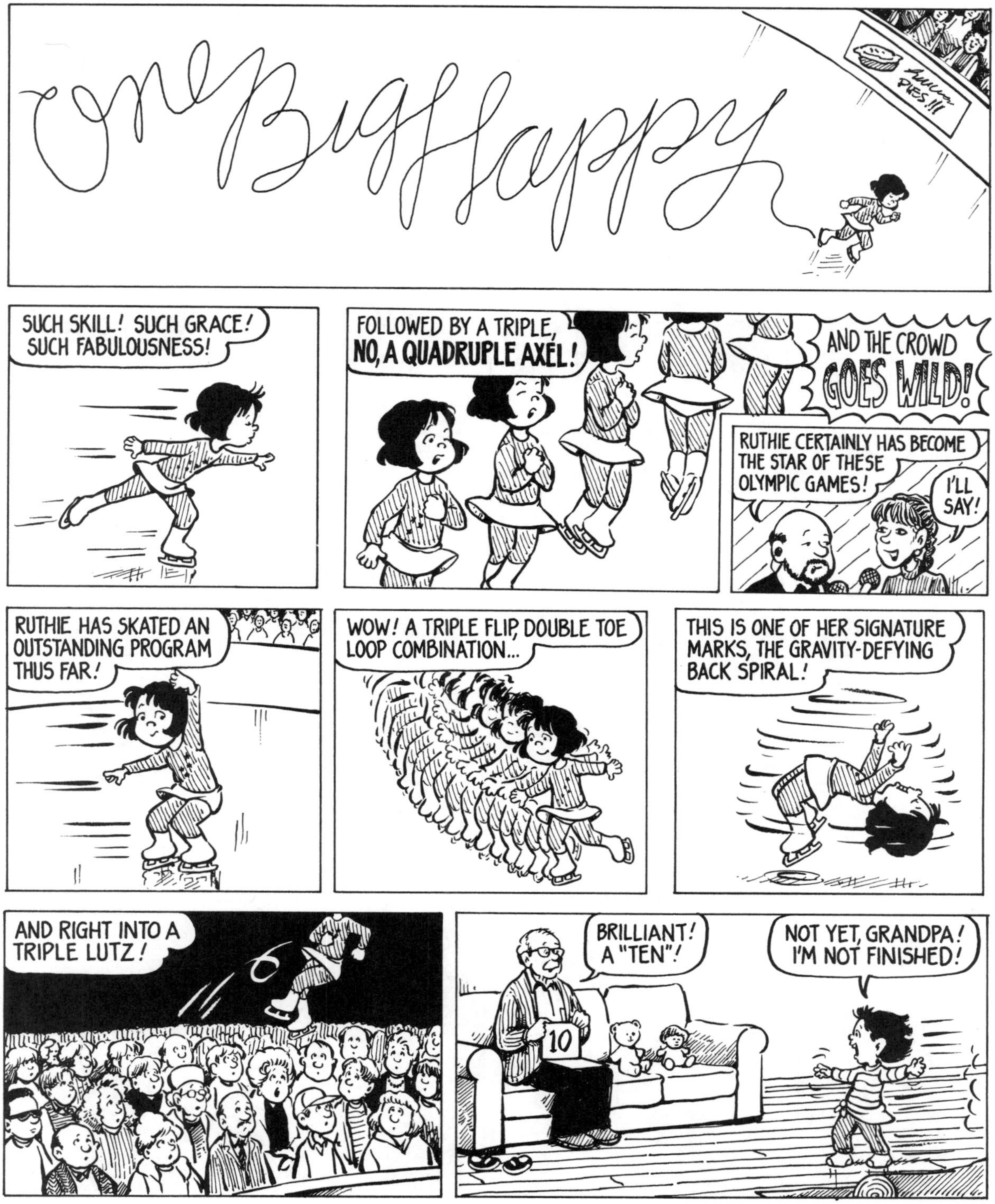
One Big Happy
SUCH SKILL! SUCH GRACE! SUCH FABULOUSNESS!
FOLLOWED BY A TRIPLE, NO, A QUADRUPLE AXEL!
AND THE CROWD GOES WILD!
RUTHIE CERTAINLY HAS BECOME THE STAR OF THESE OLYMPIC GAMES!
I'LL SAY!
RUTHIE HAS SKATED AN OUTSTANDING PROGRAM THUS FAR!
WOW! A TRIPLE FLIP, DOUBLE TOE LOOP COMBINATION...
THIS IS ONE OF HER SIGNATURE MARKS, THE GRAVITY-DEFYING BACK SPIRAL!
AND RIGHT INTO A TRIPLE LUTZ!
BRILLIANT! A "TEN"!
10
NOT YET, GRANDPA! I'M NOT FINISHED!

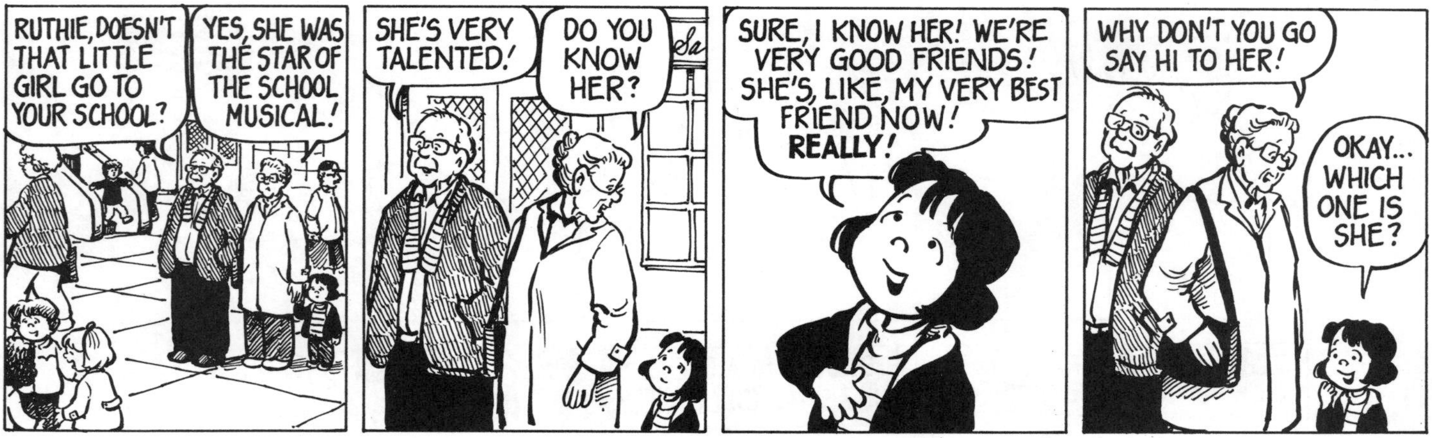
RUTHIE, DOESN'T THAT LITTLE GIRL GO TO YOUR SCHOOL?
YES, SHE WAS THE STAR OF THE SCHOOL MUSICAL!
SHE'S VERY TALENTED!
DO YOU KNOW HER?
SURE, I KNOW HER! WE'RE VERY GOOD FRIENDS! SHE'S, LIKE, MY VERY BEST FRIEND NOW! **REALLY**!
WHY DON'T YOU GO SAY HI TO HER!
OKAY... WHICH ONE IS SHE?

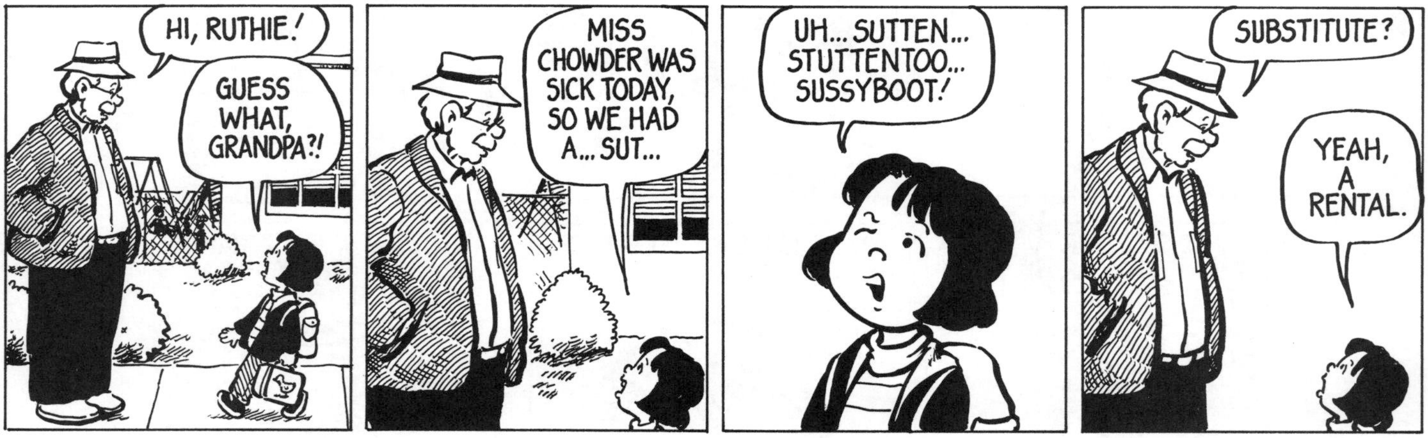
HI, RUTHIE!
GUESS WHAT, GRANDPA?!
MISS CHOWDER WAS SICK TODAY, SO WE HAD A... SUT...
UH... SUTTEN... STUTTENTOO... SUSSYBOOT!
SUBSTITUTE?
YEAH, A RENTAL.

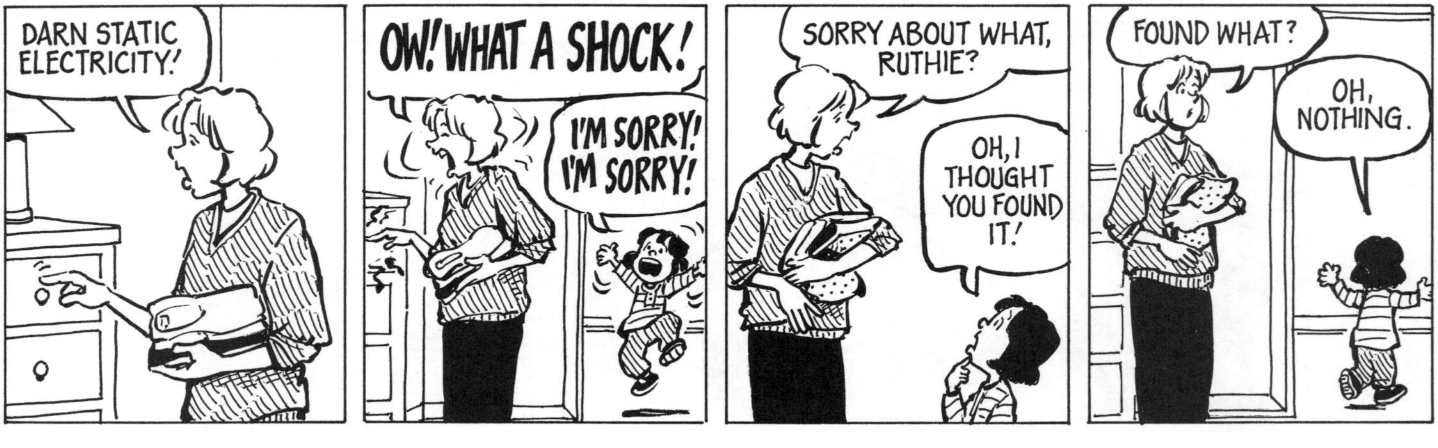
DARN STATIC ELECTRICITY!
OW! WHAT A SHOCK!
I'M SORRY! I'M SORRY!
SORRY ABOUT WHAT, RUTHIE?
OH, I THOUGHT YOU FOUND IT!
FOUND WHAT?
OH, NOTHING.

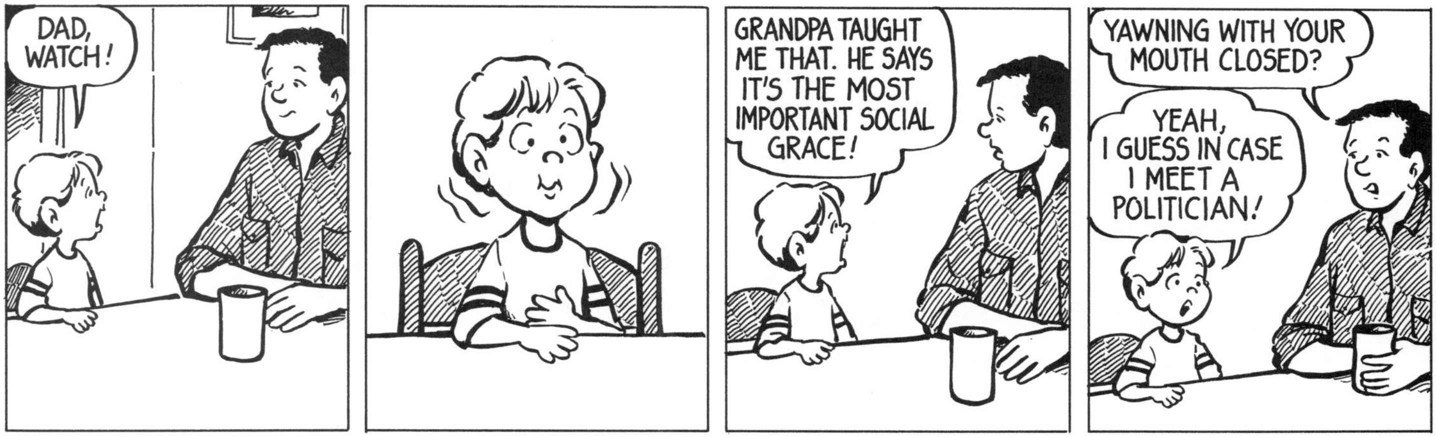
DAD, WATCH!
GRANDPA TAUGHT ME THAT. HE SAYS IT'S THE MOST IMPORTANT SOCIAL GRACE!
YAWNING WITH YOUR MOUTH CLOSED?
YEAH, I GUESS IN CASE I MEET A POLITICIAN!

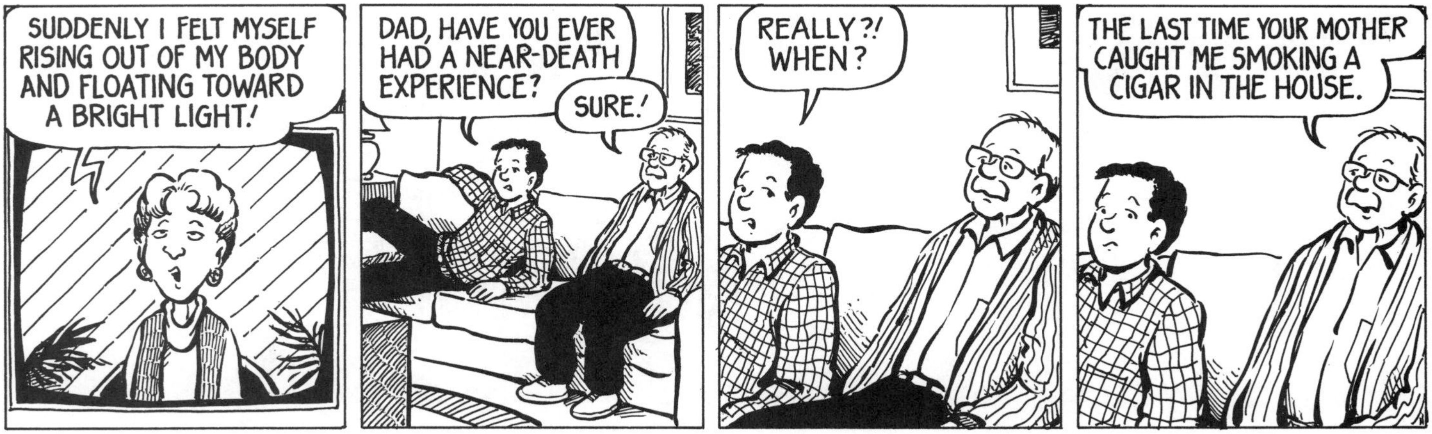
SUDDENLY I FELT MYSELF RISING OUT OF MY BODY AND FLOATING TOWARD A BRIGHT LIGHT!
DAD, HAVE YOU EVER HAD A NEAR-DEATH EXPERIENCE?
SURE!
REALLY?! WHEN?
THE LAST TIME YOUR MOTHER CAUGHT ME SMOKING A CIGAR IN THE HOUSE.

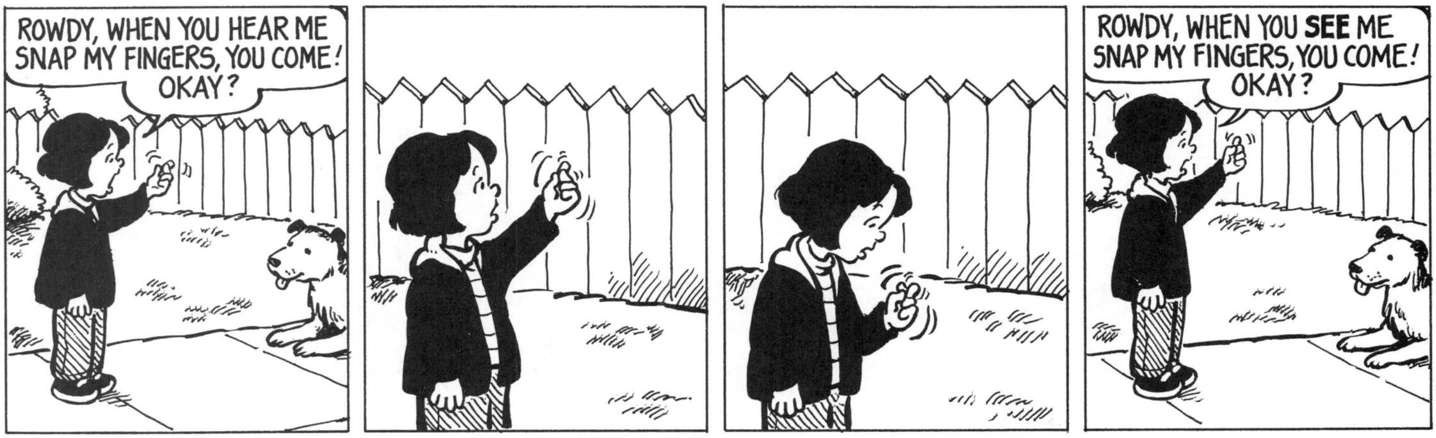
ROWDY, WHEN YOU HEAR ME SNAP MY FINGERS, YOU COME! OKAY?
ROWDY, WHEN YOU **SEE** ME SNAP MY FINGERS, YOU COME! OKAY?

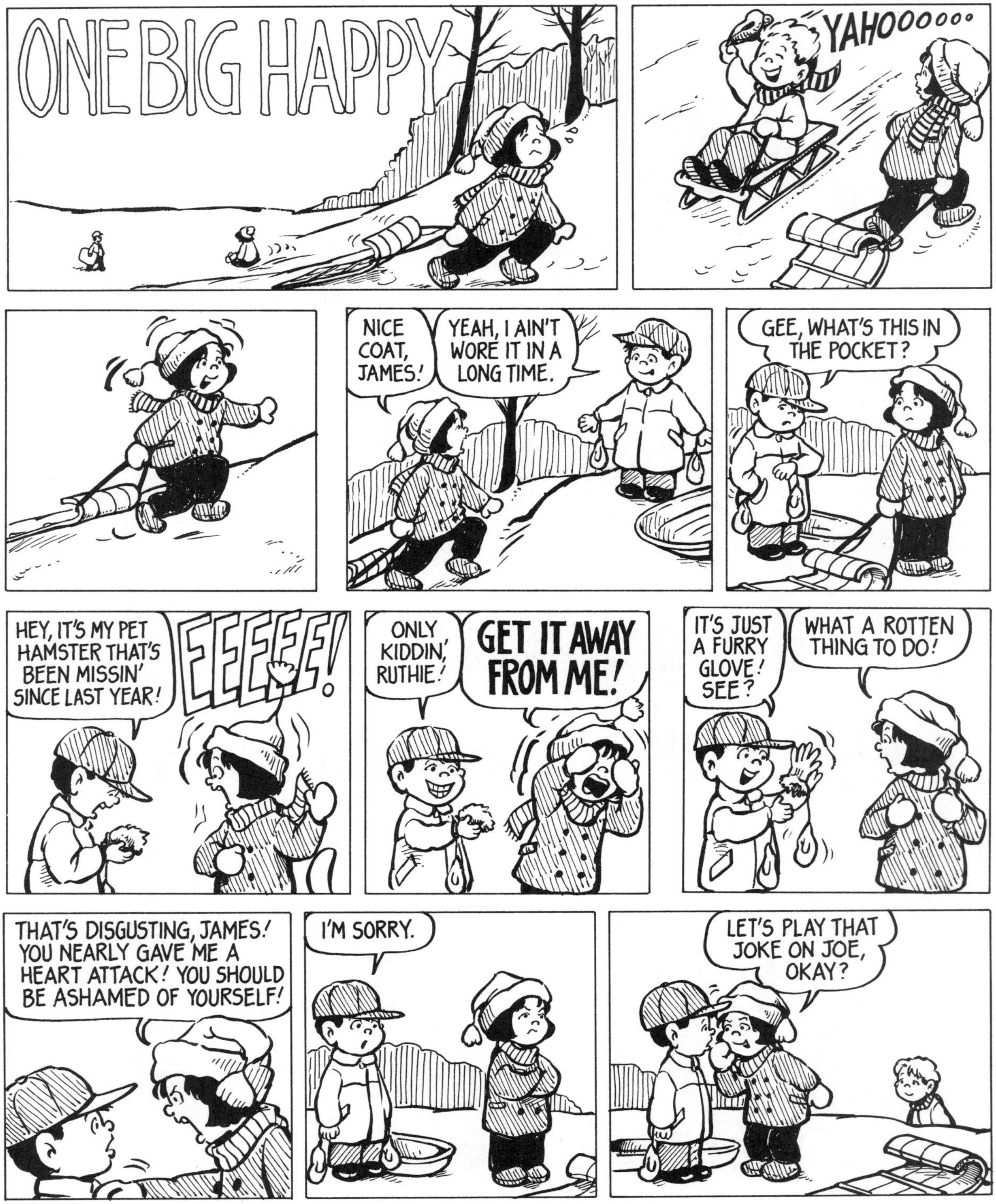
ONE BIG HAPPY
YAHOOOOOO
NICE COAT, JAMES!
YEAH, I AIN'T WORE IT IN A LONG TIME.
GEE, WHAT'S THIS IN THE POCKET?
HEY, IT'S MY PET HAMSTER THAT'S BEEN MISSIN' SINCE LAST YEAR!
EEEEEE!
ONLY KIDDIN', RUTHIE!
GET IT AWAY FROM ME!
IT'S JUST A FURRY GLOVE! SEE?
WHAT A ROTTEN THING TO DO!
THAT'S DISGUSTING, JAMES! YOU NEARLY GAVE ME A HEART ATTACK! YOU SHOULD BE ASHAMED OF YOURSELF!
I'M SORRY.
LET'S PLAY THAT JOKE ON JOE, OKAY?

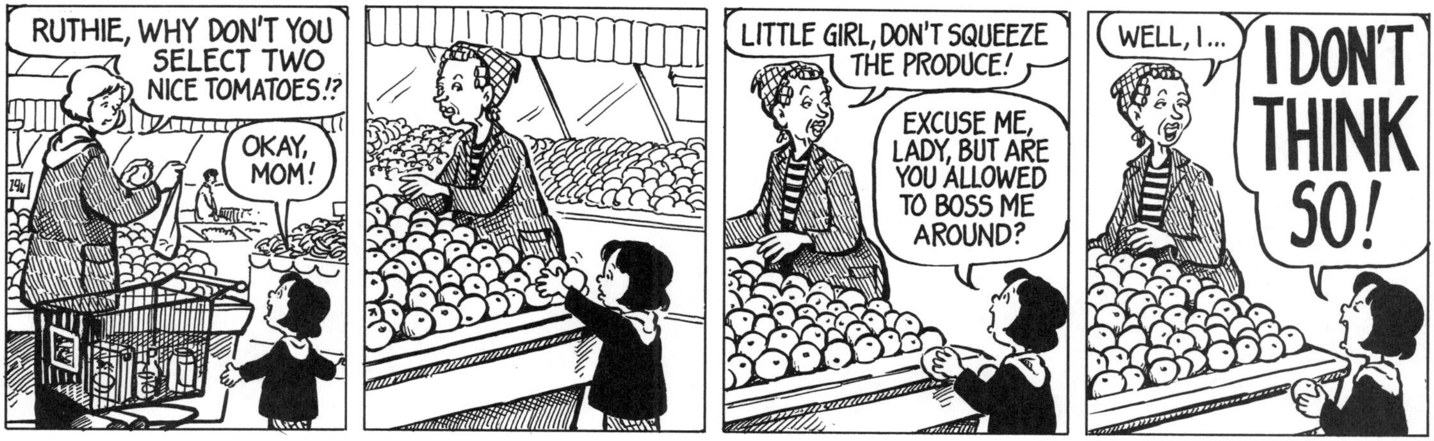
RUTHIE, WHY DON'T YOU SELECT TWO NICE TOMATOES!?
OKAY, MOM!
LITTLE GIRL, DON'T SQUEEZE THE PRODUCE!
EXCUSE ME, LADY, BUT ARE YOU ALLOWED TO BOSS ME AROUND?
WELL, I...
I DON'T THINK SO!

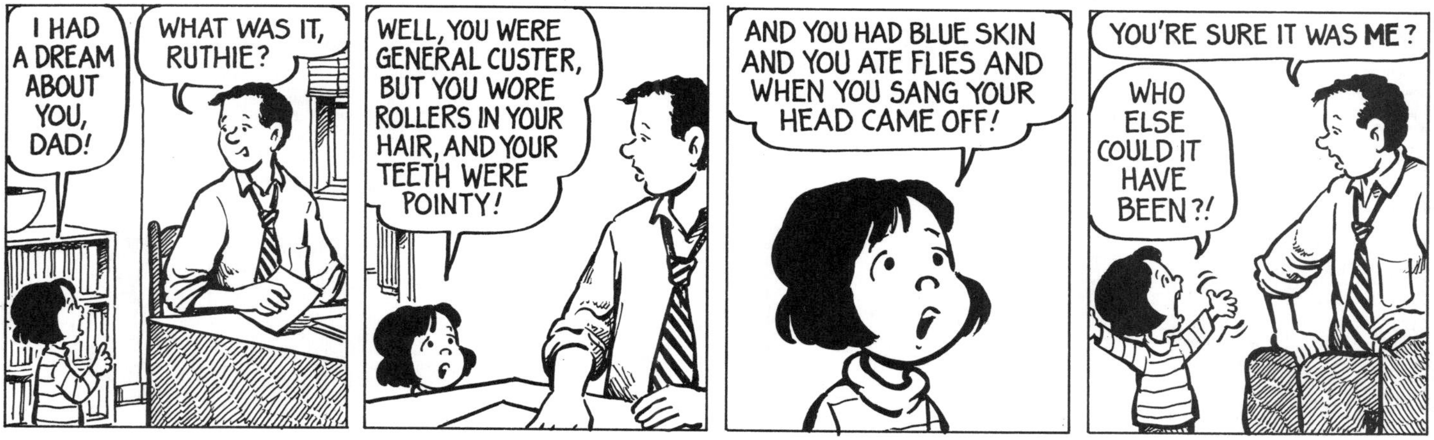
I HAD A DREAM ABOUT YOU, DAD!
WHAT WAS IT, RUTHIE?
WELL, YOU WERE GENERAL CUSTER, BUT YOU WORE ROLLERS IN YOUR HAIR, AND YOUR TEETH WERE POINTY!
AND YOU HAD BLUE SKIN AND YOU ATE FLIES AND WHEN YOU SANG YOUR HEAD CAME OFF!
YOU'RE SURE IT WAS ME?
WHO ELSE COULD IT HAVE BEEN?!

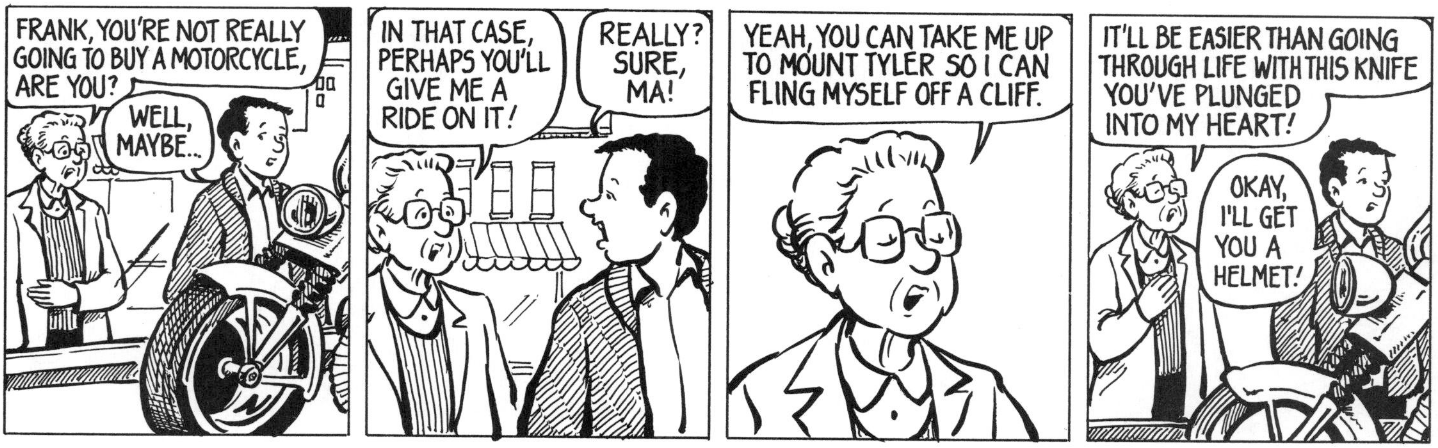
FRANK, YOU'RE NOT REALLY GOING TO BUY A MOTORCYCLE, ARE YOU?
WELL, MAYBE...
IN THAT CASE, PERHAPS YOU'LL GIVE ME A RIDE ON IT!
REALLY? SURE, MA!
YEAH, YOU CAN TAKE ME UP TO MOUNT TYLER SO I CAN FLING MYSELF OFF A CLIFF.
IT'LL BE EASIER THAN GOING THROUGH LIFE WITH THIS KNIFE YOU'VE PLUNGED INTO MY HEART!
OKAY, I'LL GET YOU A HELMET!

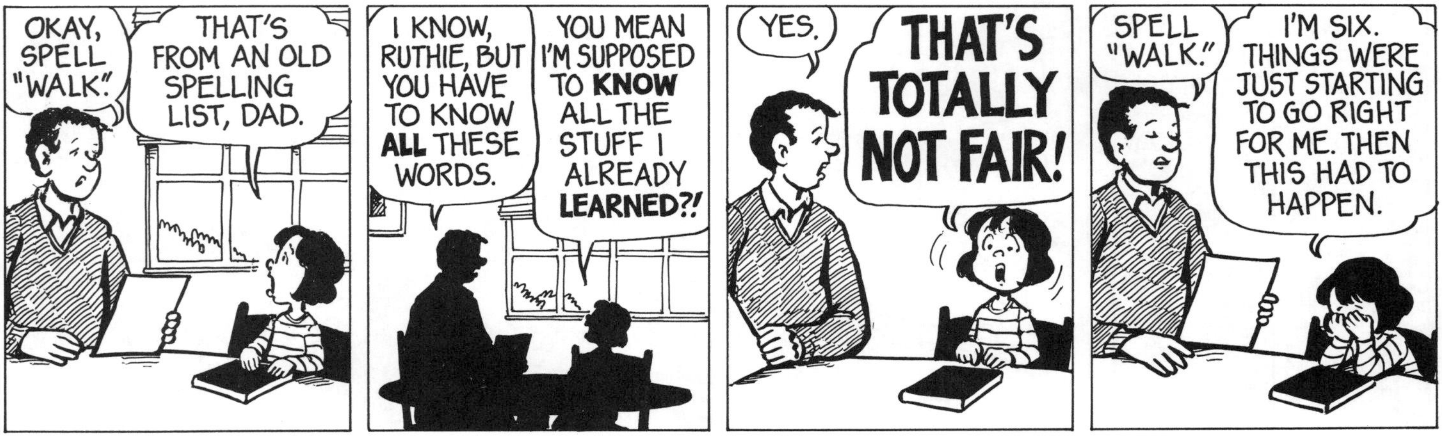
OKAY, SPELL "WALK."
THAT'S FROM AN OLD SPELLING LIST, DAD.
I KNOW, RUTHIE, BUT YOU HAVE TO KNOW ALL THESE WORDS.
YOU MEAN I'M SUPPOSED TO KNOW ALL THE STUFF I ALREADY LEARNED?!
YES.
THAT'S TOTALLY NOT FAIR!
SPELL "WALK."
I'M SIX. THINGS WERE JUST STARTING TO GO RIGHT FOR ME. THEN THIS HAD TO HAPPEN.

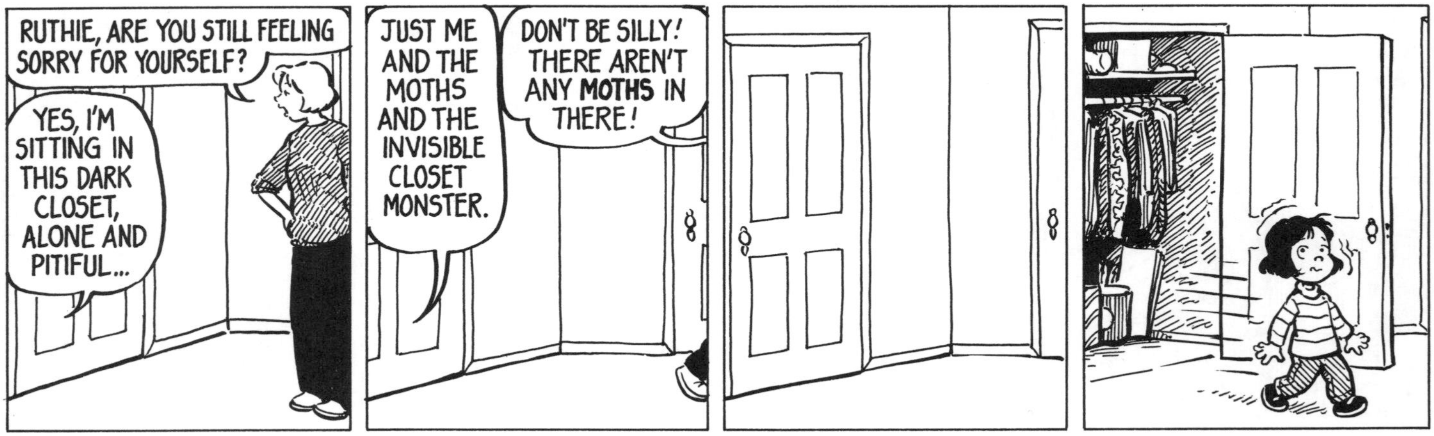
RUTHIE, ARE YOU STILL FEELING SORRY FOR YOURSELF?
YES, I'M SITTING IN THIS DARK CLOSET, ALONE AND PITIFUL...
JUST ME AND THE MOTHS AND THE INVISIBLE CLOSET MONSTER.
DON'T BE SILLY! THERE AREN'T ANY MOTHS IN THERE!

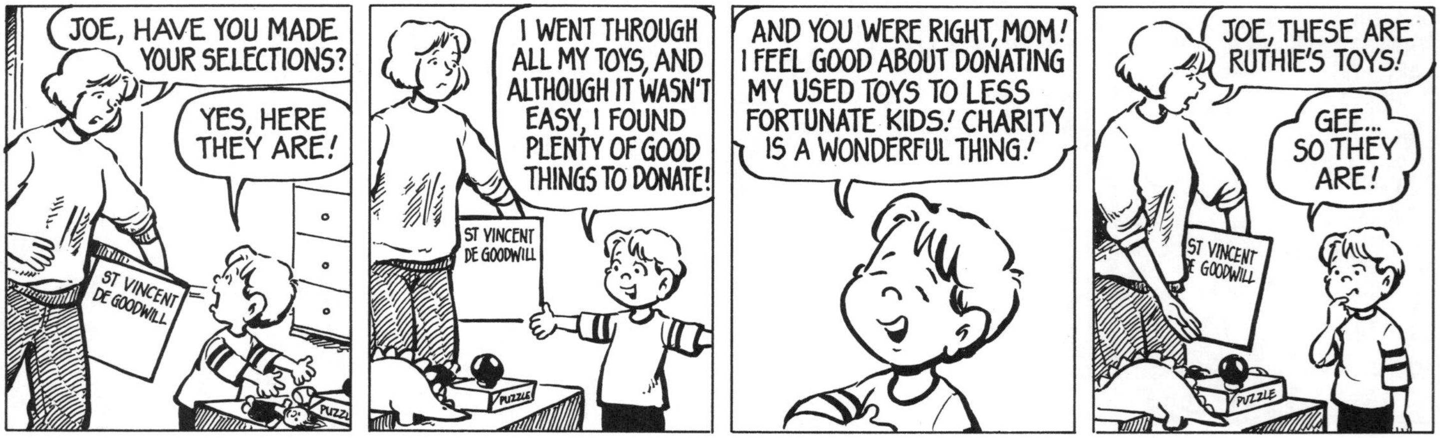
JOE, HAVE YOU MADE YOUR SELECTIONS?
YES, HERE THEY ARE!
ST VINCENT DE GOODWILL
I WENT THROUGH ALL MY TOYS, AND ALTHOUGH IT WASN'T EASY, I FOUND PLENTY OF GOOD THINGS TO DONATE!
AND YOU WERE RIGHT, MOM! I FEEL GOOD ABOUT DONATING MY USED TOYS TO LESS FORTUNATE KIDS! CHARITY IS A WONDERFUL THING!
JOE, THESE ARE RUTHIE'S TOYS!
GEE... SO THEY ARE!
PUZZLE

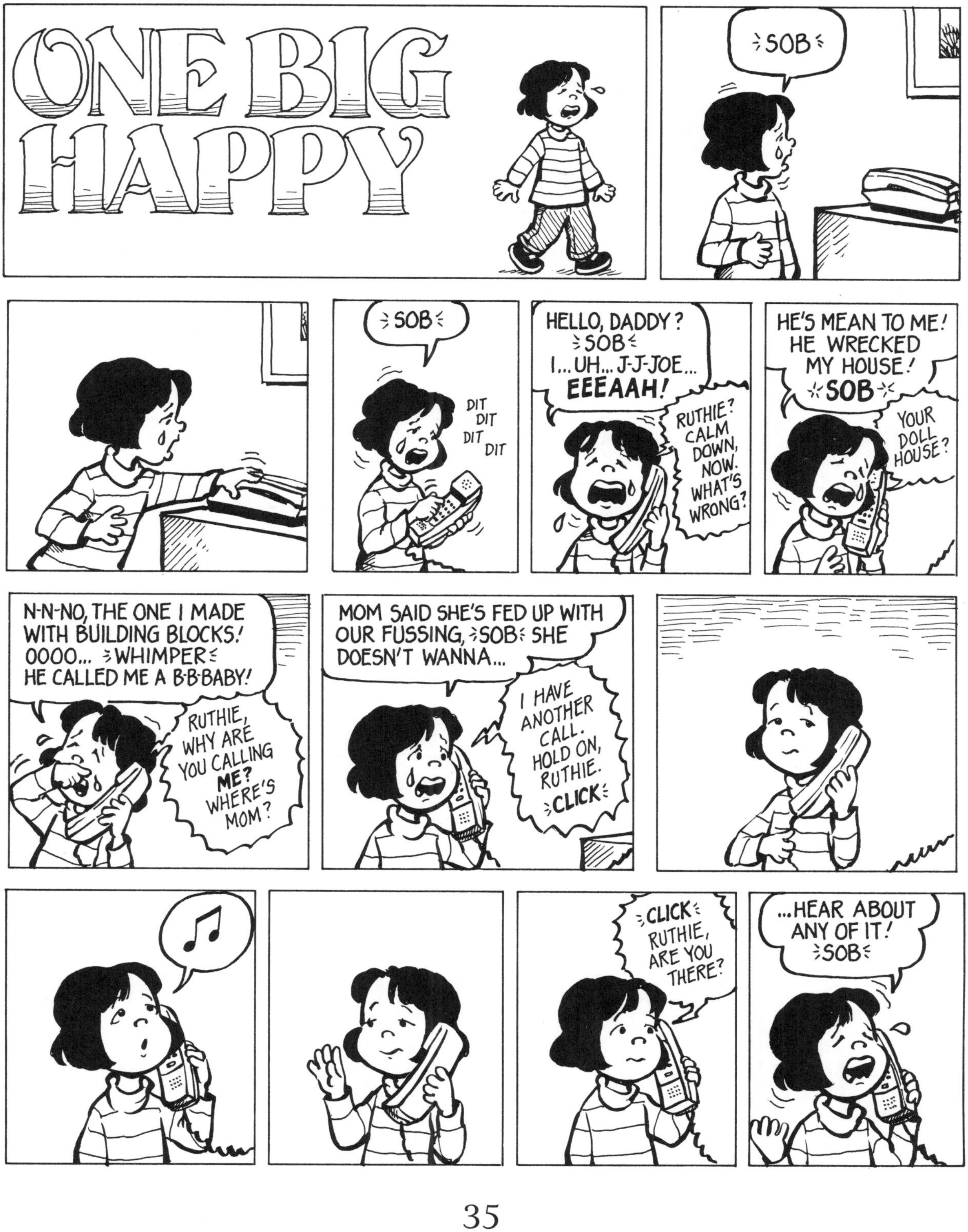
ONE BIG HAPPY
SOB
SOB
DIT DIT DIT DIT
HELLO, DADDY? SOB I... UH... J-J-JOE... EEEAAH!
RUTHIE? CALM DOWN, NOW. WHAT'S WRONG?
HE'S MEAN TO ME! HE WRECKED MY HOUSE! SOB
YOUR DOLL HOUSE?
N-N-NO, THE ONE I MADE WITH BUILDING BLOCKS! OOOO... WHIMPER HE CALLED ME A B-B-BABY!
RUTHIE, WHY ARE YOU CALLING ME? WHERE'S MOM?
MOM SAID SHE'S FED UP WITH OUR FUSSING, SOB SHE DOESN'T WANNA...
I HAVE ANOTHER CALL. HOLD ON, RUTHIE. CLICK
♫
CLICK RUTHIE, ARE YOU THERE?
...HEAR ABOUT ANY OF IT! SOB

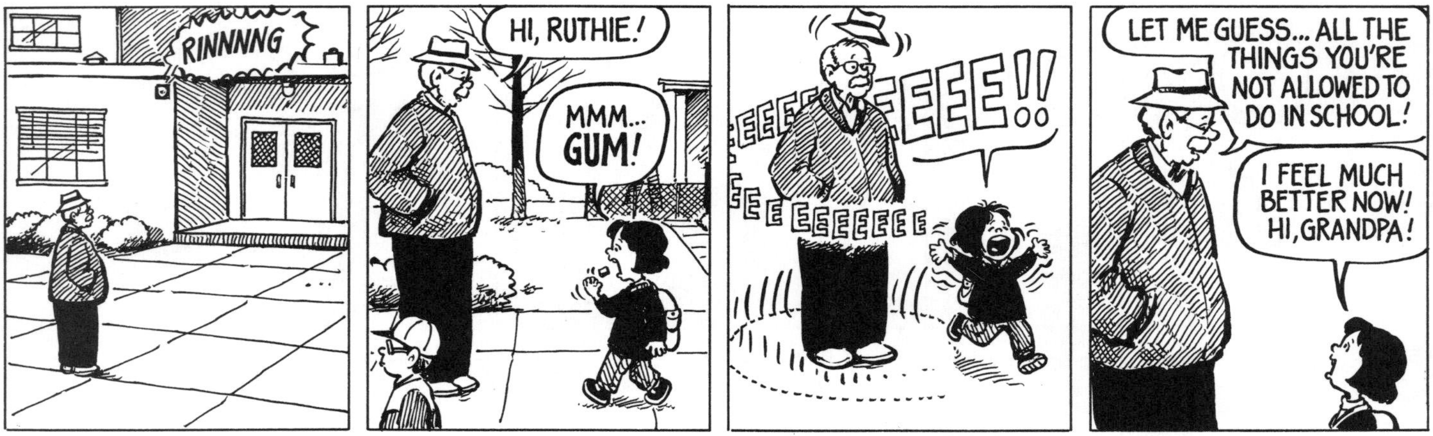
RINNNNG
HI, RUTHIE!
MMM... GUM!
EEEEEEEEEE!!
LET ME GUESS... ALL THE THINGS YOU'RE NOT ALLOWED TO DO IN SCHOOL!
I FEEL MUCH BETTER NOW! HI, GRANDPA!

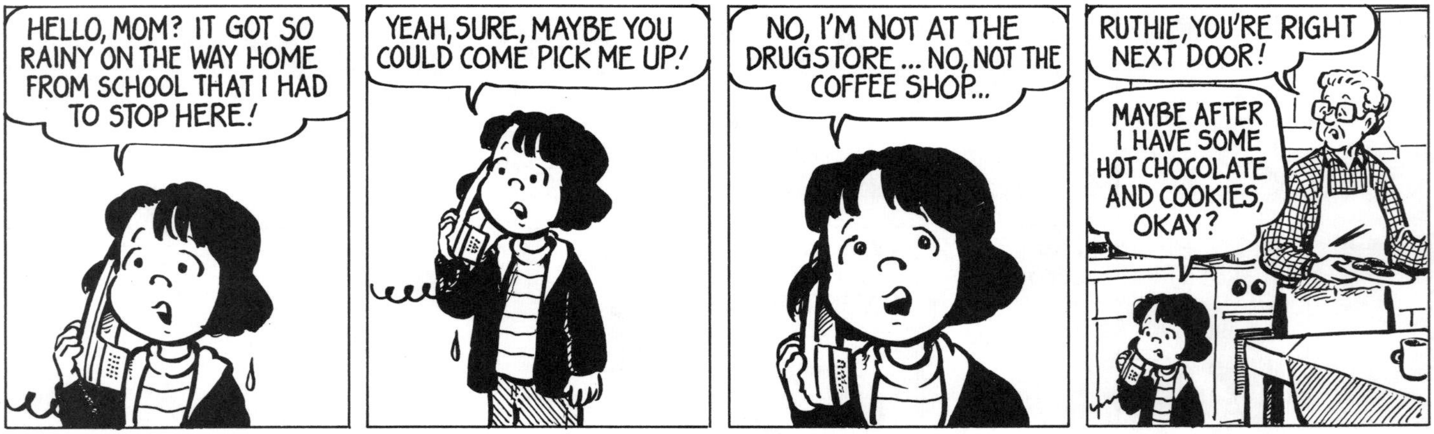
HELLO, MOM? IT GOT SO RAINY ON THE WAY HOME FROM SCHOOL THAT I HAD TO STOP HERE!
YEAH, SURE, MAYBE YOU COULD COME PICK ME UP!
NO, I'M NOT AT THE DRUGSTORE ... NO, NOT THE COFFEE SHOP...
RUTHIE, YOU'RE RIGHT NEXT DOOR!
MAYBE AFTER I HAVE SOME HOT CHOCOLATE AND COOKIES, OKAY?

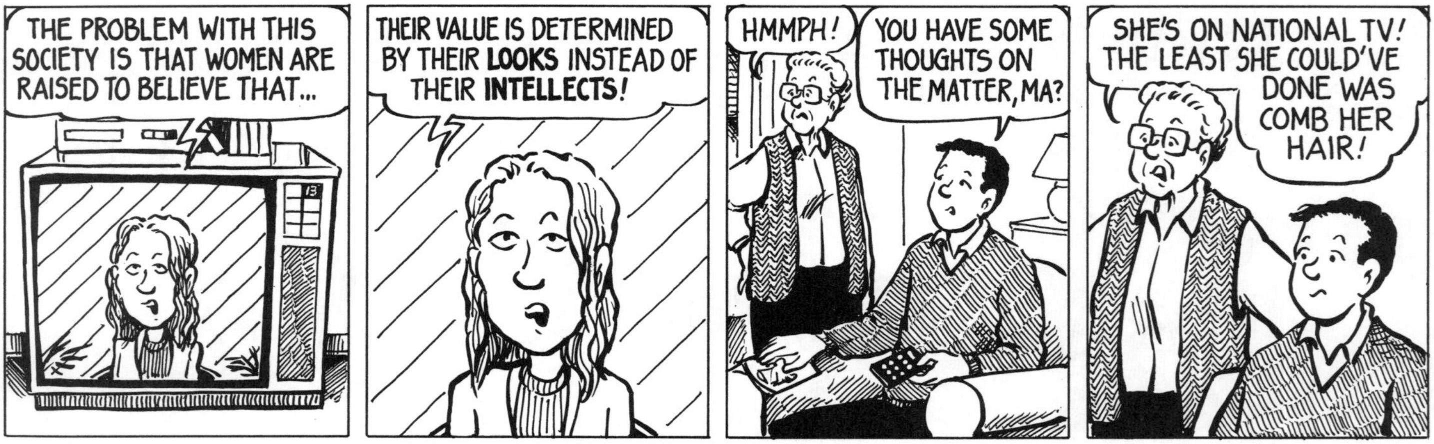
THE PROBLEM WITH THIS SOCIETY IS THAT WOMEN ARE RAISED TO BELIEVE THAT...
THEIR VALUE IS DETERMINED BY THEIR **LOOKS** INSTEAD OF THEIR **INTELLECTS**!
HMMPH!
YOU HAVE SOME THOUGHTS ON THE MATTER, MA?
SHE'S ON NATIONAL TV! THE LEAST SHE COULD'VE DONE WAS COMB HER HAIR!

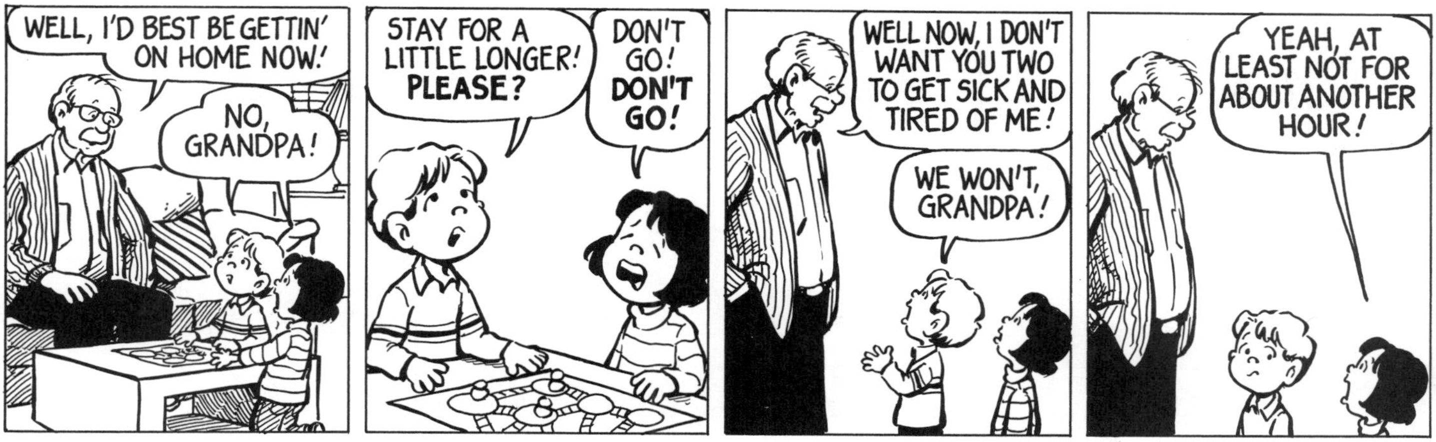
WELL, I'D BEST BE GETTIN' ON HOME NOW!
NO, GRANDPA!
STAY FOR A LITTLE LONGER! **PLEASE?**
DON'T GO! **DON'T GO!**
WELL NOW, I DON'T WANT YOU TWO TO GET SICK AND TIRED OF ME!
WE WON'T, GRANDPA!
YEAH, AT LEAST NOT FOR ABOUT ANOTHER HOUR!

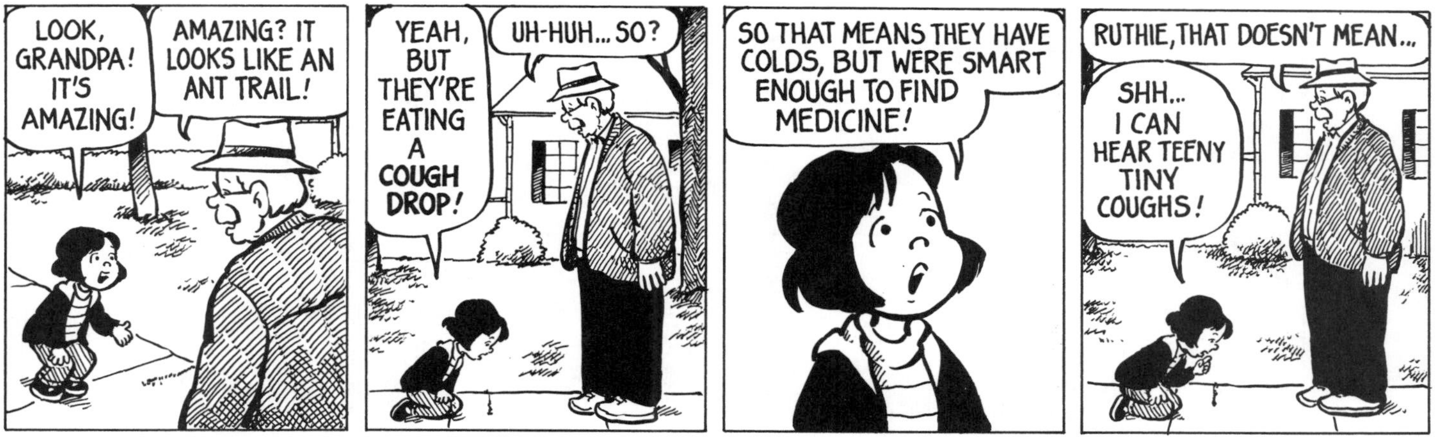
LOOK, GRANDPA! IT'S AMAZING!
AMAZING? IT LOOKS LIKE AN ANT TRAIL!
YEAH, BUT THEY'RE EATING A **COUGH DROP!**
UH-HUH... SO?
SO THAT MEANS THEY HAVE COLDS, BUT WERE SMART ENOUGH TO FIND MEDICINE!
RUTHIE, THAT DOESN'T MEAN...
SHH... I CAN HEAR TEENY TINY COUGHS!

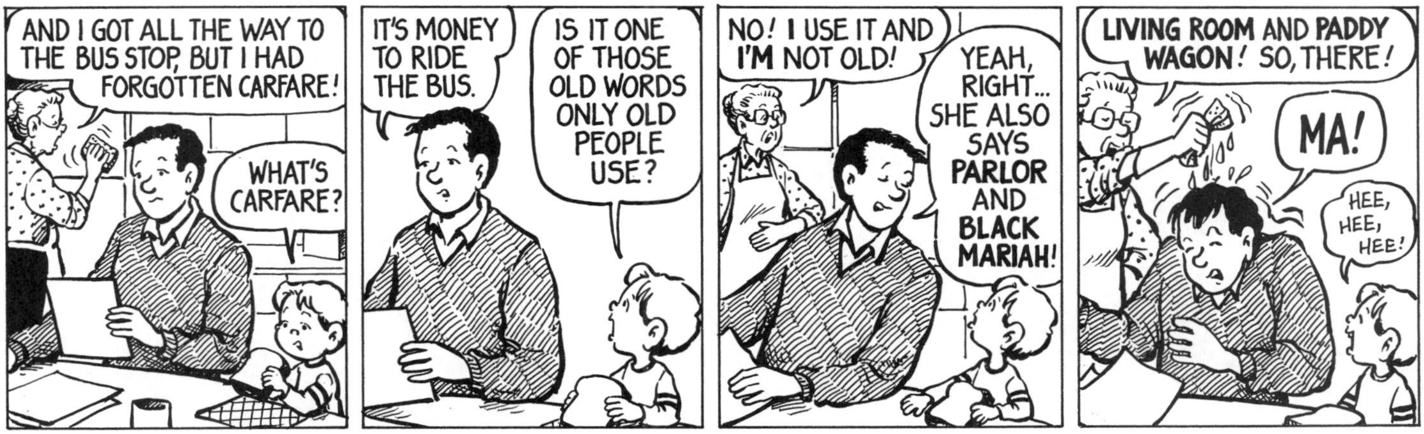
AND I GOT ALL THE WAY TO THE BUS STOP, BUT I HAD FORGOTTEN CARFARE!
WHAT'S CARFARE?
IT'S MONEY TO RIDE THE BUS.
IS IT ONE OF THOSE OLD WORDS ONLY OLD PEOPLE USE?
NO! I USE IT AND **I'M** NOT OLD!
YEAH, RIGHT... SHE ALSO SAYS **PARLOR** AND **BLACK MARIAH!**
LIVING ROOM AND **PADDY WAGON!** SO, THERE!
MA!
HEE, HEE, HEE!

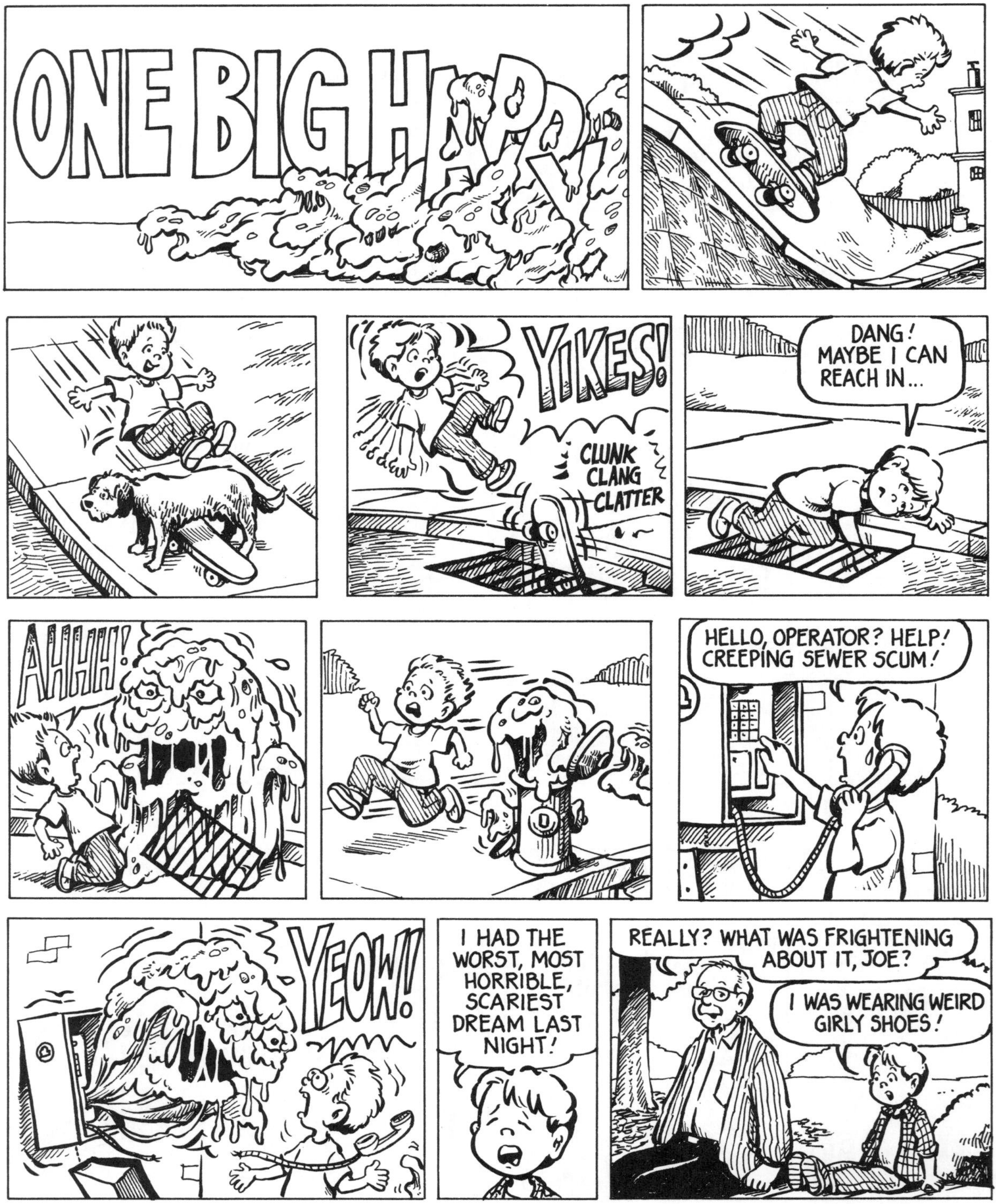
ONE BIG HAPPY
YIKES!
CLUNK CLANG CLATTER
DANG! MAYBE I CAN REACH IN...
AHHH!
HELLO, OPERATOR? HELP! CREEPING SEWER SCUM!
YEOW!
I HAD THE WORST, MOST HORRIBLE, SCARIEST DREAM LAST NIGHT!
REALLY? WHAT WAS FRIGHTENING ABOUT IT, JOE?
I WAS WEARING WEIRD GIRLY SHOES!

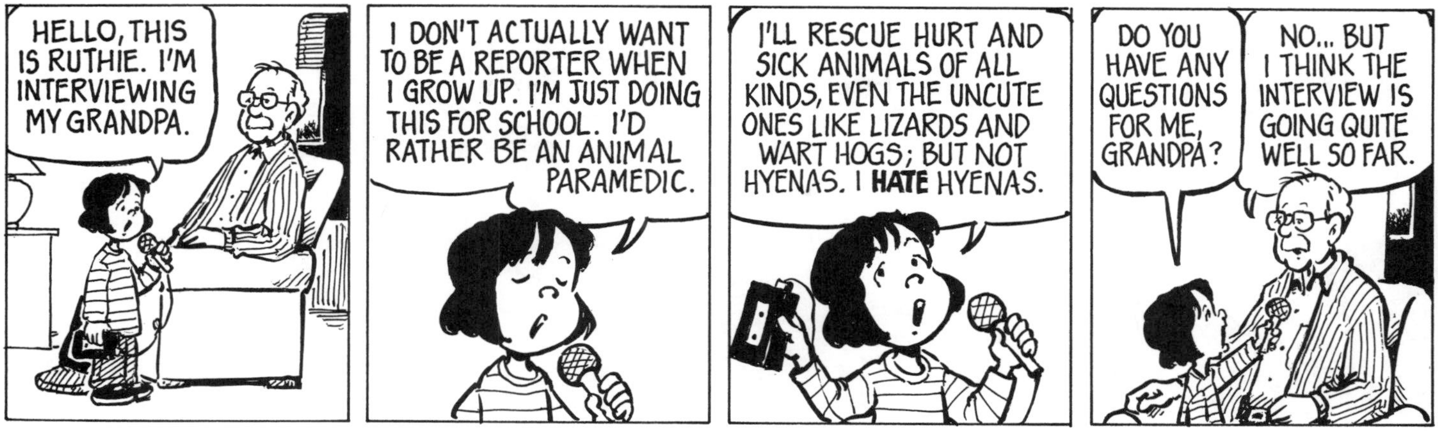
HELLO, THIS IS RUTHIE. I'M INTERVIEWING MY GRANDPA.
I DON'T ACTUALLY WANT TO BE A REPORTER WHEN I GROW UP. I'M JUST DOING THIS FOR SCHOOL. I'D RATHER BE AN ANIMAL PARAMEDIC.
I'LL RESCUE HURT AND SICK ANIMALS OF ALL KINDS, EVEN THE UNCUTE ONES LIKE LIZARDS AND WART HOGS; BUT NOT HYENAS. I **HATE** HYENAS.
DO YOU HAVE ANY QUESTIONS FOR ME, GRANDPA?
NO... BUT I THINK THE INTERVIEW IS GOING QUITE WELL SO FAR.

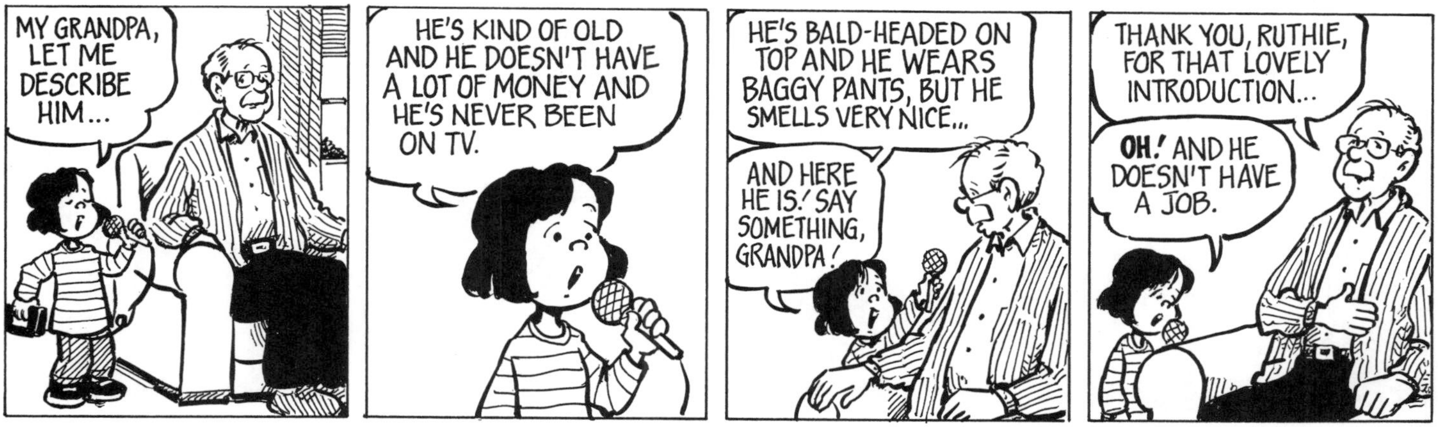
MY GRANDPA, LET ME DESCRIBE HIM...
HE'S KIND OF OLD AND HE DOESN'T HAVE A LOT OF MONEY AND HE'S NEVER BEEN ON TV.
HE'S BALD-HEADED ON TOP AND HE WEARS BAGGY PANTS, BUT HE SMELLS VERY NICE...
AND HERE HE IS! SAY SOMETHING, GRANDPA!
THANK YOU, RUTHIE, FOR THAT LOVELY INTRODUCTION...
OH! AND HE DOESN'T HAVE A JOB.

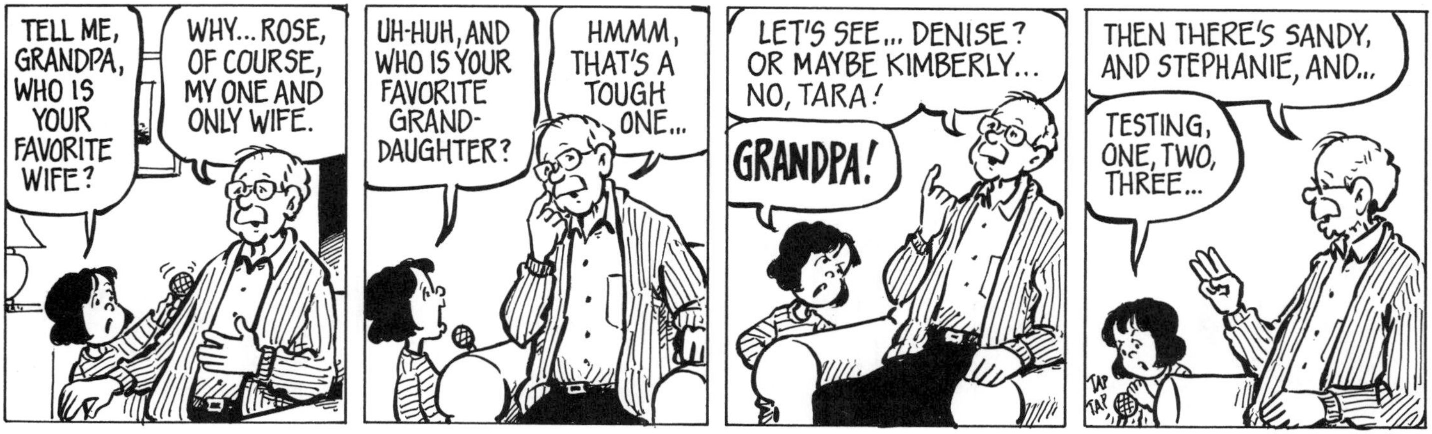
TELL ME, GRANDPA, WHO IS YOUR FAVORITE WIFE?
WHY... ROSE, OF COURSE, MY ONE AND ONLY WIFE.
UH-HUH, AND WHO IS YOUR FAVORITE GRAND-DAUGHTER?
HMMM, THAT'S A TOUGH ONE...
LET'S SEE... DENISE? OR MAYBE KIMBERLY... NO, TARA!
GRANDPA!
THEN THERE'S SANDY, AND STEPHANIE, AND...
TESTING, ONE, TWO, THREE...
TAP TAP

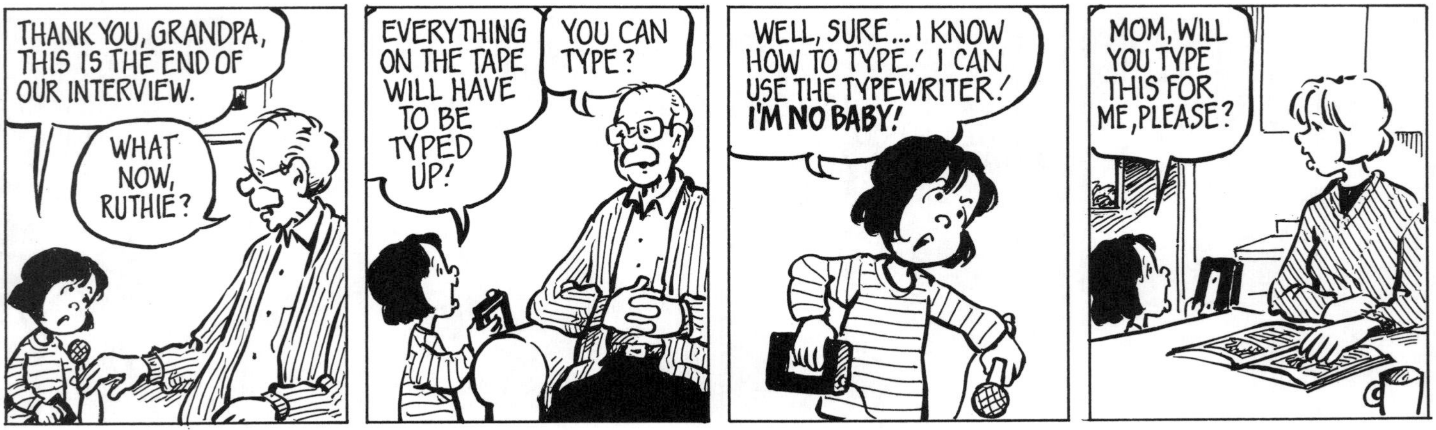
THANK YOU, GRANDPA, THIS IS THE END OF OUR INTERVIEW.
WHAT NOW, RUTHIE?
EVERYTHING ON THE TAPE WILL HAVE TO BE TYPED UP!
YOU CAN TYPE?
WELL, SURE... I KNOW HOW TO TYPE! I CAN USE THE TYPEWRITER! **I'M NO BABY!**
MOM, WILL YOU TYPE THIS FOR ME, PLEASE?

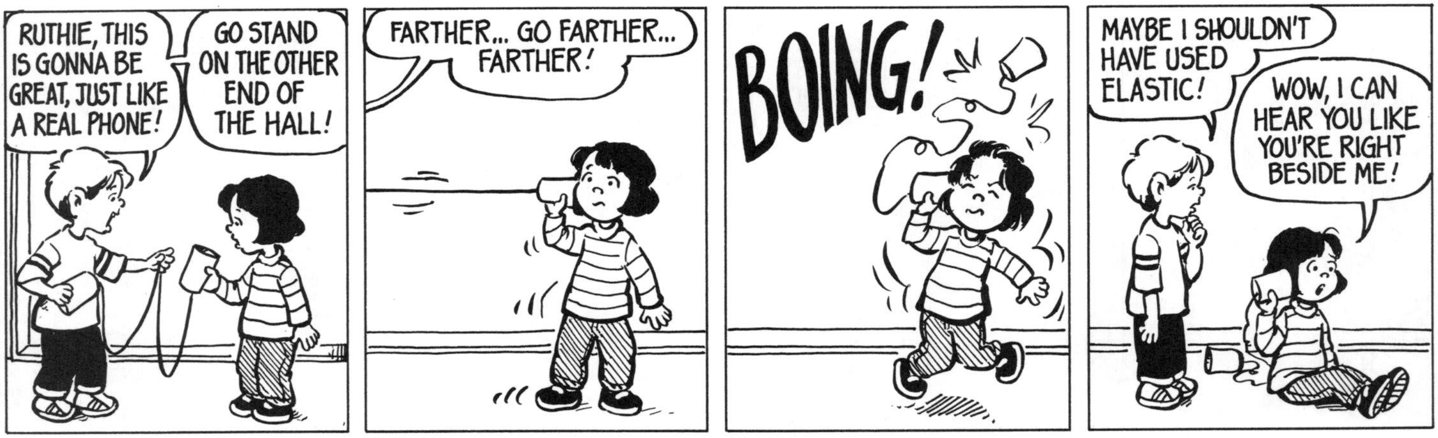
RUTHIE, THIS IS GONNA BE GREAT, JUST LIKE A REAL PHONE!
GO STAND ON THE OTHER END OF THE HALL!
FARTHER... GO FARTHER... FARTHER!
BOING!
MAYBE I SHOULDN'T HAVE USED ELASTIC!
WOW, I CAN HEAR YOU LIKE YOU'RE RIGHT BESIDE ME!

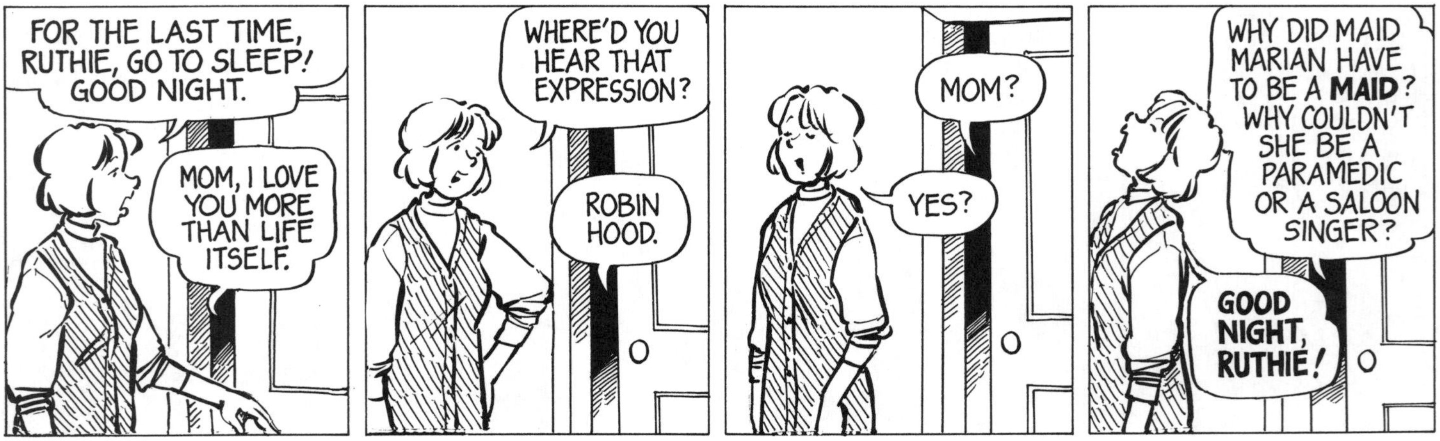
FOR THE LAST TIME, RUTHIE, GO TO SLEEP! GOOD NIGHT.
MOM, I LOVE YOU MORE THAN LIFE ITSELF.
WHERE'D YOU HEAR THAT EXPRESSION?
ROBIN HOOD.
MOM?
YES?
WHY DID MAID MARIAN HAVE TO BE A **MAID**? WHY COULDN'T SHE BE A PARAMEDIC OR A SALOON SINGER?
GOOD NIGHT, RUTHIE!

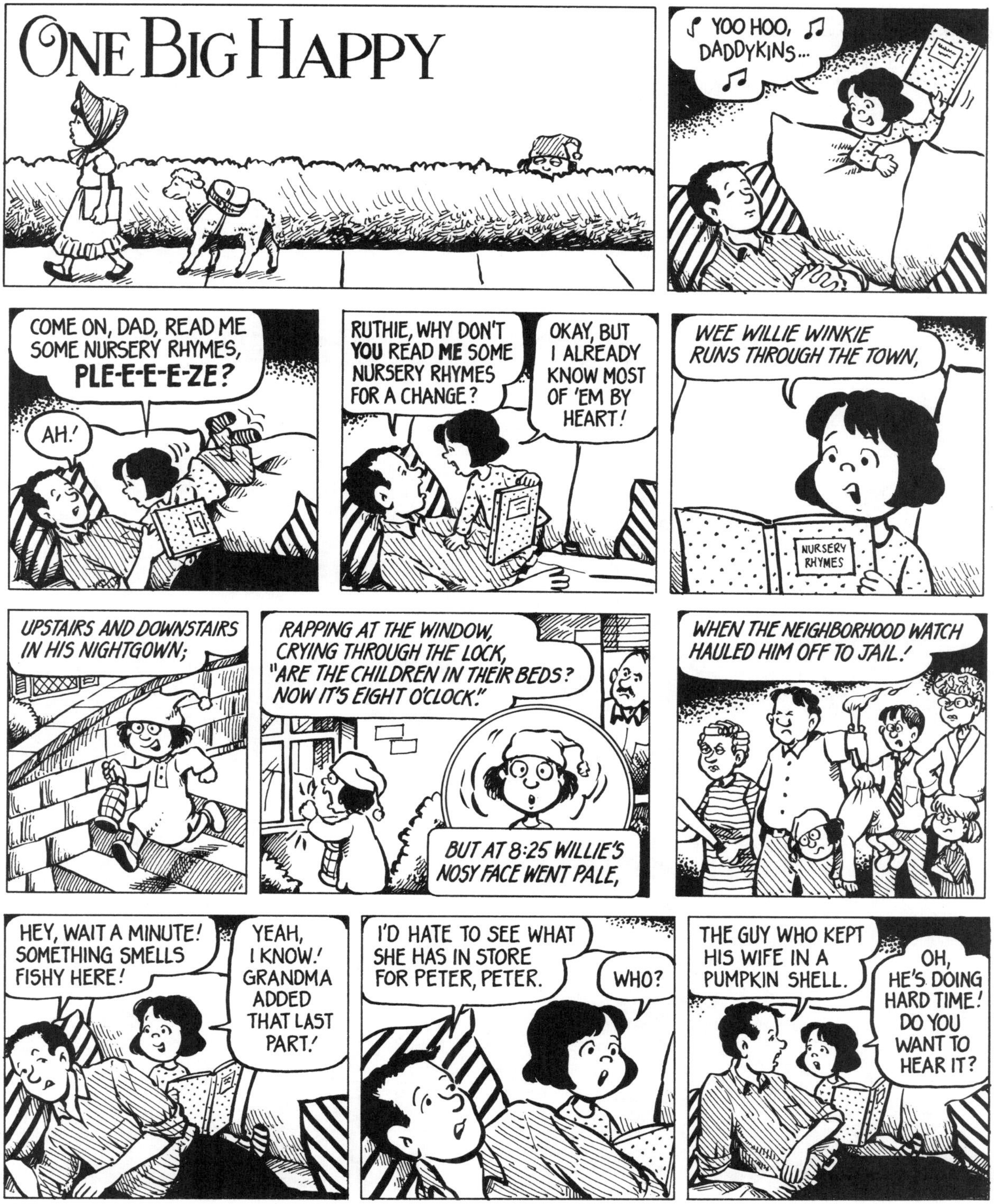
ONE BIG HAPPY
YOO HOO, DADDYKINS...
COME ON, DAD, READ ME SOME NURSERY RHYMES, PLE-E-E-E-ZE?
AH!
RUTHIE, WHY DON'T YOU READ ME SOME NURSERY RHYMES FOR A CHANGE?
OKAY, BUT I ALREADY KNOW MOST OF 'EM BY HEART!
WEE WILLIE WINKIE RUNS THROUGH THE TOWN,
NURSERY RHYMES
UPSTAIRS AND DOWNSTAIRS IN HIS NIGHTGOWN;
RAPPING AT THE WINDOW, CRYING THROUGH THE LOCK, "ARE THE CHILDREN IN THEIR BEDS? NOW IT'S EIGHT O'CLOCK."
BUT AT 8:25 WILLIE'S NOSY FACE WENT PALE,
WHEN THE NEIGHBORHOOD WATCH HAULED HIM OFF TO JAIL!
HEY, WAIT A MINUTE! SOMETHING SMELLS FISHY HERE!
YEAH, I KNOW! GRANDMA ADDED THAT LAST PART!
I'D HATE TO SEE WHAT SHE HAS IN STORE FOR PETER, PETER.
WHO?
THE GUY WHO KEPT HIS WIFE IN A PUMPKIN SHELL.
OH, HE'S DOING HARD TIME! DO YOU WANT TO HEAR IT?

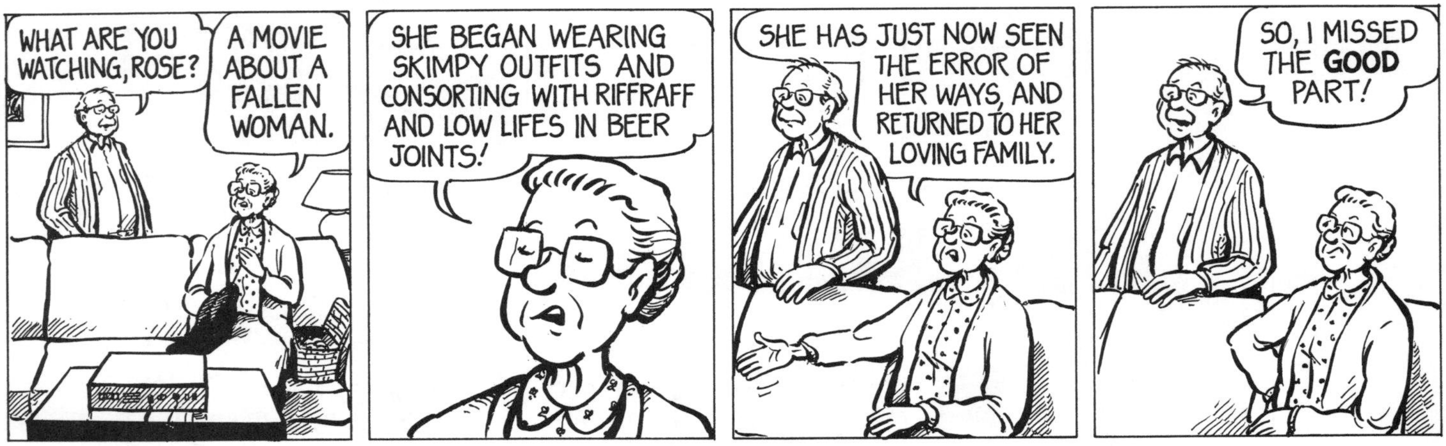
WHAT ARE YOU WATCHING, ROSE?
A MOVIE ABOUT A FALLEN WOMAN.
SHE BEGAN WEARING SKIMPY OUTFITS AND CONSORTING WITH RIFFRAFF AND LOW LIFES IN BEER JOINTS!
SHE HAS JUST NOW SEEN THE ERROR OF HER WAYS, AND RETURNED TO HER LOVING FAMILY.
SO, I MISSED THE **GOOD** PART!

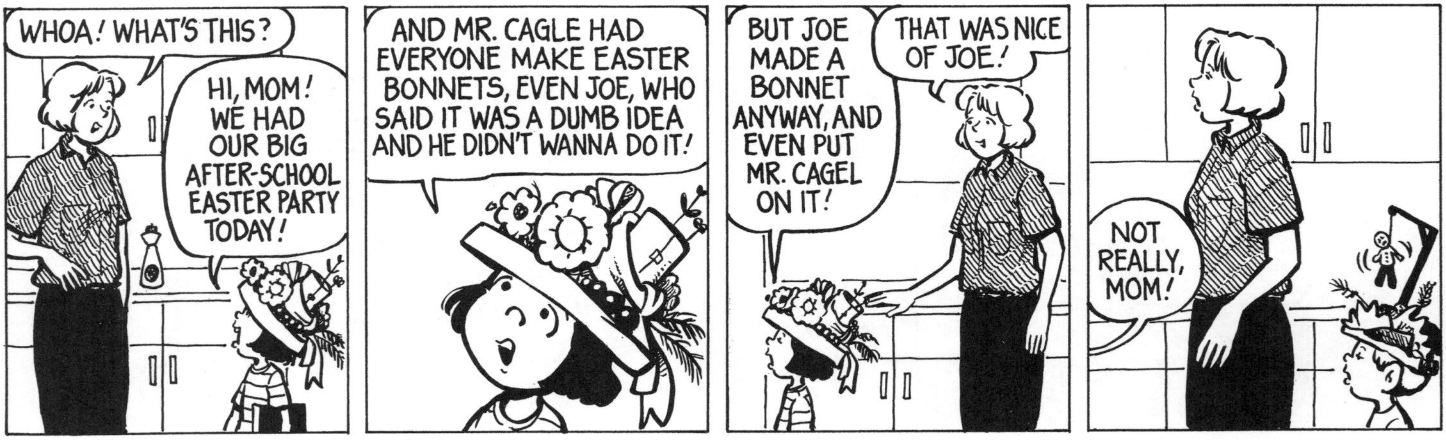
WHOA! WHAT'S THIS?
HI, MOM! WE HAD OUR BIG AFTER-SCHOOL EASTER PARTY TODAY!
AND MR. CAGLE HAD EVERYONE MAKE EASTER BONNETS, EVEN JOE, WHO SAID IT WAS A DUMB IDEA AND HE DIDN'T WANNA DO IT!
BUT JOE MADE A BONNET ANYWAY, AND EVEN PUT MR. CAGEL ON IT!
THAT WAS NICE OF JOE!
NOT REALLY, MOM!

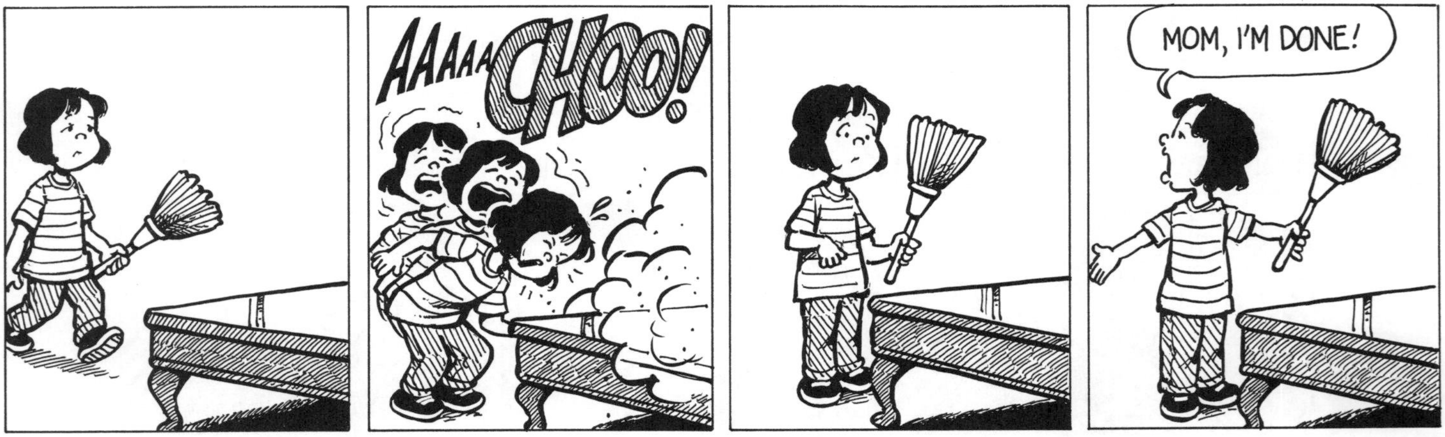
AAAAACHOO!
MOM, I'M DONE!

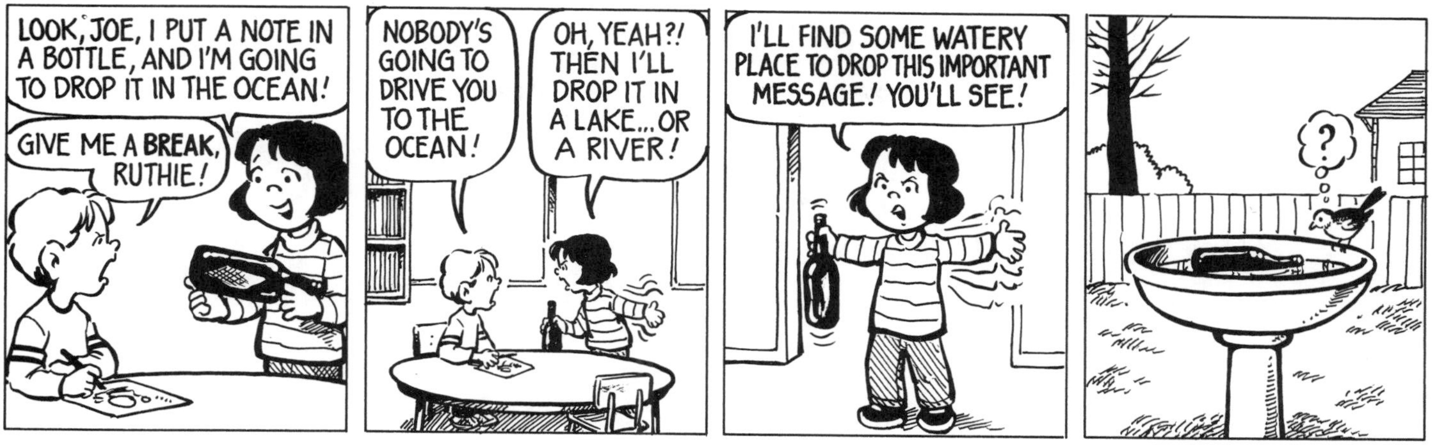
LOOK, JOE, I PUT A NOTE IN A BOTTLE, AND I'M GOING TO DROP IT IN THE OCEAN!
GIVE ME A **BREAK**, RUTHIE!
NOBODY'S GOING TO DRIVE YOU TO THE OCEAN!
OH, YEAH?! THEN I'LL DROP IT IN A LAKE... OR A RIVER!
I'LL FIND SOME WATERY PLACE TO DROP THIS IMPORTANT MESSAGE! YOU'LL SEE!
?

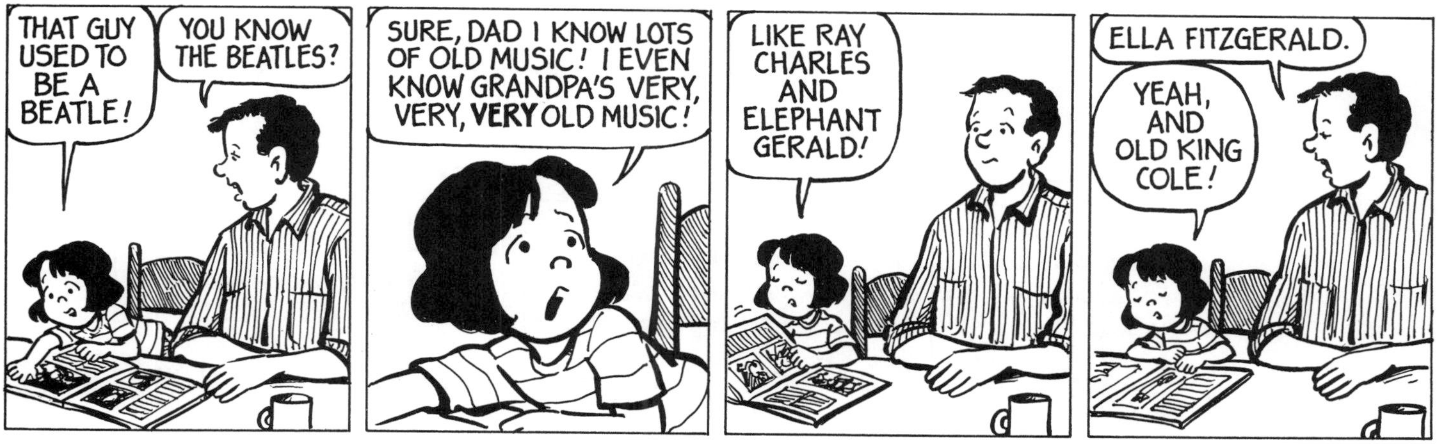
THAT GUY USED TO BE A BEATLE!
YOU KNOW THE BEATLES?
SURE, DAD I KNOW LOTS OF OLD MUSIC! I EVEN KNOW GRANDPA'S VERY, VERY, **VERY** OLD MUSIC!
LIKE RAY CHARLES AND ELEPHANT GERALD!
ELLA FITZGERALD.
YEAH, AND OLD KING COLE!

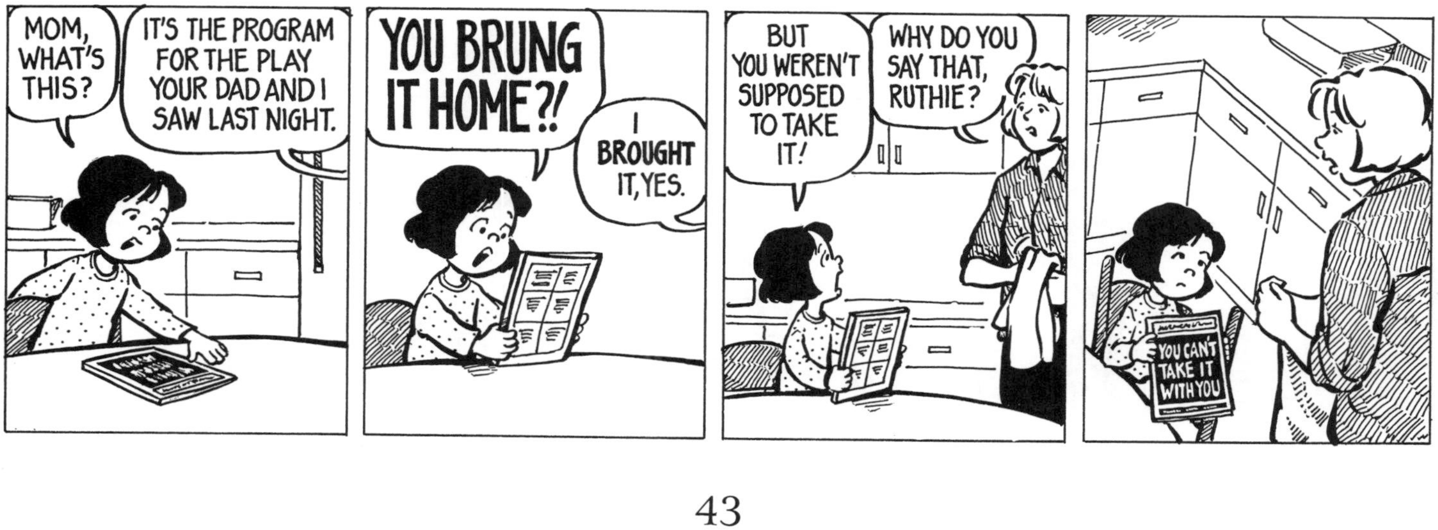
MOM, WHAT'S THIS?
IT'S THE PROGRAM FOR THE PLAY YOUR DAD AND I SAW LAST NIGHT.
YOU BRUNG IT HOME?!
I **BROUGHT** IT, YES.
BUT YOU WEREN'T SUPPOSED TO TAKE IT!
WHY DO YOU SAY THAT, RUTHIE?
YOU CAN'T TAKE IT WITH YOU

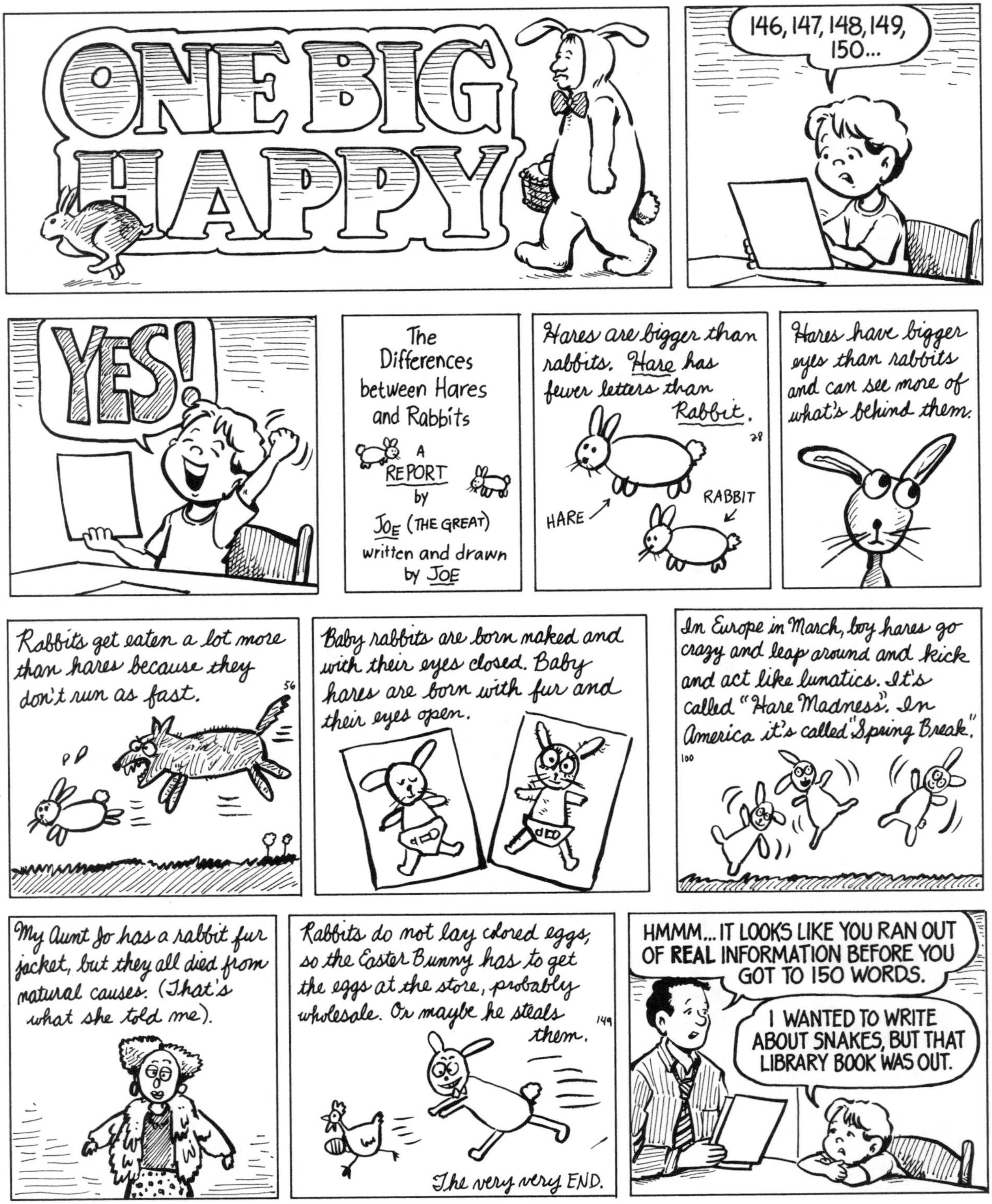

ONE BIG HAPPY
146, 147, 148, 149, 150...
YES!
The Differences between Hares and Rabbits
A REPORT by JOE (THE GREAT)
written and drawn by JOE
Hares are bigger than rabbits. Hare has fewer letters than Rabbit.
28
HARE
RABBIT
Hares have bigger eyes than rabbits and can see more of what's behind them.
Rabbits get eaten a lot more than hares because they don't run as fast.
56
Baby rabbits are born naked and with their eyes closed. Baby hares are born with fur and their eyes open.
In Europe in March, boy hares go crazy and leap around and kick and act like lunatics. It's called "Hare Madness". In America it's called "Spring Break".
100
My Aunt Jo has a rabbit fur jacket, but they all died from natural causes. (That's what she told me).
Rabbits do not lay colored eggs, so the Easter Bunny has to get the eggs at the store, probably wholesale. Or maybe he steals them.
149
The very very END.
HMMM... IT LOOKS LIKE YOU RAN OUT OF REAL INFORMATION BEFORE YOU GOT TO 150 WORDS.
I WANTED TO WRITE ABOUT SNAKES, BUT THAT LIBRARY BOOK WAS OUT.

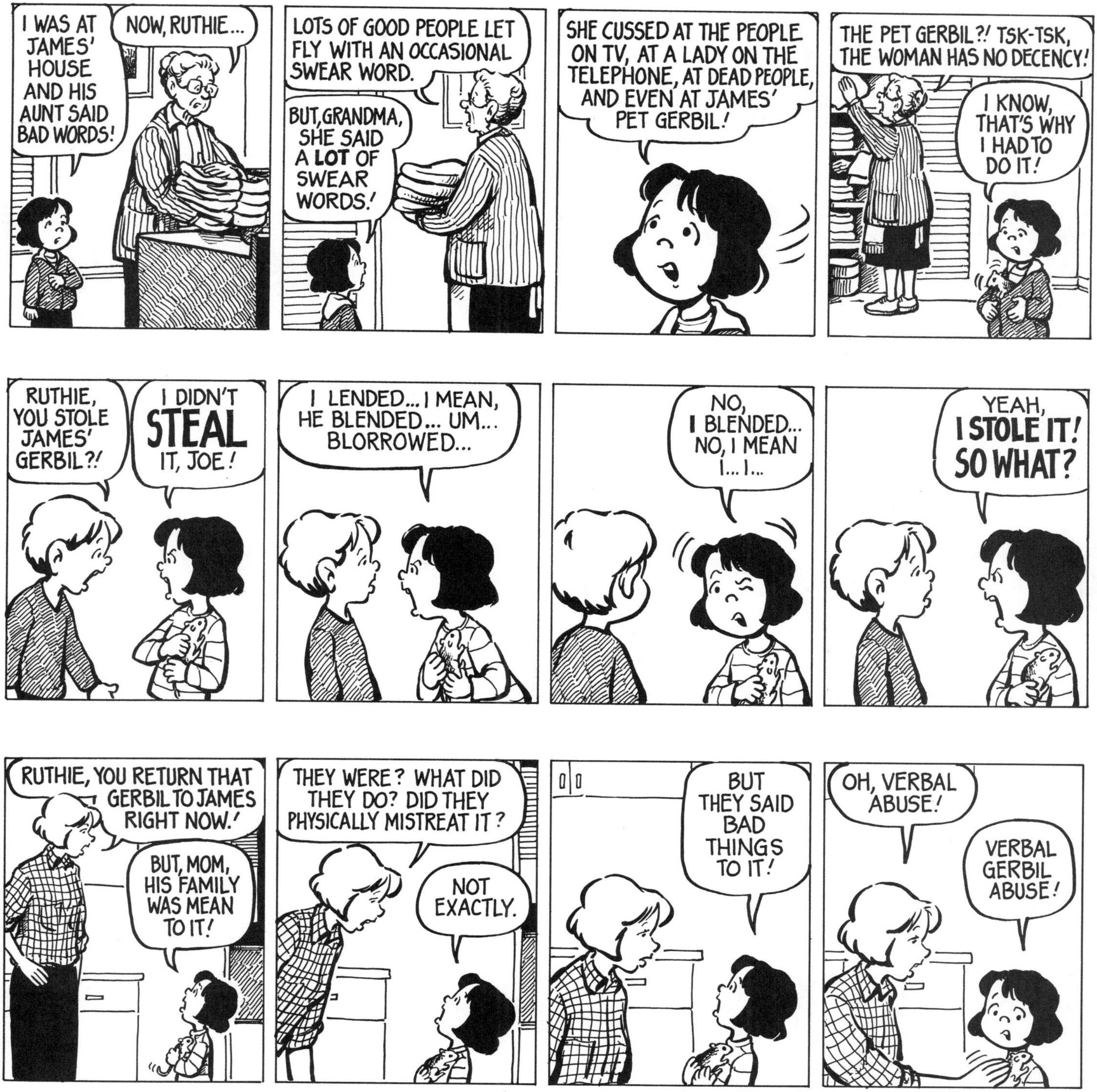
I WAS AT JAMES' HOUSE AND HIS AUNT SAID BAD WORDS!
NOW, RUTHIE...
LOTS OF GOOD PEOPLE LET FLY WITH AN OCCASIONAL SWEAR WORD.
BUT, GRANDMA, SHE SAID A **LOT** OF SWEAR WORDS!
SHE CUSSED AT THE PEOPLE ON TV, AT A LADY ON THE TELEPHONE, AT DEAD PEOPLE, AND EVEN AT JAMES' PET GERBIL!
THE PET GERBIL?! TSK-TSK, THE WOMAN HAS NO DECENCY!
I KNOW, THAT'S WHY I HAD TO DO IT!
RUTHIE, YOU STOLE JAMES' GERBIL?!
I DIDN'T **STEAL** IT, JOE!
I LENDED... I MEAN, HE BLENDED... UM... BLORROWED...
NO, **I** BLENDED... NO, I MEAN I... I...
YEAH, **I STOLE IT! SO WHAT?**
RUTHIE, YOU RETURN THAT GERBIL TO JAMES RIGHT NOW!
BUT, MOM, HIS FAMILY WAS MEAN TO IT!
THEY WERE? WHAT DID THEY DO? DID THEY PHYSICALLY MISTREAT IT?
NOT EXACTLY.
BUT THEY SAID BAD THINGS TO IT!
OH, VERBAL ABUSE!
VERBAL GERBIL ABUSE!

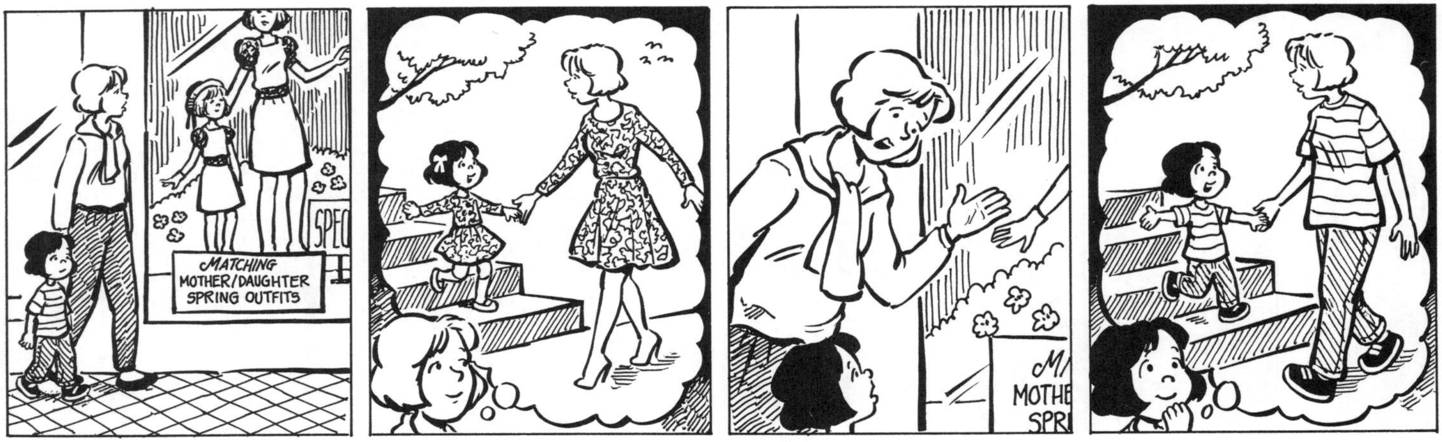
MATCHING
MOTHER/DAUGHTER
SPRING OUTFITS

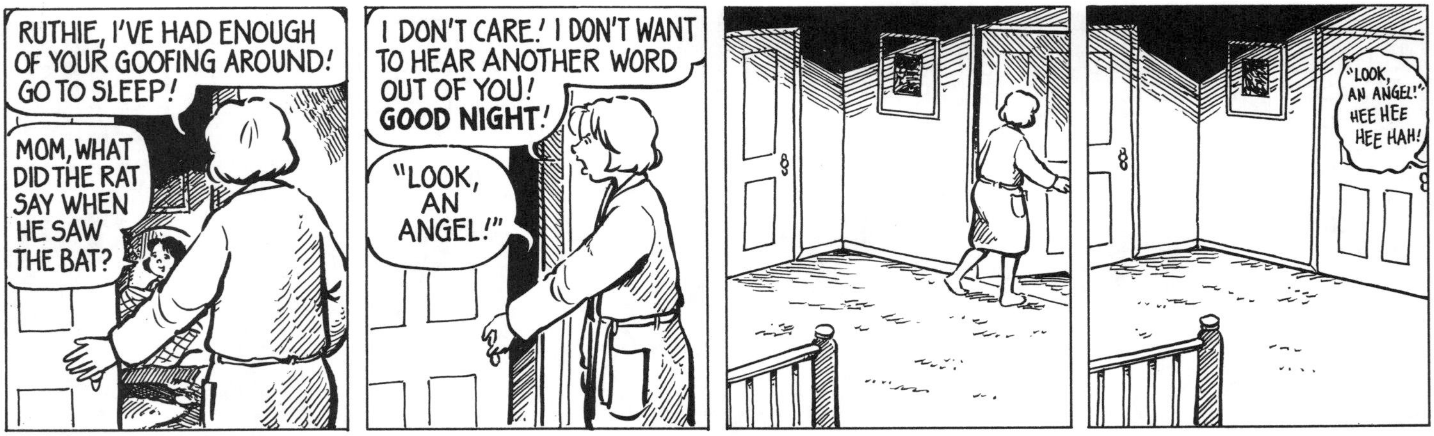
RUTHIE, I'VE HAD ENOUGH OF YOUR GOOFING AROUND! GO TO SLEEP!
MOM, WHAT DID THE RAT SAY WHEN HE SAW THE BAT?
I DON'T CARE! I DON'T WANT TO HEAR ANOTHER WORD OUT OF YOU! GOOD NIGHT!
"LOOK, AN ANGEL!"
"LOOK, AN ANGEL!" HEE HEE HEE HAH!

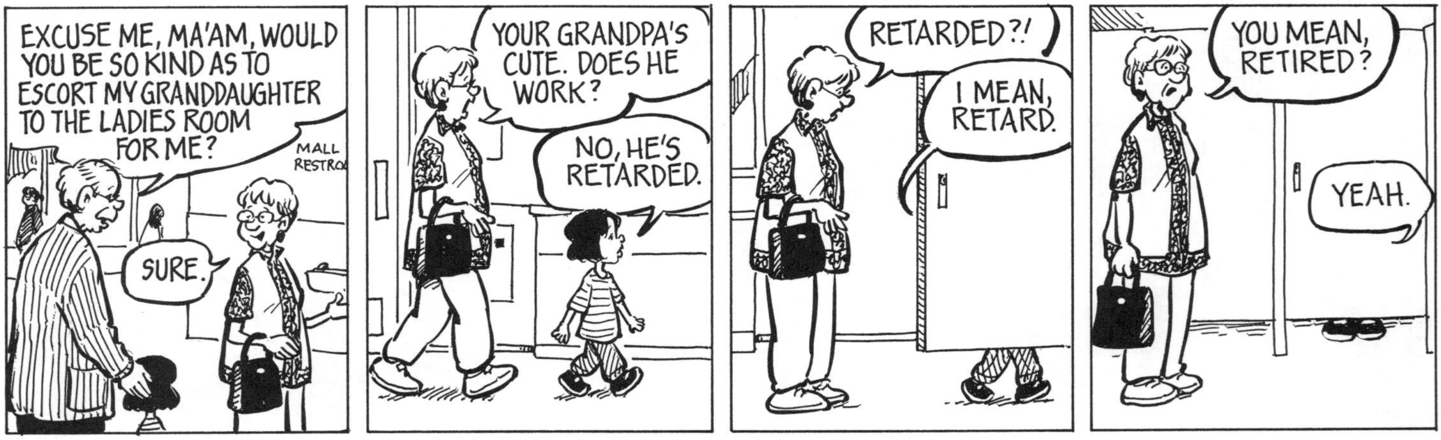
EXCUSE ME, MA'AM, WOULD YOU BE SO KIND AS TO ESCORT MY GRANDDAUGHTER TO THE LADIES ROOM FOR ME?
MALL
SURE.
YOUR GRANDPA'S CUTE. DOES HE WORK?
NO, HE'S RETARDED.
RETARDED?!
I MEAN, RETARD.
YOU MEAN, RETIRED?
YEAH.

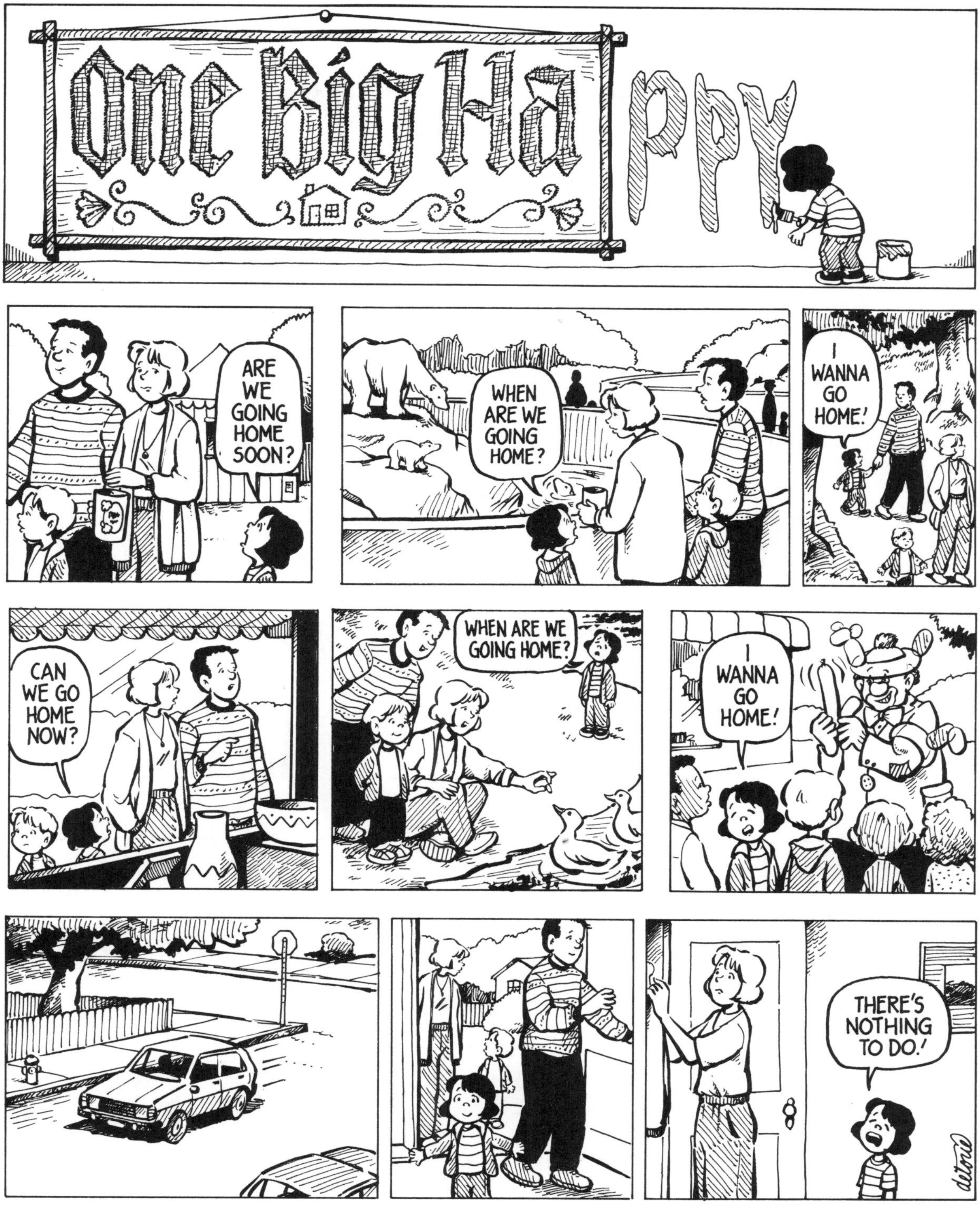
One Big Ha
PPY
ARE WE GOING HOME SOON?
WHEN ARE WE GOING HOME?
I WANNA GO HOME!
CAN WE GO HOME NOW?
WHEN ARE WE GOING HOME?
I WANNA GO HOME!
THERE'S NOTHING TO DO!
detorie

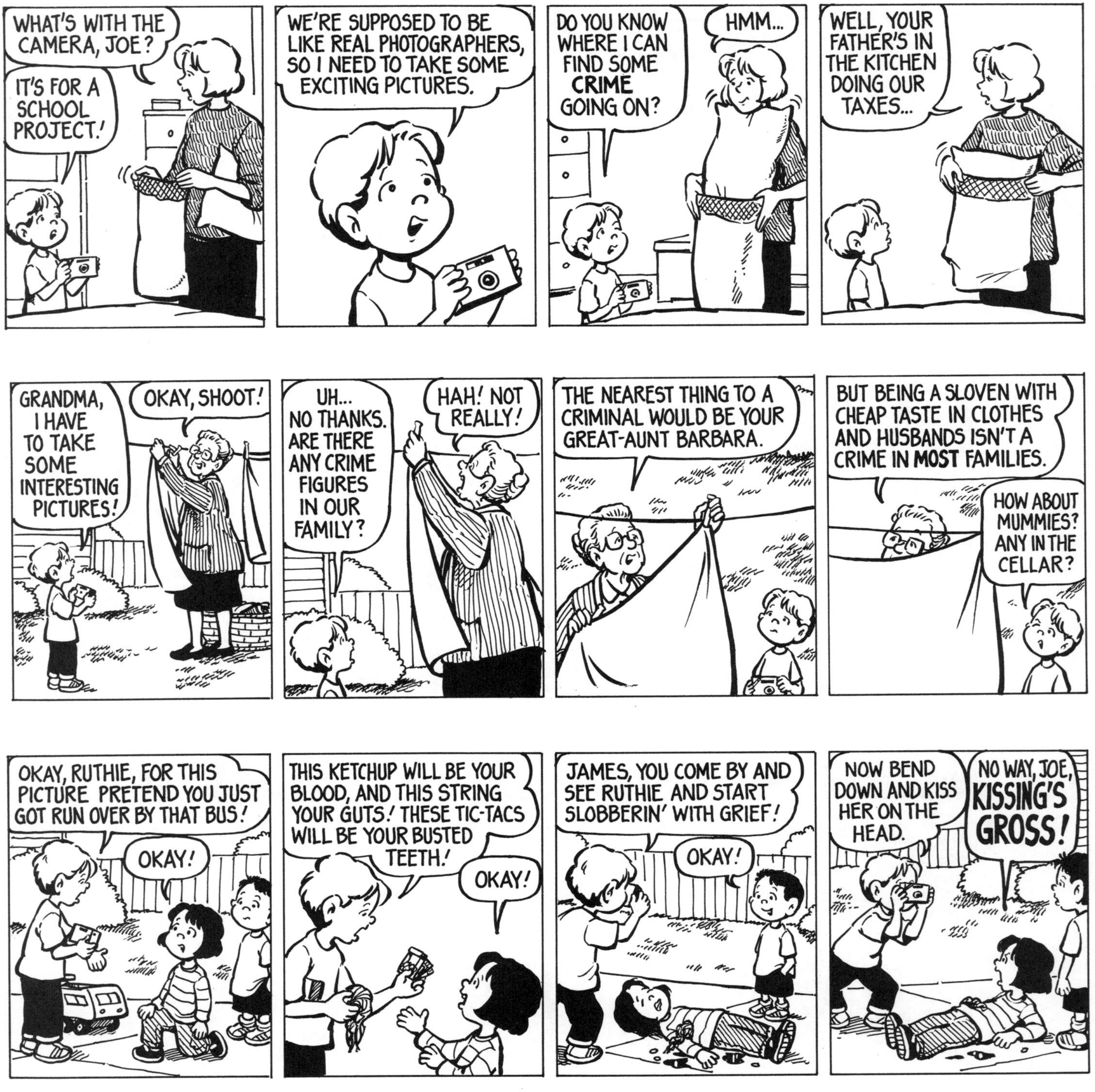
WHAT'S WITH THE CAMERA, JOE?
IT'S FOR A SCHOOL PROJECT!
WE'RE SUPPOSED TO BE LIKE REAL PHOTOGRAPHERS, SO I NEED TO TAKE SOME EXCITING PICTURES.
DO YOU KNOW WHERE I CAN FIND SOME CRIME GOING ON?
HMM...
WELL, YOUR FATHER'S IN THE KITCHEN DOING OUR TAXES...
GRANDMA, I HAVE TO TAKE SOME INTERESTING PICTURES!
OKAY, SHOOT!
UH... NO THANKS. ARE THERE ANY CRIME FIGURES IN OUR FAMILY?
HAH! NOT REALLY!
THE NEAREST THING TO A CRIMINAL WOULD BE YOUR GREAT-AUNT BARBARA.
BUT BEING A SLOVEN WITH CHEAP TASTE IN CLOTHES AND HUSBANDS ISN'T A CRIME IN MOST FAMILIES.
HOW ABOUT MUMMIES? ANY IN THE CELLAR?
OKAY, RUTHIE, FOR THIS PICTURE PRETEND YOU JUST GOT RUN OVER BY THAT BUS!
OKAY!
THIS KETCHUP WILL BE YOUR BLOOD, AND THIS STRING YOUR GUTS! THESE TIC-TACS WILL BE YOUR BUSTED TEETH!
OKAY!
JAMES, YOU COME BY AND SEE RUTHIE AND START SLOBBERIN' WITH GRIEF!
OKAY!
NOW BEND DOWN AND KISS HER ON THE HEAD.
NO WAY, JOE, KISSING'S GROSS!

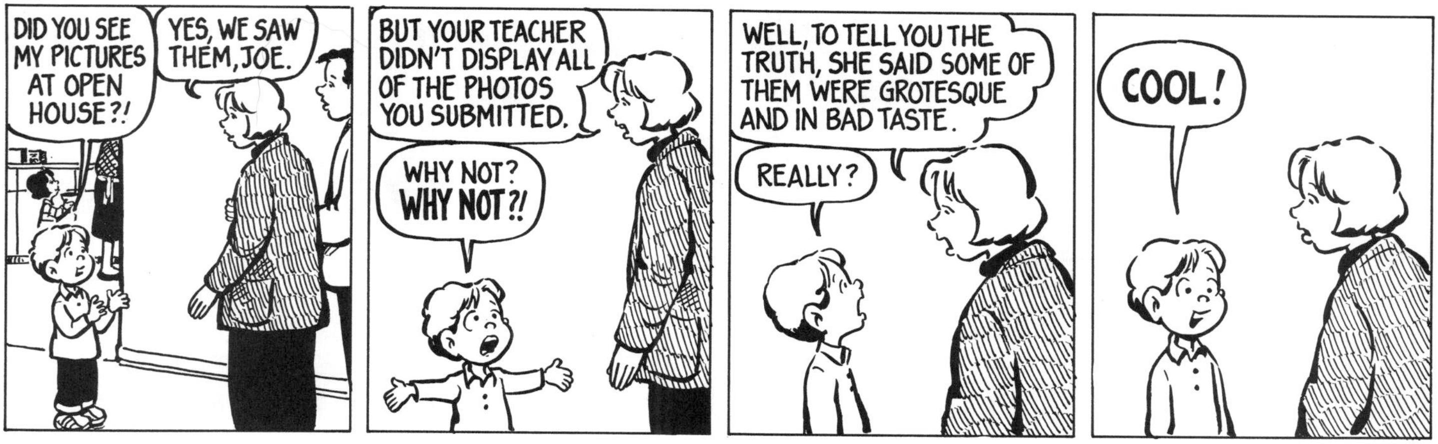
DID YOU SEE MY PICTURES AT OPEN HOUSE?!
YES, WE SAW THEM, JOE.
BUT YOUR TEACHER DIDN'T DISPLAY ALL OF THE PHOTOS YOU SUBMITTED.
WHY NOT? WHY NOT?!
WELL, TO TELL YOU THE TRUTH, SHE SAID SOME OF THEM WERE GROTESQUE AND IN BAD TASTE.
REALLY?
COOL!

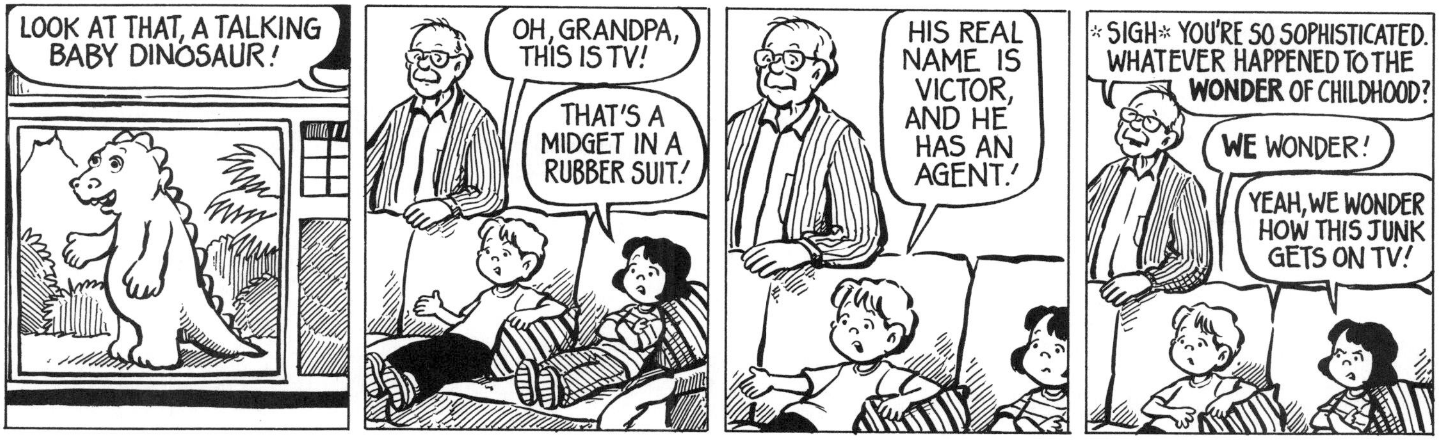
LOOK AT THAT, A TALKING BABY DINOSAUR!
OH, GRANDPA, THIS IS TV!
THAT'S A MIDGET IN A RUBBER SUIT!
HIS REAL NAME IS VICTOR, AND HE HAS AN AGENT!
SIGH YOU'RE SO SOPHISTICATED. WHATEVER HAPPENED TO THE WONDER OF CHILDHOOD?
WE WONDER!
YEAH, WE WONDER HOW THIS JUNK GETS ON TV!

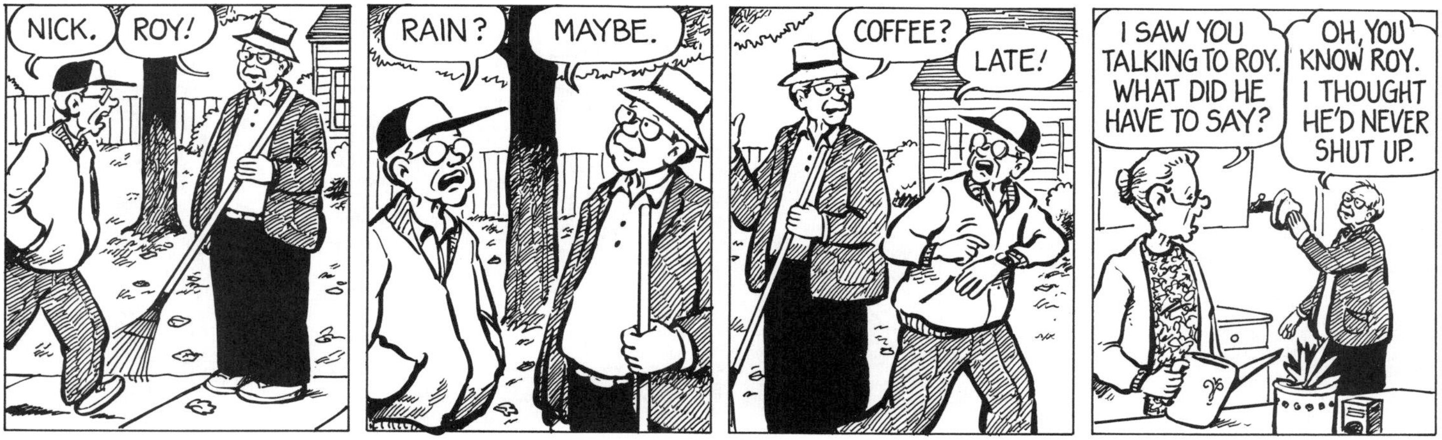
NICK.
ROY!
RAIN?
MAYBE.
COFFEE?
LATE!
I SAW YOU TALKING TO ROY. WHAT DID HE HAVE TO SAY?
OH, YOU KNOW ROY. I THOUGHT HE'D NEVER SHUT UP.

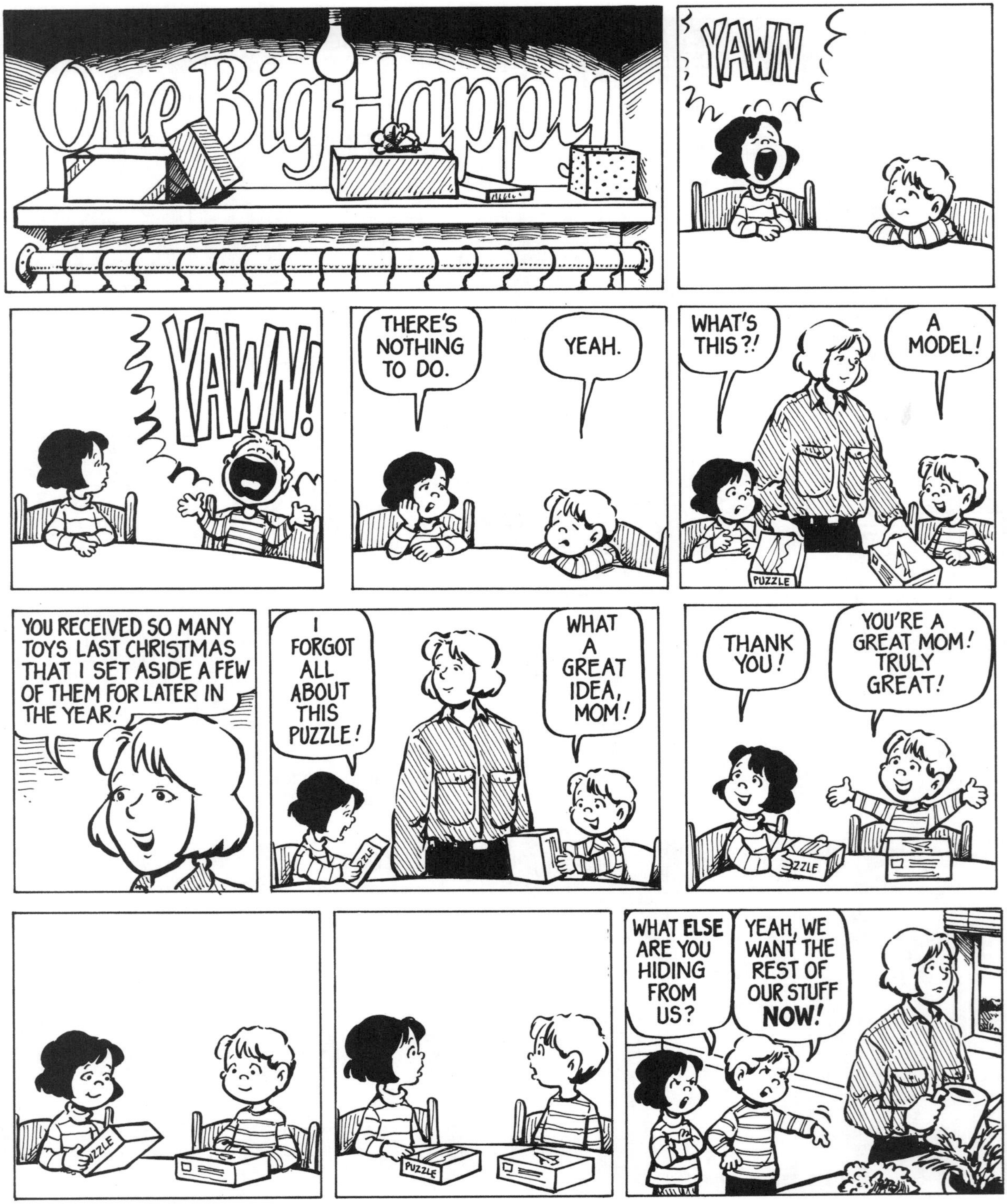
One Big Happy
YAWN
YAWN!
THERE'S NOTHING TO DO.
YEAH.
WHAT'S THIS?!
A MODEL!
PUZZLE
YOU RECEIVED SO MANY TOYS LAST CHRISTMAS THAT I SET ASIDE A FEW OF THEM FOR LATER IN THE YEAR!
I FORGOT ALL ABOUT THIS PUZZLE!
WHAT A GREAT IDEA, MOM!
THANK YOU!
YOU'RE A GREAT MOM! TRULY GREAT!
PUZZLE
WHAT ELSE ARE YOU HIDING FROM US?
YEAH, WE WANT THE REST OF OUR STUFF NOW!

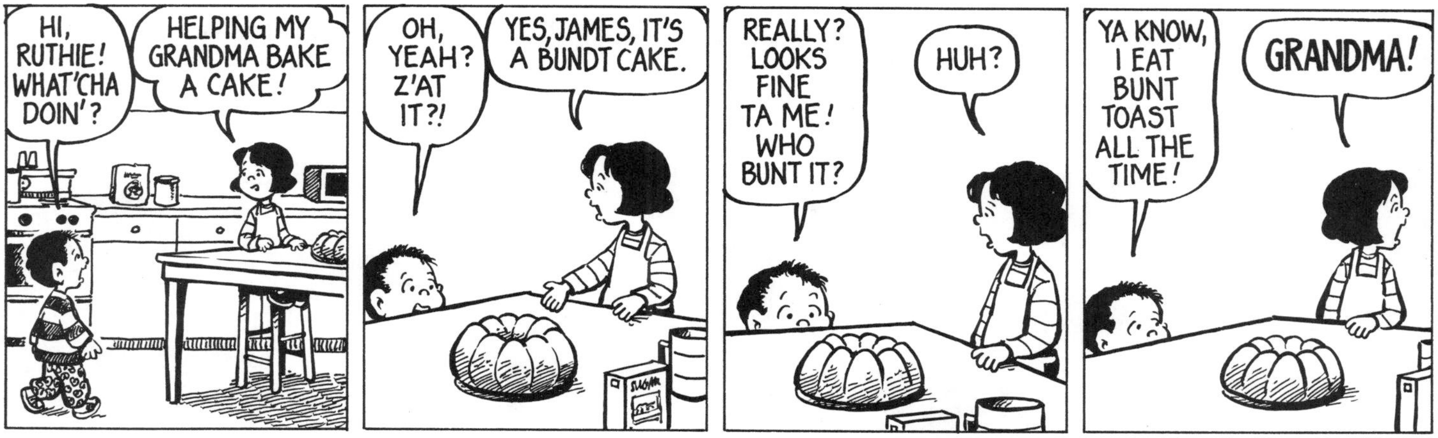
HI, RUTHIE! WHAT'CHA DOIN'?
HELPING MY GRANDMA BAKE A CAKE!
OH, YEAH? Z'AT IT?!
YES, JAMES, IT'S A BUNDT CAKE.
REALLY? LOOKS FINE TA ME! WHO BUNT IT?
HUH?
YA KNOW, I EAT BUNT TOAST ALL THE TIME!
GRANDMA!

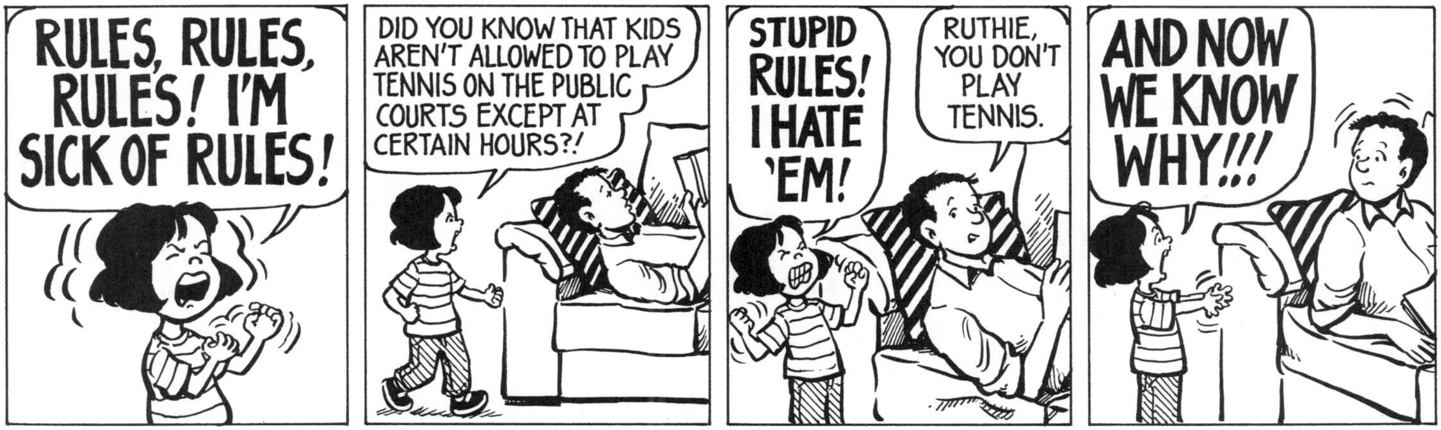
RULES, RULES, RULES! I'M SICK OF RULES!
DID YOU KNOW THAT KIDS AREN'T ALLOWED TO PLAY TENNIS ON THE PUBLIC COURTS EXCEPT AT CERTAIN HOURS?!
STUPID RULES! I HATE 'EM!
RUTHIE, YOU DON'T PLAY TENNIS.
AND NOW WE KNOW WHY!!!

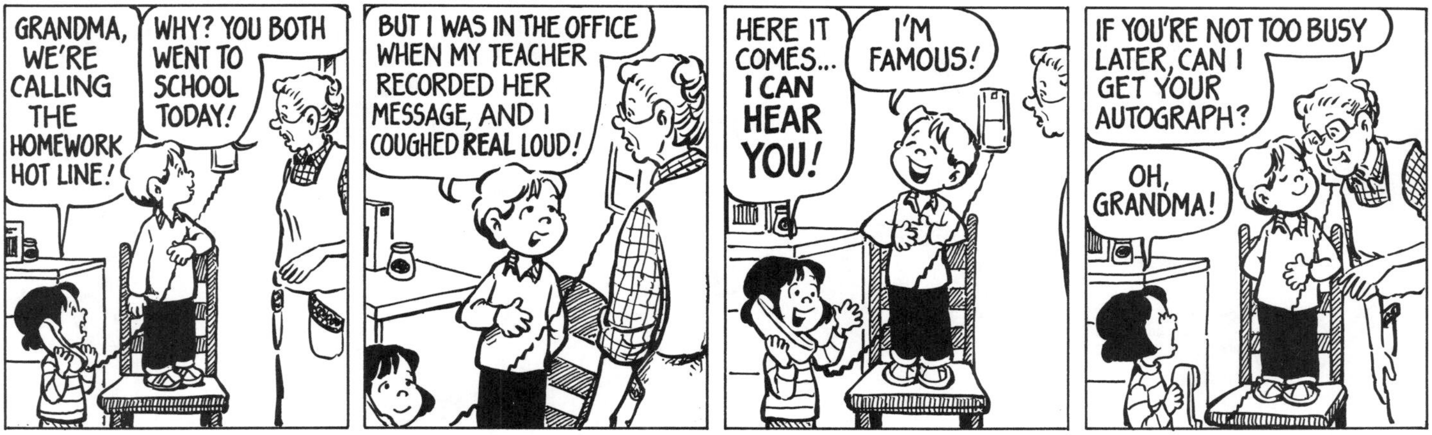
GRANDMA, WE'RE CALLING THE HOMEWORK HOT LINE!
WHY? YOU BOTH WENT TO SCHOOL TODAY!
BUT I WAS IN THE OFFICE WHEN MY TEACHER RECORDED HER MESSAGE, AND I COUGHED REAL LOUD!
HERE IT COMES... I CAN HEAR YOU!
I'M FAMOUS!
IF YOU'RE NOT TOO BUSY LATER, CAN I GET YOUR AUTOGRAPH?
OH, GRANDMA!

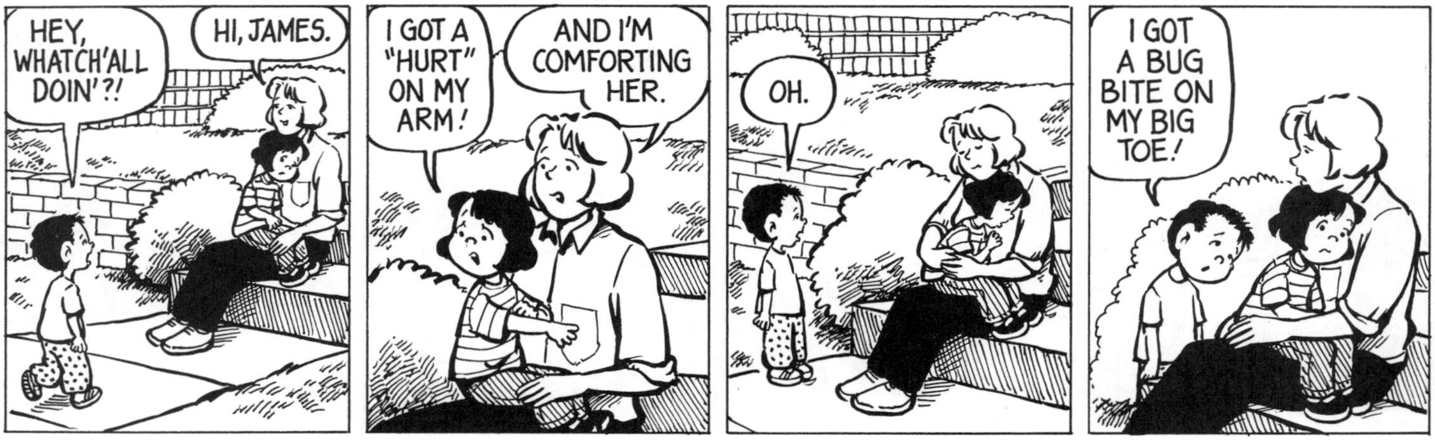
HEY, WHATCH'ALL DOIN'?!
HI, JAMES.
I GOT A "HURT" ON MY ARM!
AND I'M COMFORTING HER.
OH.
I GOT A BUG BITE ON MY BIG TOE!

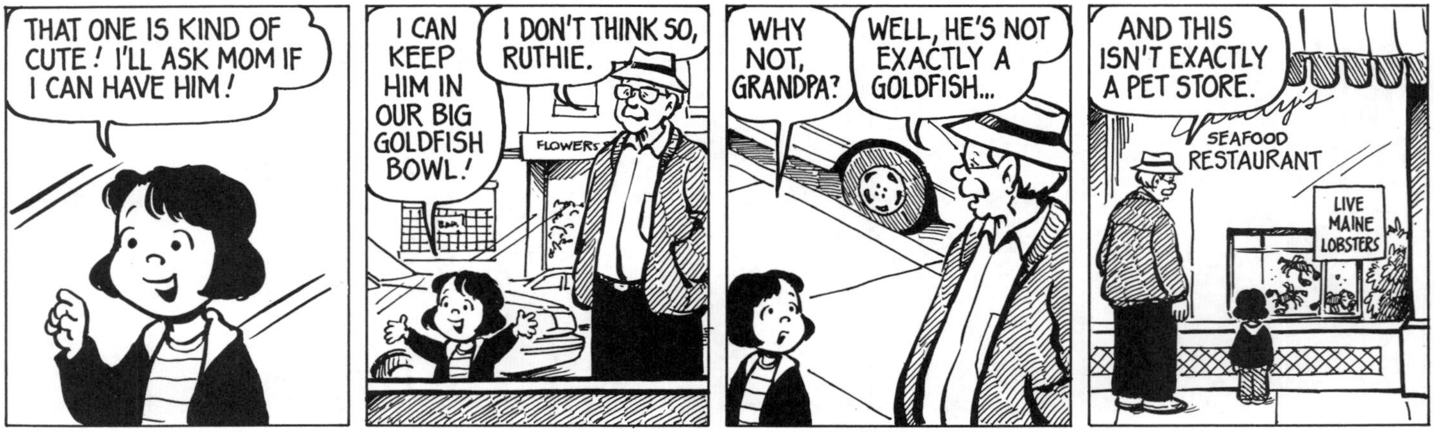
THAT ONE IS KIND OF CUTE! I'LL ASK MOM IF I CAN HAVE HIM!
I CAN KEEP HIM IN OUR BIG GOLDFISH BOWL!
I DON'T THINK SO, RUTHIE.
FLOWERS
WHY NOT, GRANDPA?
WELL, HE'S NOT EXACTLY A GOLDFISH...
AND THIS ISN'T EXACTLY A PET STORE.
SEAFOOD
RESTAURANT
LIVE MAINE LOBSTERS

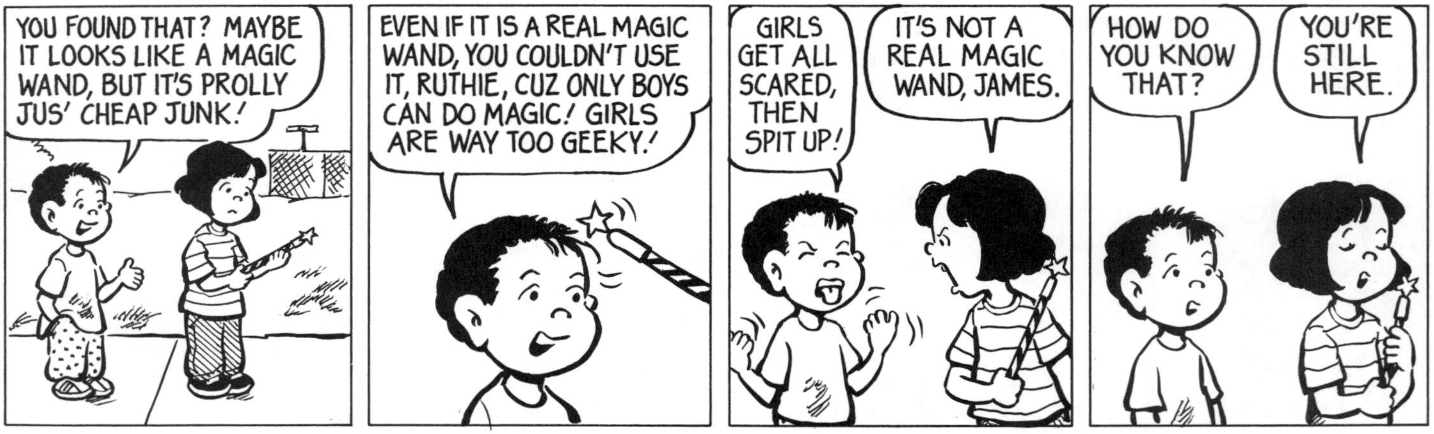
YOU FOUND THAT? MAYBE IT LOOKS LIKE A MAGIC WAND, BUT IT'S PROLLY JUS' CHEAP JUNK!
EVEN IF IT IS A REAL MAGIC WAND, YOU COULDN'T USE IT, RUTHIE, CUZ ONLY BOYS CAN DO MAGIC! GIRLS ARE WAY TOO GEEKY!
GIRLS GET ALL SCARED, THEN SPIT UP!
IT'S NOT A REAL MAGIC WAND, JAMES.
HOW DO YOU KNOW THAT?
YOU'RE STILL HERE.

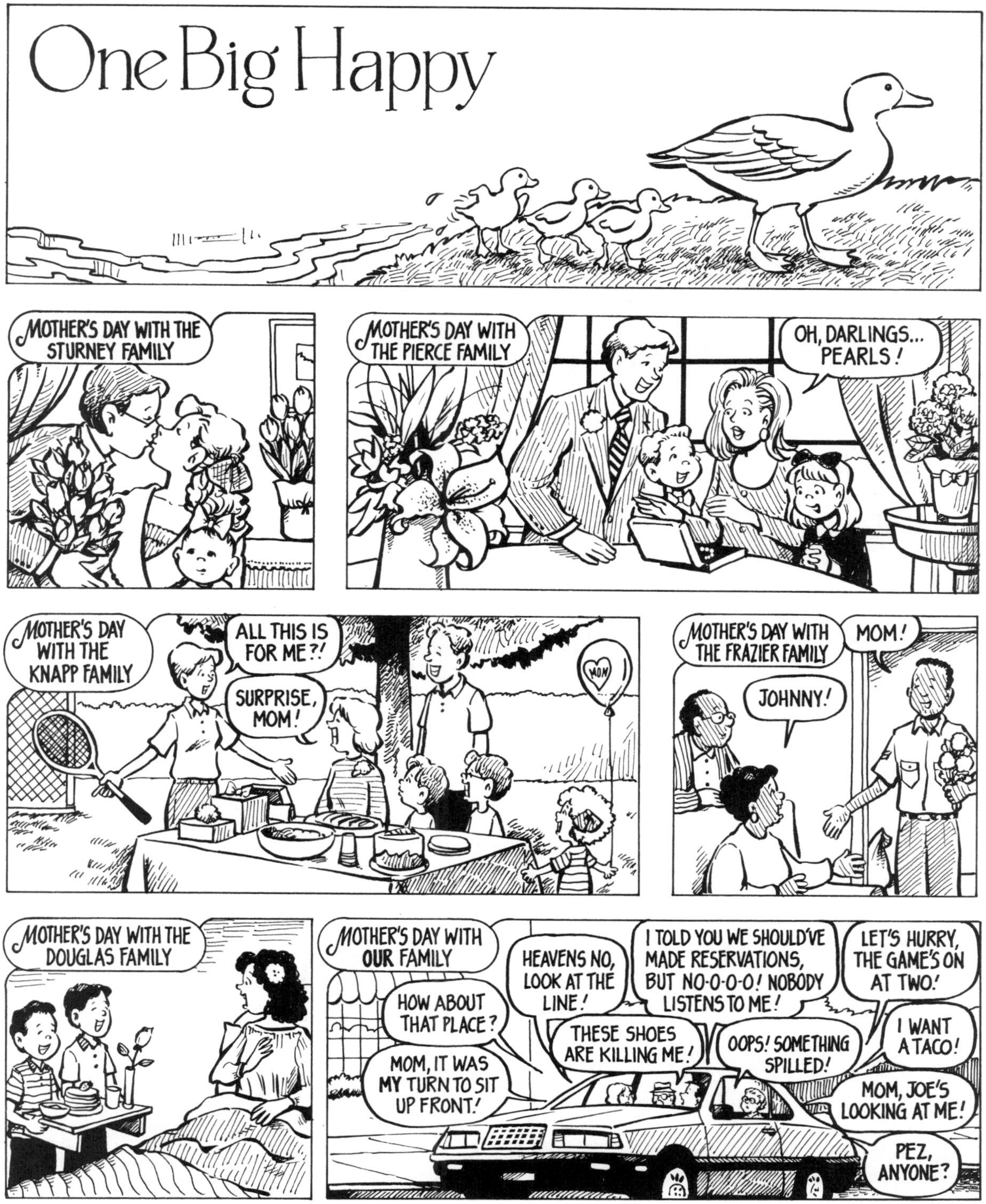
One Big Happy
MOTHER'S DAY WITH THE STURNEY FAMILY
MOTHER'S DAY WITH THE PIERCE FAMILY
OH, DARLINGS... PEARLS!
MOTHER'S DAY WITH THE KNAPP FAMILY
ALL THIS IS FOR ME?!
SURPRISE, MOM!
MOM
MOTHER'S DAY WITH THE FRAZIER FAMILY
MOM!
JOHNNY!
MOTHER'S DAY WITH THE DOUGLAS FAMILY
MOTHER'S DAY WITH **OUR** FAMILY
HOW ABOUT THAT PLACE?
HEAVENS NO, LOOK AT THE LINE!
I TOLD YOU WE SHOULD'VE MADE RESERVATIONS, BUT NO-O-O-O! NOBODY LISTENS TO ME!
LET'S HURRY, THE GAME'S ON AT TWO!
MOM, IT WAS **MY** TURN TO SIT UP FRONT!
THESE SHOES ARE KILLING ME!
OOPS! SOMETHING SPILLED!
I WANT A TACO!
MOM, JOE'S LOOKING AT ME!
PEZ, ANYONE?

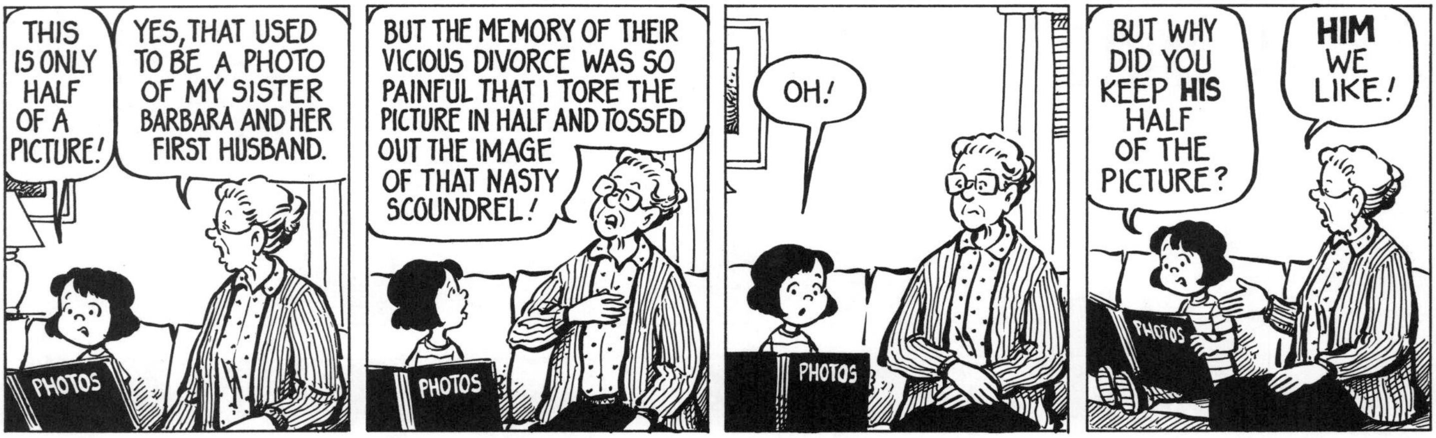
THIS IS ONLY HALF OF A PICTURE!
YES, THAT USED TO BE A PHOTO OF MY SISTER BARBARA AND HER FIRST HUSBAND.
BUT THE MEMORY OF THEIR VICIOUS DIVORCE WAS SO PAINFUL THAT I TORE THE PICTURE IN HALF AND TOSSED OUT THE IMAGE OF THAT NASTY SCOUNDREL!
PHOTOS
OH!
PHOTOS
BUT WHY DID YOU KEEP **HIS** HALF OF THE PICTURE?
HIM WE LIKE!
PHOTOS

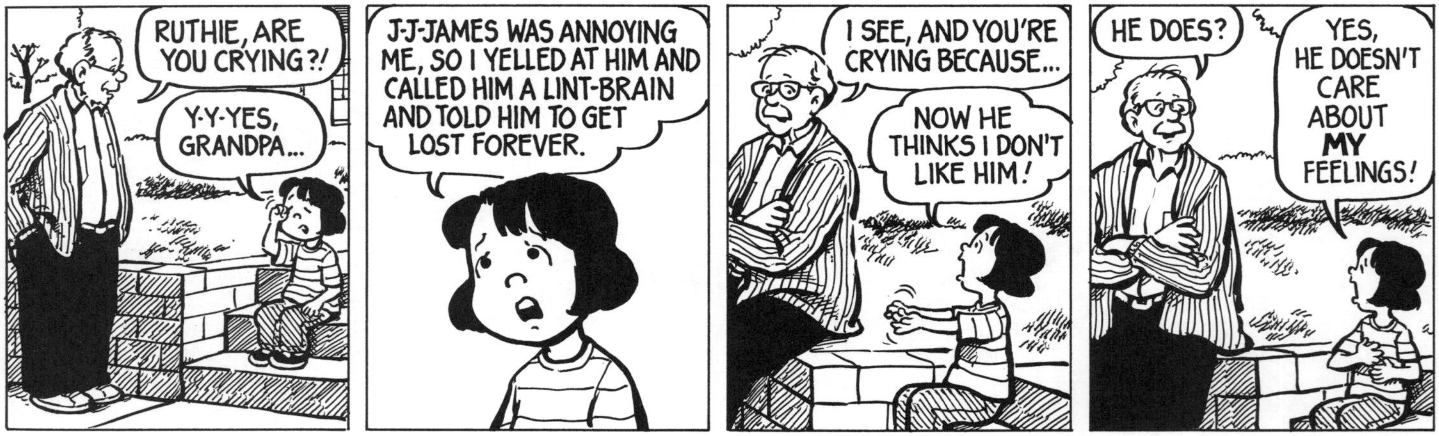
RUTHIE, ARE YOU CRYING?!
Y-Y-YES, GRANDPA...
J-J-JAMES WAS ANNOYING ME, SO I YELLED AT HIM AND CALLED HIM A LINT-BRAIN AND TOLD HIM TO GET LOST FOREVER.
I SEE, AND YOU'RE CRYING BECAUSE...
NOW HE THINKS I DON'T LIKE HIM!
HE DOES?
YES, HE DOESN'T CARE ABOUT **MY** FEELINGS!

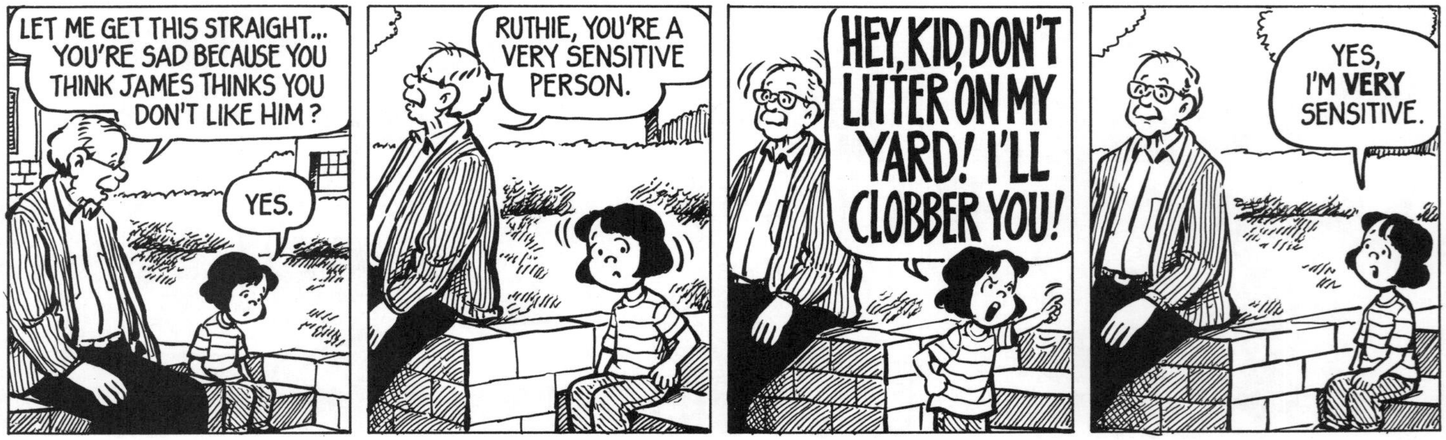
LET ME GET THIS STRAIGHT... YOU'RE SAD BECAUSE YOU THINK JAMES THINKS YOU DON'T LIKE HIM?
YES.
RUTHIE, YOU'RE A VERY SENSITIVE PERSON.
HEY, KID, DON'T LITTER ON MY YARD! I'LL CLOBBER YOU!
YES, I'M **VERY** SENSITIVE.

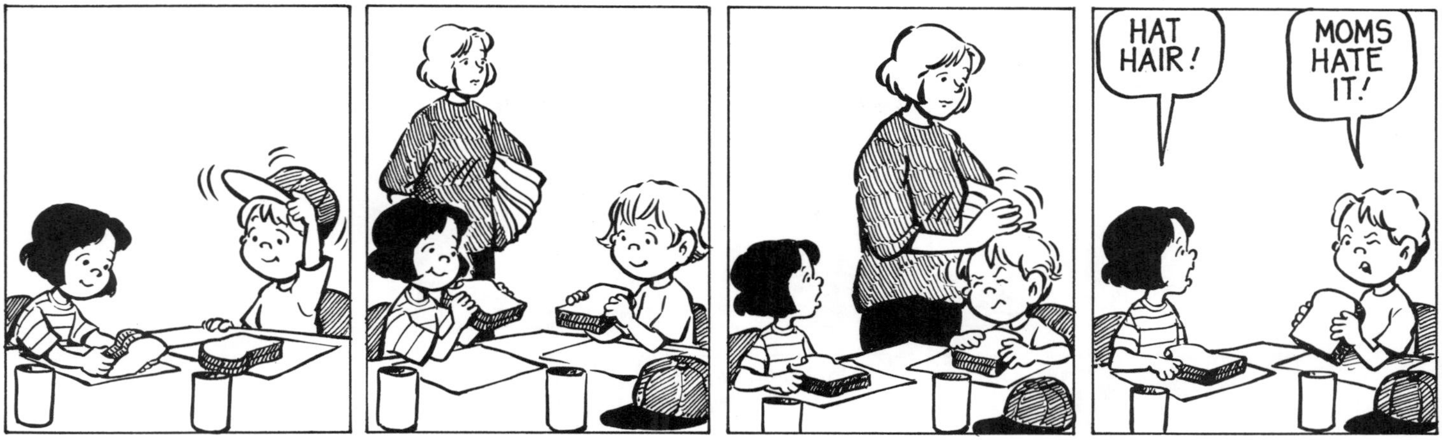
HAT HAIR!
MOMS HATE IT!

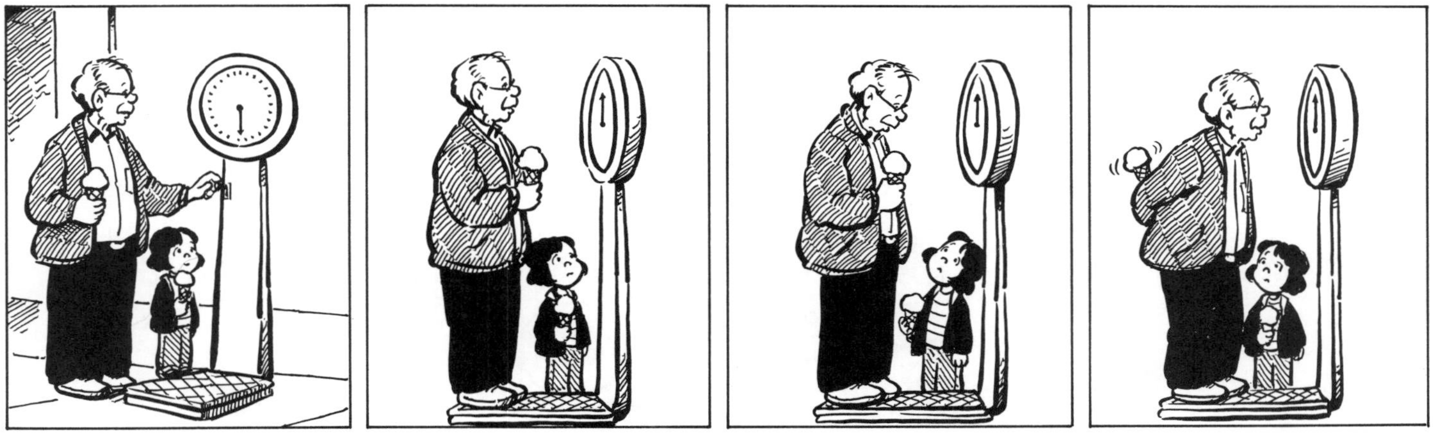

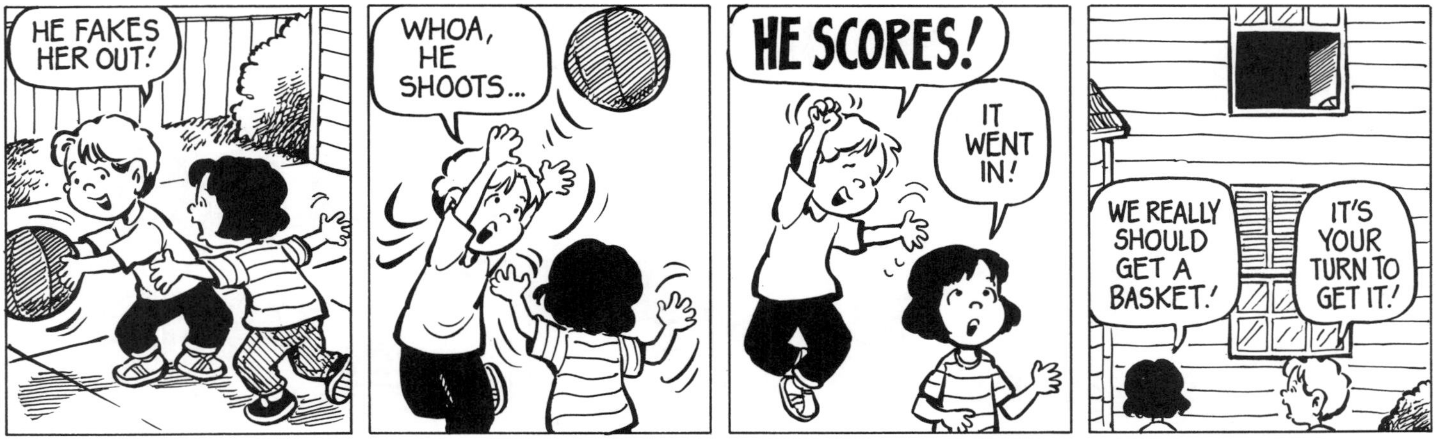
HE FAKES HER OUT!
WHOA, HE SHOOTS...
HE SCORES!
IT WENT IN!
WE REALLY SHOULD GET A BASKET!
IT'S YOUR TURN TO GET IT!

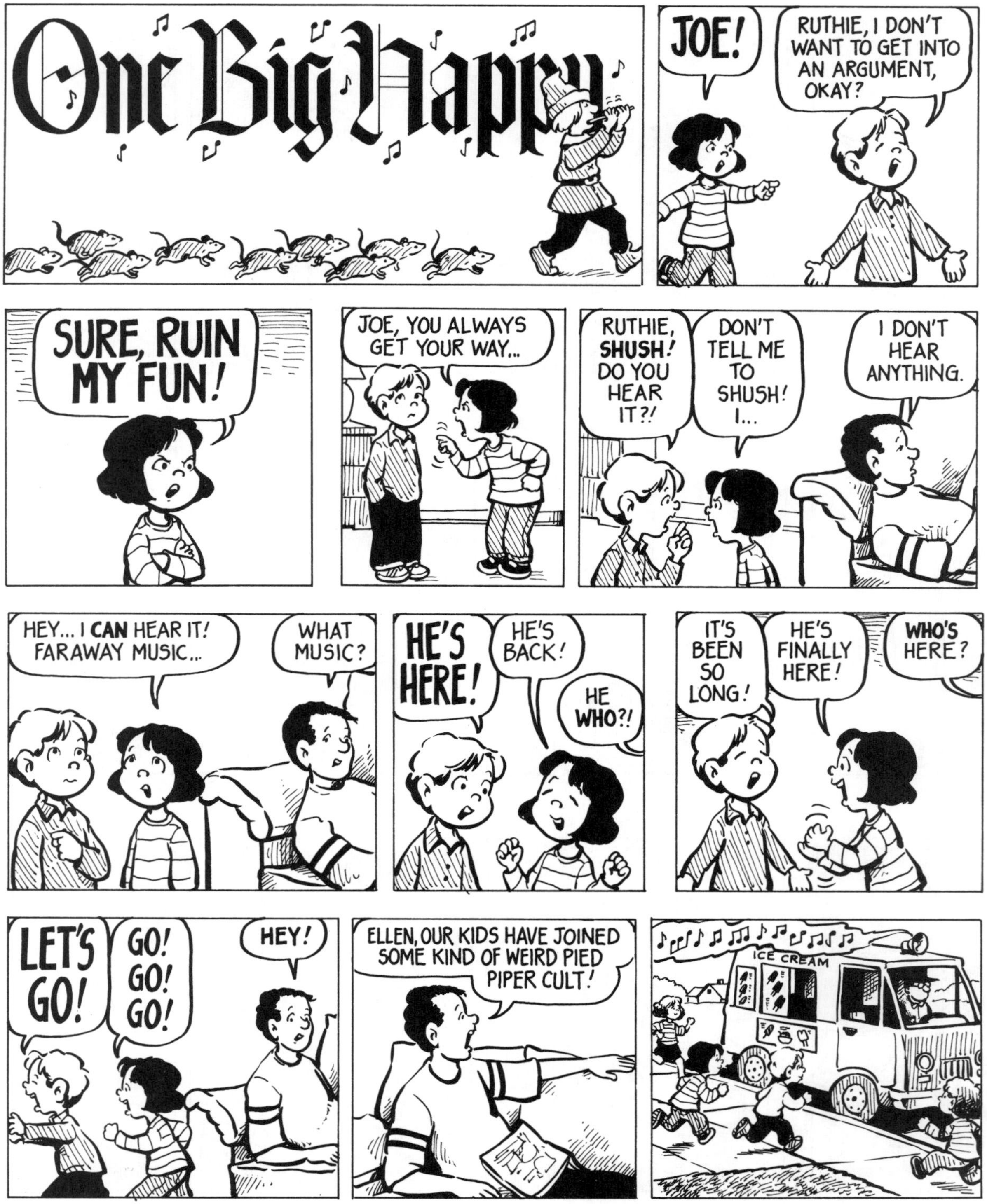
One Big Happy
JOE!
RUTHIE, I DON'T WANT TO GET INTO AN ARGUMENT, OKAY?
SURE, RUIN MY FUN!
JOE, YOU ALWAYS GET YOUR WAY...
RUTHIE, SHUSH! DO YOU HEAR IT?!
DON'T TELL ME TO SHUSH! I...
I DON'T HEAR ANYTHING.
HEY... I CAN HEAR IT! FARAWAY MUSIC...
WHAT MUSIC?
HE'S HERE!
HE'S BACK!
HE WHO?!
IT'S BEEN SO LONG!
HE'S FINALLY HERE!
WHO'S HERE?
LET'S GO!
GO! GO! GO!
HEY!
ELLEN, OUR KIDS HAVE JOINED SOME KIND OF WEIRD PIED PIPER CULT!
ICE CREAM

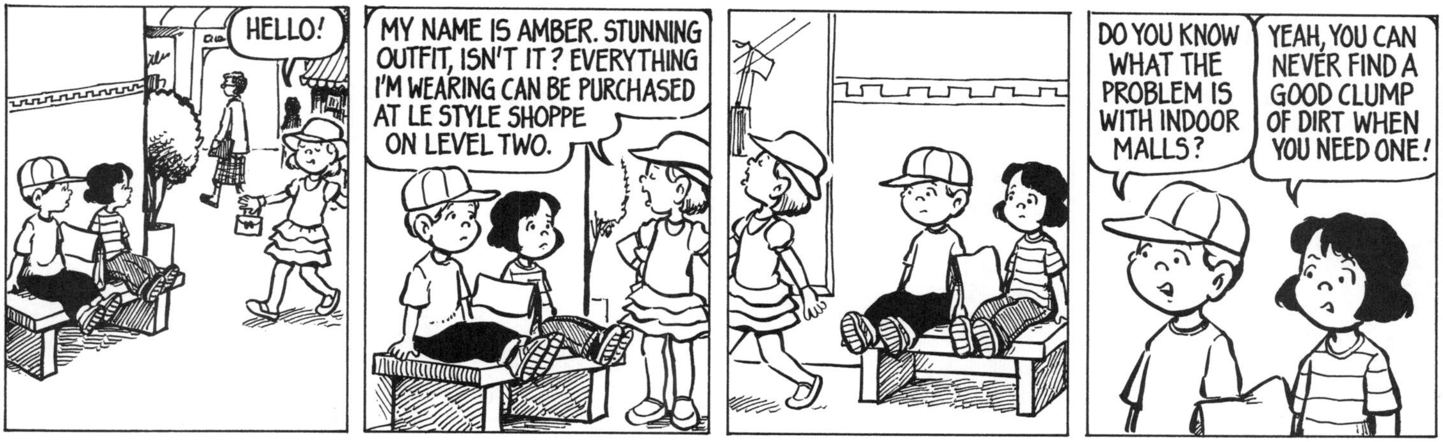
HELLO!
MY NAME IS AMBER. STUNNING OUTFIT, ISN'T IT? EVERYTHING I'M WEARING CAN BE PURCHASED AT LE STYLE SHOPPE ON LEVEL TWO.
DO YOU KNOW WHAT THE PROBLEM IS WITH INDOOR MALLS?
YEAH, YOU CAN NEVER FIND A GOOD CLUMP OF DIRT WHEN YOU NEED ONE!

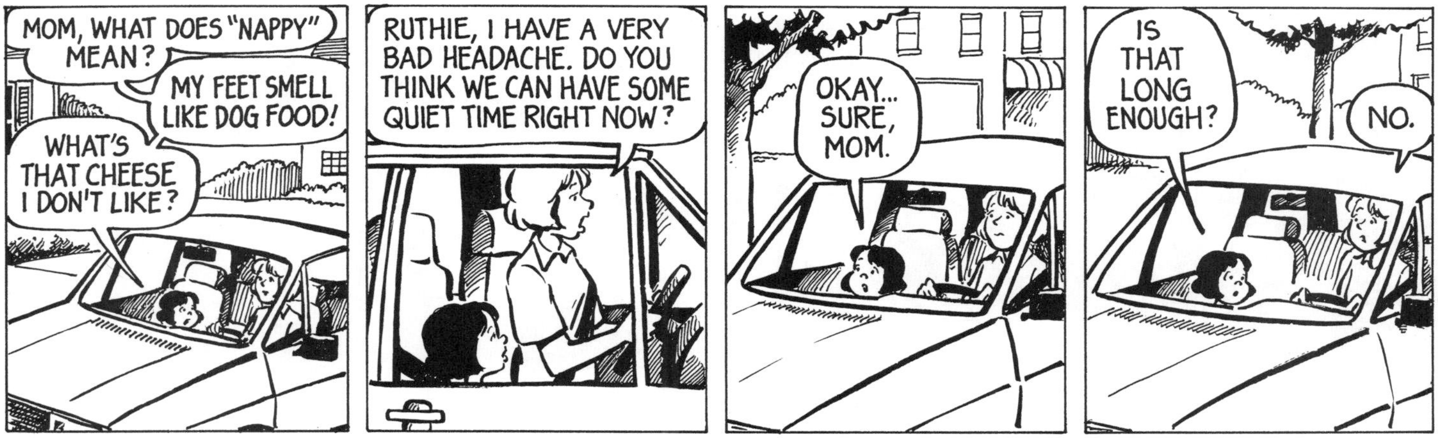
MOM, WHAT DOES "NAPPY" MEAN?
MY FEET SMELL LIKE DOG FOOD!
WHAT'S THAT CHEESE I DON'T LIKE?
RUTHIE, I HAVE A VERY BAD HEADACHE. DO YOU THINK WE CAN HAVE SOME QUIET TIME RIGHT NOW?
OKAY... SURE, MOM.
IS THAT LONG ENOUGH?
NO.

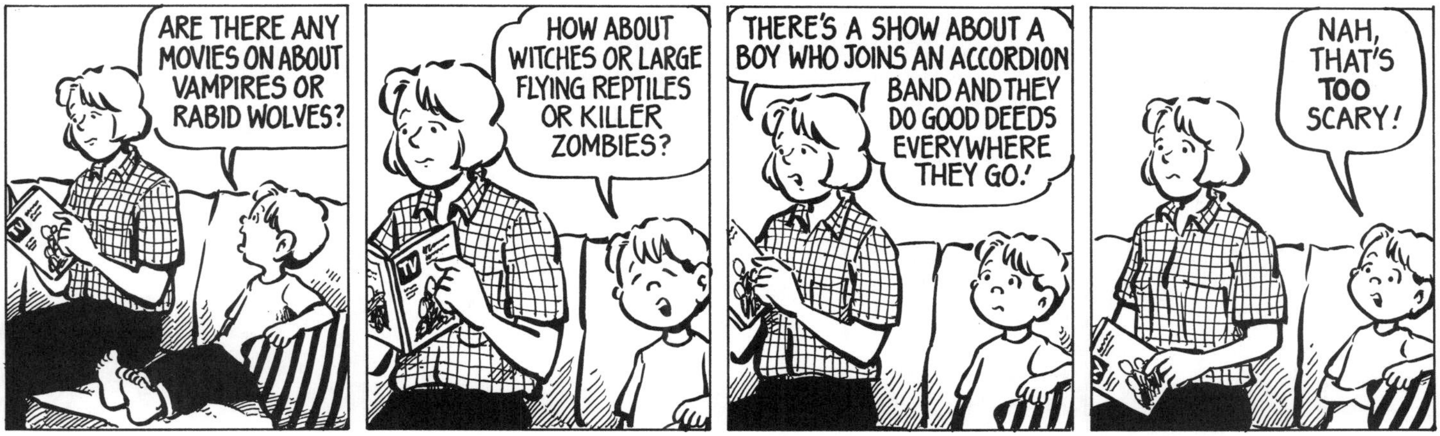
ARE THERE ANY MOVIES ON ABOUT VAMPIRES OR RABID WOLVES?
HOW ABOUT WITCHES OR LARGE FLYING REPTILES OR KILLER ZOMBIES?
THERE'S A SHOW ABOUT A BOY WHO JOINS AN ACCORDION BAND AND THEY DO GOOD DEEDS EVERYWHERE THEY GO!
NAH, THAT'S TOO SCARY!

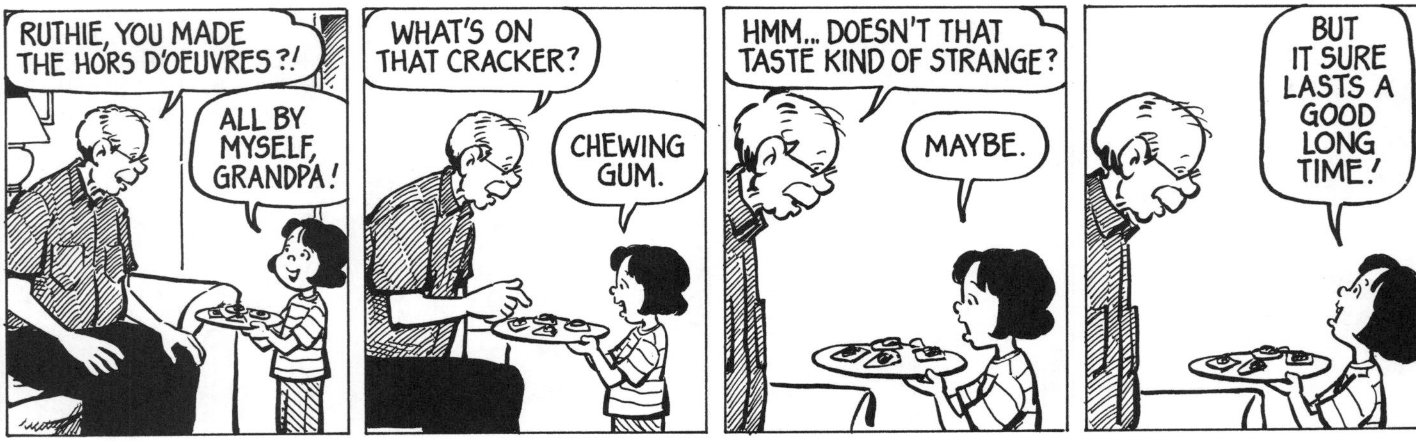
RUTHIE, YOU MADE THE HORS D'OEUVRES ?!
ALL BY MYSELF, GRANDPA!
WHAT'S ON THAT CRACKER?
CHEWING GUM.
HMM... DOESN'T THAT TASTE KIND OF STRANGE?
MAYBE.
BUT IT SURE LASTS A GOOD LONG TIME!

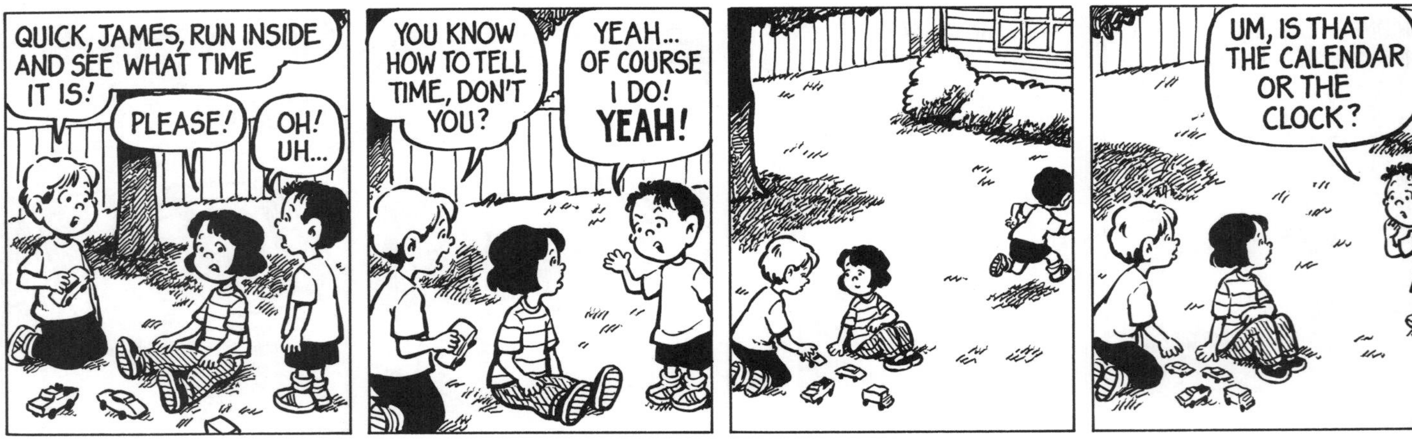
QUICK, JAMES, RUN INSIDE AND SEE WHAT TIME IT IS!
PLEASE!
OH! UH...
YOU KNOW HOW TO TELL TIME, DON'T YOU?
YEAH... OF COURSE I DO! **YEAH**!
UM, IS THAT THE CALENDAR OR THE CLOCK?

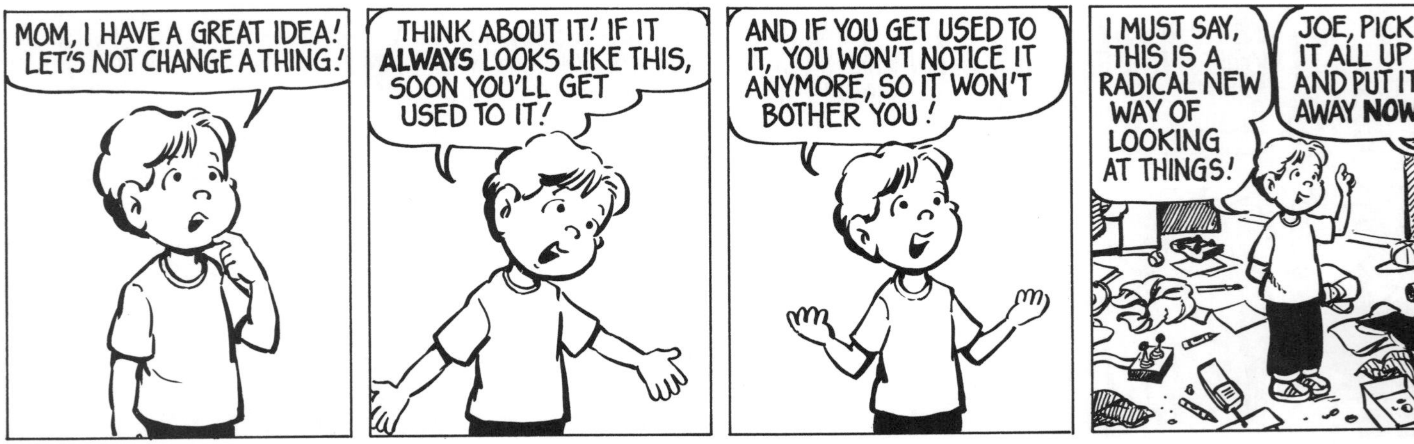
MOM, I HAVE A GREAT IDEA! LET'S NOT CHANGE A THING!
THINK ABOUT IT! IF IT **ALWAYS** LOOKS LIKE THIS, SOON YOU'LL GET USED TO IT!
AND IF YOU GET USED TO IT, YOU WON'T NOTICE IT ANYMORE, SO IT WON'T BOTHER YOU!
I MUST SAY, THIS IS A RADICAL NEW WAY OF LOOKING AT THINGS!
JOE, PICK IT ALL UP AND PUT IT AWAY **NOW**!

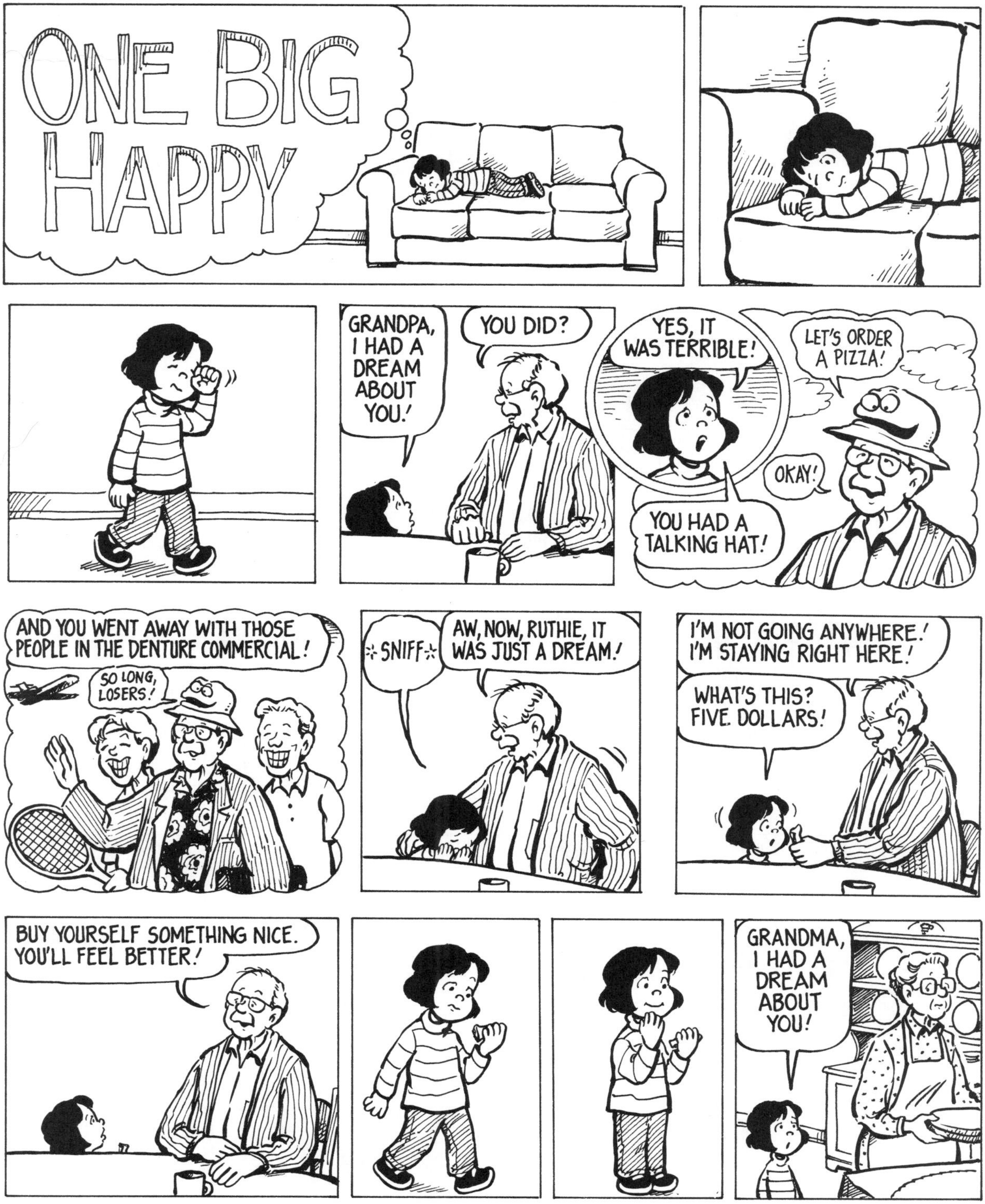

ONE BIG HAPPY
GRANDPA, I HAD A DREAM ABOUT YOU!
YOU DID?
YES, IT WAS TERRIBLE!
YOU HAD A TALKING HAT!
LET'S ORDER A PIZZA!
OKAY!
AND YOU WENT AWAY WITH THOSE PEOPLE IN THE DENTURE COMMERCIAL!
SO LONG, LOSERS!
SNIFF
AW, NOW, RUTHIE, IT WAS JUST A DREAM!
I'M NOT GOING ANYWHERE! I'M STAYING RIGHT HERE!
WHAT'S THIS? FIVE DOLLARS!
BUY YOURSELF SOMETHING NICE. YOU'LL FEEL BETTER!
GRANDMA, I HAD A DREAM ABOUT YOU!

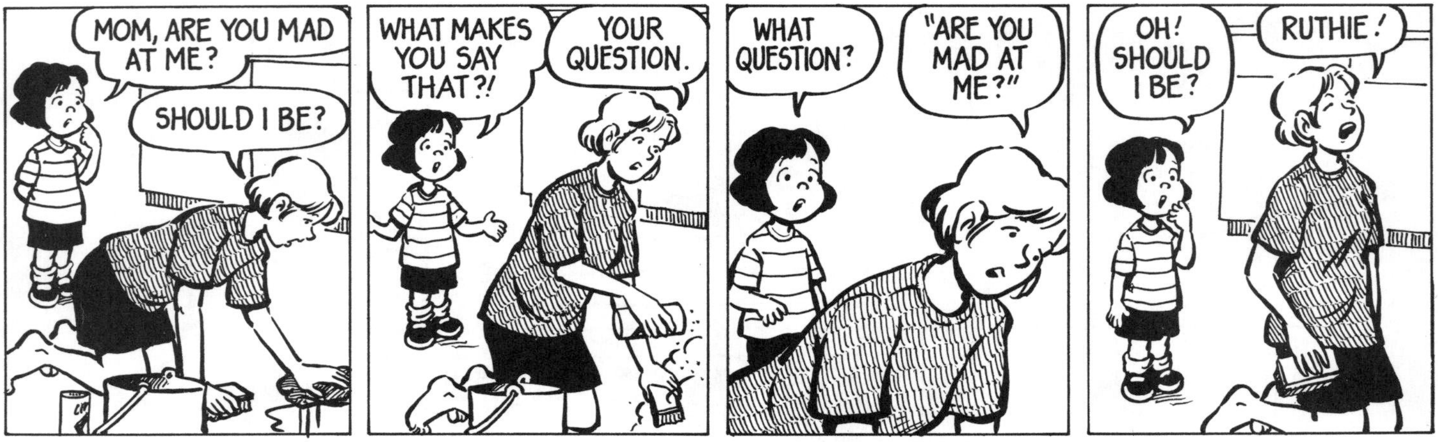
MOM, ARE YOU MAD AT ME?
SHOULD I BE?
WHAT MAKES YOU SAY THAT?!
YOUR QUESTION.
WHAT QUESTION?
"ARE YOU MAD AT ME?"
OH! SHOULD I BE?
RUTHIE!

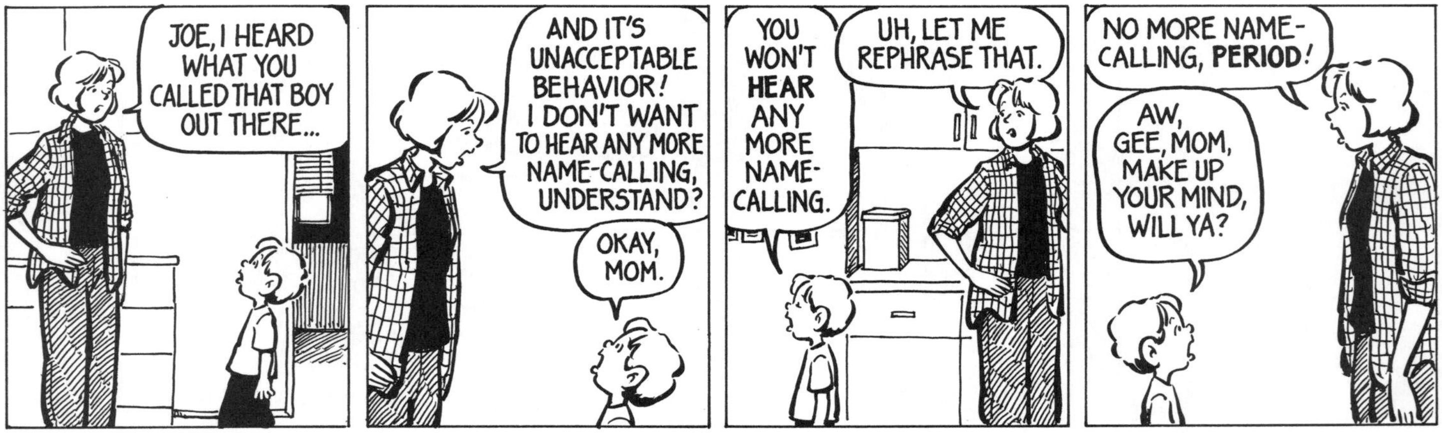
JOE, I HEARD WHAT YOU CALLED THAT BOY OUT THERE...
AND IT'S UNACCEPTABLE BEHAVIOR! I DON'T WANT TO HEAR ANY MORE NAME-CALLING, UNDERSTAND?
OKAY, MOM.
YOU WON'T **HEAR** ANY MORE NAME-CALLING.
UH, LET ME REPHRASE THAT.
NO MORE NAME-CALLING, **PERIOD**!
AW, GEE, MOM, MAKE UP YOUR MIND, WILL YA?

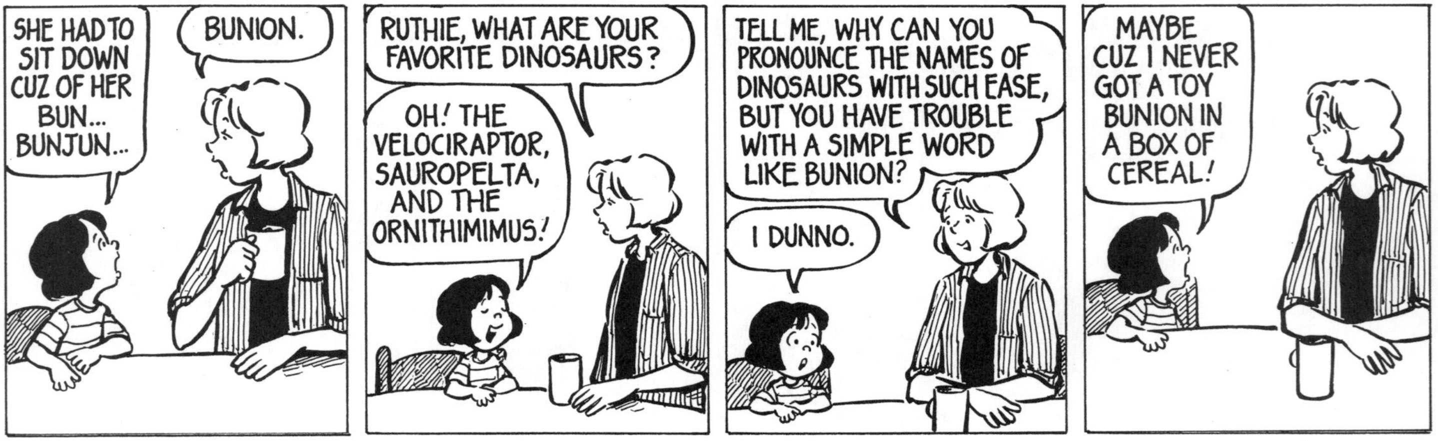
SHE HAD TO SIT DOWN CUZ OF HER BUN... BUNJUN...
BUNION.
RUTHIE, WHAT ARE YOUR FAVORITE DINOSAURS?
OH! THE VELOCIRAPTOR, SAUROPELTA, AND THE ORNITHIMIMUS!
TELL ME, WHY CAN YOU PRONOUNCE THE NAMES OF DINOSAURS WITH SUCH EASE, BUT YOU HAVE TROUBLE WITH A SIMPLE WORD LIKE BUNION?
I DUNNO.
MAYBE CUZ I NEVER GOT A TOY BUNION IN A BOX OF CEREAL!

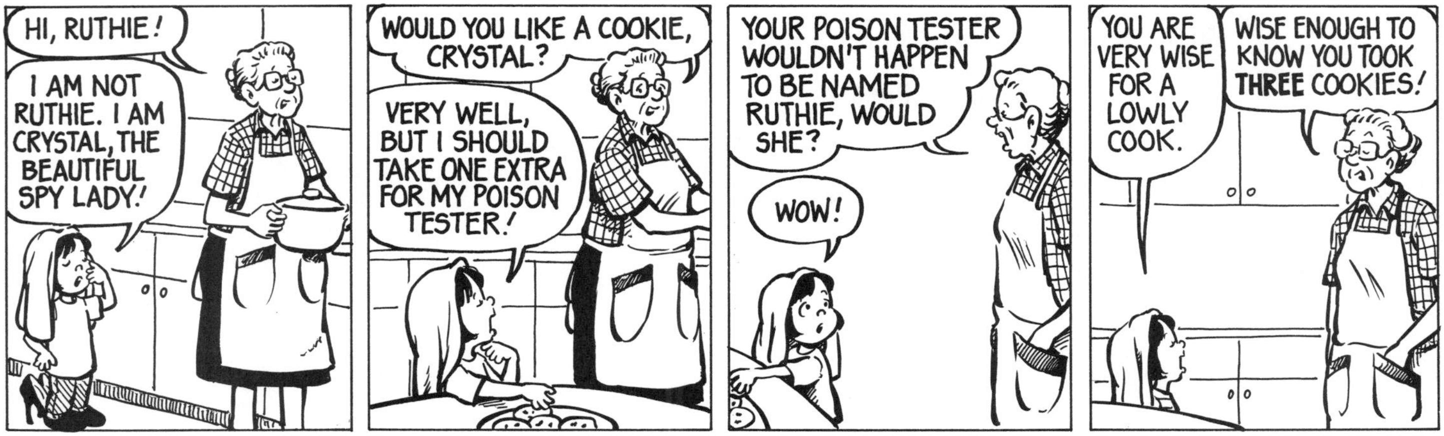
HI, RUTHIE!
I AM NOT RUTHIE. I AM CRYSTAL, THE BEAUTIFUL SPY LADY!
WOULD YOU LIKE A COOKIE, CRYSTAL?
VERY WELL, BUT I SHOULD TAKE ONE EXTRA FOR MY POISON TESTER!
YOUR POISON TESTER WOULDN'T HAPPEN TO BE NAMED RUTHIE, WOULD SHE?
WOW!
YOU ARE VERY WISE FOR A LOWLY COOK.
WISE ENOUGH TO KNOW YOU TOOK **THREE** COOKIES!

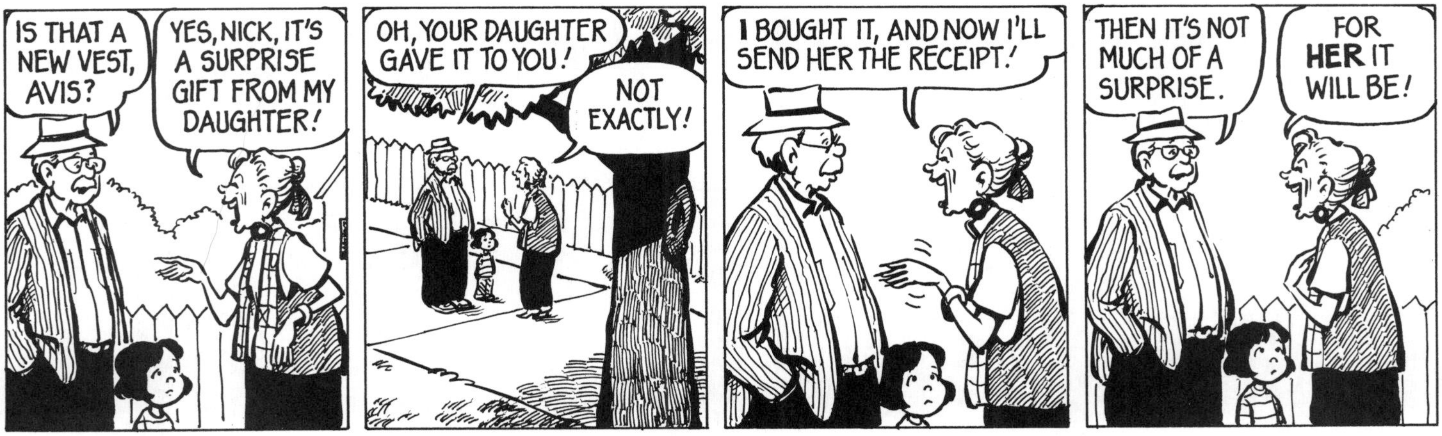
IS THAT A NEW VEST, AVIS?
YES, NICK, IT'S A SURPRISE GIFT FROM MY DAUGHTER!
OH, YOUR DAUGHTER GAVE IT TO YOU!
NOT EXACTLY!
I BOUGHT IT, AND NOW I'LL SEND HER THE RECEIPT!
THEN IT'S NOT MUCH OF A SURPRISE.
FOR **HER** IT WILL BE!

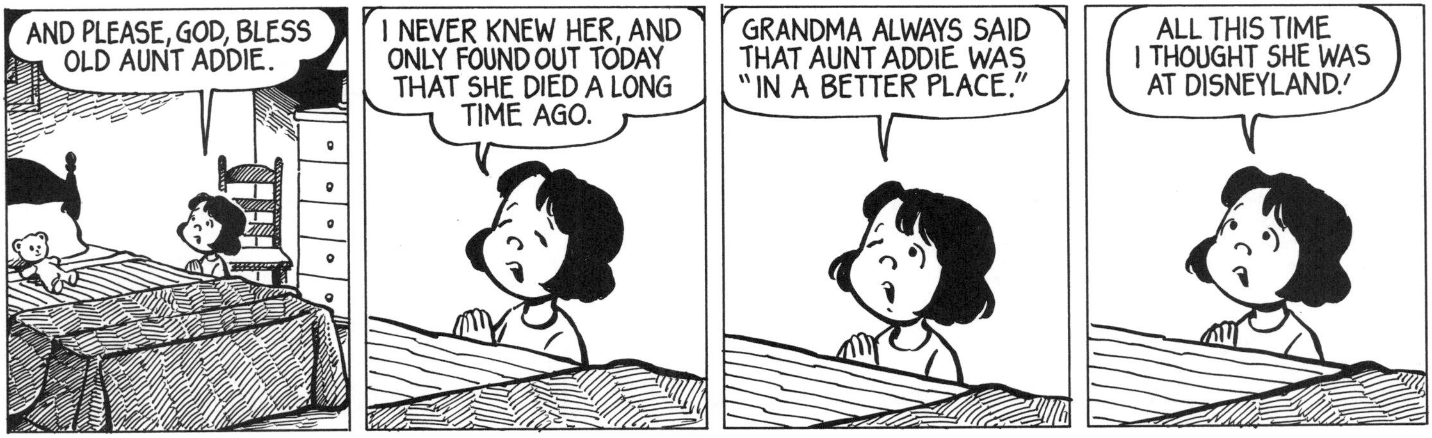
AND PLEASE, GOD, BLESS OLD AUNT ADDIE.
I NEVER KNEW HER, AND ONLY FOUND OUT TODAY THAT SHE DIED A LONG TIME AGO.
GRANDMA ALWAYS SAID THAT AUNT ADDIE WAS "IN A BETTER PLACE."
ALL THIS TIME I THOUGHT SHE WAS AT DISNEYLAND!

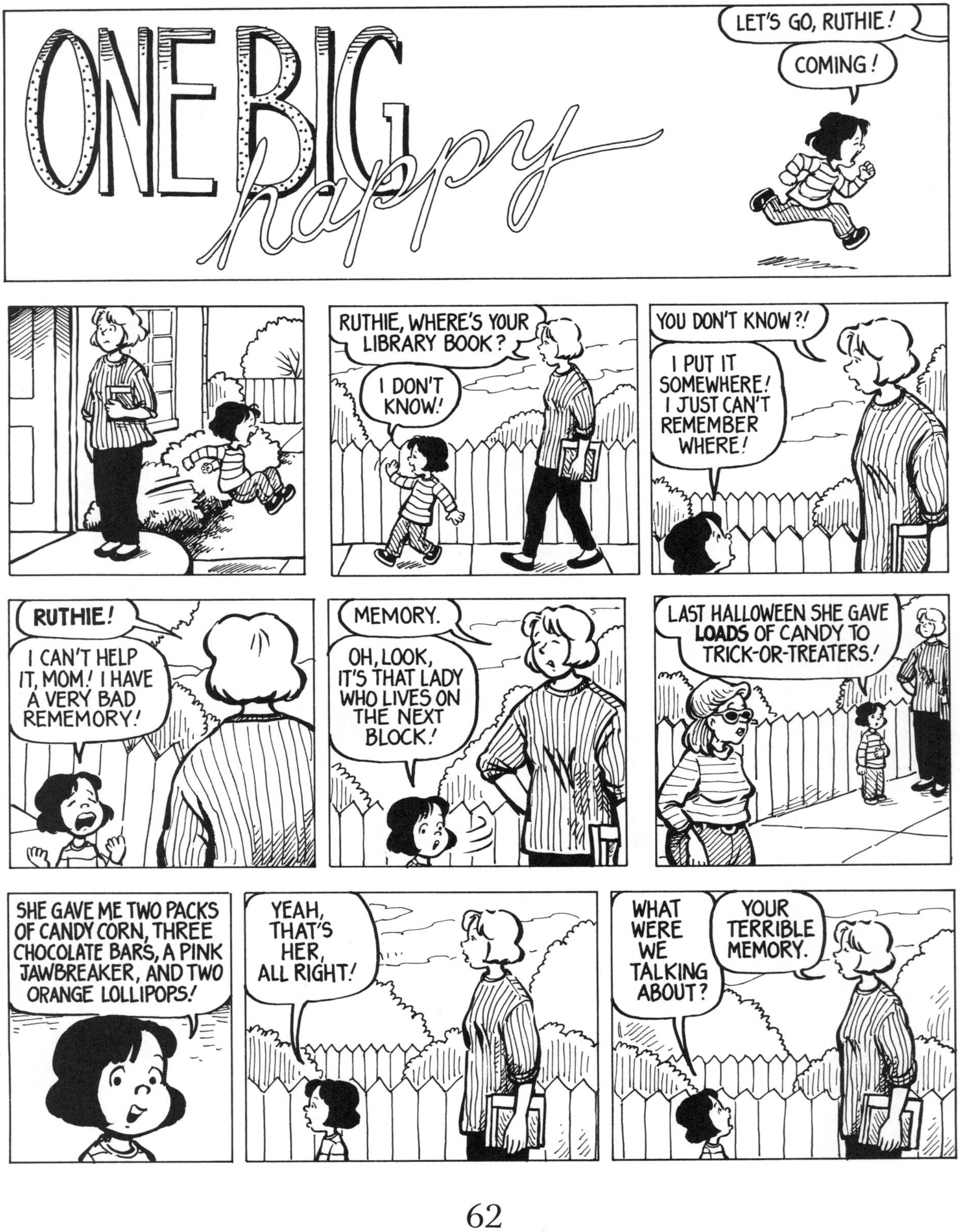
ONE BIG happy
LET'S GO, RUTHIE!
COMING!
RUTHIE, WHERE'S YOUR LIBRARY BOOK?
I DON'T KNOW!
YOU DON'T KNOW?!
I PUT IT SOMEWHERE! I JUST CAN'T REMEMBER WHERE!
RUTHIE!
I CAN'T HELP IT, MOM! I HAVE A VERY BAD REMEMORY!
MEMORY.
OH, LOOK, IT'S THAT LADY WHO LIVES ON THE NEXT BLOCK!
LAST HALLOWEEN SHE GAVE LOADS OF CANDY TO TRICK-OR-TREATERS!
SHE GAVE ME TWO PACKS OF CANDY CORN, THREE CHOCOLATE BARS, A PINK JAWBREAKER, AND TWO ORANGE LOLLIPOPS!
YEAH, THAT'S HER, ALL RIGHT!
WHAT WERE WE TALKING ABOUT?
YOUR TERRIBLE MEMORY.

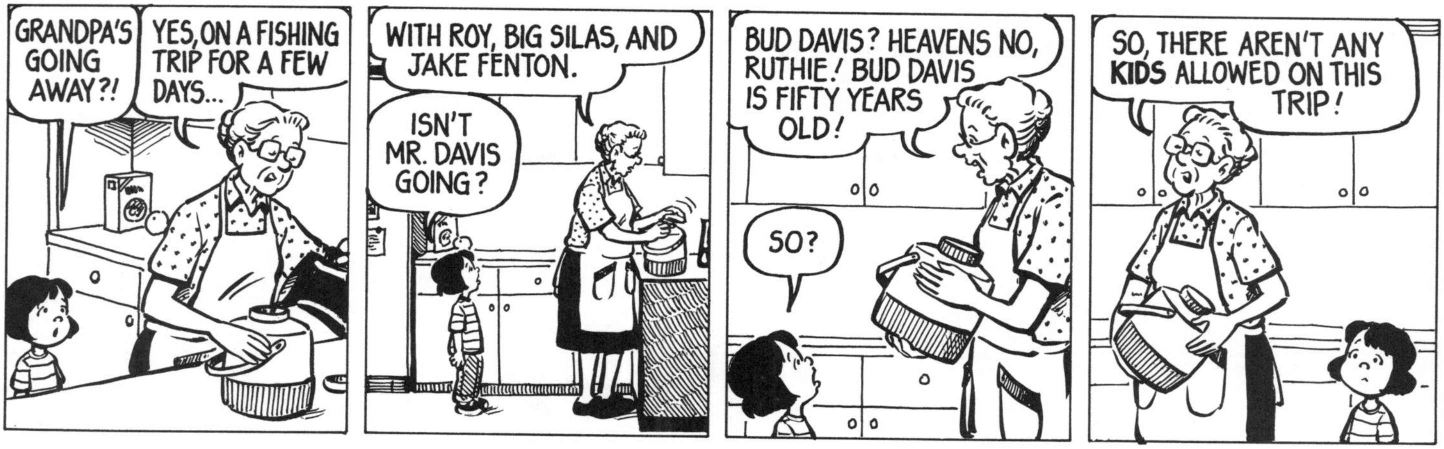
GRANDPA'S GOING AWAY?!
YES, ON A FISHING TRIP FOR A FEW DAYS...
WITH ROY, BIG SILAS, AND JAKE FENTON.
ISN'T MR. DAVIS GOING?
BUD DAVIS? HEAVENS NO, RUTHIE! BUD DAVIS IS FIFTY YEARS OLD!
SO?
SO, THERE AREN'T ANY KIDS ALLOWED ON THIS TRIP!

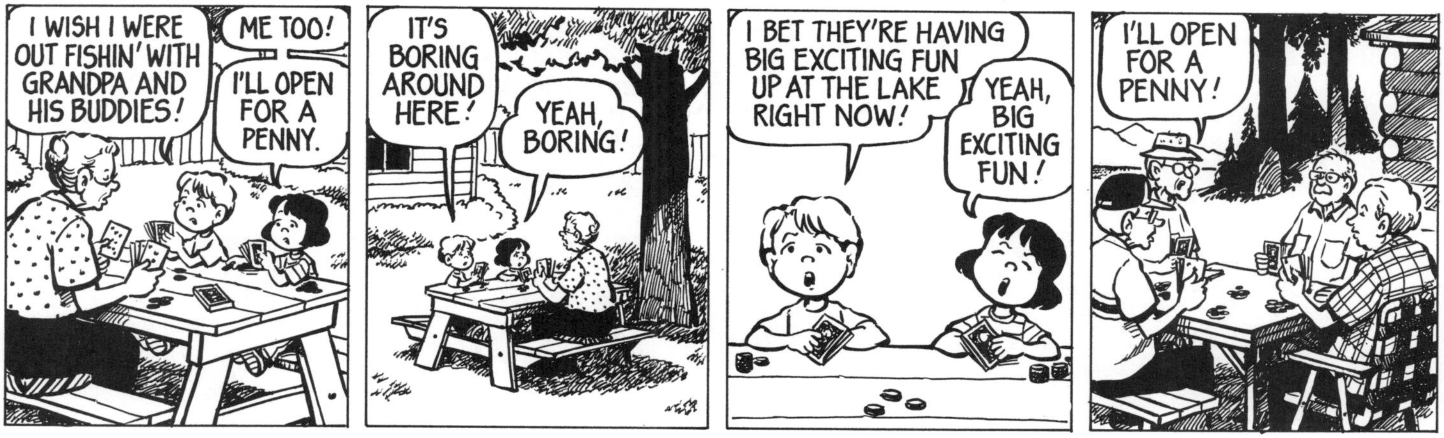
I WISH I WERE OUT FISHIN' WITH GRANDPA AND HIS BUDDIES!
ME TOO!
I'LL OPEN FOR A PENNY.
IT'S BORING AROUND HERE!
YEAH, BORING!
I BET THEY'RE HAVING BIG EXCITING FUN UP AT THE LAKE RIGHT NOW!
YEAH, BIG EXCITING FUN!
I'LL OPEN FOR A PENNY!

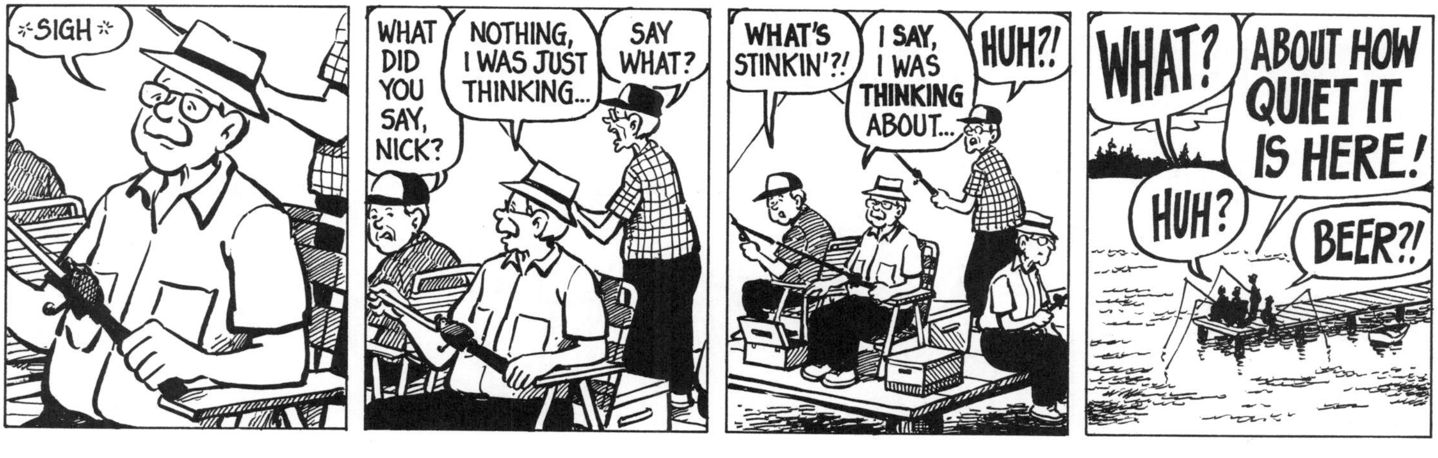
SIGH
WHAT DID YOU SAY, NICK?
NOTHING, I WAS JUST THINKING...
SAY WHAT?
WHAT'S STINKIN'?!
I SAY, I WAS THINKING ABOUT...
HUH?!
WHAT?
ABOUT HOW QUIET IT IS HERE!
HUH?
BEER?!

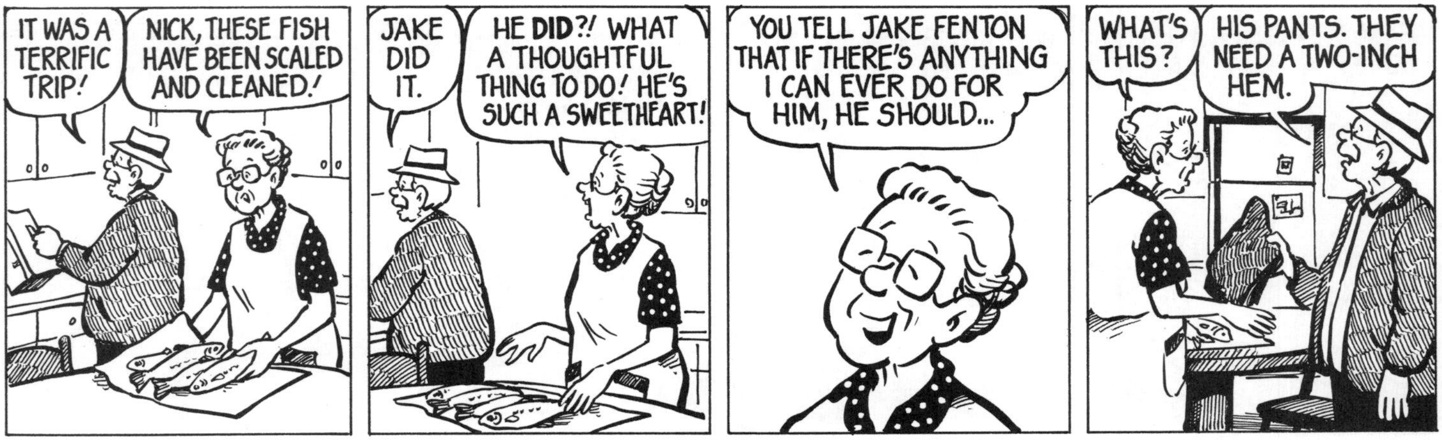
IT WAS A TERRIFIC TRIP!
NICK, THESE FISH HAVE BEEN SCALED AND CLEANED!
JAKE DID IT.
HE DID?! WHAT A THOUGHTFUL THING TO DO! HE'S SUCH A SWEETHEART!
YOU TELL JAKE FENTON THAT IF THERE'S ANYTHING I CAN EVER DO FOR HIM, HE SHOULD...
WHAT'S THIS?
HIS PANTS. THEY NEED A TWO-INCH HEM.

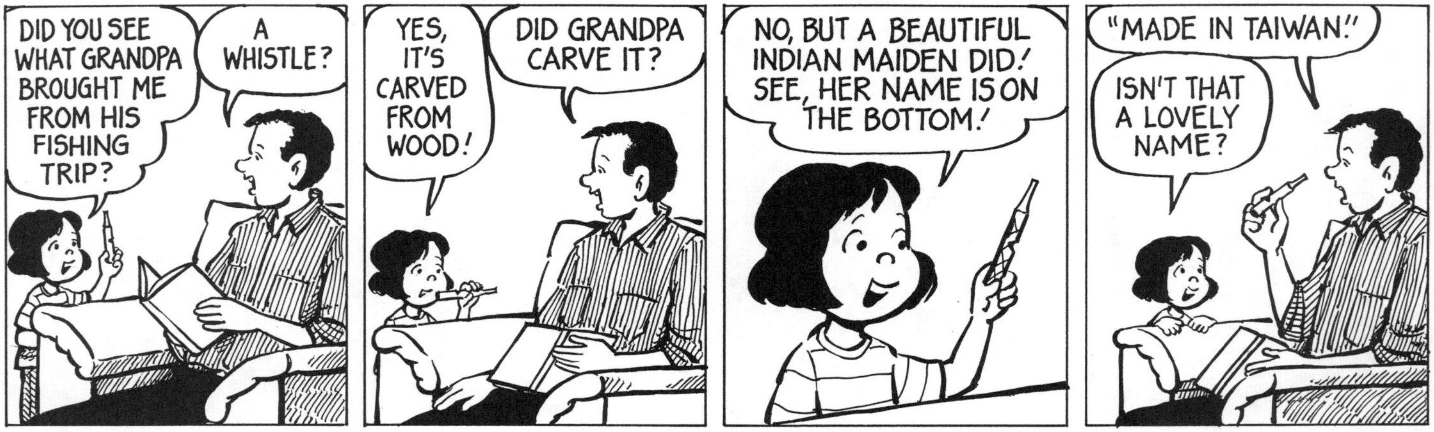
DID YOU SEE WHAT GRANDPA BROUGHT ME FROM HIS FISHING TRIP?
A WHISTLE?
YES, IT'S CARVED FROM WOOD!
DID GRANDPA CARVE IT?
NO, BUT A BEAUTIFUL INDIAN MAIDEN DID! SEE, HER NAME IS ON THE BOTTOM!
"MADE IN TAIWAN."
ISN'T THAT A LOVELY NAME?

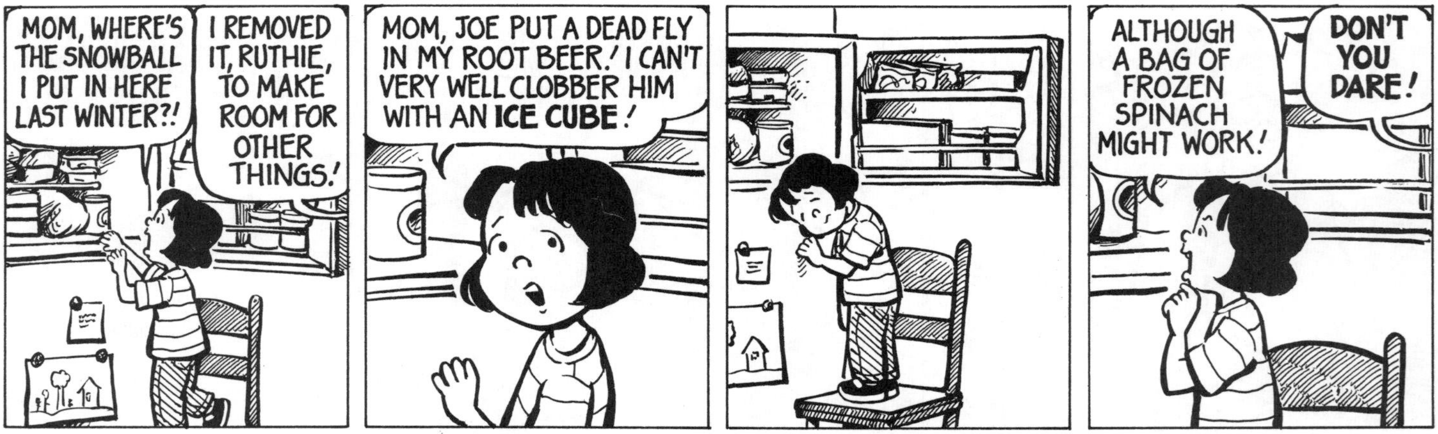
MOM, WHERE'S THE SNOWBALL I PUT IN HERE LAST WINTER?!
I REMOVED IT, RUTHIE, TO MAKE ROOM FOR OTHER THINGS!
MOM, JOE PUT A DEAD FLY IN MY ROOT BEER! I CAN'T VERY WELL CLOBBER HIM WITH AN ICE CUBE!
ALTHOUGH A BAG OF FROZEN SPINACH MIGHT WORK!
DON'T YOU DARE!

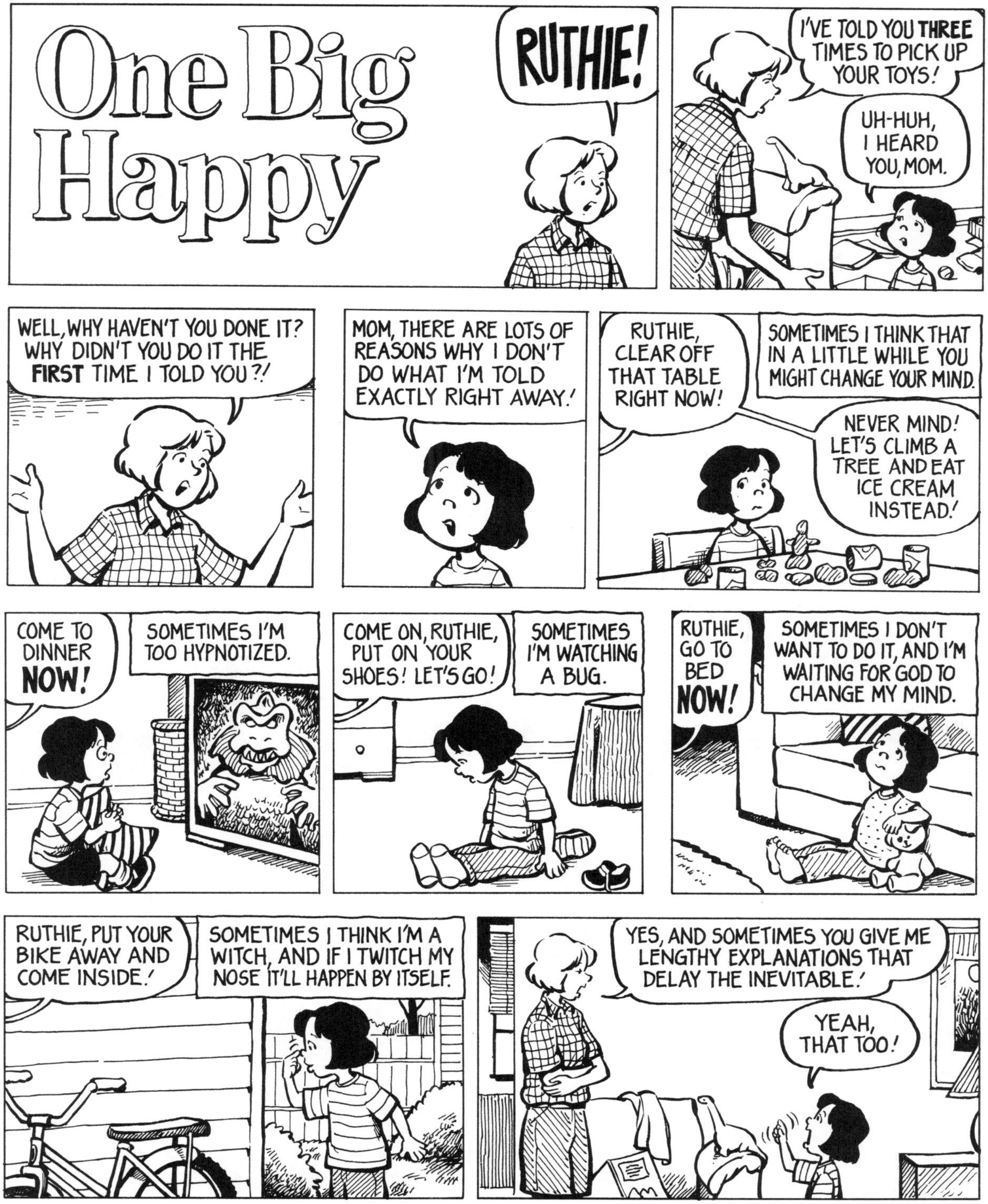
One Big Happy
RUTHIE!
I'VE TOLD YOU THREE TIMES TO PICK UP YOUR TOYS!
UH-HUH, I HEARD YOU, MOM.
WELL, WHY HAVEN'T YOU DONE IT? WHY DIDN'T YOU DO IT THE FIRST TIME I TOLD YOU?!
MOM, THERE ARE LOTS OF REASONS WHY I DON'T DO WHAT I'M TOLD EXACTLY RIGHT AWAY!
RUTHIE, CLEAR OFF THAT TABLE RIGHT NOW!
SOMETIMES I THINK THAT IN A LITTLE WHILE YOU MIGHT CHANGE YOUR MIND.
NEVER MIND! LET'S CLIMB A TREE AND EAT ICE CREAM INSTEAD!
COME TO DINNER NOW!
SOMETIMES I'M TOO HYPNOTIZED.
COME ON, RUTHIE, PUT ON YOUR SHOES! LET'S GO!
SOMETIMES I'M WATCHING A BUG.
RUTHIE, GO TO BED NOW!
SOMETIMES I DON'T WANT TO DO IT, AND I'M WAITING FOR GOD TO CHANGE MY MIND.
RUTHIE, PUT YOUR BIKE AWAY AND COME INSIDE!
SOMETIMES I THINK I'M A WITCH, AND IF I TWITCH MY NOSE IT'LL HAPPEN BY ITSELF.
YES, AND SOMETIMES YOU GIVE ME LENGTHY EXPLANATIONS THAT DELAY THE INEVITABLE!
YEAH, THAT TOO!

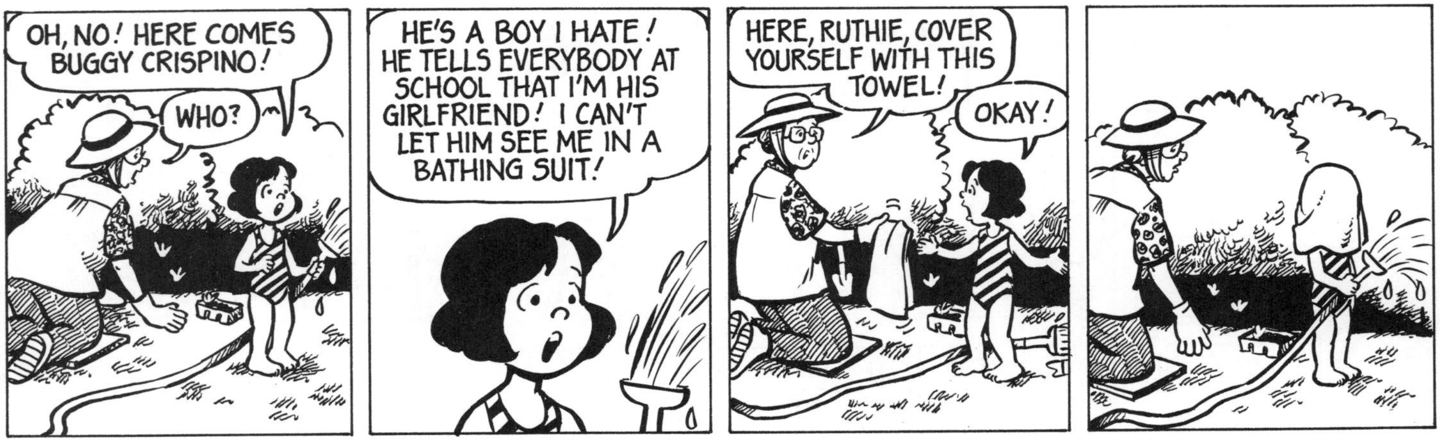
OH, NO! HERE COMES BUGGY CRISPINO!
WHO?
HE'S A BOY I HATE! HE TELLS EVERYBODY AT SCHOOL THAT I'M HIS GIRLFRIEND! I CAN'T LET HIM SEE ME IN A BATHING SUIT!
HERE, RUTHIE, COVER YOURSELF WITH THIS TOWEL!
OKAY!

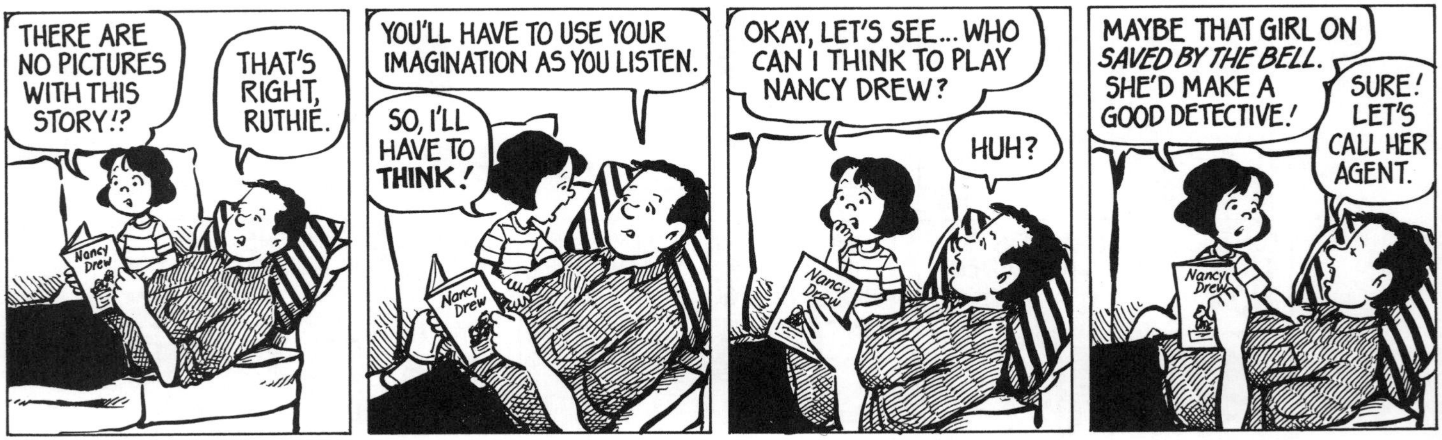
THERE ARE NO PICTURES WITH THIS STORY!?
THAT'S RIGHT, RUTHIE.
YOU'LL HAVE TO USE YOUR IMAGINATION AS YOU LISTEN.
SO, I'LL HAVE TO **THINK**!
Nancy Drew
OKAY, LET'S SEE... WHO CAN I THINK TO PLAY NANCY DREW?
HUH?
MAYBE THAT GIRL ON *SAVED BY THE BELL*. SHE'D MAKE A GOOD DETECTIVE!
SURE! LET'S CALL HER AGENT.

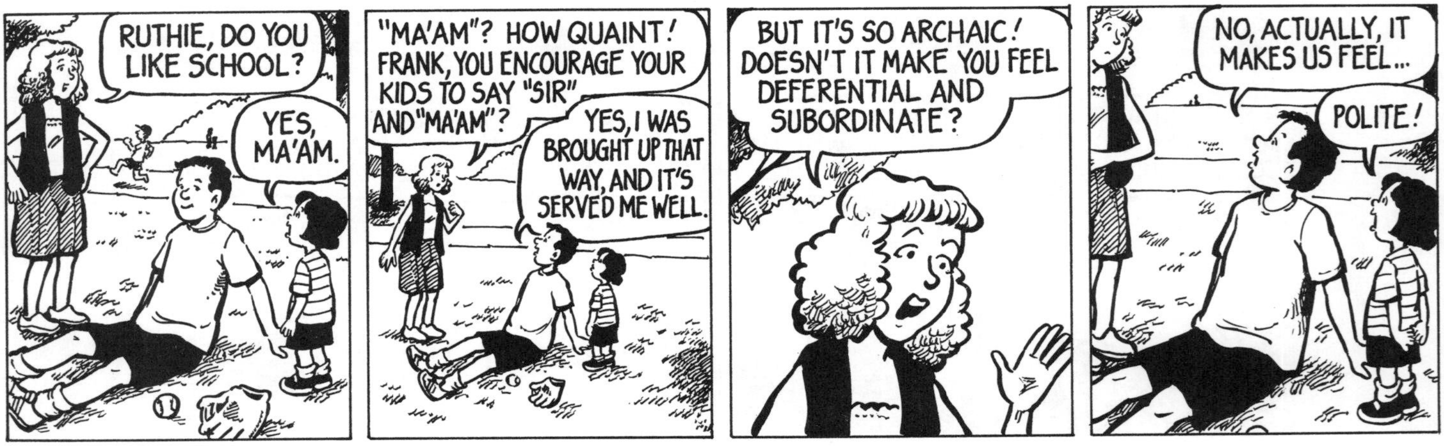
RUTHIE, DO YOU LIKE SCHOOL?
YES, MA'AM.
"MA'AM"? HOW QUAINT! FRANK, YOU ENCOURAGE YOUR KIDS TO SAY "SIR" AND "MA'AM"?
YES, I WAS BROUGHT UP THAT WAY, AND IT'S SERVED ME WELL.
BUT IT'S SO ARCHAIC! DOESN'T IT MAKE YOU FEEL DEFERENTIAL AND SUBORDINATE?
NO, ACTUALLY, IT MAKES US FEEL...
POLITE!

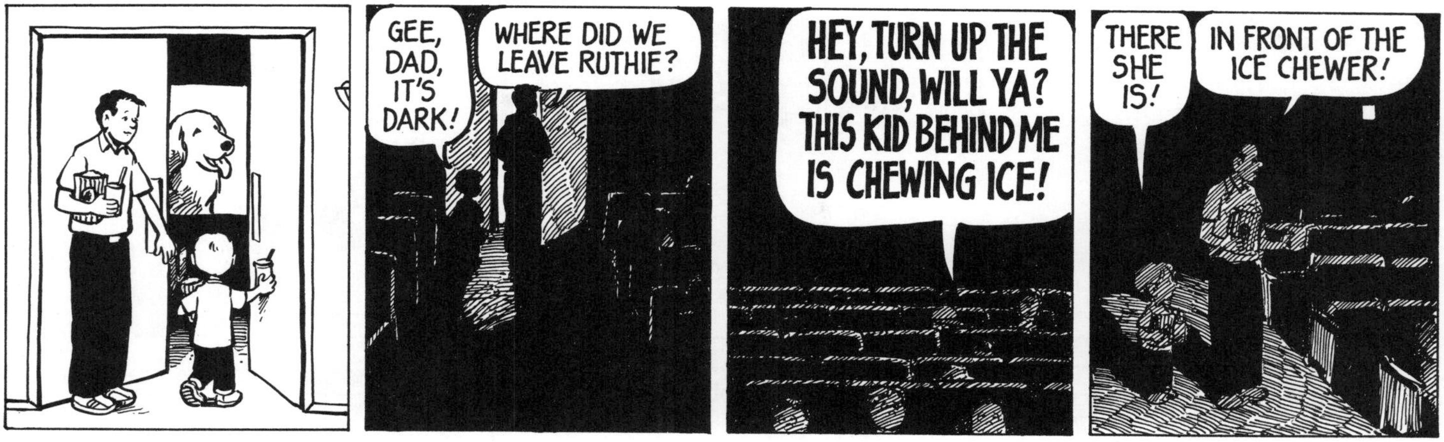
GEE, DAD, IT'S DARK!
WHERE DID WE LEAVE RUTHIE?
HEY, TURN UP THE SOUND, WILL YA? THIS KID BEHIND ME IS CHEWING ICE!
THERE SHE IS!
IN FRONT OF THE ICE CHEWER!

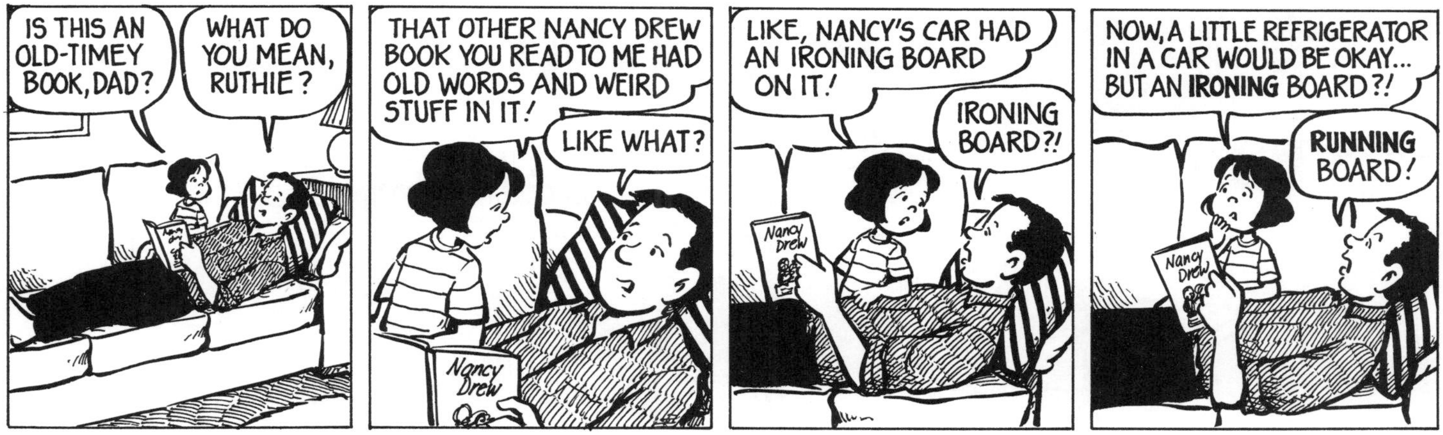
IS THIS AN OLD-TIMEY BOOK, DAD?
WHAT DO YOU MEAN, RUTHIE?
Nancy Drew
THAT OTHER NANCY DREW BOOK YOU READ TO ME HAD OLD WORDS AND WEIRD STUFF IN IT!
LIKE WHAT?
Nancy Drew
LIKE, NANCY'S CAR HAD AN IRONING BOARD ON IT!
IRONING BOARD?!
Nancy Drew
NOW, A LITTLE REFRIGERATOR IN A CAR WOULD BE OKAY... BUT AN **IRONING** BOARD?!
RUNNING BOARD!
Nancy Drew

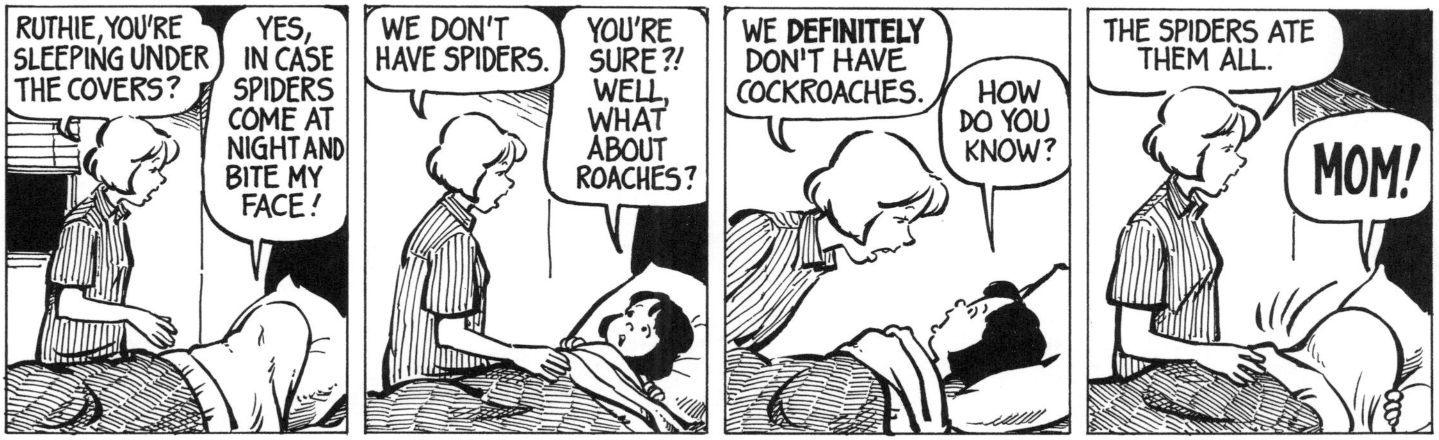
RUTHIE, YOU'RE SLEEPING UNDER THE COVERS?
YES, IN CASE SPIDERS COME AT NIGHT AND BITE MY FACE!
WE DON'T HAVE SPIDERS.
YOU'RE SURE?! WELL, WHAT ABOUT ROACHES?
WE **DEFINITELY** DON'T HAVE COCKROACHES.
HOW DO YOU KNOW?
THE SPIDERS ATE THEM ALL.
MOM!

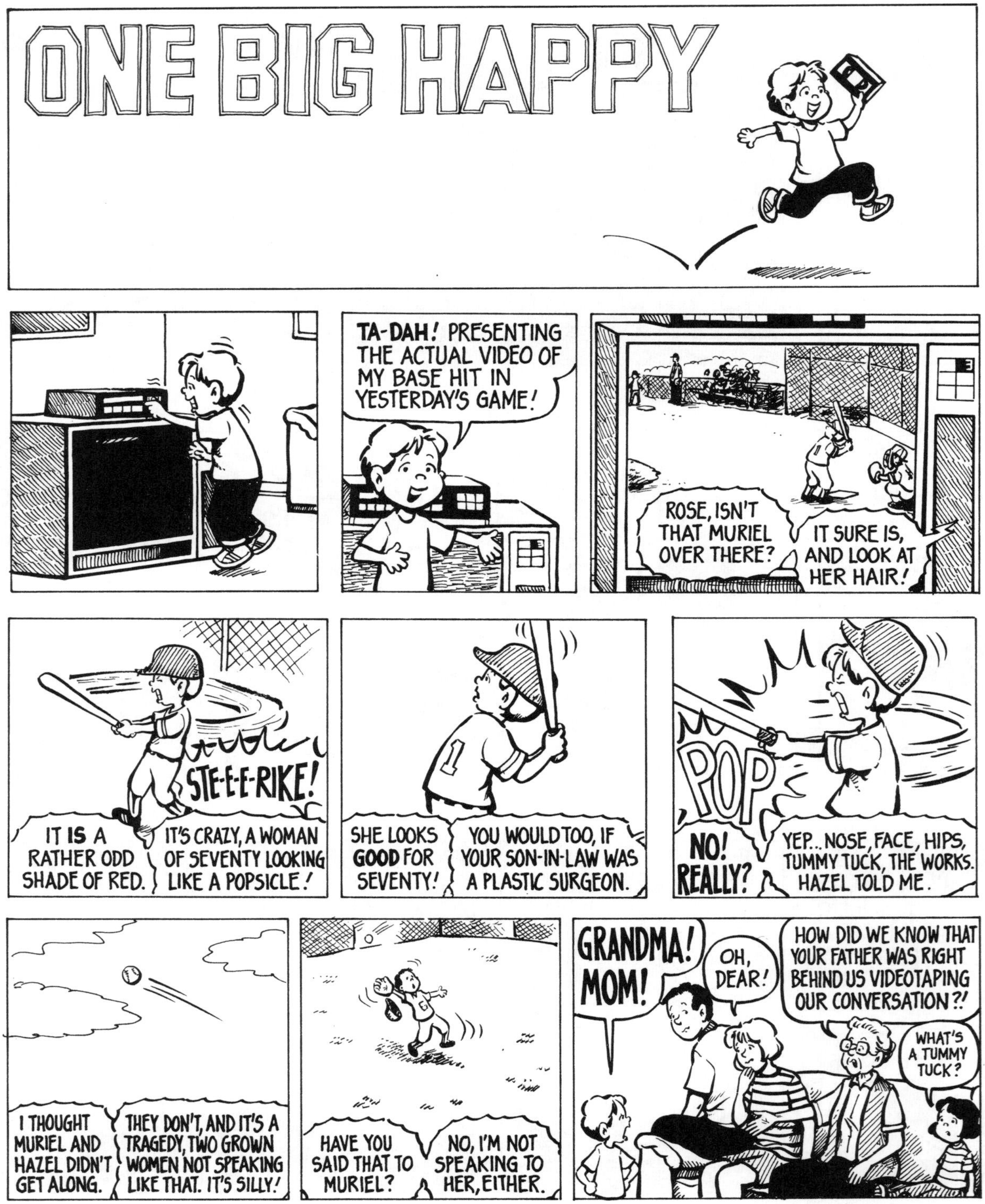
ONE BIG HAPPY
TA-DAH! PRESENTING THE ACTUAL VIDEO OF MY BASE HIT IN YESTERDAY'S GAME!
ROSE, ISN'T THAT MURIEL OVER THERE?
IT SURE IS, AND LOOK AT HER HAIR!
STE-E-E-RIKE!
IT IS A RATHER ODD SHADE OF RED.
IT'S CRAZY, A WOMAN OF SEVENTY LOOKING LIKE A POPSICLE!
SHE LOOKS GOOD FOR SEVENTY!
YOU WOULD TOO, IF YOUR SON-IN-LAW WAS A PLASTIC SURGEON.
POP
NO! REALLY?
YEP... NOSE, FACE, HIPS, TUMMY TUCK, THE WORKS. HAZEL TOLD ME.
I THOUGHT MURIEL AND HAZEL DIDN'T GET ALONG.
THEY DON'T, AND IT'S A TRAGEDY, TWO GROWN WOMEN NOT SPEAKING LIKE THAT. IT'S SILLY!
HAVE YOU SAID THAT TO MURIEL?
NO, I'M NOT SPEAKING TO HER, EITHER.
GRANDMA! MOM!
OH, DEAR!
HOW DID WE KNOW THAT YOUR FATHER WAS RIGHT BEHIND US VIDEOTAPING OUR CONVERSATION?!
WHAT'S A TUMMY TUCK?

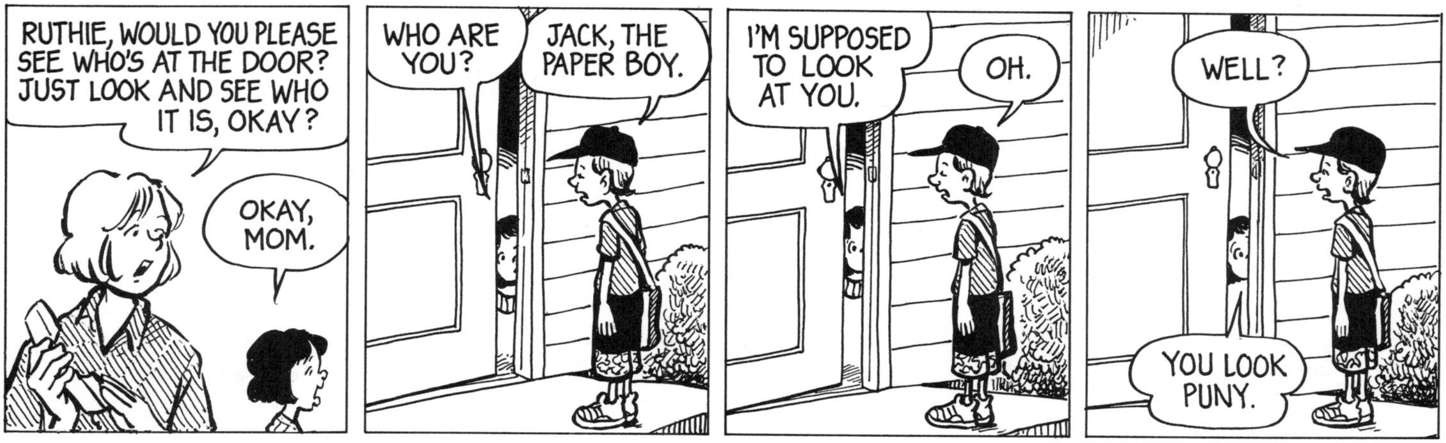
RUTHIE, WOULD YOU PLEASE SEE WHO'S AT THE DOOR? JUST LOOK AND SEE WHO IT IS, OKAY?
OKAY, MOM.
WHO ARE YOU?
JACK, THE PAPER BOY.
I'M SUPPOSED TO LOOK AT YOU.
OH.
WELL?
YOU LOOK PUNY.

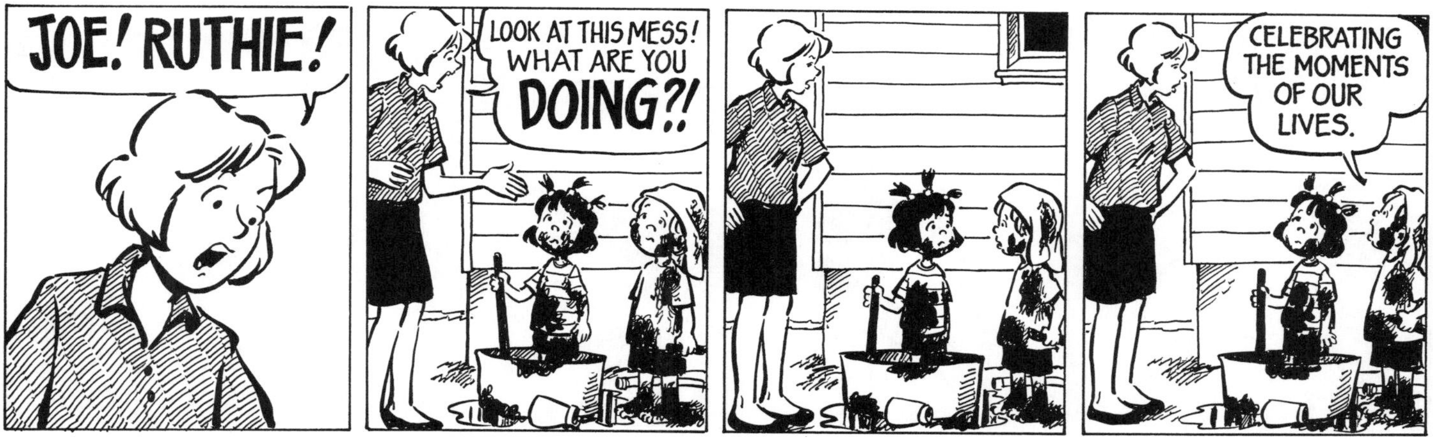
JOE! RUTHIE!
LOOK AT THIS MESS! WHAT ARE YOU DOING?!
CELEBRATING THE MOMENTS OF OUR LIVES.

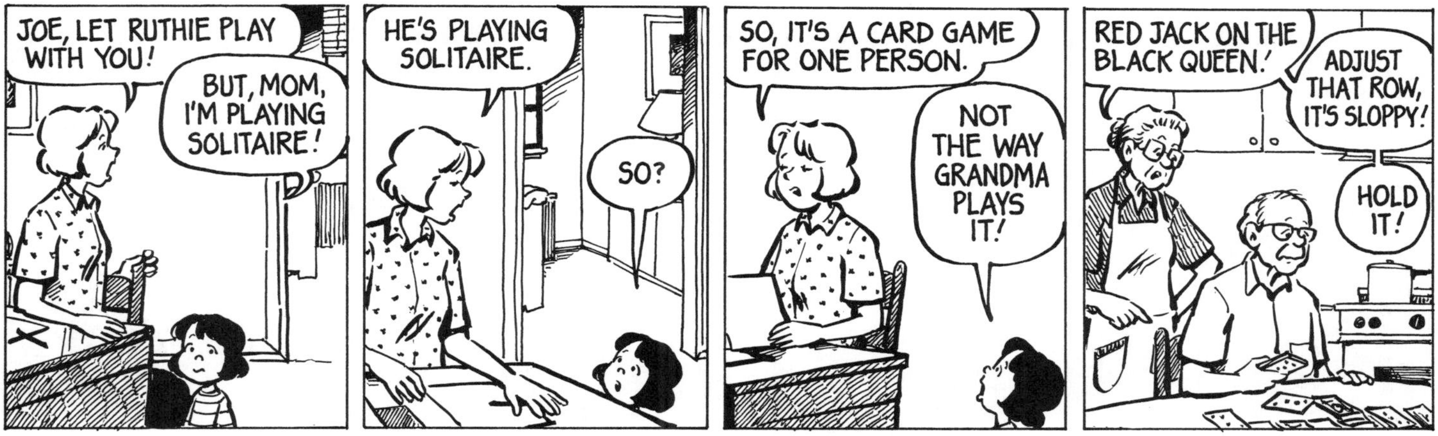
JOE, LET RUTHIE PLAY WITH YOU!
BUT, MOM, I'M PLAYING SOLITAIRE!
HE'S PLAYING SOLITAIRE.
SO?
SO, IT'S A CARD GAME FOR ONE PERSON.
NOT THE WAY GRANDMA PLAYS IT!
RED JACK ON THE BLACK QUEEN!
ADJUST THAT ROW, IT'S SLOPPY!
HOLD IT!

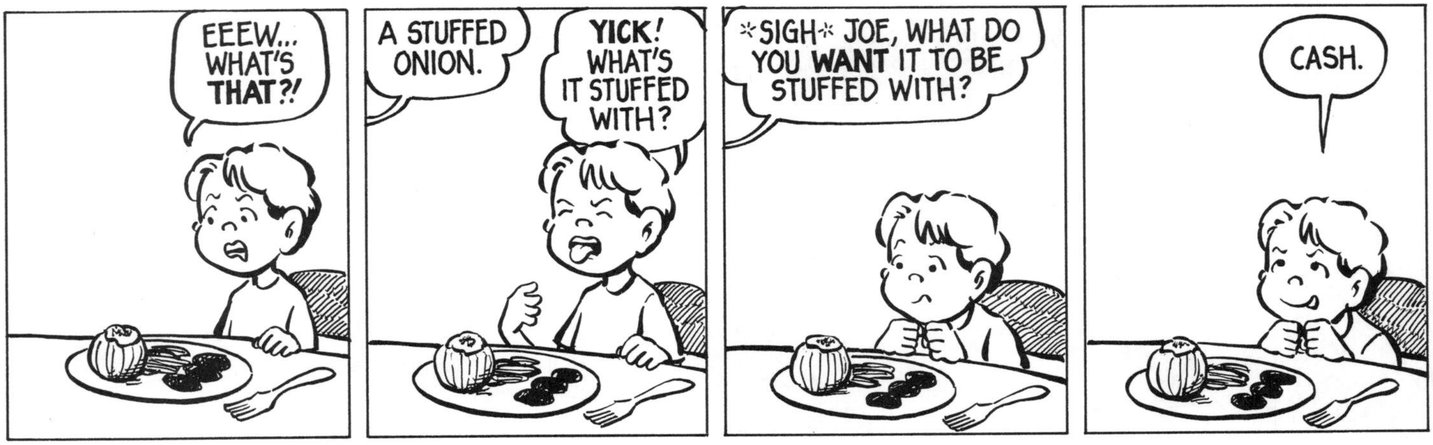
EEEW... WHAT'S **THAT**?!
A STUFFED ONION.
YICK! WHAT'S IT STUFFED WITH?
SIGH JOE, WHAT DO YOU **WANT** IT TO BE STUFFED WITH?
CASH.

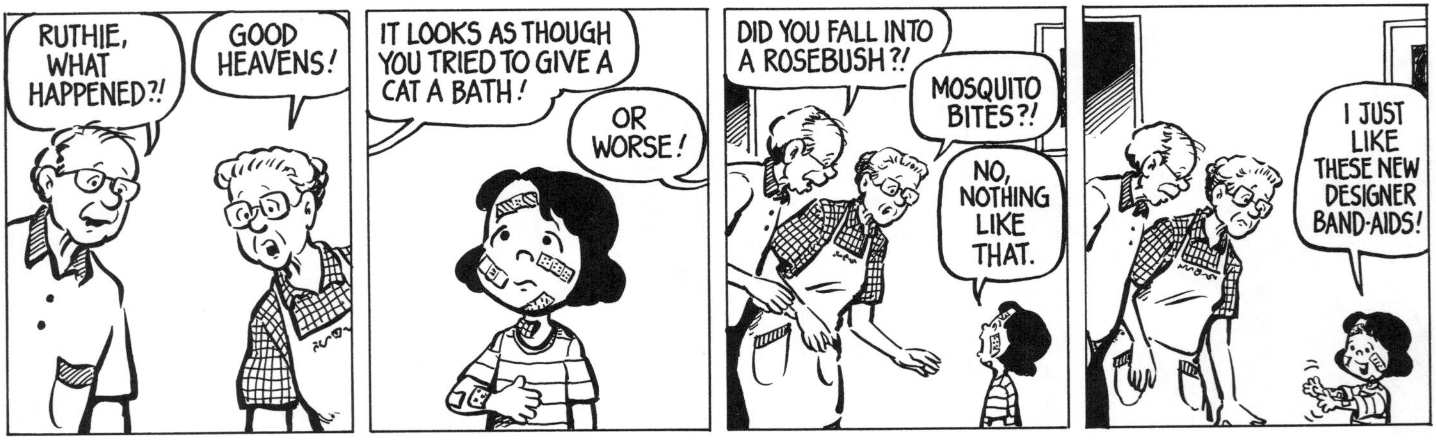
RUTHIE, WHAT HAPPENED?!
GOOD HEAVENS!
IT LOOKS AS THOUGH YOU TRIED TO GIVE A CAT A BATH!
OR WORSE!
DID YOU FALL INTO A ROSEBUSH?!
MOSQUITO BITES?!
NO, NOTHING LIKE THAT.
I JUST LIKE THESE NEW DESIGNER BAND-AIDS!

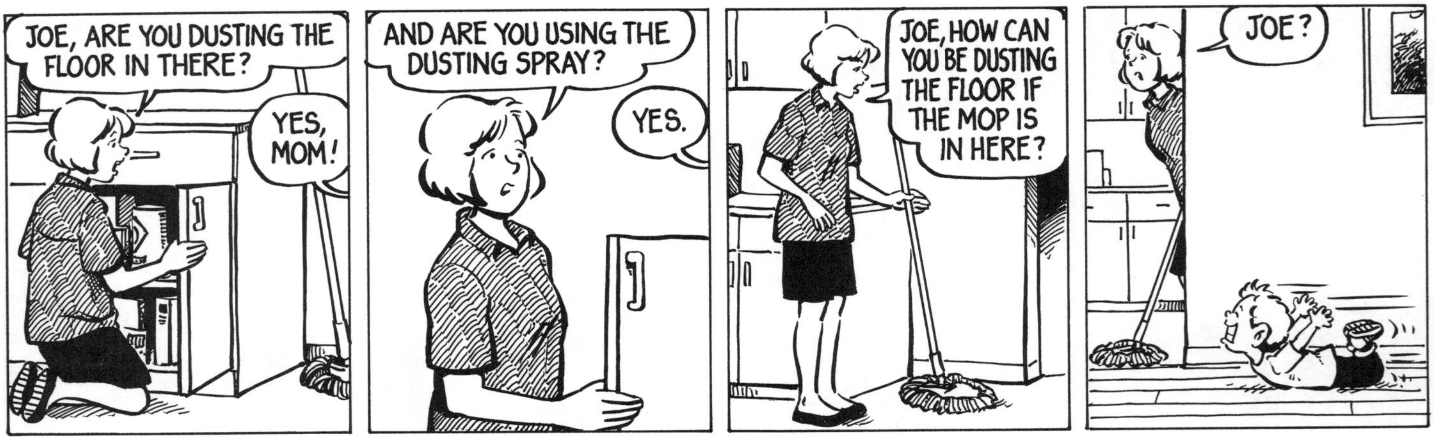
JOE, ARE YOU DUSTING THE FLOOR IN THERE?
YES, MOM!
AND ARE YOU USING THE DUSTING SPRAY?
YES.
JOE, HOW CAN YOU BE DUSTING THE FLOOR IF THE MOP IS IN HERE?
JOE?

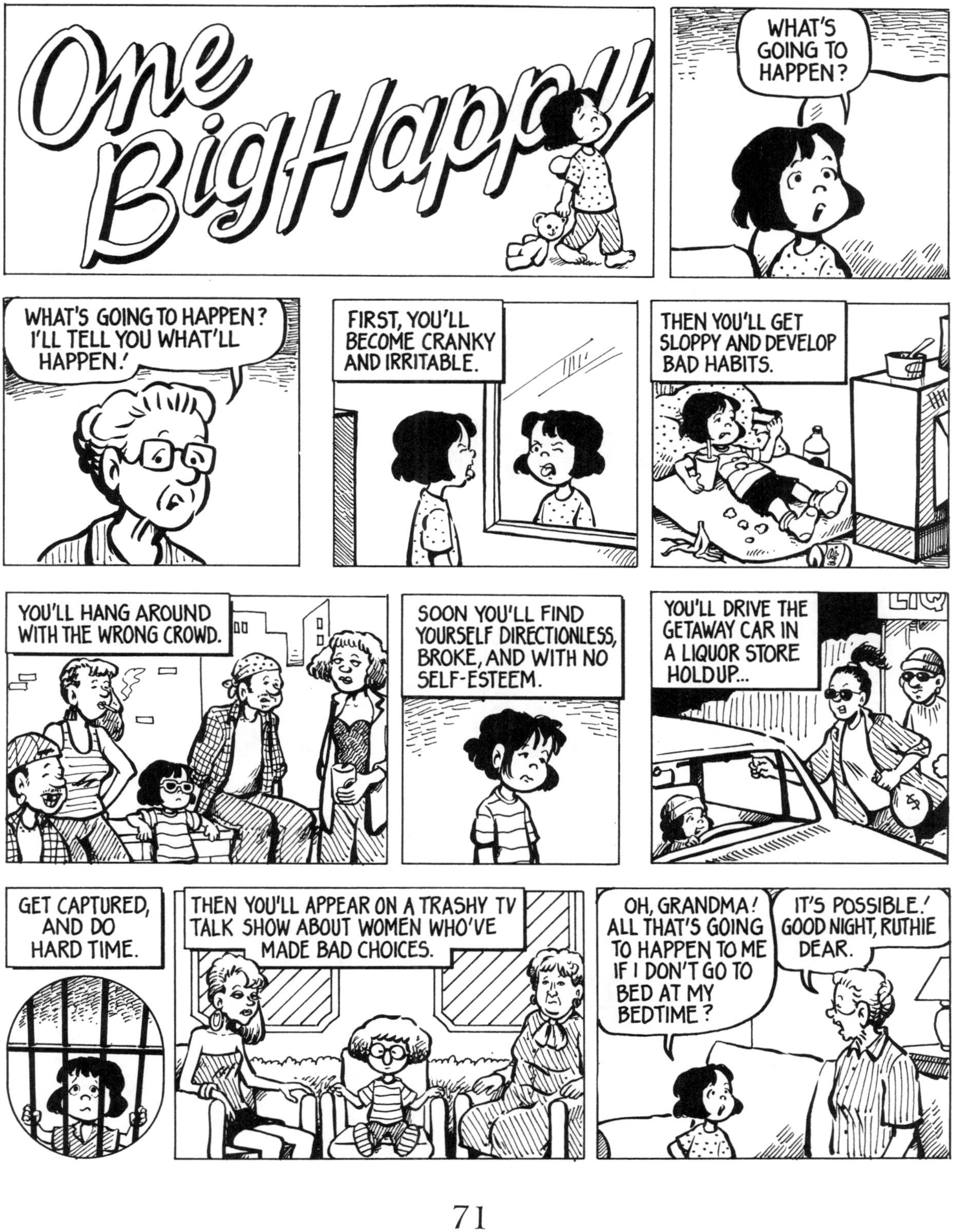
One Big Happy
WHAT'S GOING TO HAPPEN?
WHAT'S GOING TO HAPPEN? I'LL TELL YOU WHAT'LL HAPPEN!
FIRST, YOU'LL BECOME CRANKY AND IRRITABLE.
THEN YOU'LL GET SLOPPY AND DEVELOP BAD HABITS.
YOU'LL HANG AROUND WITH THE WRONG CROWD.
SOON YOU'LL FIND YOURSELF DIRECTIONLESS, BROKE, AND WITH NO SELF-ESTEEM.
YOU'LL DRIVE THE GETAWAY CAR IN A LIQUOR STORE HOLDUP...
GET CAPTURED, AND DO HARD TIME.
THEN YOU'LL APPEAR ON A TRASHY TV TALK SHOW ABOUT WOMEN WHO'VE MADE BAD CHOICES.
OH, GRANDMA! ALL THAT'S GOING TO HAPPEN TO ME IF I DON'T GO TO BED AT MY BEDTIME?
IT'S POSSIBLE! GOOD NIGHT, RUTHIE DEAR.

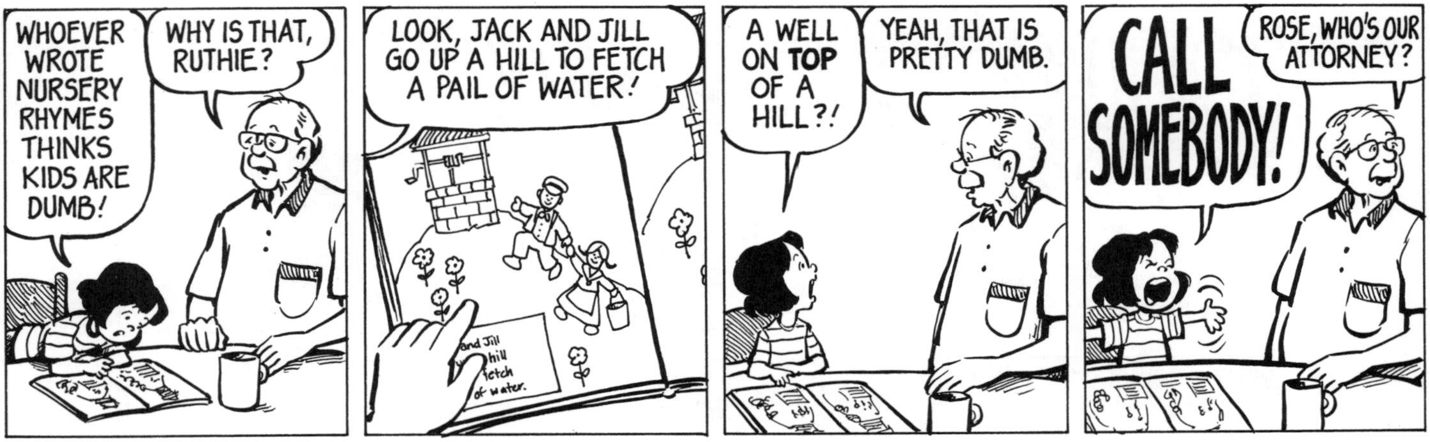
WHOEVER WROTE NURSERY RHYMES THINKS KIDS ARE DUMB!
WHY IS THAT, RUTHIE?
LOOK, JACK AND JILL GO UP A HILL TO FETCH A PAIL OF WATER!
A WELL ON **TOP** OF A HILL?!
YEAH, THAT IS PRETTY DUMB.
CALL SOMEBODY!
ROSE, WHO'S OUR ATTORNEY?

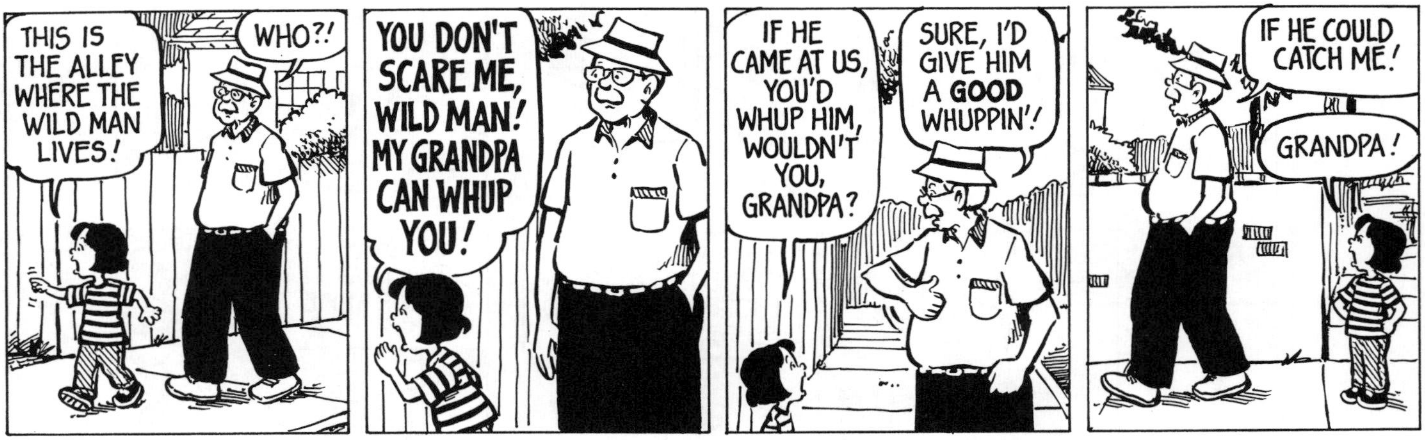
THIS IS THE ALLEY WHERE THE WILD MAN LIVES!
WHO?!
YOU DON'T SCARE ME, WILD MAN! MY GRANDPA CAN WHUP YOU!
IF HE CAME AT US, YOU'D WHUP HIM, WOULDN'T YOU, GRANDPA?
SURE, I'D GIVE HIM A **GOOD** WHUPPIN'!
IF HE COULD CATCH ME!
GRANDPA!

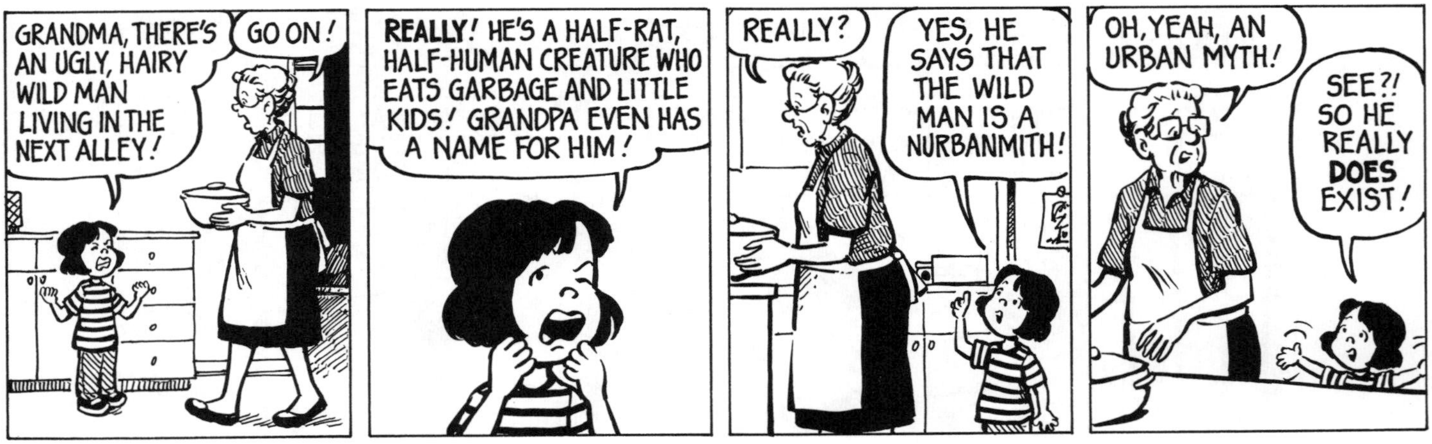
GRANDMA, THERE'S AN UGLY, HAIRY WILD MAN LIVING IN THE NEXT ALLEY!
GO ON!
REALLY! HE'S A HALF-RAT, HALF-HUMAN CREATURE WHO EATS GARBAGE AND LITTLE KIDS! GRANDPA EVEN HAS A NAME FOR HIM!
REALLY?
YES, HE SAYS THAT THE WILD MAN IS A NURBANMITH!
OH, YEAH, AN URBAN MYTH!
SEE?! SO HE REALLY **DOES** EXIST!

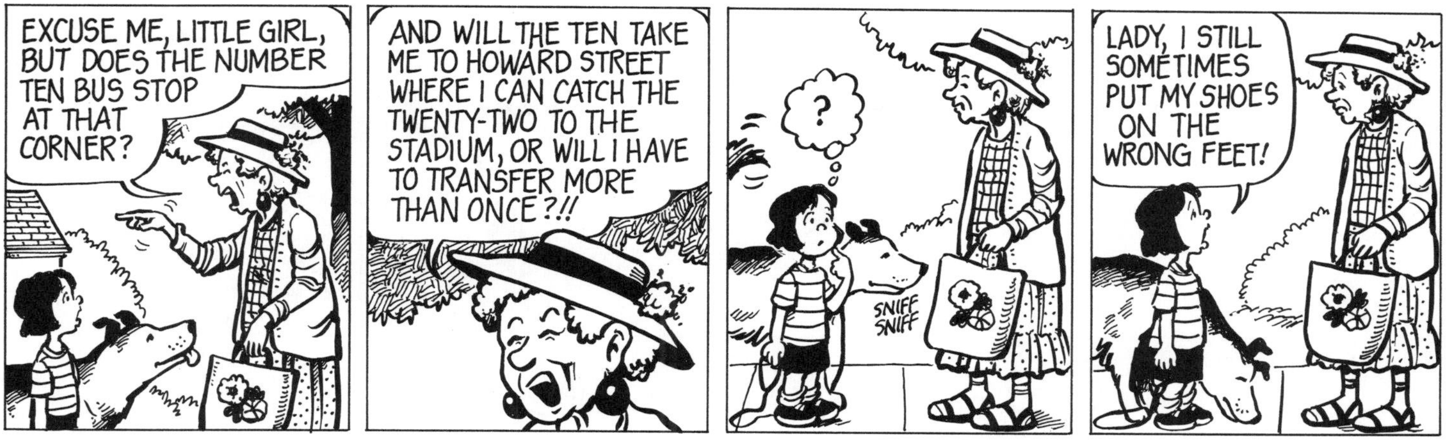
EXCUSE ME, LITTLE GIRL, BUT DOES THE NUMBER TEN BUS STOP AT THAT CORNER?
AND WILL THE TEN TAKE ME TO HOWARD STREET WHERE I CAN CATCH THE TWENTY-TWO TO THE STADIUM, OR WILL I HAVE TO TRANSFER MORE THAN ONCE?!!
?
SNIFF SNIFF
LADY, I STILL SOMETIMES PUT MY SHOES ON THE WRONG FEET!

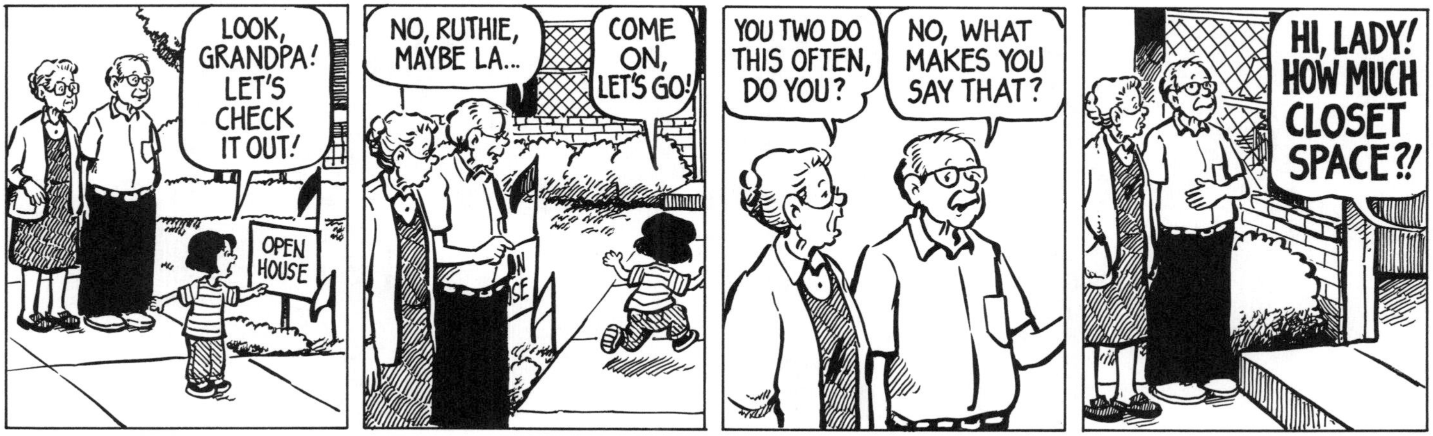
LOOK, GRANDPA! LET'S CHECK IT OUT!
OPEN HOUSE
NO, RUTHIE, MAYBE LA...
COME ON, LET'S GO!
YOU TWO DO THIS OFTEN, DO YOU?
NO, WHAT MAKES YOU SAY THAT?
HI, LADY! HOW MUCH CLOSET SPACE?!

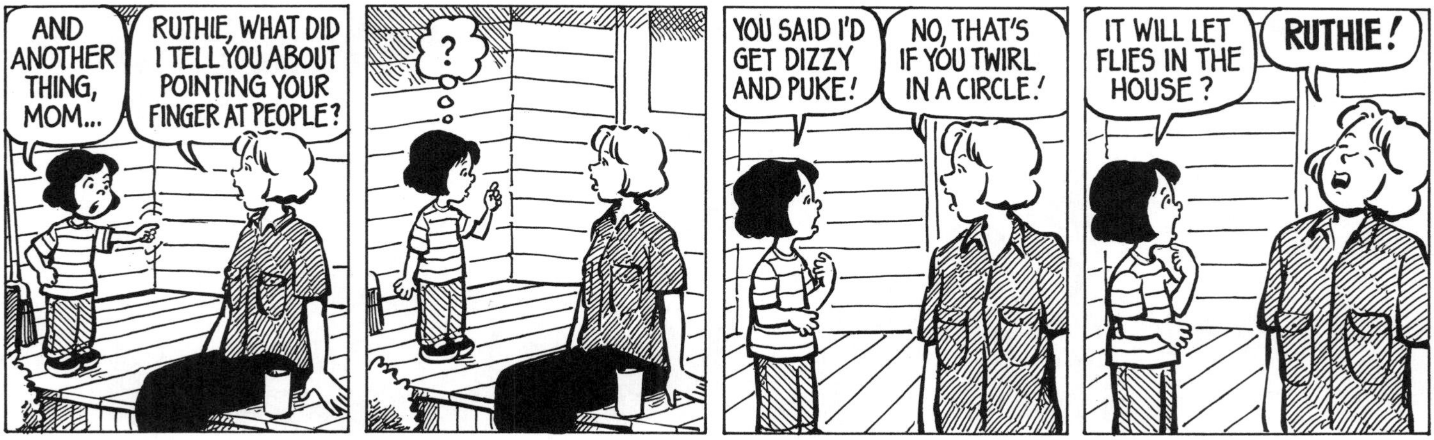
AND ANOTHER THING, MOM...
RUTHIE, WHAT DID I TELL YOU ABOUT POINTING YOUR FINGER AT PEOPLE?
?
YOU SAID I'D GET DIZZY AND PUKE!
NO, THAT'S IF YOU TWIRL IN A CIRCLE!
IT WILL LET FLIES IN THE HOUSE?
RUTHIE!

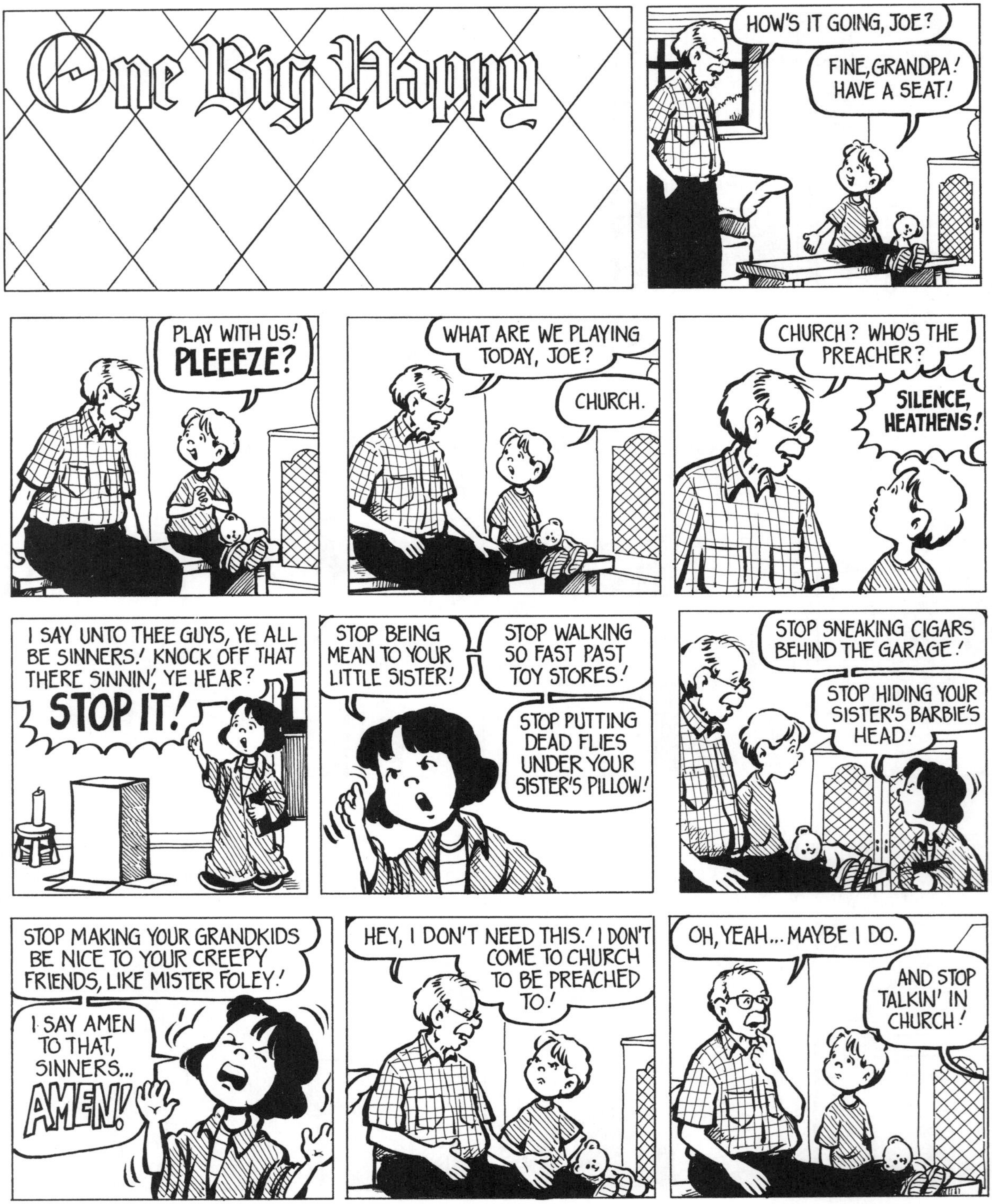
One Big Happy
HOW'S IT GOING, JOE?
FINE, GRANDPA! HAVE A SEAT!
PLAY WITH US! PLEEEZE?
WHAT ARE WE PLAYING TODAY, JOE?
CHURCH.
CHURCH? WHO'S THE PREACHER?
SILENCE, HEATHENS!
I SAY UNTO THEE GUYS, YE ALL BE SINNERS! KNOCK OFF THAT THERE SINNIN', YE HEAR? STOP IT!
STOP BEING MEAN TO YOUR LITTLE SISTER!
STOP WALKING SO FAST PAST TOY STORES!
STOP PUTTING DEAD FLIES UNDER YOUR SISTER'S PILLOW!
STOP SNEAKING CIGARS BEHIND THE GARAGE!
STOP HIDING YOUR SISTER'S BARBIE'S HEAD!
STOP MAKING YOUR GRANDKIDS BE NICE TO YOUR CREEPY FRIENDS, LIKE MISTER FOLEY!
I SAY AMEN TO THAT, SINNERS... AMEN!
HEY, I DON'T NEED THIS! I DON'T COME TO CHURCH TO BE PREACHED TO!
OH, YEAH... MAYBE I DO.
AND STOP TALKIN' IN CHURCH!

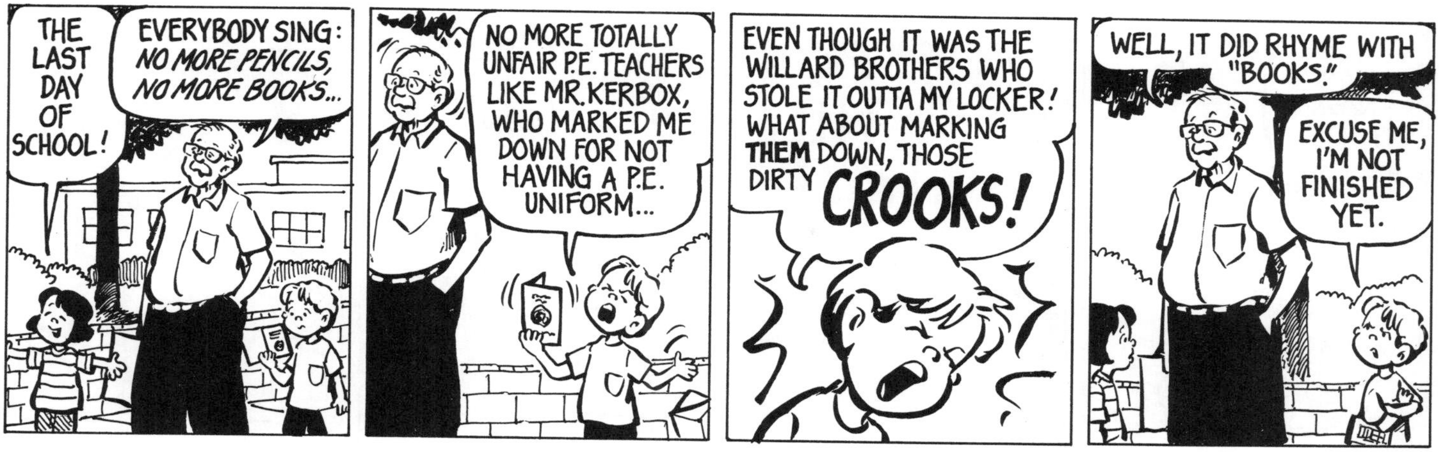
THE LAST DAY OF SCHOOL!
EVERYBODY SING: NO MORE PENCILS, NO MORE BOOKS...
NO MORE TOTALLY UNFAIR P.E. TEACHERS LIKE MR. KERBOX, WHO MARKED ME DOWN FOR NOT HAVING A P.E. UNIFORM...
EVEN THOUGH IT WAS THE WILLARD BROTHERS WHO STOLE IT OUTTA MY LOCKER! WHAT ABOUT MARKING THEM DOWN, THOSE DIRTY CROOKS!
WELL, IT DID RHYME WITH "BOOKS."
EXCUSE ME, I'M NOT FINISHED YET.

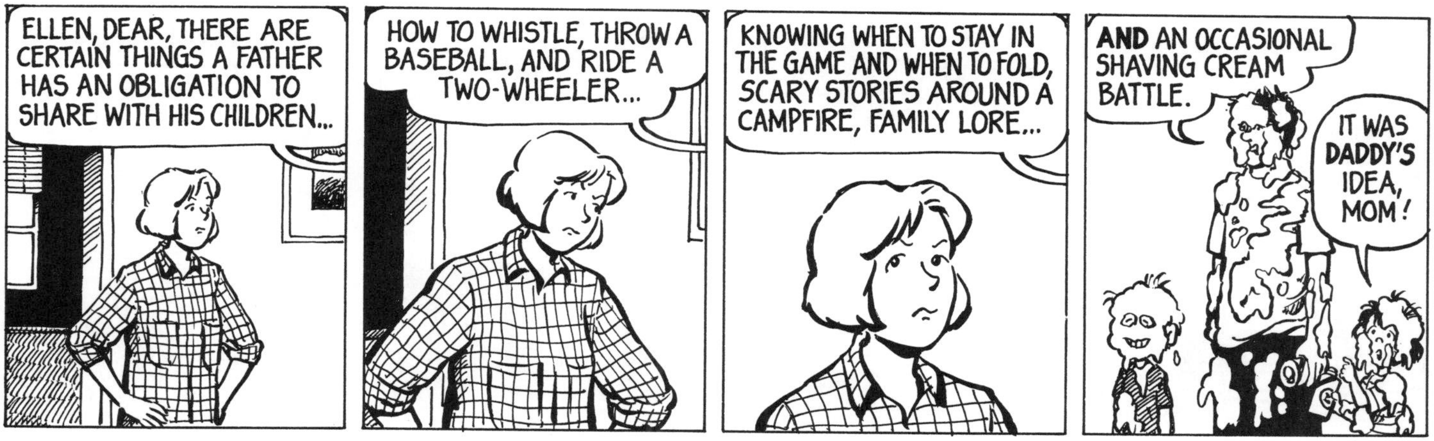
ELLEN, DEAR, THERE ARE CERTAIN THINGS A FATHER HAS AN OBLIGATION TO SHARE WITH HIS CHILDREN...
HOW TO WHISTLE, THROW A BASEBALL, AND RIDE A TWO-WHEELER...
KNOWING WHEN TO STAY IN THE GAME AND WHEN TO FOLD, SCARY STORIES AROUND A CAMPFIRE, FAMILY LORE...
AND AN OCCASIONAL SHAVING CREAM BATTLE.
IT WAS DADDY'S IDEA, MOM!

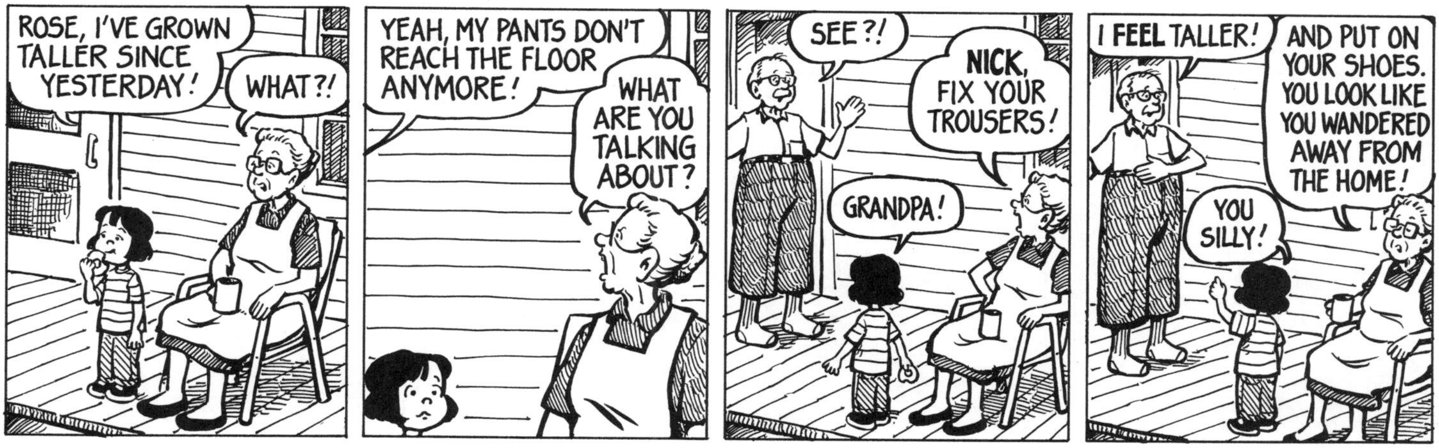
ROSE, I'VE GROWN TALLER SINCE YESTERDAY!
WHAT?!
YEAH, MY PANTS DON'T REACH THE FLOOR ANYMORE!
WHAT ARE YOU TALKING ABOUT?
SEE?!
NICK, FIX YOUR TROUSERS!
GRANDPA!
I FEEL TALLER!
AND PUT ON YOUR SHOES. YOU LOOK LIKE YOU WANDERED AWAY FROM THE HOME!
YOU SILLY!

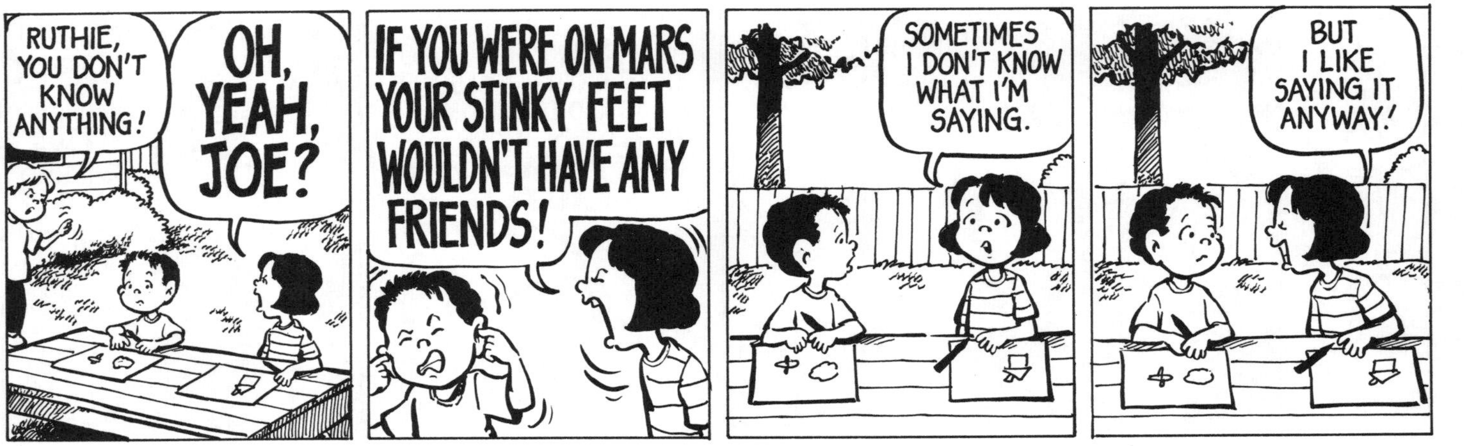
RUTHIE, YOU DON'T KNOW ANYTHING!
OH, YEAH, JOE?
IF YOU WERE ON MARS YOUR STINKY FEET WOULDN'T HAVE ANY FRIENDS!
SOMETIMES I DON'T KNOW WHAT I'M SAYING.
BUT I LIKE SAYING IT ANYWAY!

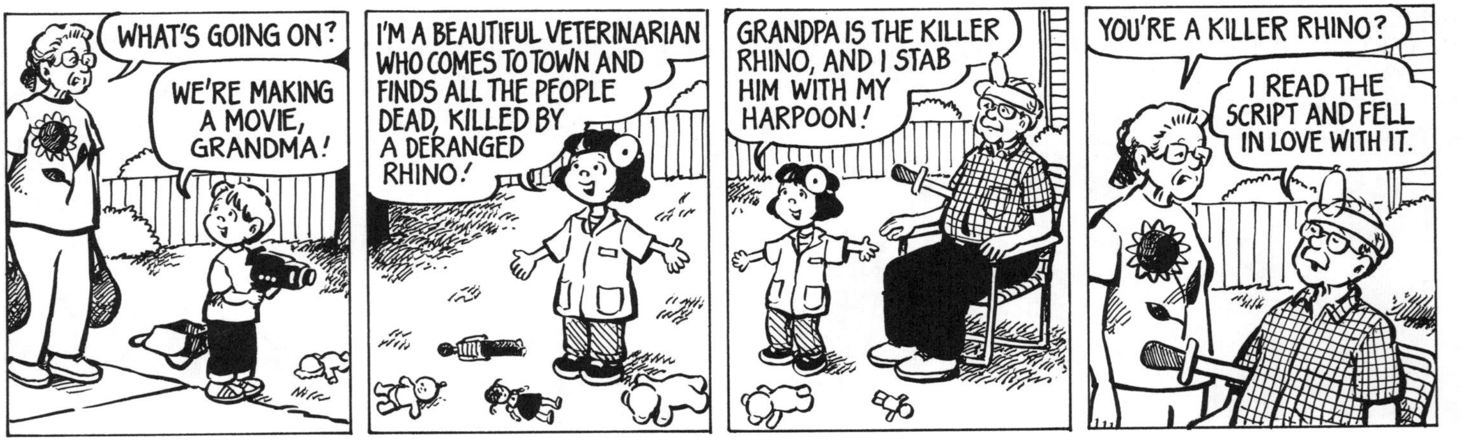
WHAT'S GOING ON?
WE'RE MAKING A MOVIE, GRANDMA!
I'M A BEAUTIFUL VETERINARIAN WHO COMES TO TOWN AND FINDS ALL THE PEOPLE DEAD, KILLED BY A DERANGED RHINO!
GRANDPA IS THE KILLER RHINO, AND I STAB HIM WITH MY HARPOON!
YOU'RE A KILLER RHINO?
I READ THE SCRIPT AND FELL IN LOVE WITH IT.

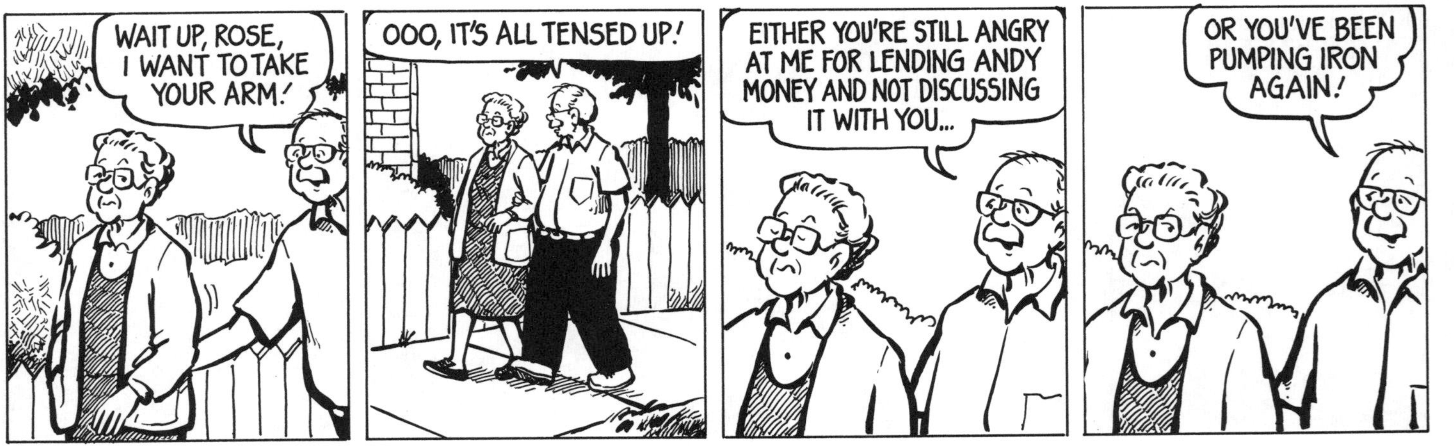
WAIT UP, ROSE, I WANT TO TAKE YOUR ARM!
OOO, IT'S ALL TENSED UP!
EITHER YOU'RE STILL ANGRY AT ME FOR LENDING ANDY MONEY AND NOT DISCUSSING IT WITH YOU...
OR YOU'VE BEEN PUMPING IRON AGAIN!

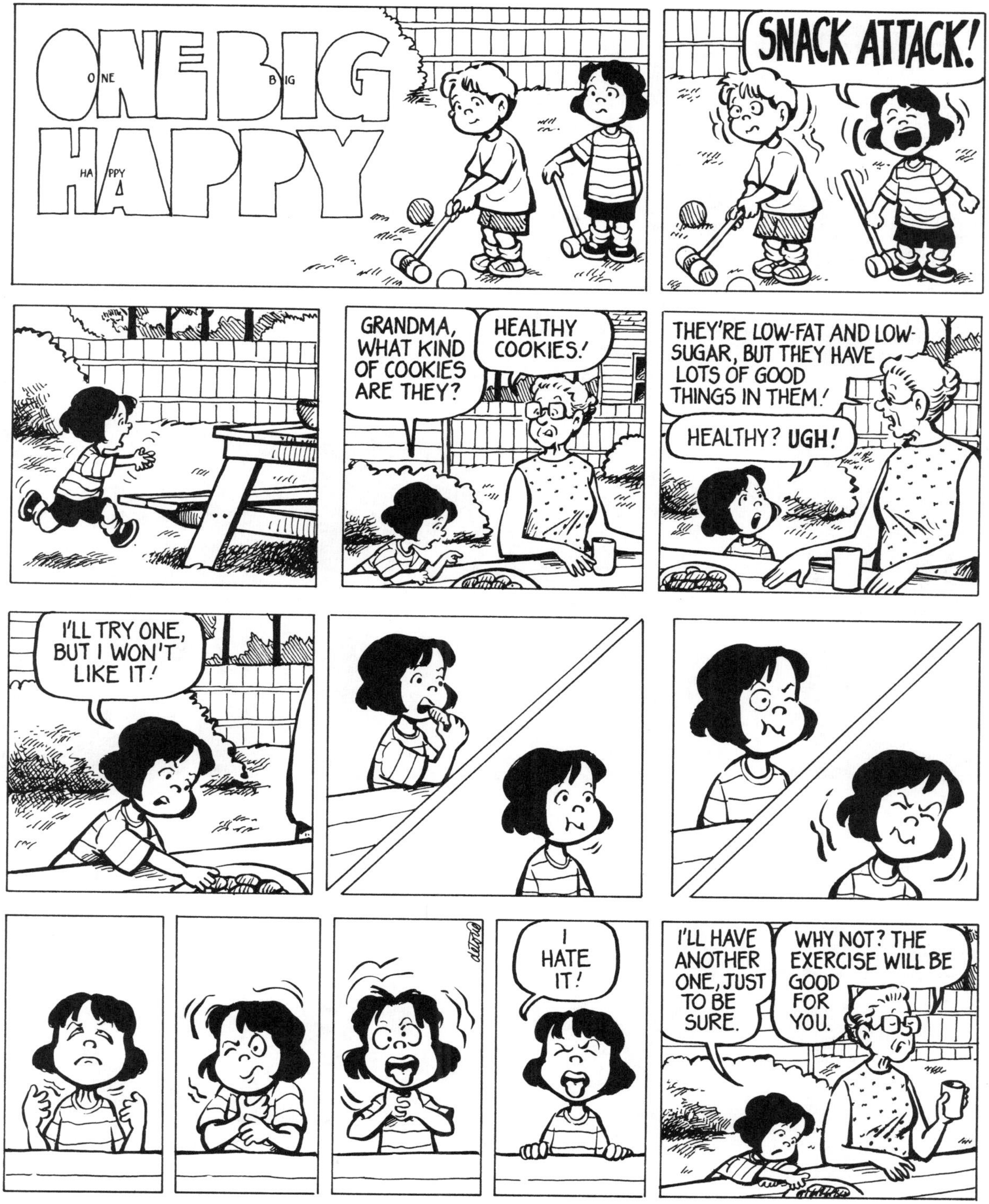
ONE BIG HAPPY
SNACK ATTACK!
GRANDMA, WHAT KIND OF COOKIES ARE THEY?
HEALTHY COOKIES!
THEY'RE LOW-FAT AND LOW-SUGAR, BUT THEY HAVE LOTS OF GOOD THINGS IN THEM!
HEALTHY? UGH!
I'LL TRY ONE, BUT I WON'T LIKE IT!
I HATE IT!
I'LL HAVE ANOTHER ONE, JUST TO BE SURE.
WHY NOT? THE EXERCISE WILL BE GOOD FOR YOU.

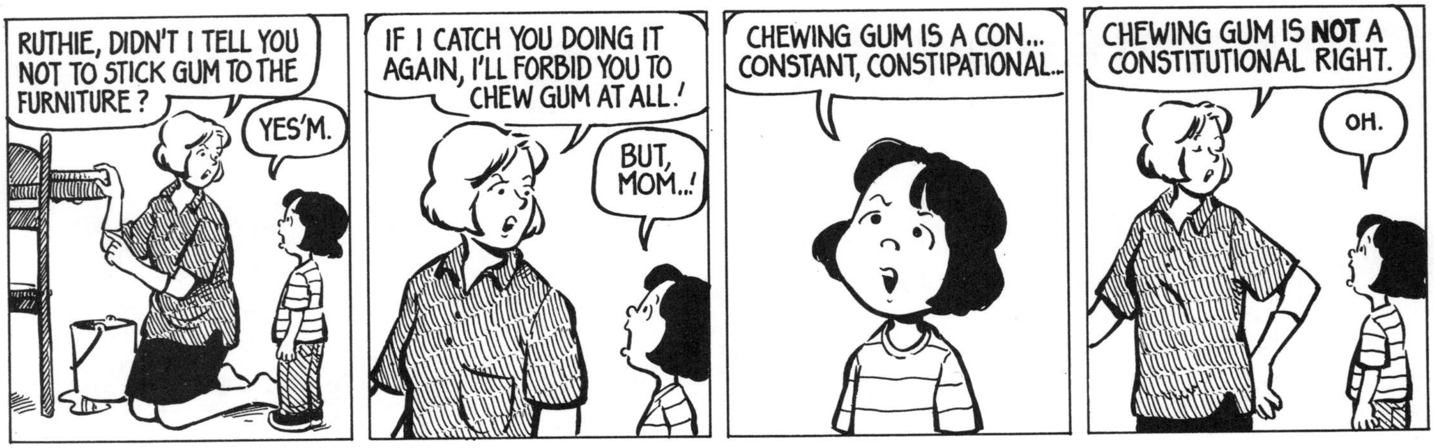
RUTHIE, DIDN'T I TELL YOU NOT TO STICK GUM TO THE FURNITURE?
YES'M.
IF I CATCH YOU DOING IT AGAIN, I'LL FORBID YOU TO CHEW GUM AT ALL!
BUT, MOM..!
CHEWING GUM IS A CON... CONSTANT, CONSTIPATIONAL...
CHEWING GUM IS NOT A CONSTITUTIONAL RIGHT.
OH.

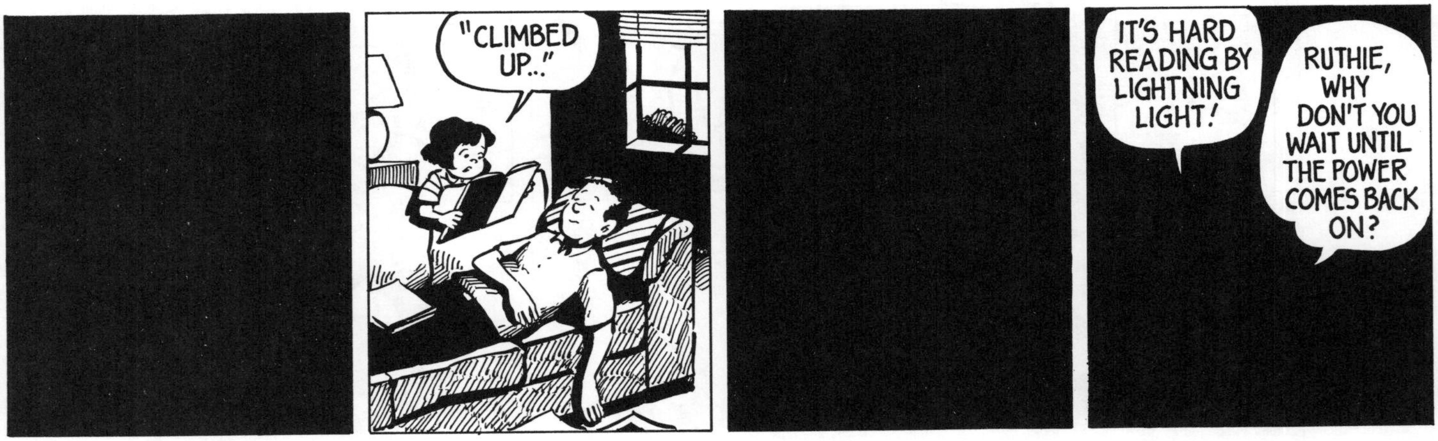
"CLIMBED UP.."
IT'S HARD READING BY LIGHTNING LIGHT!
RUTHIE, WHY DON'T YOU WAIT UNTIL THE POWER COMES BACK ON?

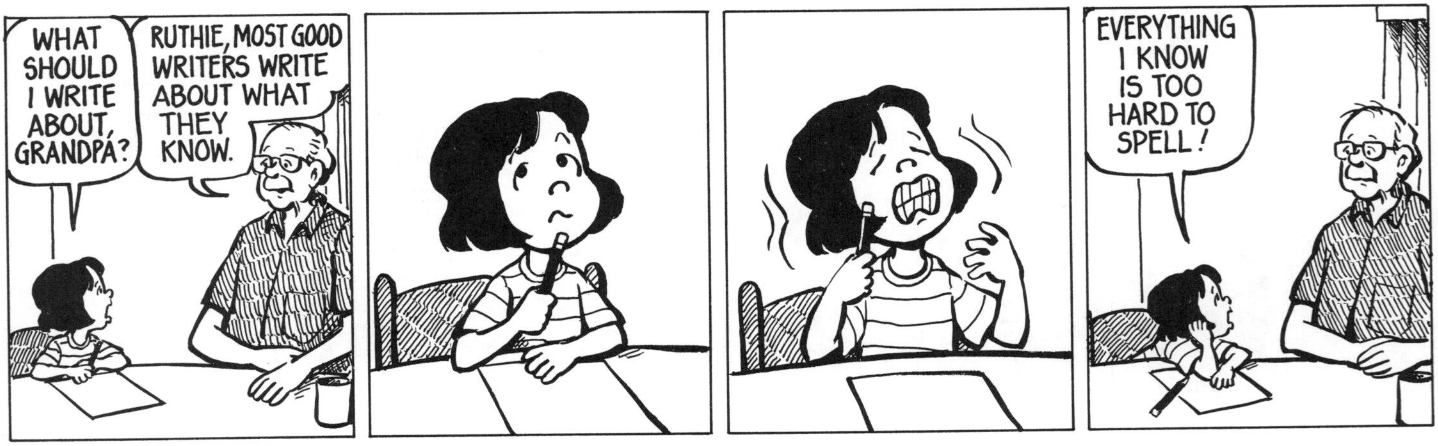
WHAT SHOULD I WRITE ABOUT, GRANDPA?
RUTHIE, MOST GOOD WRITERS WRITE ABOUT WHAT THEY KNOW.
EVERYTHING I KNOW IS TOO HARD TO SPELL!

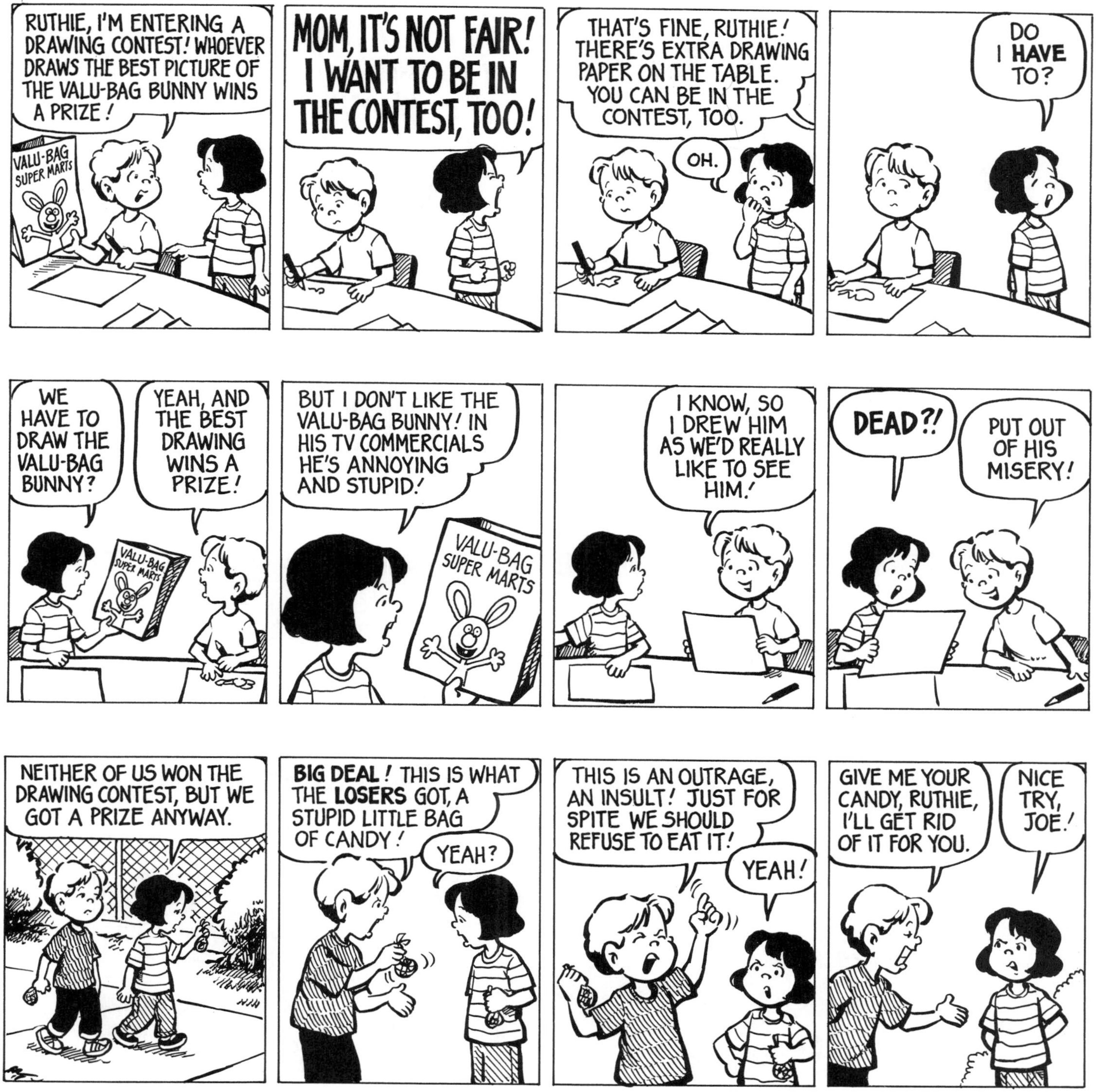

RUTHIE, I'M ENTERING A DRAWING CONTEST! WHOEVER DRAWS THE BEST PICTURE OF THE VALU-BAG BUNNY WINS A PRIZE!
VALU-BAG SUPER MARTS
MOM, IT'S NOT FAIR! I WANT TO BE IN THE CONTEST, TOO!
THAT'S FINE, RUTHIE! THERE'S EXTRA DRAWING PAPER ON THE TABLE. YOU CAN BE IN THE CONTEST, TOO.
OH.
DO I **HAVE** TO?
WE HAVE TO DRAW THE VALU-BAG BUNNY?
YEAH, AND THE BEST DRAWING WINS A PRIZE!
VALU-BAG SUPER MARTS
BUT I DON'T LIKE THE VALU-BAG BUNNY! IN HIS TV COMMERCIALS HE'S ANNOYING AND STUPID!
VALU-BAG SUPER MARTS
I KNOW, SO I DREW HIM AS WE'D REALLY LIKE TO SEE HIM!
DEAD?!
PUT OUT OF HIS MISERY!
NEITHER OF US WON THE DRAWING CONTEST, BUT WE GOT A PRIZE ANYWAY.
BIG DEAL! THIS IS WHAT THE **LOSERS** GOT, A STUPID LITTLE BAG OF CANDY!
YEAH?
THIS IS AN OUTRAGE, AN INSULT! JUST FOR SPITE WE SHOULD REFUSE TO EAT IT!
YEAH!
GIVE ME YOUR CANDY, RUTHIE, I'LL GET RID OF IT FOR YOU.
NICE TRY, JOE!

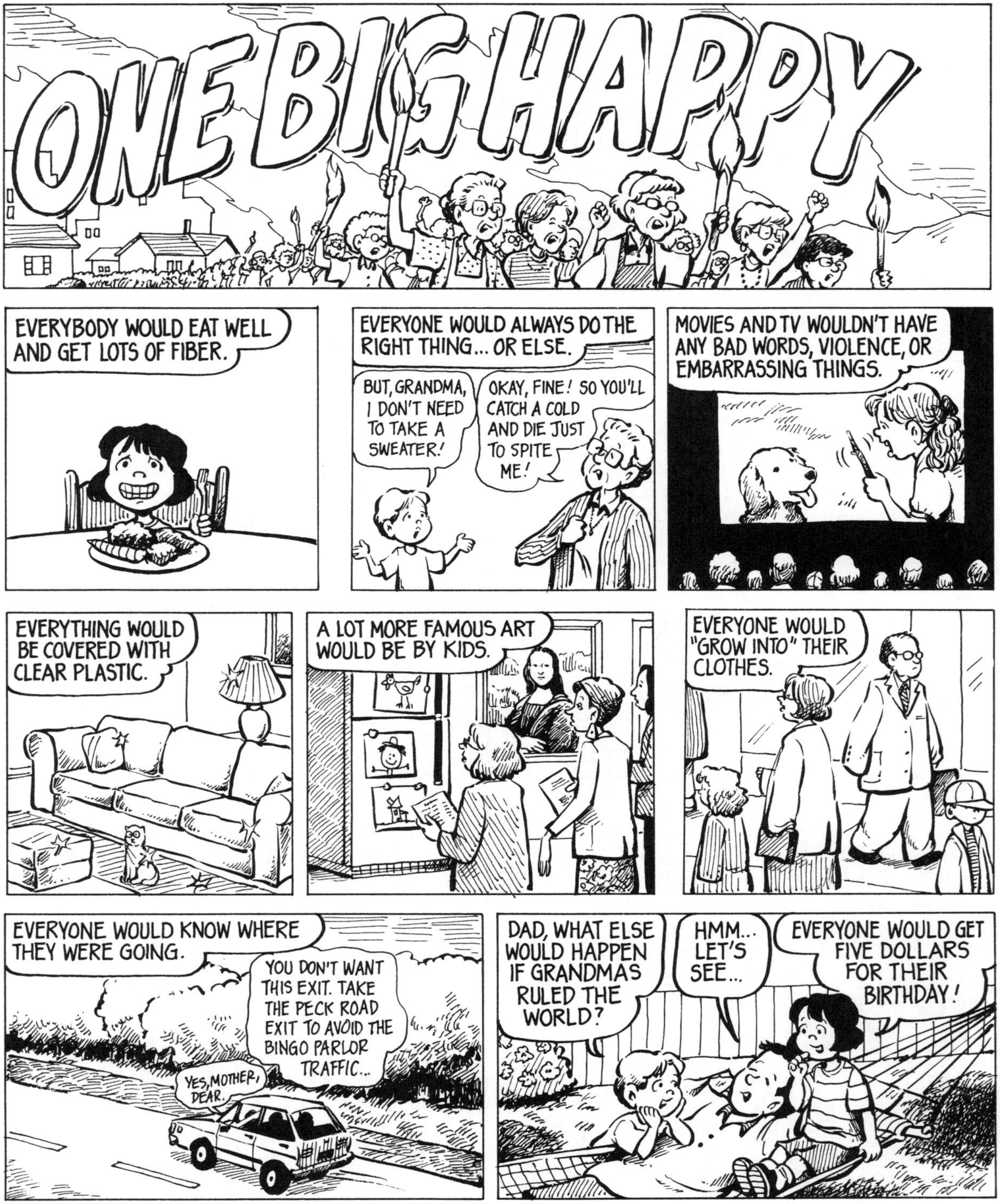
ONE BIG HAPPY
EVERYBODY WOULD EAT WELL AND GET LOTS OF FIBER.
EVERYONE WOULD ALWAYS DO THE RIGHT THING... OR ELSE.
BUT, GRANDMA, I DON'T NEED TO TAKE A SWEATER!
OKAY, FINE! SO YOU'LL CATCH A COLD AND DIE JUST TO SPITE ME!
MOVIES AND TV WOULDN'T HAVE ANY BAD WORDS, VIOLENCE, OR EMBARRASSING THINGS.
EVERYTHING WOULD BE COVERED WITH CLEAR PLASTIC.
A LOT MORE FAMOUS ART WOULD BE BY KIDS.
EVERYONE WOULD "GROW INTO" THEIR CLOTHES.
EVERYONE WOULD KNOW WHERE THEY WERE GOING.
YOU DON'T WANT THIS EXIT. TAKE THE PECK ROAD EXIT TO AVOID THE BINGO PARLOR TRAFFIC...
YES, MOTHER, DEAR.
DAD, WHAT ELSE WOULD HAPPEN IF GRANDMAS RULED THE WORLD?
HMM... LET'S SEE...
EVERYONE WOULD GET FIVE DOLLARS FOR THEIR BIRTHDAY!

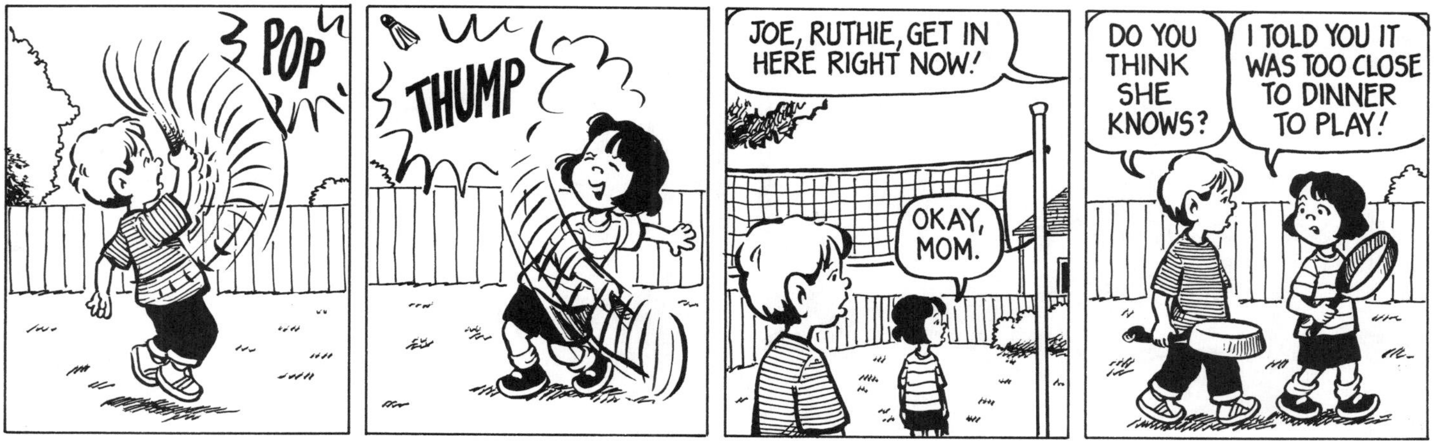
POP
THUMP
JOE, RUTHIE, GET IN HERE RIGHT NOW!
OKAY, MOM.
DO YOU THINK SHE KNOWS?
I TOLD YOU IT WAS TOO CLOSE TO DINNER TO PLAY!

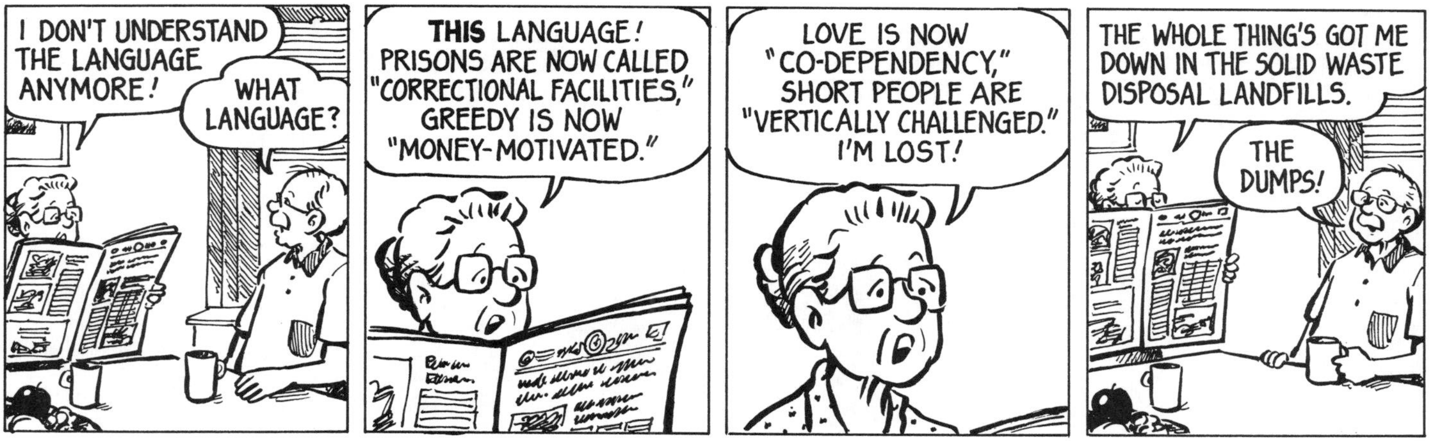
I DON'T UNDERSTAND THE LANGUAGE ANYMORE!
WHAT LANGUAGE?
THIS LANGUAGE! PRISONS ARE NOW CALLED "CORRECTIONAL FACILITIES," GREEDY IS NOW "MONEY-MOTIVATED."
LOVE IS NOW "CO-DEPENDENCY," SHORT PEOPLE ARE "VERTICALLY CHALLENGED." I'M LOST!
THE WHOLE THING'S GOT ME DOWN IN THE SOLID WASTE DISPOSAL LANDFILLS.
THE DUMPS!

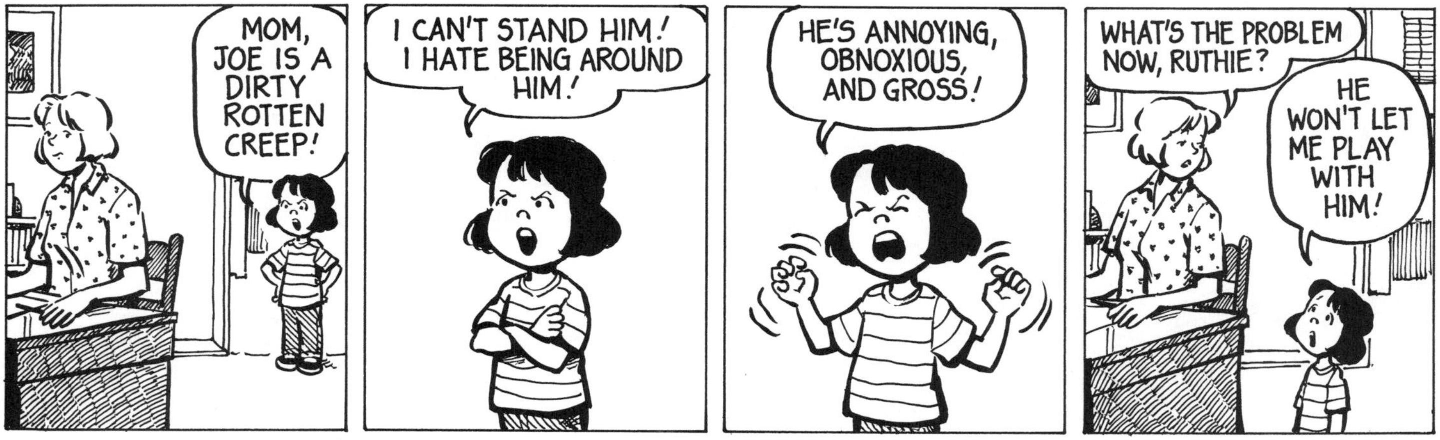
MOM, JOE IS A DIRTY ROTTEN CREEP!
I CAN'T STAND HIM! I HATE BEING AROUND HIM!
HE'S ANNOYING, OBNOXIOUS, AND GROSS!
WHAT'S THE PROBLEM NOW, RUTHIE?
HE WON'T LET ME PLAY WITH HIM!

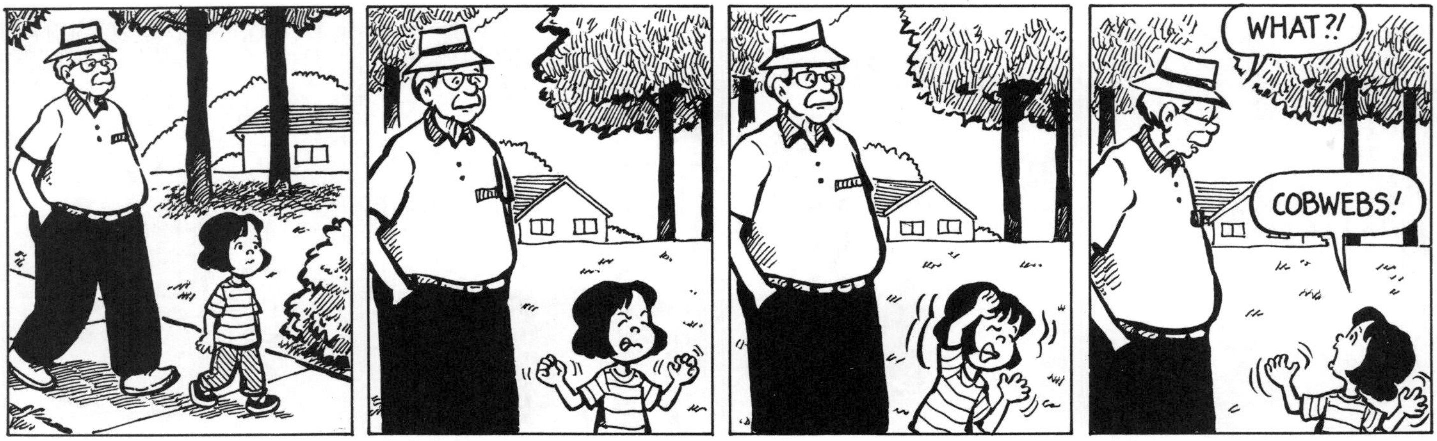
WHAT?!
COBWEBS!

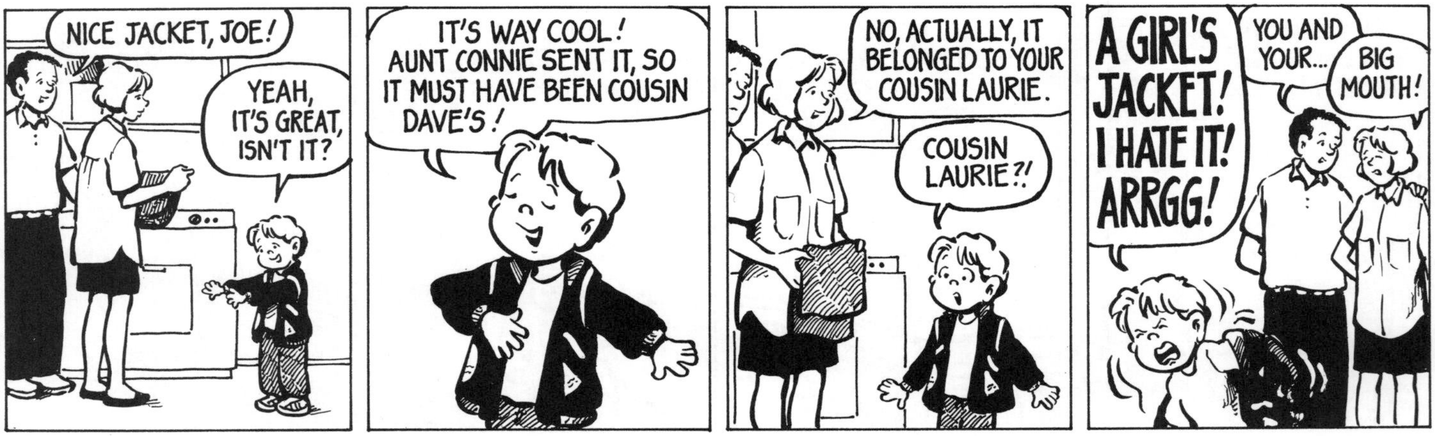
NICE JACKET, JOE!
YEAH, IT'S GREAT, ISN'T IT?
IT'S WAY COOL! AUNT CONNIE SENT IT, SO IT MUST HAVE BEEN COUSIN DAVE'S!
NO, ACTUALLY, IT BELONGED TO YOUR COUSIN LAURIE.
COUSIN LAURIE?!
A GIRL'S JACKET! I HATE IT! ARRGG!
YOU AND YOUR...
BIG MOUTH!

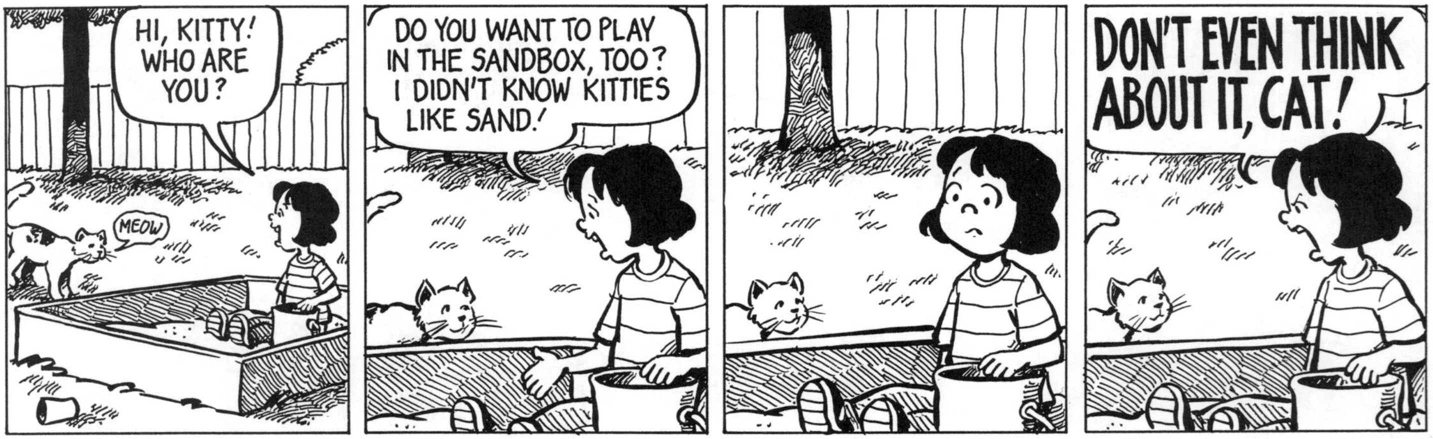
HI, KITTY! WHO ARE YOU?
MEOW
DO YOU WANT TO PLAY IN THE SANDBOX, TOO? I DIDN'T KNOW KITTIES LIKE SAND!
DON'T EVEN THINK ABOUT IT, CAT!

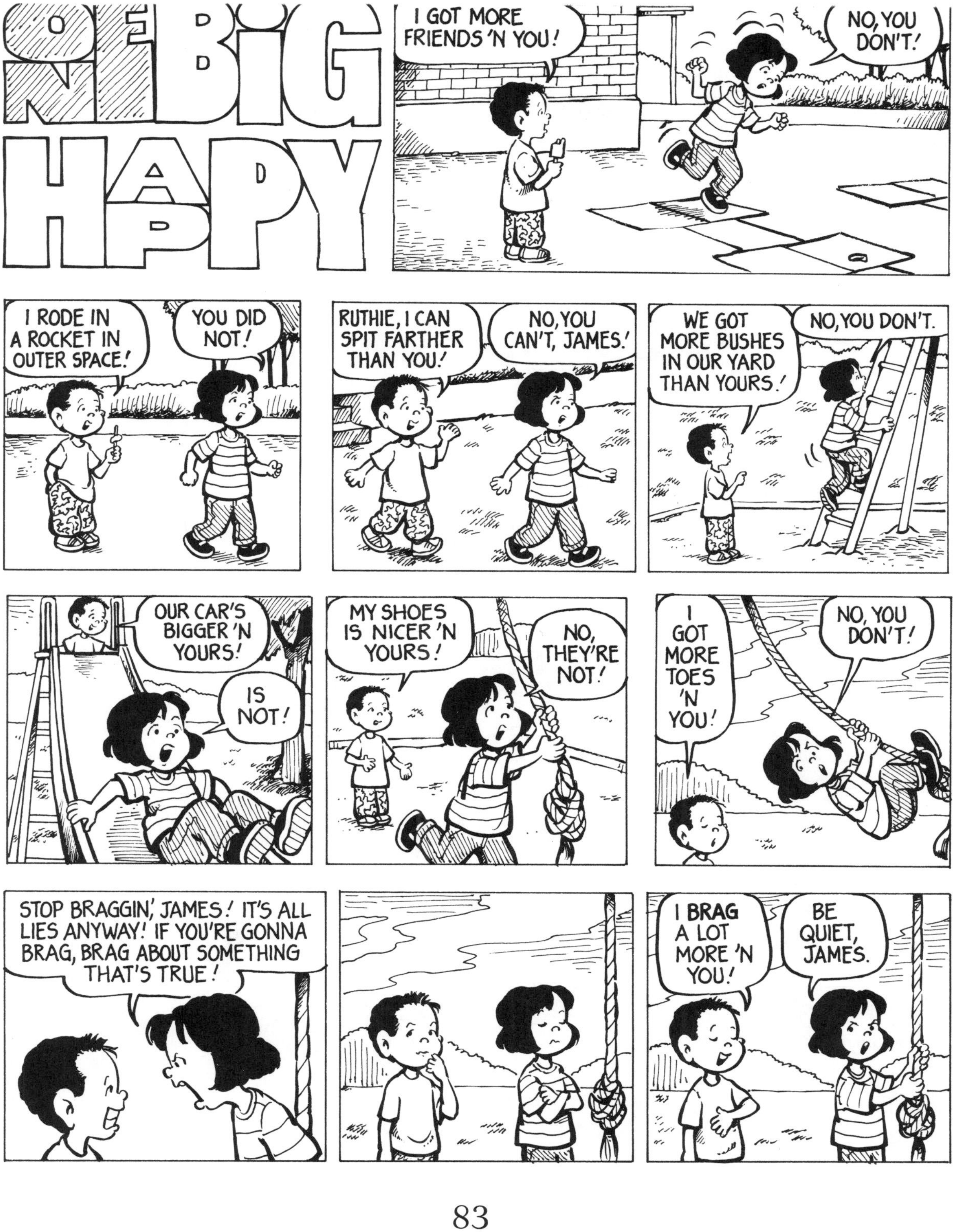
ONE BIG HAPPY
I GOT MORE FRIENDS 'N YOU!
NO, YOU DON'T!
I RODE IN A ROCKET IN OUTER SPACE!
YOU DID NOT!
RUTHIE, I CAN SPIT FARTHER THAN YOU!
NO, YOU CAN'T, JAMES!
WE GOT MORE BUSHES IN OUR YARD THAN YOURS!
NO, YOU DON'T.
OUR CAR'S BIGGER 'N YOURS!
IS NOT!
MY SHOES IS NICER 'N YOURS!
NO, THEY'RE NOT!
I GOT MORE TOES 'N YOU!
NO, YOU DON'T!
STOP BRAGGIN', JAMES! IT'S ALL LIES ANYWAY! IF YOU'RE GONNA BRAG, BRAG ABOUT SOMETHING THAT'S TRUE!
I **BRAG** A LOT MORE 'N YOU!
BE QUIET, JAMES.

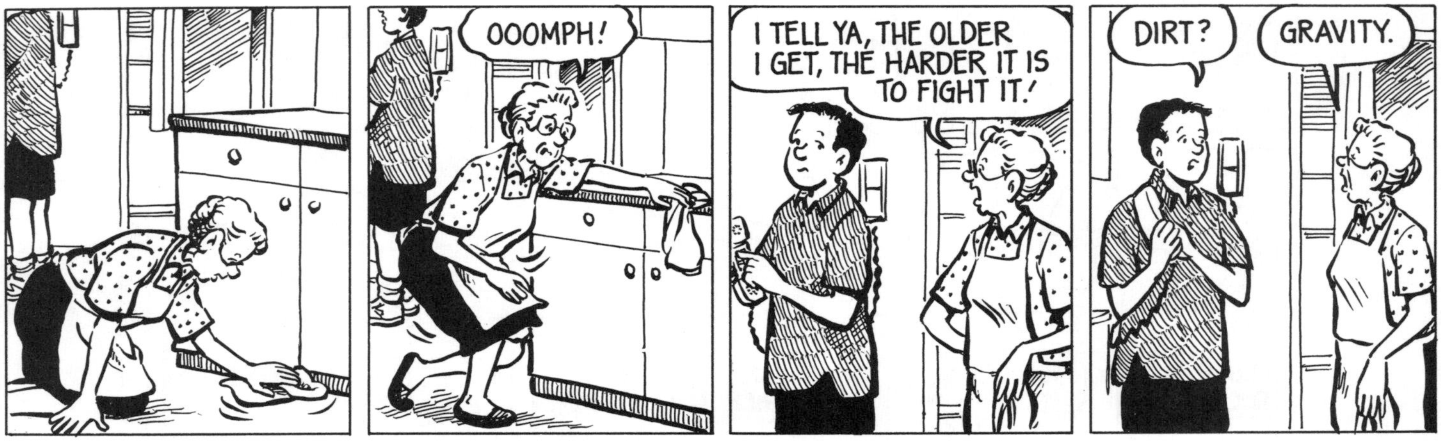
OOOMPH!
I TELL YA, THE OLDER I GET, THE HARDER IT IS TO FIGHT IT!
DIRT?
GRAVITY.

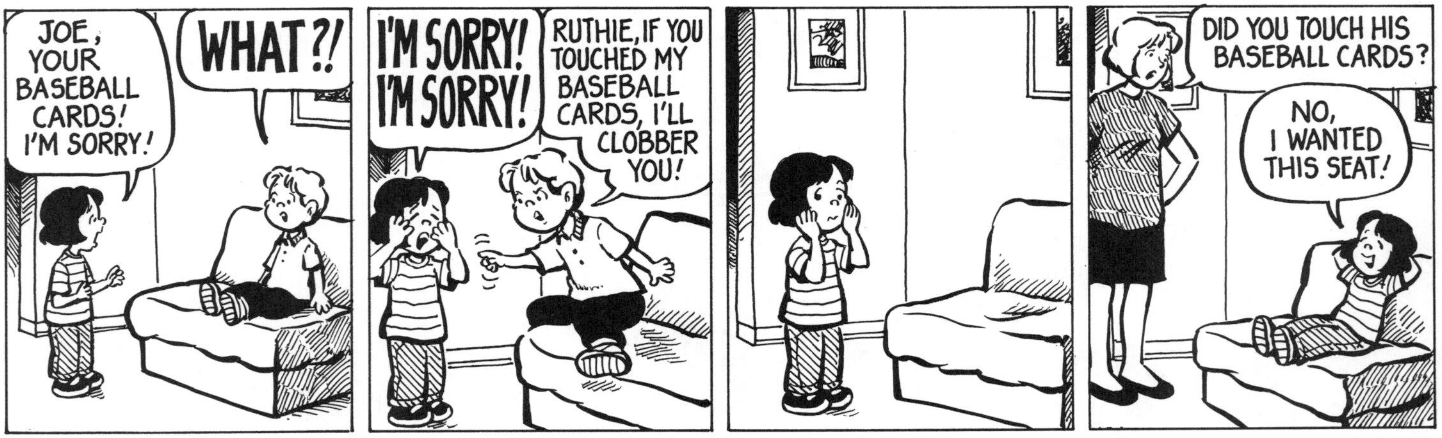
JOE, YOUR BASEBALL CARDS! I'M SORRY!
WHAT?!
I'M SORRY! I'M SORRY!
RUTHIE, IF YOU TOUCHED MY BASEBALL CARDS, I'LL CLOBBER YOU!
DID YOU TOUCH HIS BASEBALL CARDS?
NO, I WANTED THIS SEAT!

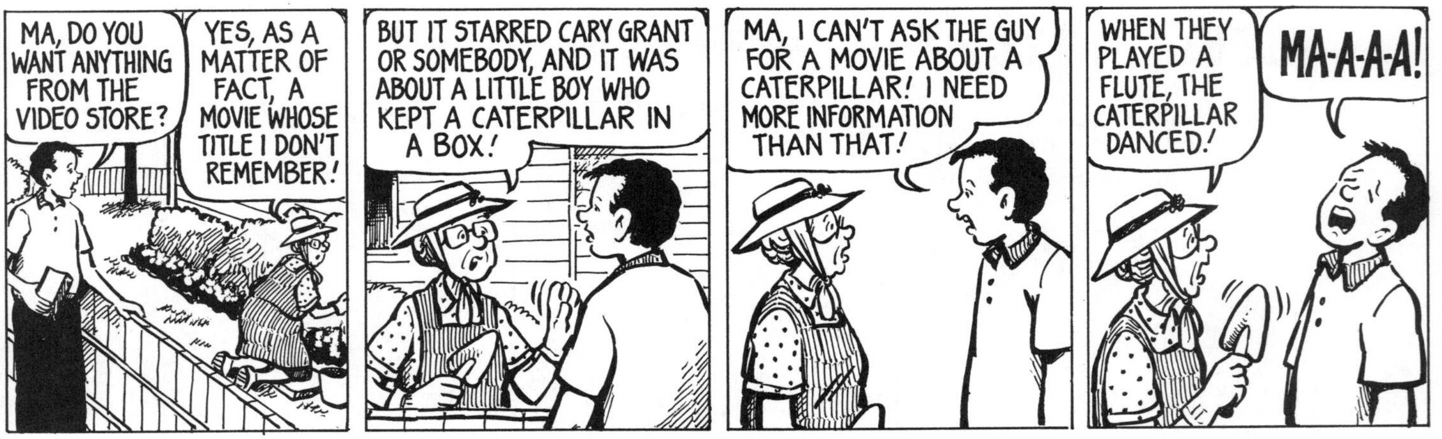
MA, DO YOU WANT ANYTHING FROM THE VIDEO STORE?
YES, AS A MATTER OF FACT, A MOVIE WHOSE TITLE I DON'T REMEMBER!
BUT IT STARRED CARY GRANT OR SOMEBODY, AND IT WAS ABOUT A LITTLE BOY WHO KEPT A CATERPILLAR IN A BOX!
MA, I CAN'T ASK THE GUY FOR A MOVIE ABOUT A CATERPILLAR! I NEED MORE INFORMATION THAN THAT!
WHEN THEY PLAYED A FLUTE, THE CATERPILLAR DANCED!
MA-A-A-A!

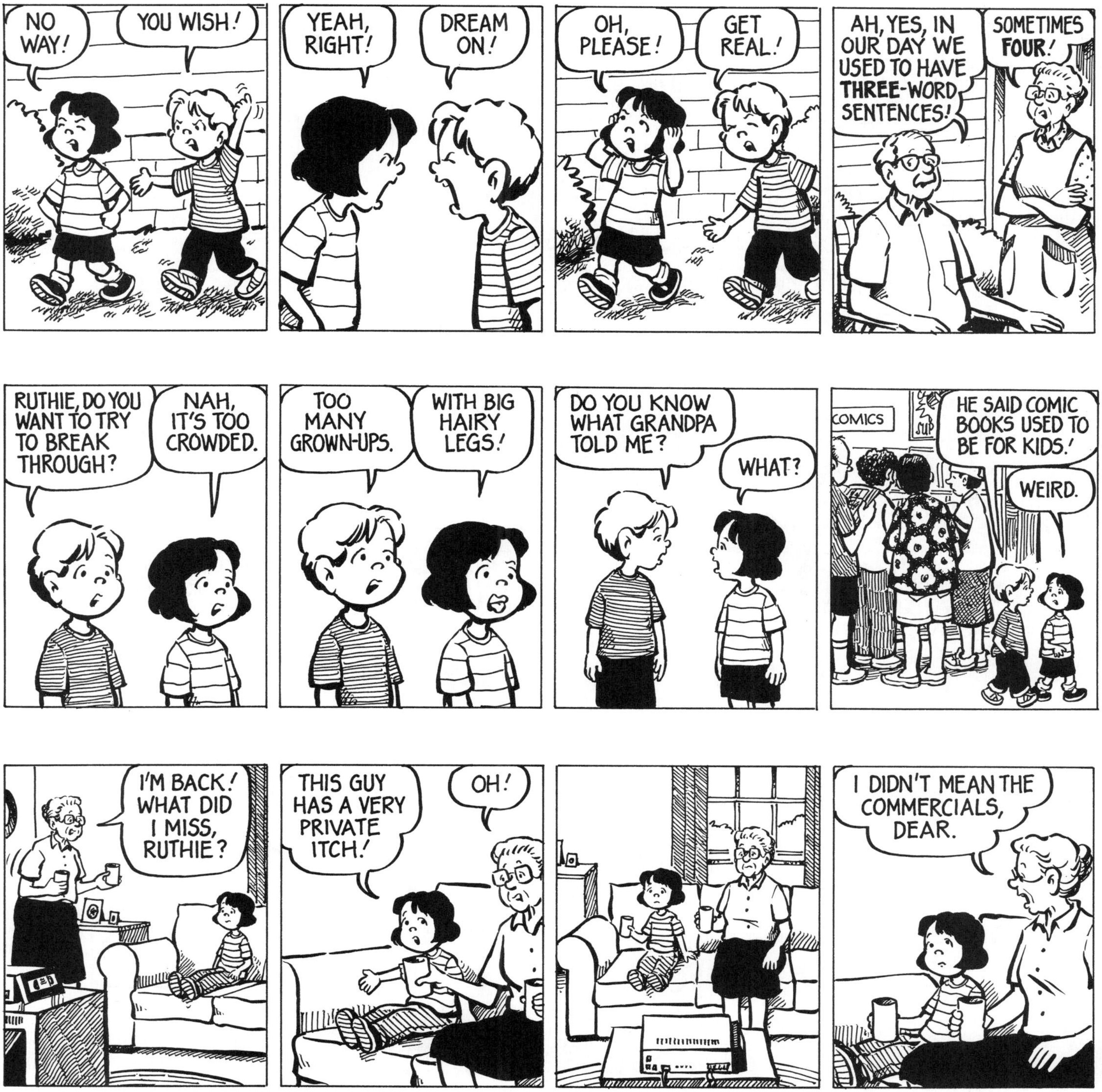
NO WAY!
YOU WISH!
YEAH, RIGHT!
DREAM ON!
OH, PLEASE!
GET REAL!
AH, YES, IN OUR DAY WE USED TO HAVE THREE-WORD SENTENCES!
SOMETIMES FOUR!
RUTHIE, DO YOU WANT TO TRY TO BREAK THROUGH?
NAH, IT'S TOO CROWDED.
TOO MANY GROWN-UPS.
WITH BIG HAIRY LEGS!
DO YOU KNOW WHAT GRANDPA TOLD ME?
WHAT?
COMICS
HE SAID COMIC BOOKS USED TO BE FOR KIDS!
WEIRD.
I'M BACK! WHAT DID I MISS, RUTHIE?
THIS GUY HAS A VERY PRIVATE ITCH!
OH!
I DIDN'T MEAN THE COMMERCIALS, DEAR.

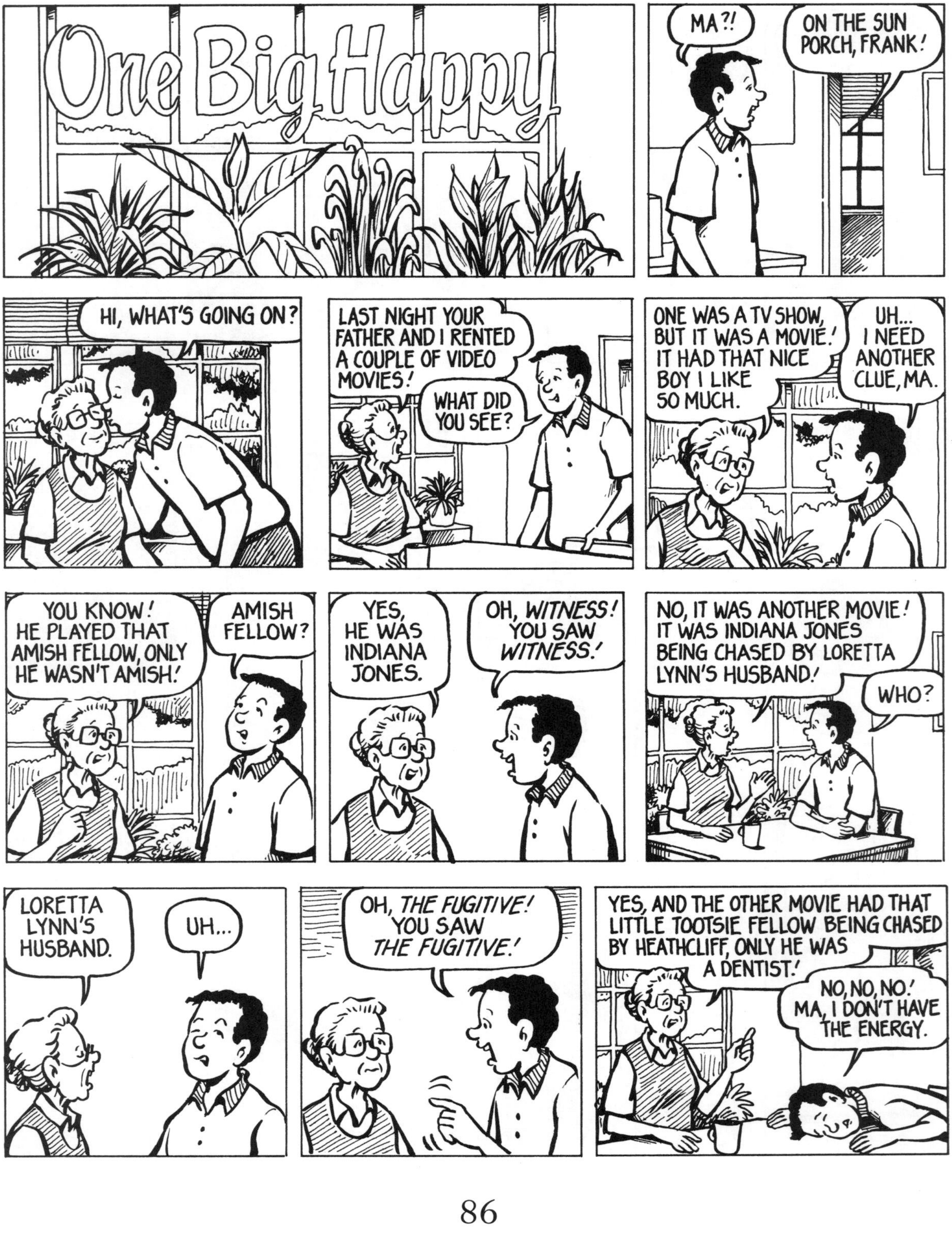
One Big Happy
MA?!
ON THE SUN PORCH, FRANK!
HI, WHAT'S GOING ON?
LAST NIGHT YOUR FATHER AND I RENTED A COUPLE OF VIDEO MOVIES!
WHAT DID YOU SEE?
ONE WAS A TV SHOW, BUT IT WAS A MOVIE! IT HAD THAT NICE BOY I LIKE SO MUCH.
UH... I NEED ANOTHER CLUE, MA.
YOU KNOW! HE PLAYED THAT AMISH FELLOW, ONLY HE WASN'T AMISH!
AMISH FELLOW?
YES, HE WAS INDIANA JONES.
OH, *WITNESS*! YOU SAW *WITNESS*!
NO, IT WAS ANOTHER MOVIE! IT WAS INDIANA JONES BEING CHASED BY LORETTA LYNN'S HUSBAND!
WHO?
LORETTA LYNN'S HUSBAND.
UH...
OH, *THE FUGITIVE*! YOU SAW *THE FUGITIVE*!
YES, AND THE OTHER MOVIE HAD THAT LITTLE TOOTSIE FELLOW BEING CHASED BY HEATHCLIFF, ONLY HE WAS A DENTIST!
NO, NO, NO! MA, I DON'T HAVE THE ENERGY.

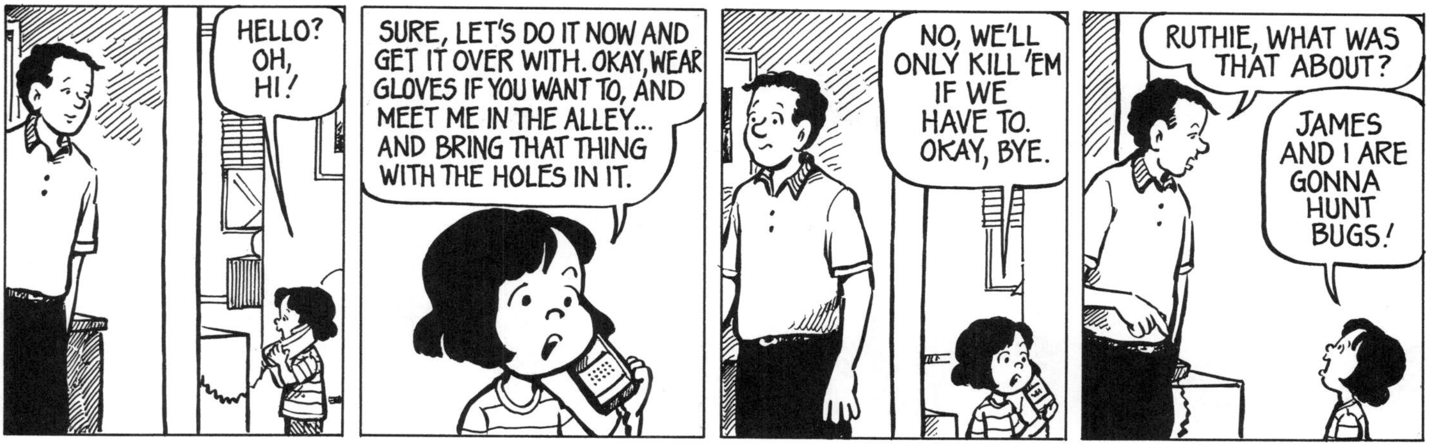
HELLO? OH, HI!
SURE, LET'S DO IT NOW AND GET IT OVER WITH. OKAY, WEAR GLOVES IF YOU WANT TO, AND MEET ME IN THE ALLEY... AND BRING THAT THING WITH THE HOLES IN IT.
NO, WE'LL ONLY KILL 'EM IF WE HAVE TO. OKAY, BYE.
RUTHIE, WHAT WAS THAT ABOUT?
JAMES AND I ARE GONNA HUNT BUGS!

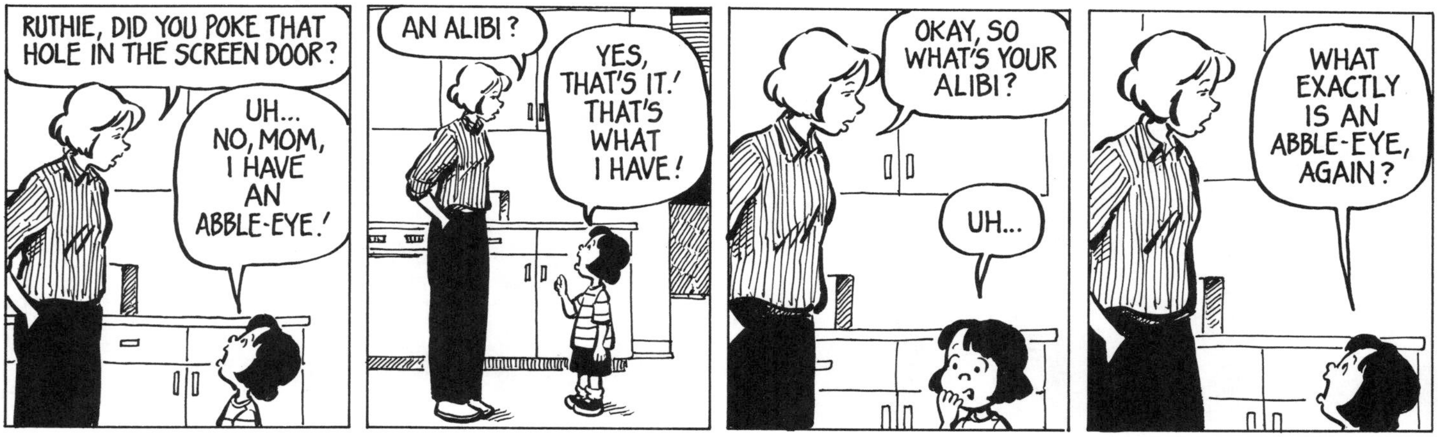
RUTHIE, DID YOU POKE THAT HOLE IN THE SCREEN DOOR?
UH... NO, MOM, I HAVE AN ABBLE-EYE!
AN ALIBI?
YES, THAT'S IT! THAT'S WHAT I HAVE!
OKAY, SO WHAT'S YOUR ALIBI?
UH...
WHAT EXACTLY IS AN ABBLE-EYE, AGAIN?

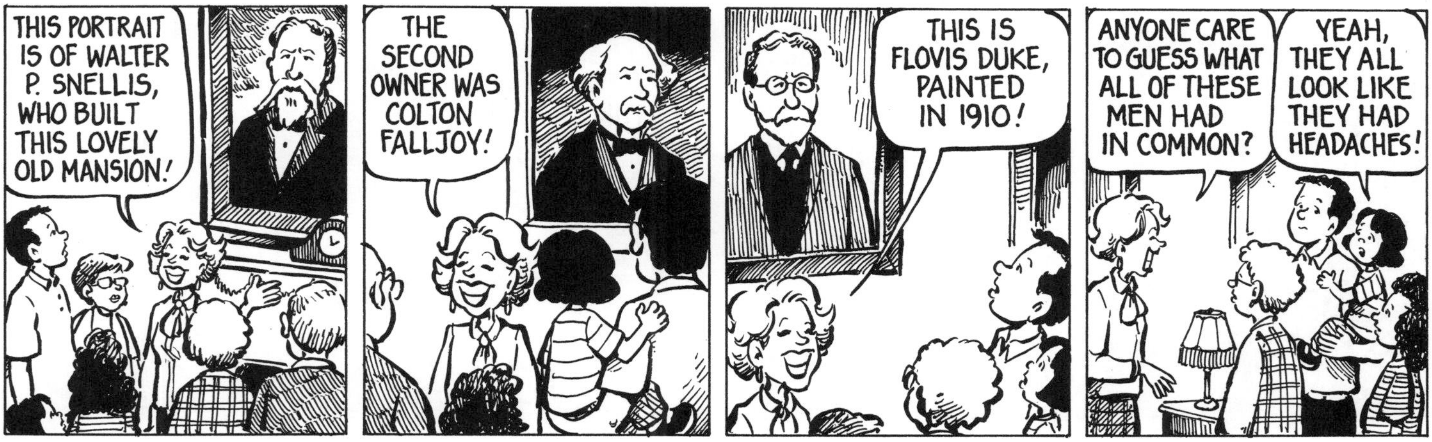
THIS PORTRAIT IS OF WALTER P. SNELLIS, WHO BUILT THIS LOVELY OLD MANSION!
THE SECOND OWNER WAS COLTON FALLJOY!
THIS IS FLOVIS DUKE, PAINTED IN 1910!
ANYONE CARE TO GUESS WHAT ALL OF THESE MEN HAD IN COMMON?
YEAH, THEY ALL LOOK LIKE THEY HAD HEADACHES!

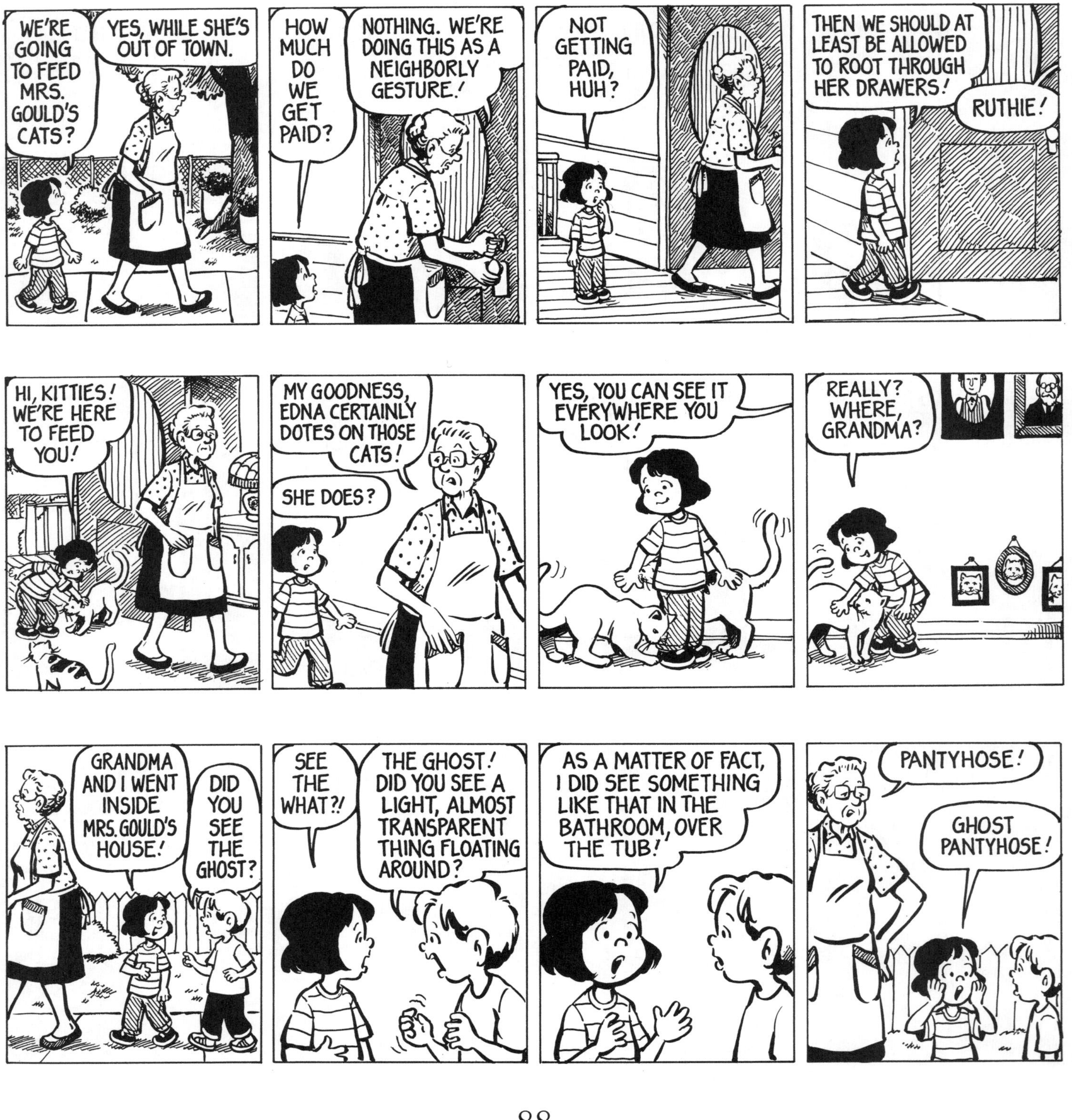
WE'RE GOING TO FEED MRS. GOULD'S CATS?
YES, WHILE SHE'S OUT OF TOWN.
HOW MUCH DO WE GET PAID?
NOTHING. WE'RE DOING THIS AS A NEIGHBORLY GESTURE!
NOT GETTING PAID, HUH?
THEN WE SHOULD AT LEAST BE ALLOWED TO ROOT THROUGH HER DRAWERS!
RUTHIE!
HI, KITTIES! WE'RE HERE TO FEED YOU!
MY GOODNESS, EDNA CERTAINLY DOTES ON THOSE CATS!
SHE DOES?
YES, YOU CAN SEE IT EVERYWHERE YOU LOOK!
REALLY? WHERE, GRANDMA?
GRANDMA AND I WENT INSIDE MRS. GOULD'S HOUSE!
DID YOU SEE THE GHOST?
SEE THE WHAT?!
THE GHOST! DID YOU SEE A LIGHT, ALMOST TRANSPARENT THING FLOATING AROUND?
AS A MATTER OF FACT, I DID SEE SOMETHING LIKE THAT IN THE BATHROOM, OVER THE TUB!
PANTYHOSE!
GHOST PANTYHOSE!

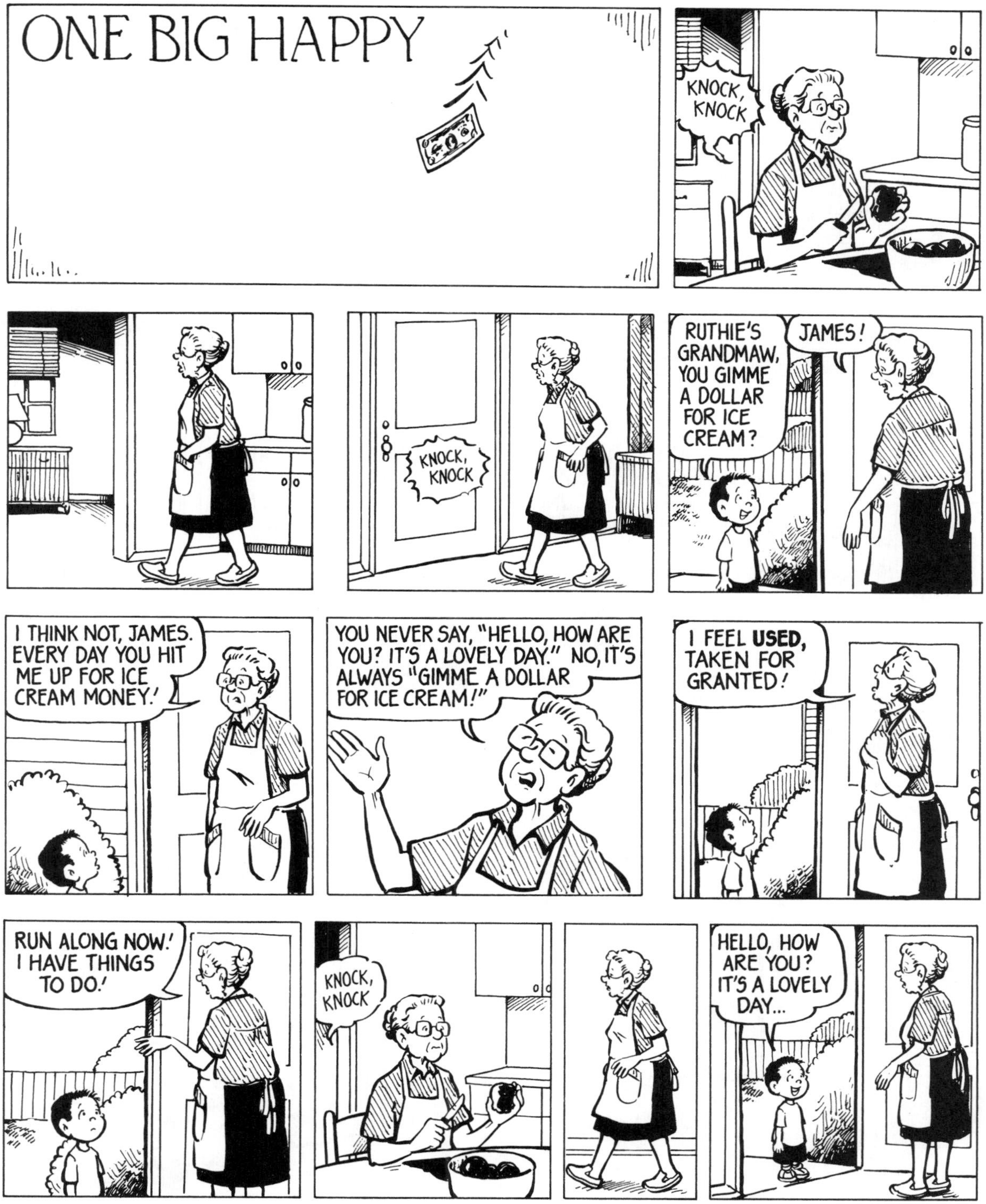
ONE BIG HAPPY
KNOCK, KNOCK
KNOCK, KNOCK
RUTHIE'S GRANDMAW, YOU GIMME A DOLLAR FOR ICE CREAM?
JAMES!
I THINK NOT, JAMES. EVERY DAY YOU HIT ME UP FOR ICE CREAM MONEY!
YOU NEVER SAY, "HELLO, HOW ARE YOU? IT'S A LOVELY DAY." NO, IT'S ALWAYS "GIMME A DOLLAR FOR ICE CREAM!"
I FEEL **USED,** TAKEN FOR GRANTED!
RUN ALONG NOW! I HAVE THINGS TO DO!
KNOCK, KNOCK
HELLO, HOW ARE YOU? IT'S A LOVELY DAY...

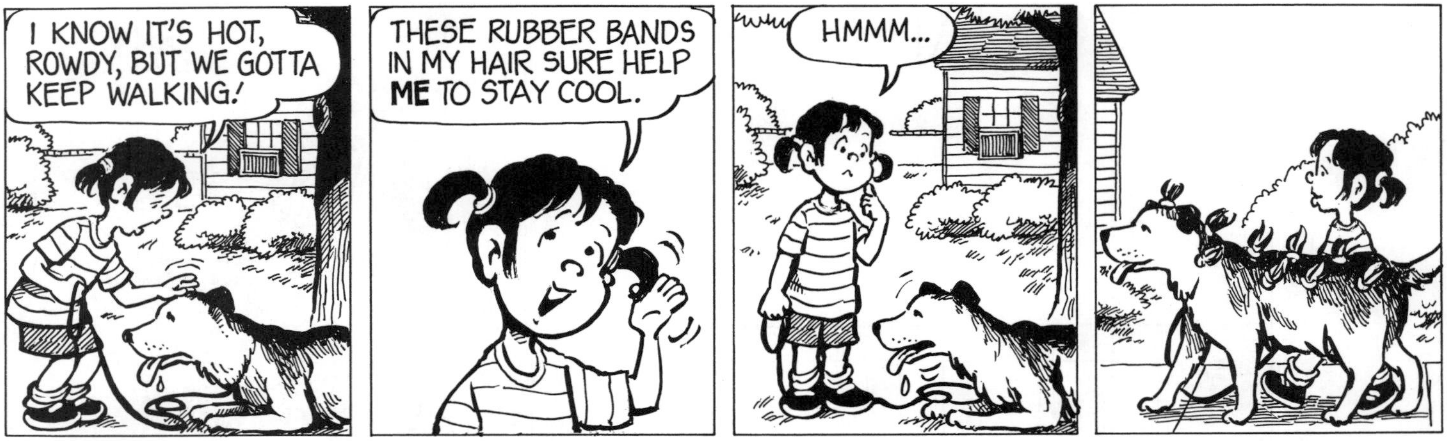
I KNOW IT'S HOT, ROWDY, BUT WE GOTTA KEEP WALKING!
THESE RUBBER BANDS IN MY HAIR SURE HELP **ME** TO STAY COOL.
HMMM...

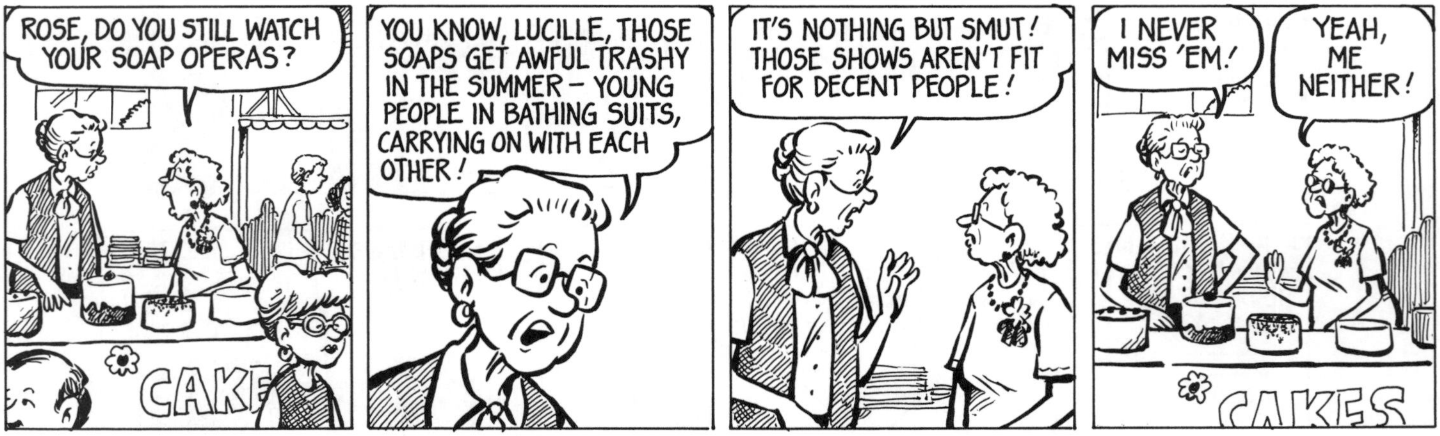
ROSE, DO YOU STILL WATCH YOUR SOAP OPERAS?
CAKE
YOU KNOW, LUCILLE, THOSE SOAPS GET AWFUL TRASHY IN THE SUMMER – YOUNG PEOPLE IN BATHING SUITS, CARRYING ON WITH EACH OTHER!
IT'S NOTHING BUT SMUT! THOSE SHOWS AREN'T FIT FOR DECENT PEOPLE!
I NEVER MISS 'EM!
YEAH, ME NEITHER!
CAKES

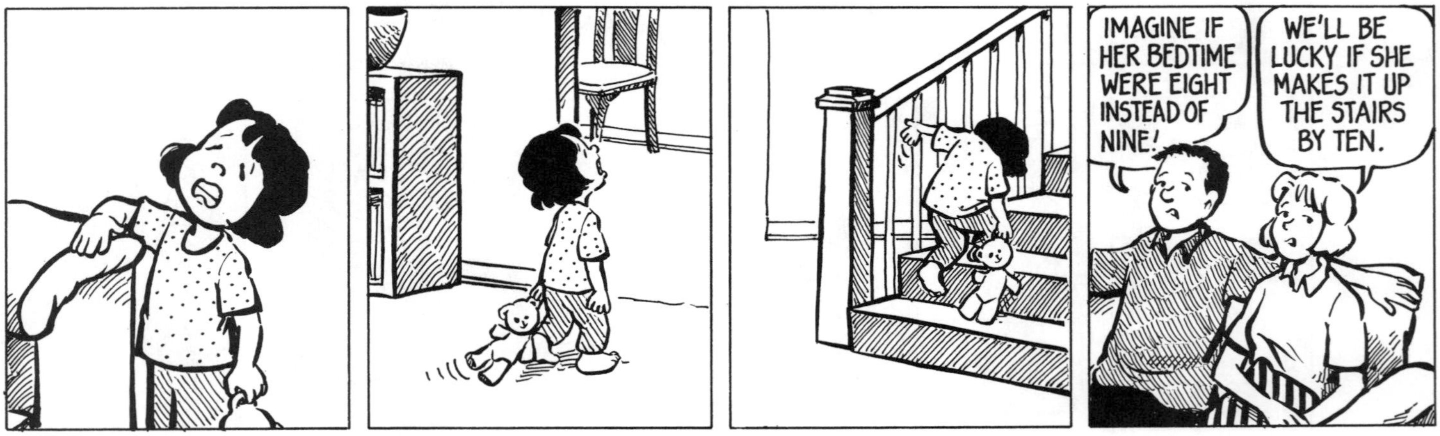
IMAGINE IF HER BEDTIME WERE EIGHT INSTEAD OF NINE!
WE'LL BE LUCKY IF SHE MAKES IT UP THE STAIRS BY TEN.

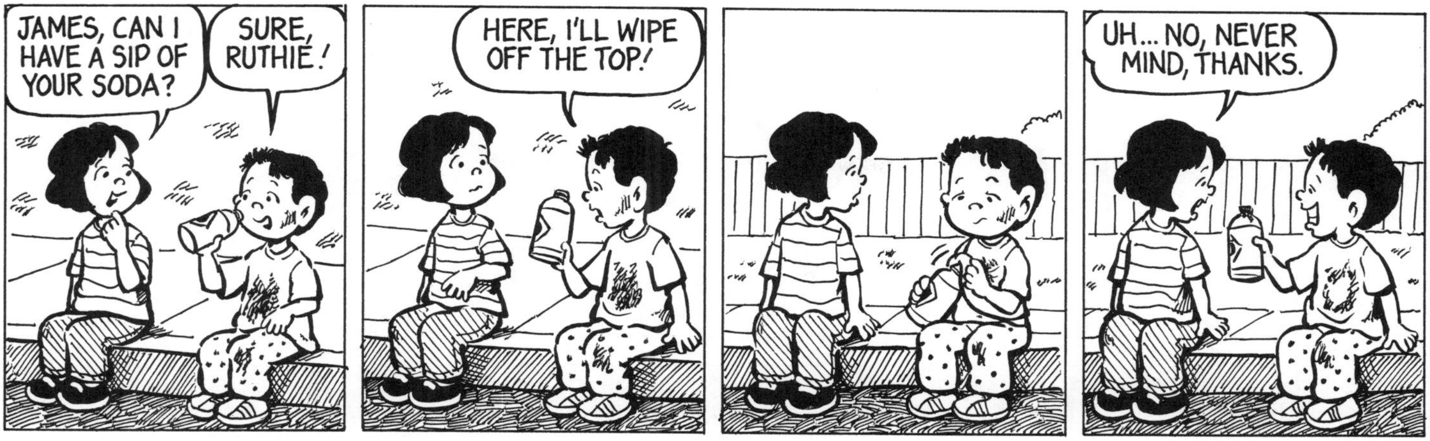
JAMES, CAN I HAVE A SIP OF YOUR SODA?
SURE, RUTHIE!
HERE, I'LL WIPE OFF THE TOP!
UH... NO, NEVER MIND, THANKS.

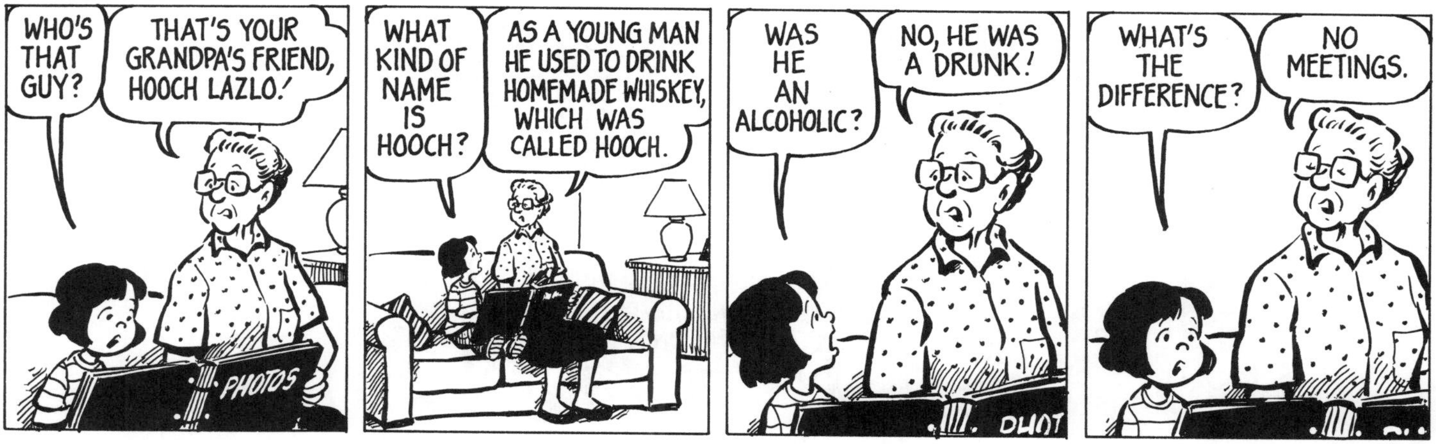
WHO'S THAT GUY?
THAT'S YOUR GRANDPA'S FRIEND, HOOCH LAZLO!
PHOTOS
WHAT KIND OF NAME IS HOOCH?
AS A YOUNG MAN HE USED TO DRINK HOMEMADE WHISKEY, WHICH WAS CALLED HOOCH.
WAS HE AN ALCOHOLIC?
NO, HE WAS A DRUNK!
WHAT'S THE DIFFERENCE?
NO MEETINGS.

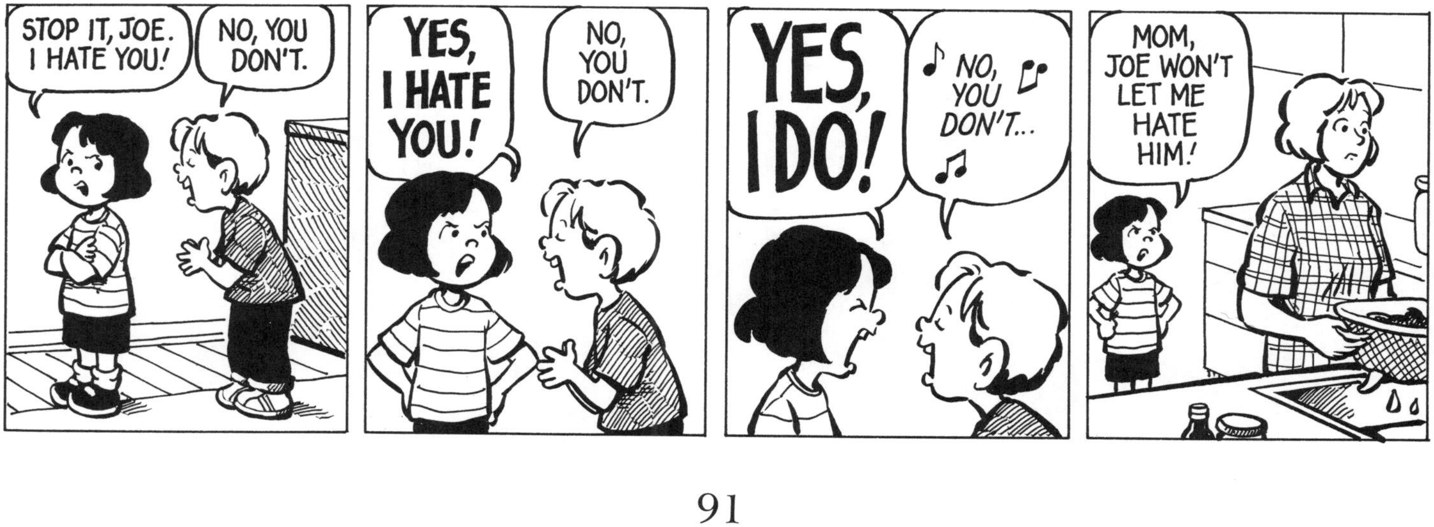
STOP IT, JOE. I HATE YOU!
NO, YOU DON'T.
YES, I HATE YOU!
NO, YOU DON'T.
YES, I DO!
NO, YOU DON'T...
MOM, JOE WON'T LET ME HATE HIM!

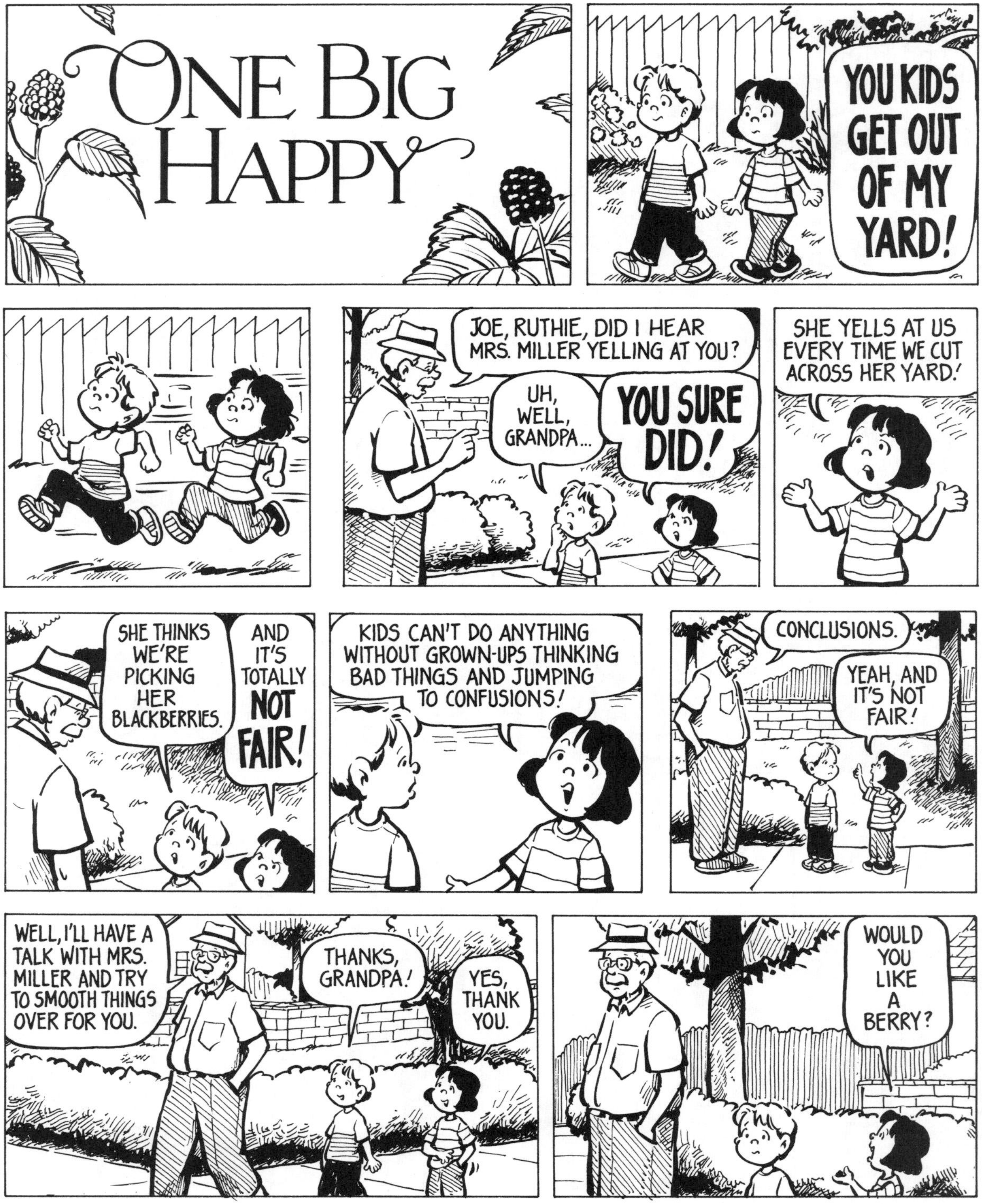
ONE BIG HAPPY
YOU KIDS GET OUT OF MY YARD!
JOE, RUTHIE, DID I HEAR MRS. MILLER YELLING AT YOU?
UH, WELL, GRANDPA...
YOU SURE DID!
SHE YELLS AT US EVERY TIME WE CUT ACROSS HER YARD!
SHE THINKS WE'RE PICKING HER BLACKBERRIES.
AND IT'S TOTALLY NOT FAIR!
KIDS CAN'T DO ANYTHING WITHOUT GROWN-UPS THINKING BAD THINGS AND JUMPING TO CONFUSIONS!
CONCLUSIONS.
YEAH, AND IT'S NOT FAIR!
WELL, I'LL HAVE A TALK WITH MRS. MILLER AND TRY TO SMOOTH THINGS OVER FOR YOU.
THANKS, GRANDPA!
YES, THANK YOU.
WOULD YOU LIKE A BERRY?

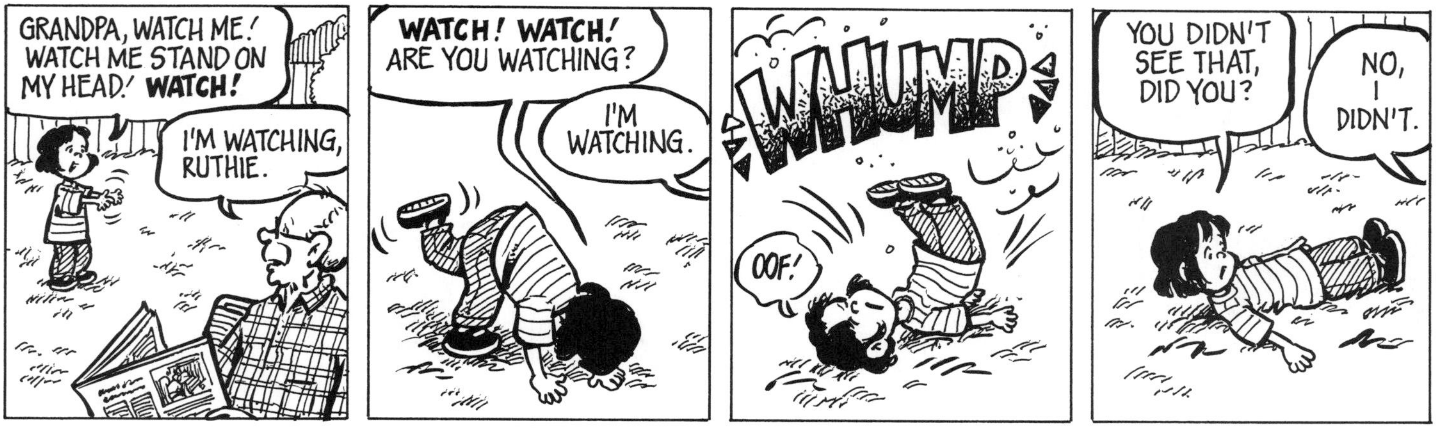
GRANDPA, WATCH ME! WATCH ME STAND ON MY HEAD! **WATCH!**
I'M WATCHING, RUTHIE.
WATCH! WATCH! ARE YOU WATCHING?
I'M WATCHING.
WHUMP
OOF!
YOU DIDN'T SEE THAT, DID YOU?
NO, I DIDN'T.

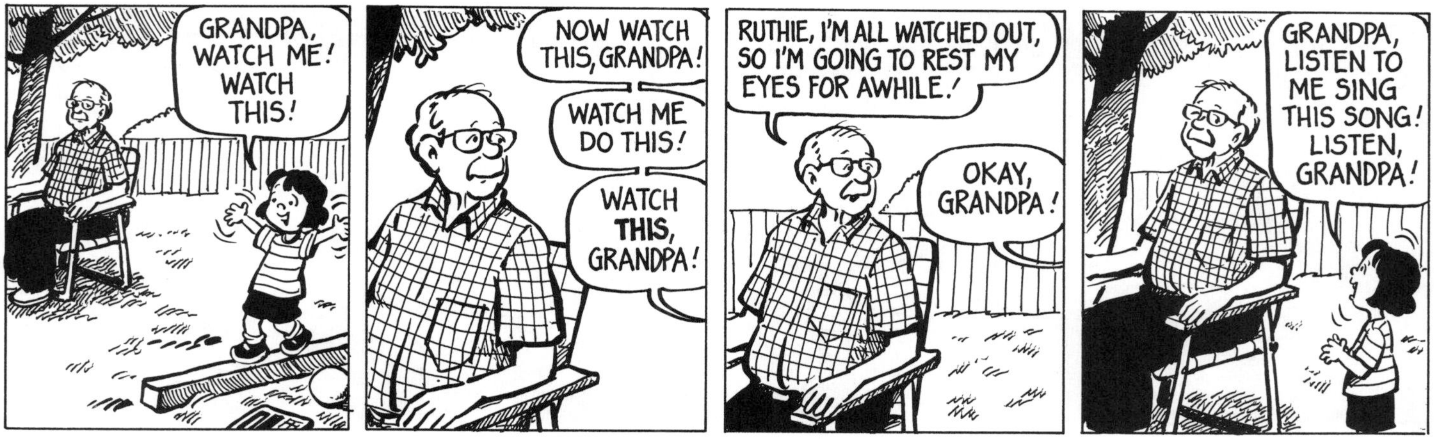
GRANDPA, WATCH ME! WATCH THIS!
NOW WATCH THIS, GRANDPA!
WATCH ME DO THIS!
WATCH **THIS**, GRANDPA!
RUTHIE, I'M ALL WATCHED OUT, SO I'M GOING TO REST MY EYES FOR AWHILE!
OKAY, GRANDPA!
GRANDPA, LISTEN TO ME SING THIS SONG! LISTEN, GRANDPA!

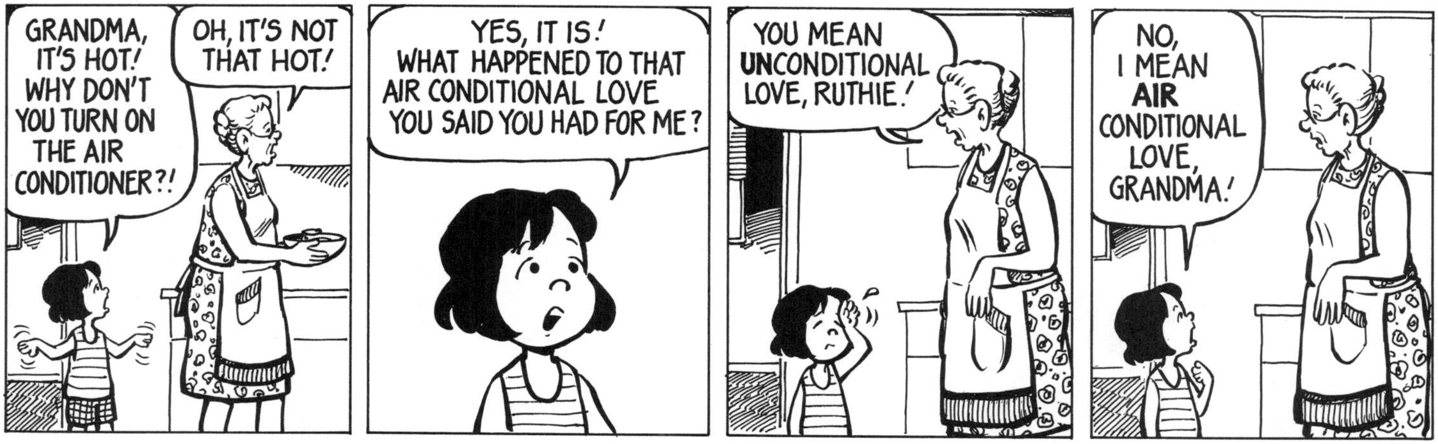
GRANDMA, IT'S HOT! WHY DON'T YOU TURN ON THE AIR CONDITIONER?!
OH, IT'S NOT THAT HOT!
YES, IT IS! WHAT HAPPENED TO THAT AIR CONDITIONAL LOVE YOU SAID YOU HAD FOR ME?
YOU MEAN **UN**CONDITIONAL LOVE, RUTHIE!
NO, I MEAN **AIR** CONDITIONAL LOVE, GRANDMA!

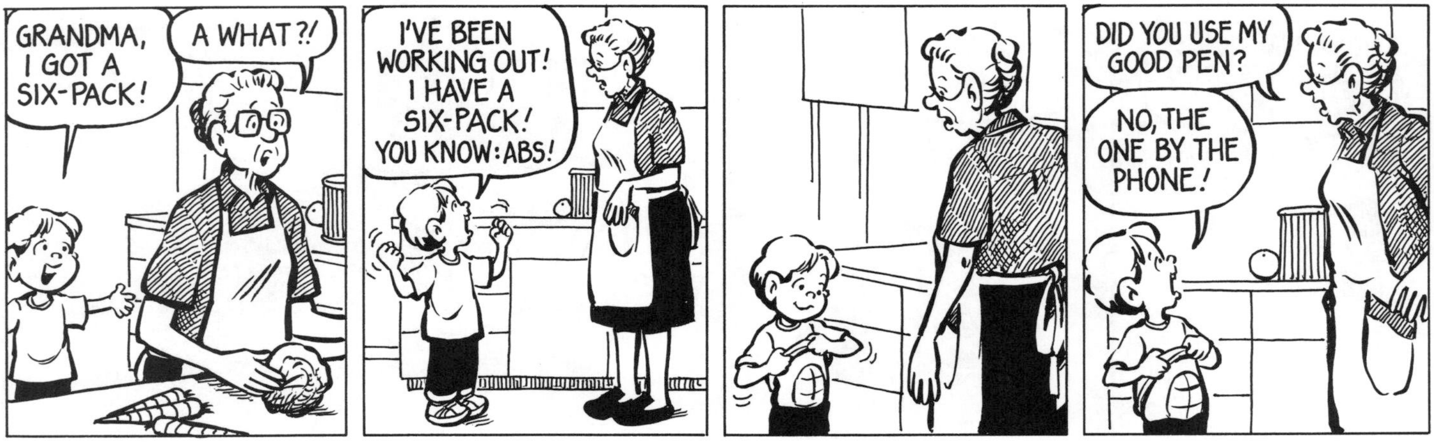
GRANDMA, I GOT A SIX-PACK!
A WHAT?!
I'VE BEEN WORKING OUT! I HAVE A SIX-PACK! YOU KNOW: ABS!
DID YOU USE MY GOOD PEN?
NO, THE ONE BY THE PHONE!

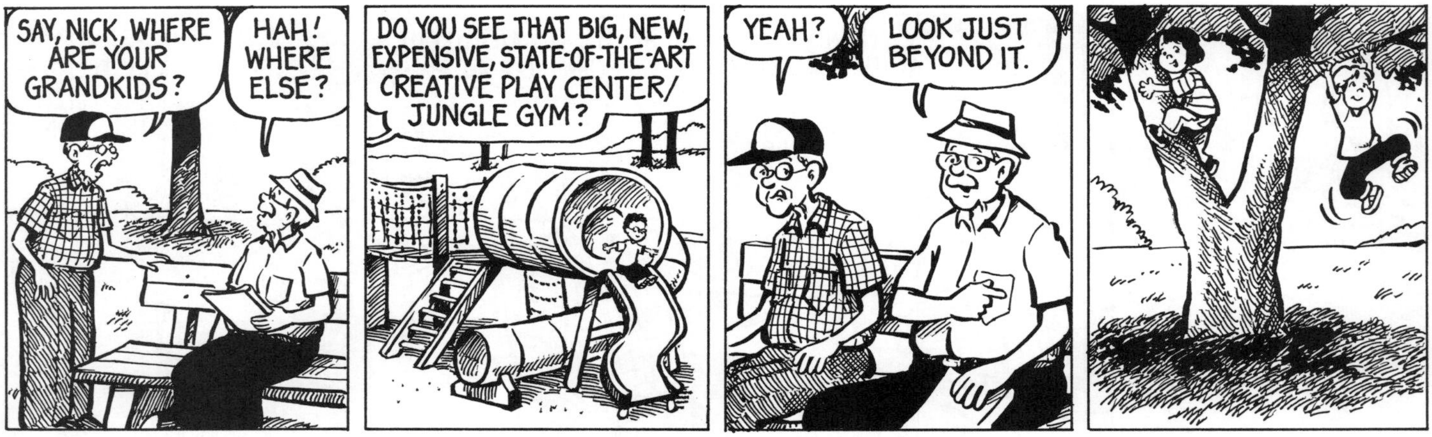
SAY, NICK, WHERE ARE YOUR GRANDKIDS?
HAH! WHERE ELSE?
DO YOU SEE THAT BIG, NEW, EXPENSIVE, STATE-OF-THE-ART CREATIVE PLAY CENTER/ JUNGLE GYM?
YEAH?
LOOK JUST BEYOND IT.

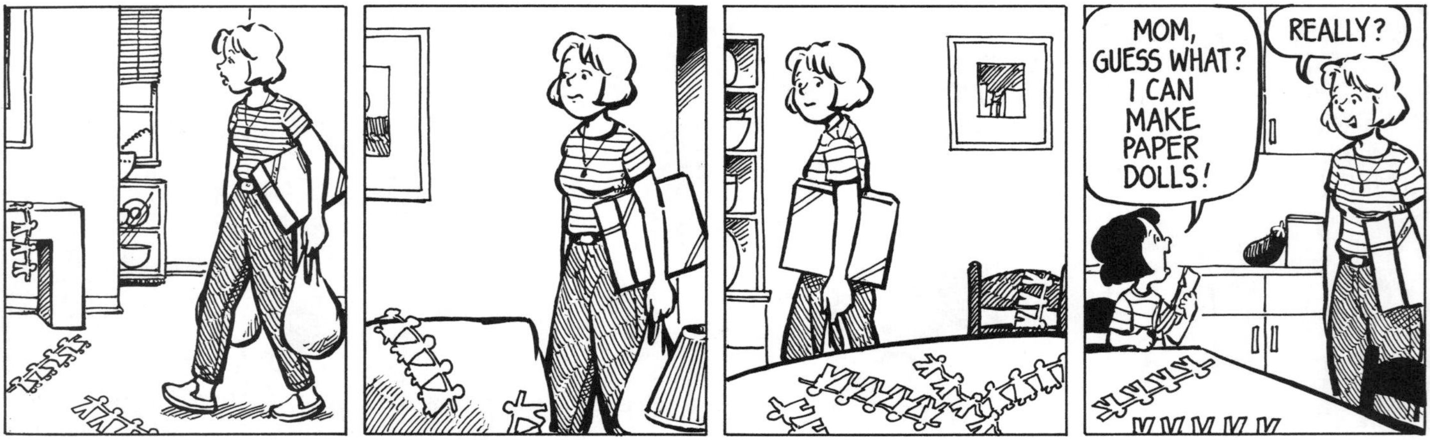
MOM, GUESS WHAT? I CAN MAKE PAPER DOLLS!
REALLY?

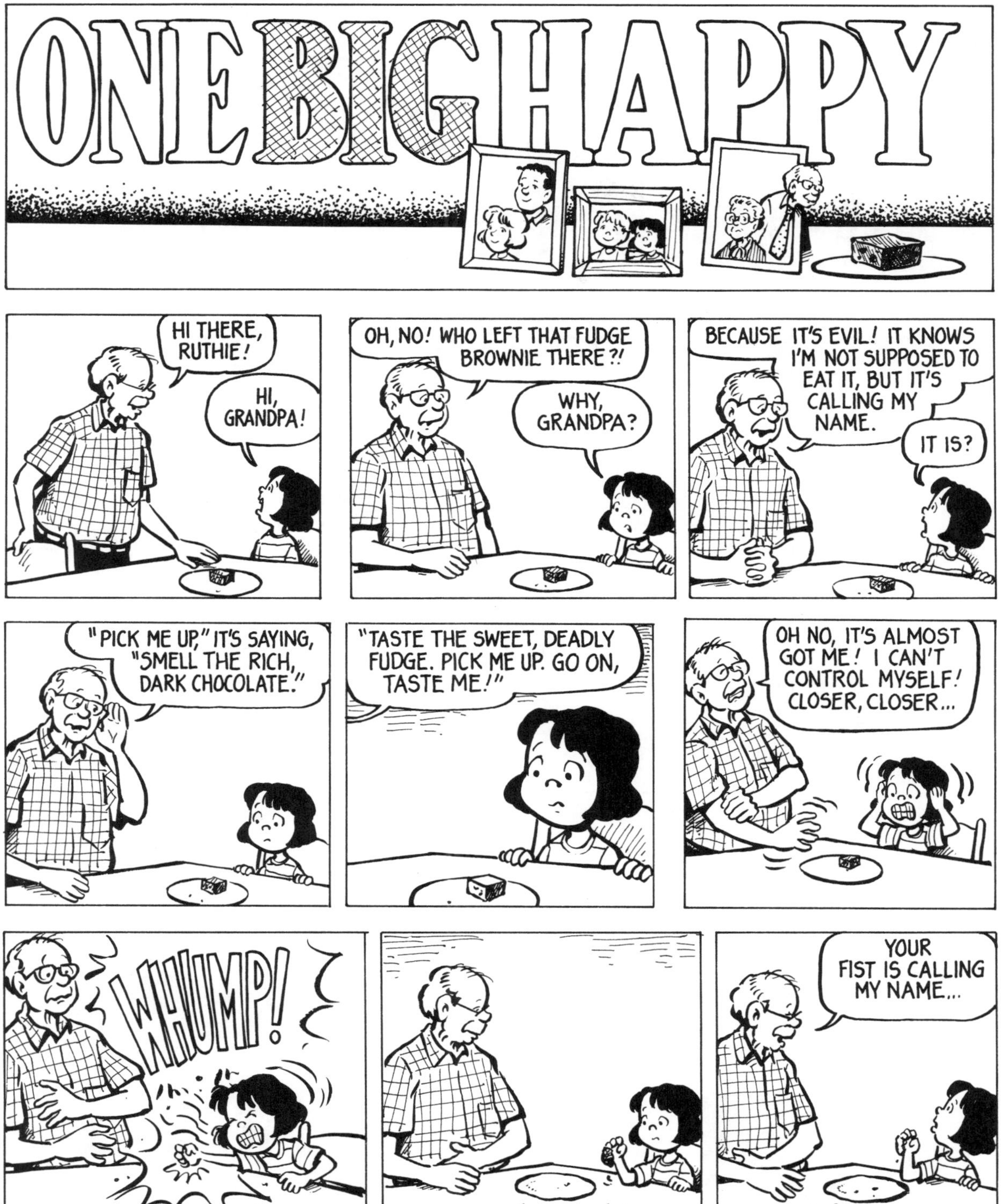
ONE BIG HAPPY
HI THERE, RUTHIE!
HI, GRANDPA!
OH, NO! WHO LEFT THAT FUDGE BROWNIE THERE?!
WHY, GRANDPA?
BECAUSE IT'S EVIL! IT KNOWS I'M NOT SUPPOSED TO EAT IT, BUT IT'S CALLING MY NAME.
IT IS?
"PICK ME UP," IT'S SAYING, "SMELL THE RICH, DARK CHOCOLATE."
"TASTE THE SWEET, DEADLY FUDGE. PICK ME UP. GO ON, TASTE ME!"
OH NO, IT'S ALMOST GOT ME! I CAN'T CONTROL MYSELF! CLOSER, CLOSER...
WHUMP!
YOUR FIST IS CALLING MY NAME...

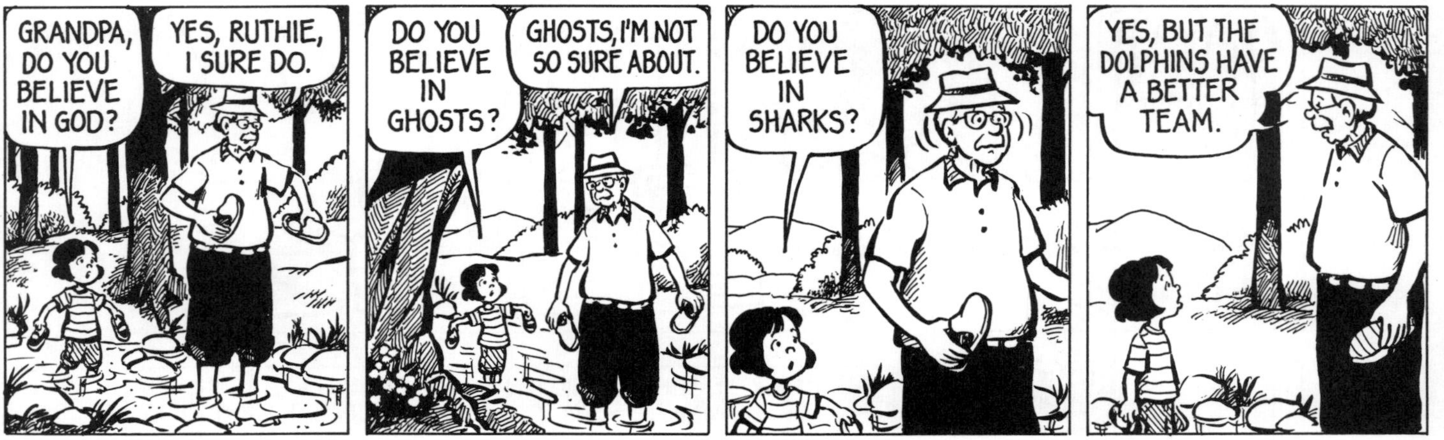
GRANDPA, DO YOU BELIEVE IN GOD?
YES, RUTHIE, I SURE DO.
DO YOU BELIEVE IN GHOSTS?
GHOSTS, I'M NOT SO SURE ABOUT.
DO YOU BELIEVE IN SHARKS?
YES, BUT THE DOLPHINS HAVE A BETTER TEAM.

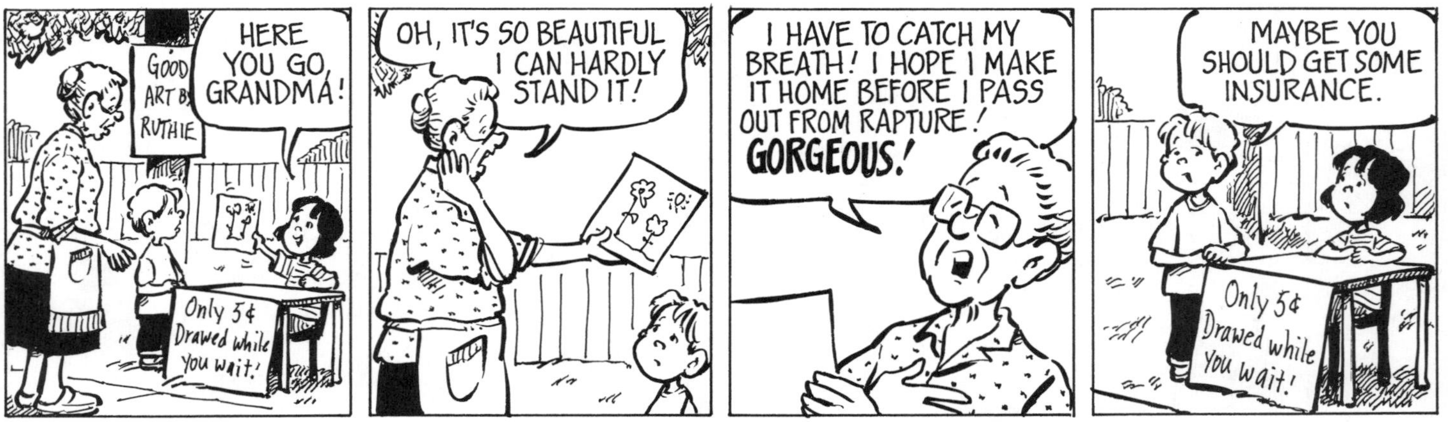
GOOD ART BY RUTHIE
HERE YOU GO, GRANDMA!
Only 5¢ Drawed while You wait!
OH, IT'S SO BEAUTIFUL I CAN HARDLY STAND IT!
I HAVE TO CATCH MY BREATH! I HOPE I MAKE IT HOME BEFORE I PASS OUT FROM RAPTURE! GORGEOUS!
MAYBE YOU SHOULD GET SOME INSURANCE.
Only 5¢ Drawed while You wait!

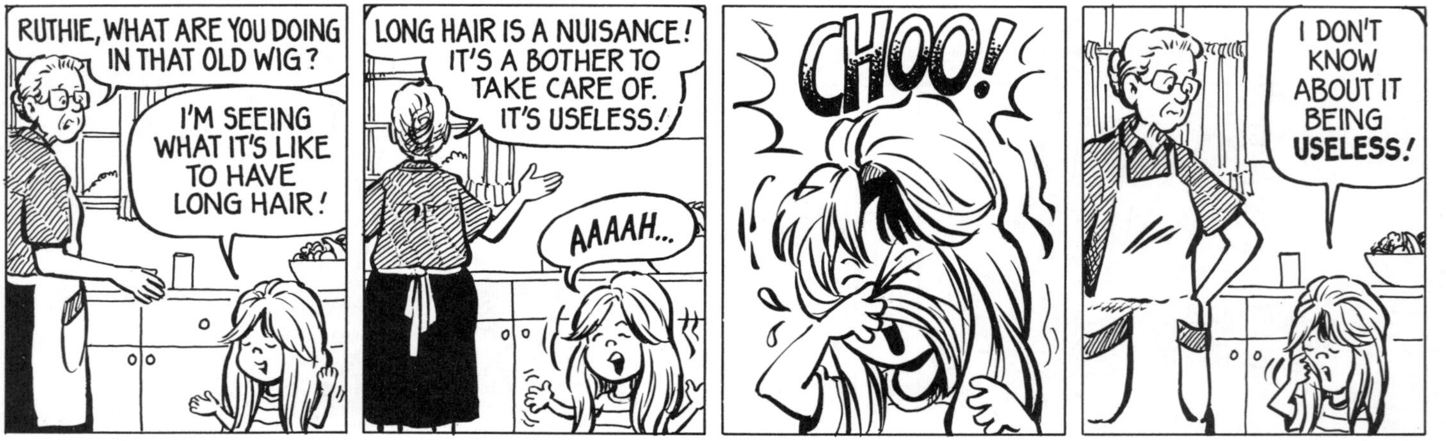
RUTHIE, WHAT ARE YOU DOING IN THAT OLD WIG?
I'M SEEING WHAT IT'S LIKE TO HAVE LONG HAIR!
LONG HAIR IS A NUISANCE! IT'S A BOTHER TO TAKE CARE OF. IT'S USELESS!
AAAAH...
CHOO!
I DON'T KNOW ABOUT IT BEING USELESS!

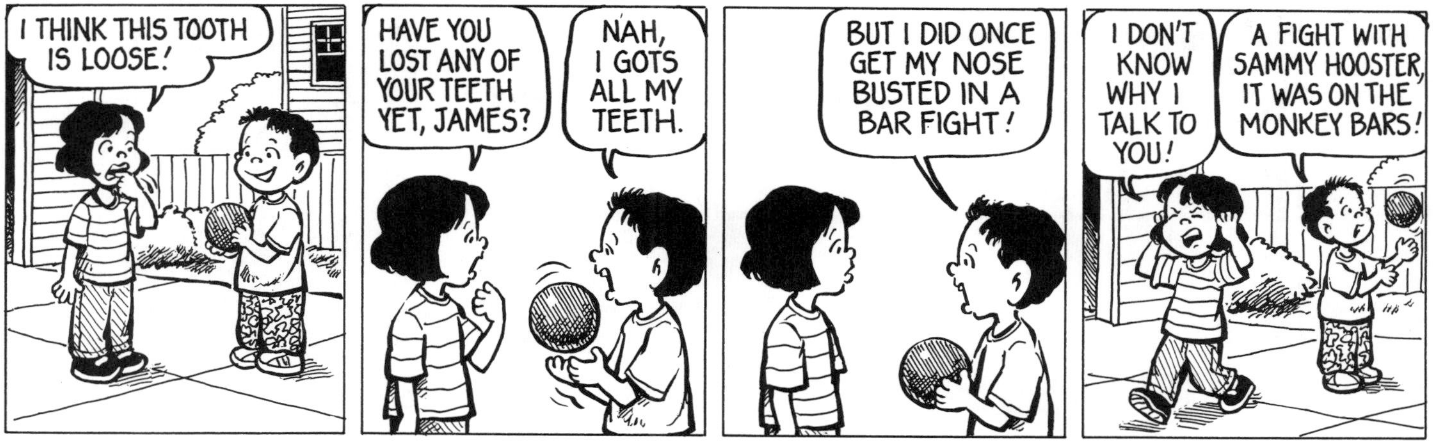
I THINK THIS TOOTH IS LOOSE!
HAVE YOU LOST ANY OF YOUR TEETH YET, JAMES?
NAH, I GOTS ALL MY TEETH.
BUT I DID ONCE GET MY NOSE BUSTED IN A BAR FIGHT!
I DON'T KNOW WHY I TALK TO YOU!
A FIGHT WITH SAMMY HOOSTER, IT WAS ON THE MONKEY BARS!

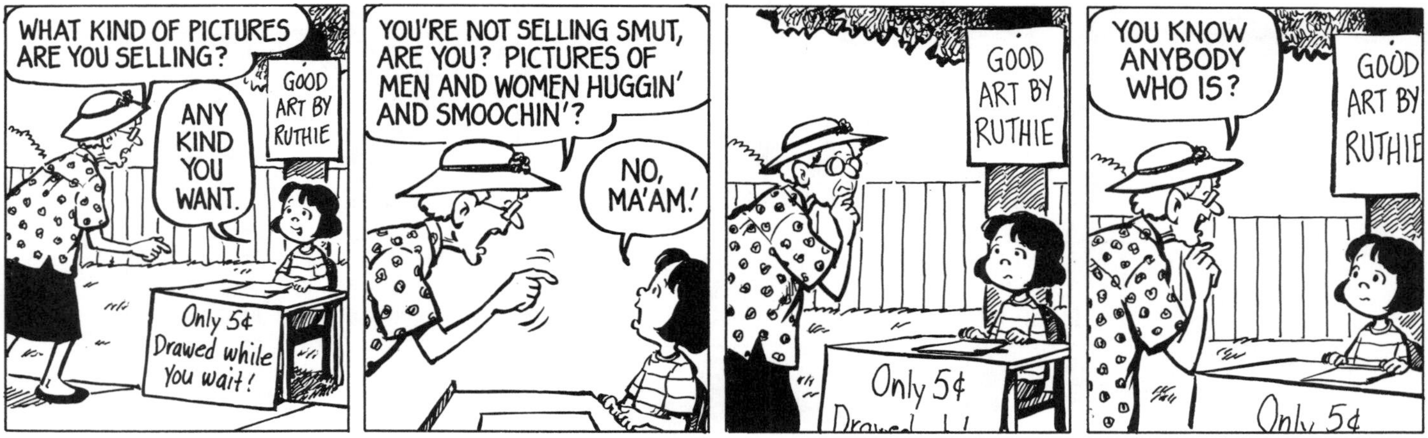
WHAT KIND OF PICTURES ARE YOU SELLING?
GOOD ART BY RUTHIE
ANY KIND YOU WANT.
Only 5¢ Drawed while you wait!
YOU'RE NOT SELLING SMUT, ARE YOU? PICTURES OF MEN AND WOMEN HUGGIN' AND SMOOCHIN'?
NO, MA'AM!
GOOD ART BY RUTHIE
Only 5¢
YOU KNOW ANYBODY WHO IS?
GOOD ART BY RUTHIE

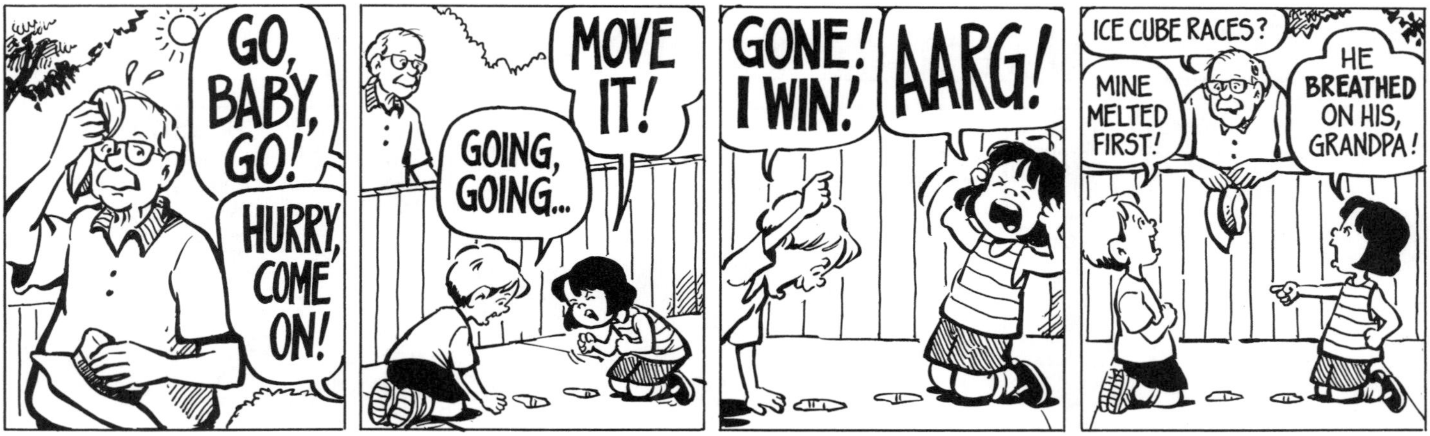
GO, BABY, GO!
HURRY, COME ON!
MOVE IT!
GOING, GOING...
GONE! I WIN!
AARG!
ICE CUBE RACES?
MINE MELTED FIRST!
HE BREATHED ON HIS, GRANDPA!

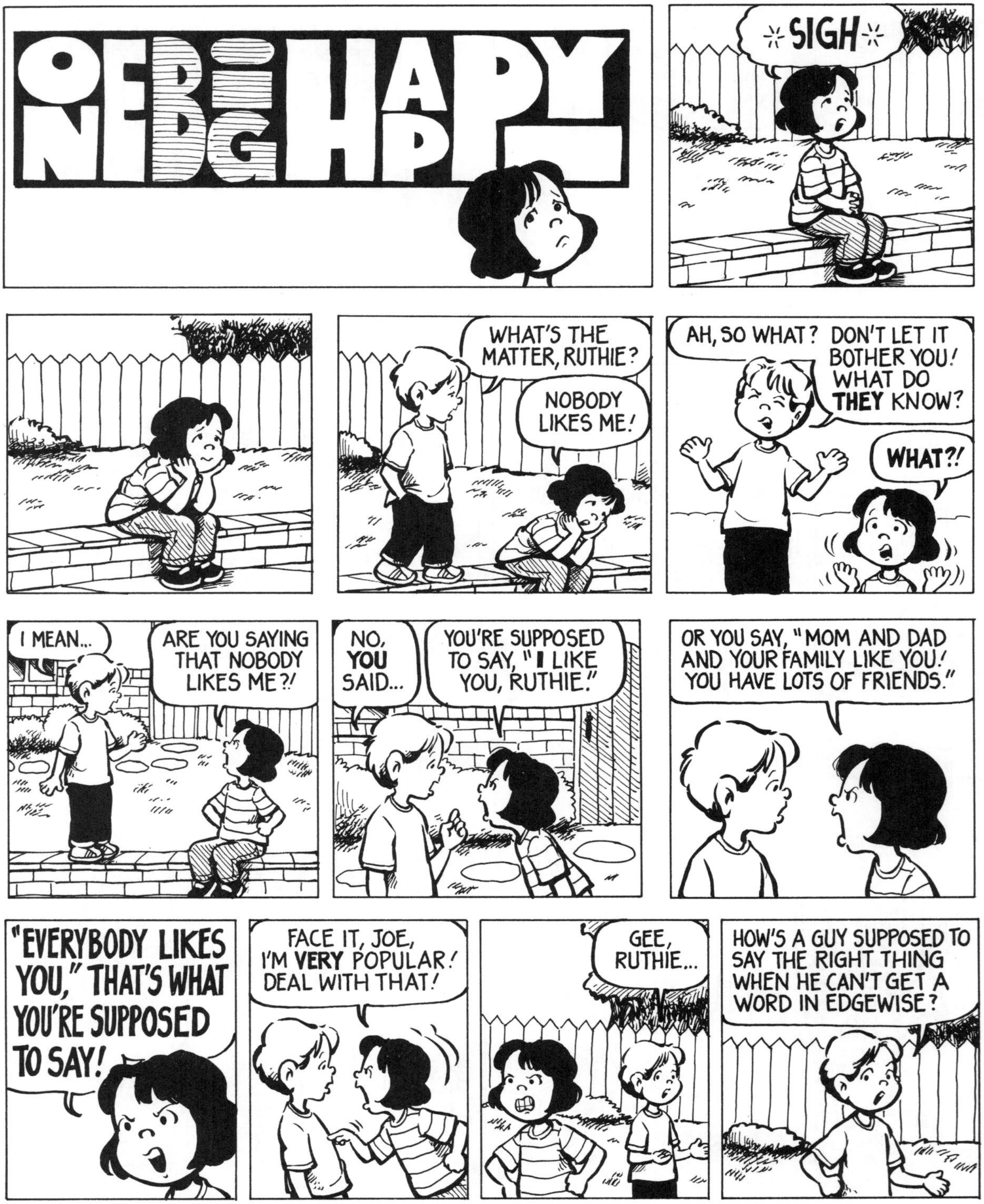
ONE BIG HAPPY
SIGH
WHAT'S THE MATTER, RUTHIE?
NOBODY LIKES ME!
AH, SO WHAT? DON'T LET IT BOTHER YOU! WHAT DO **THEY** KNOW?
WHAT?!
I MEAN...
ARE YOU SAYING THAT NOBODY LIKES ME?!
NO, **YOU** SAID...
YOU'RE SUPPOSED TO SAY, "**I** LIKE YOU, RUTHIE."
OR YOU SAY, "MOM AND DAD AND YOUR FAMILY LIKE YOU! YOU HAVE LOTS OF FRIENDS."
"EVERYBODY LIKES YOU," THAT'S WHAT YOU'RE SUPPOSED TO SAY!
FACE IT, JOE, I'M **VERY** POPULAR! DEAL WITH THAT!
GEE, RUTHIE...
HOW'S A GUY SUPPOSED TO SAY THE RIGHT THING WHEN HE CAN'T GET A WORD IN EDGEWISE?

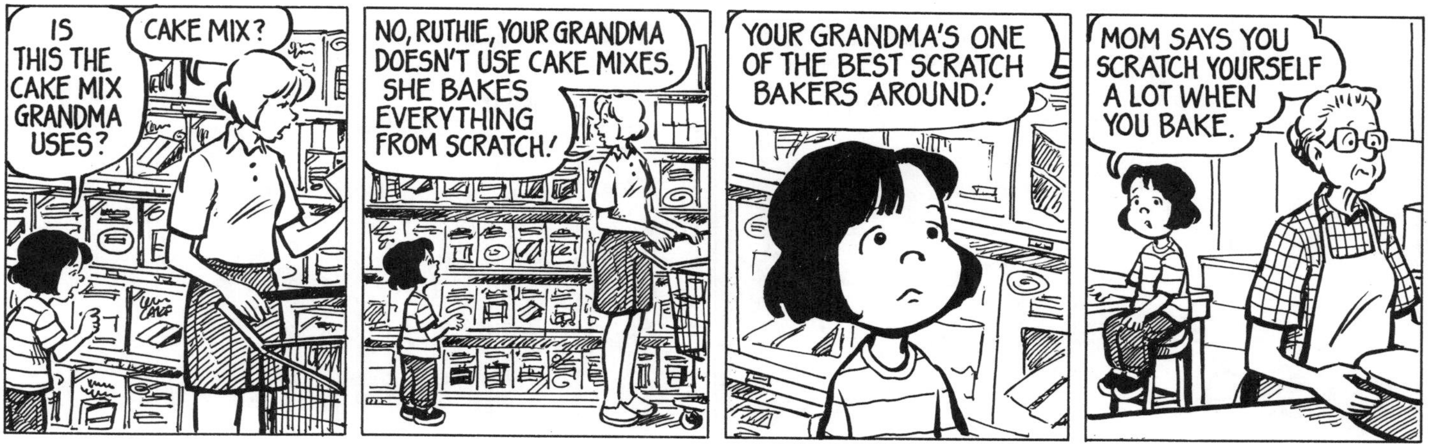
IS THIS THE CAKE MIX GRANDMA USES?
CAKE MIX?
NO, RUTHIE, YOUR GRANDMA DOESN'T USE CAKE MIXES. SHE BAKES EVERYTHING FROM SCRATCH!
YOUR GRANDMA'S ONE OF THE BEST SCRATCH BAKERS AROUND!
MOM SAYS YOU SCRATCH YOURSELF A LOT WHEN YOU BAKE.

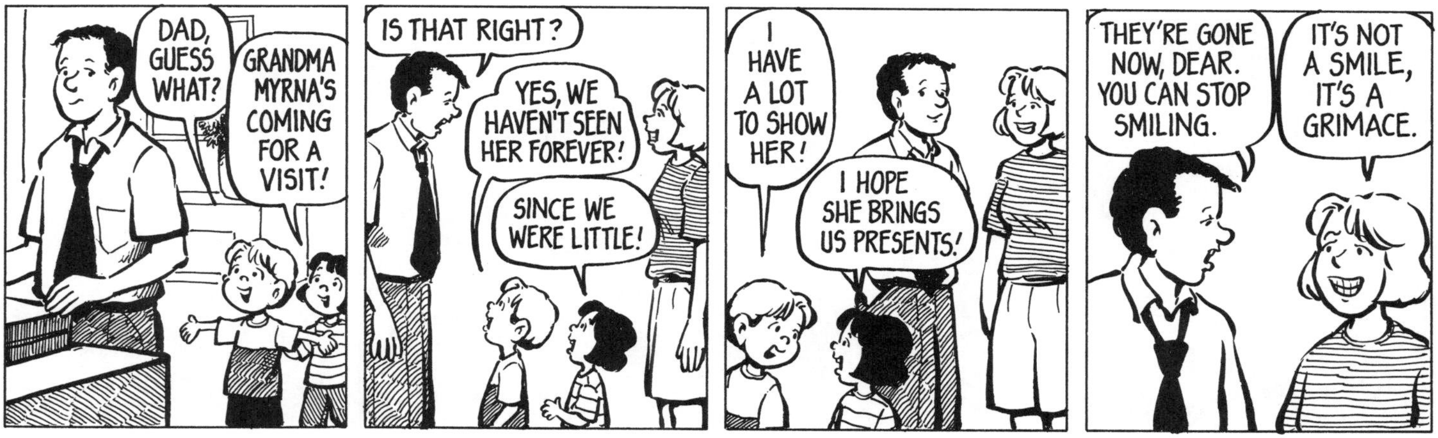
DAD, GUESS WHAT?
GRANDMA MYRNA'S COMING FOR A VISIT!
IS THAT RIGHT?
YES, WE HAVEN'T SEEN HER FOREVER!
SINCE WE WERE LITTLE!
I HAVE A LOT TO SHOW HER!
I HOPE SHE BRINGS US PRESENTS!
THEY'RE GONE NOW, DEAR. YOU CAN STOP SMILING.
IT'S NOT A SMILE, IT'S A GRIMACE.

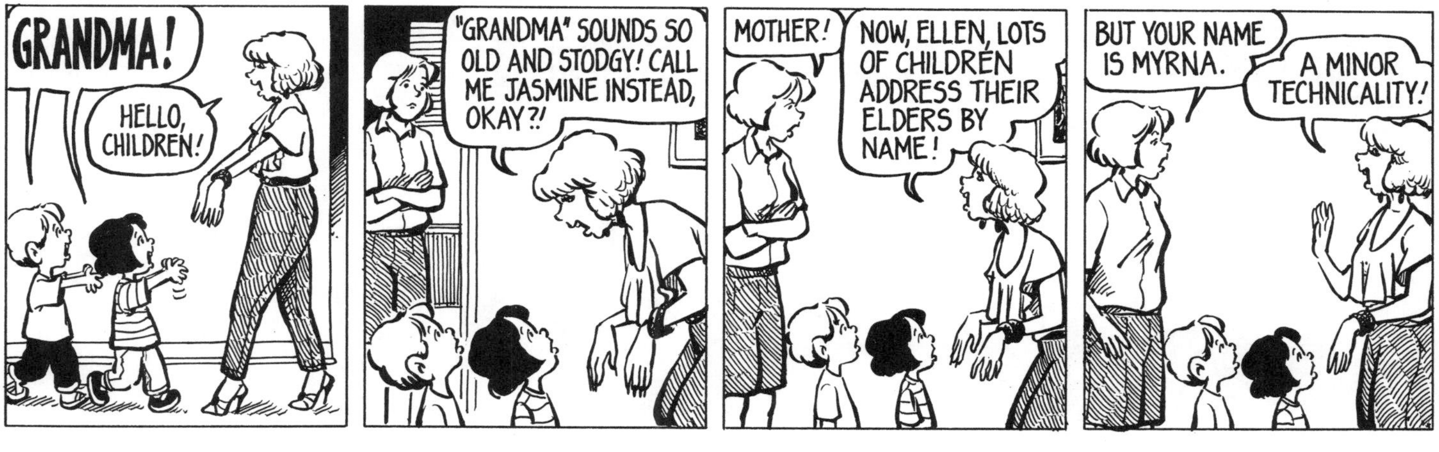
GRANDMA!
HELLO, CHILDREN!
"GRANDMA" SOUNDS SO OLD AND STODGY! CALL ME JASMINE INSTEAD, OKAY?!
MOTHER!
NOW, ELLEN, LOTS OF CHILDREN ADDRESS THEIR ELDERS BY NAME!
BUT YOUR NAME IS MYRNA.
A MINOR TECHNICALITY!

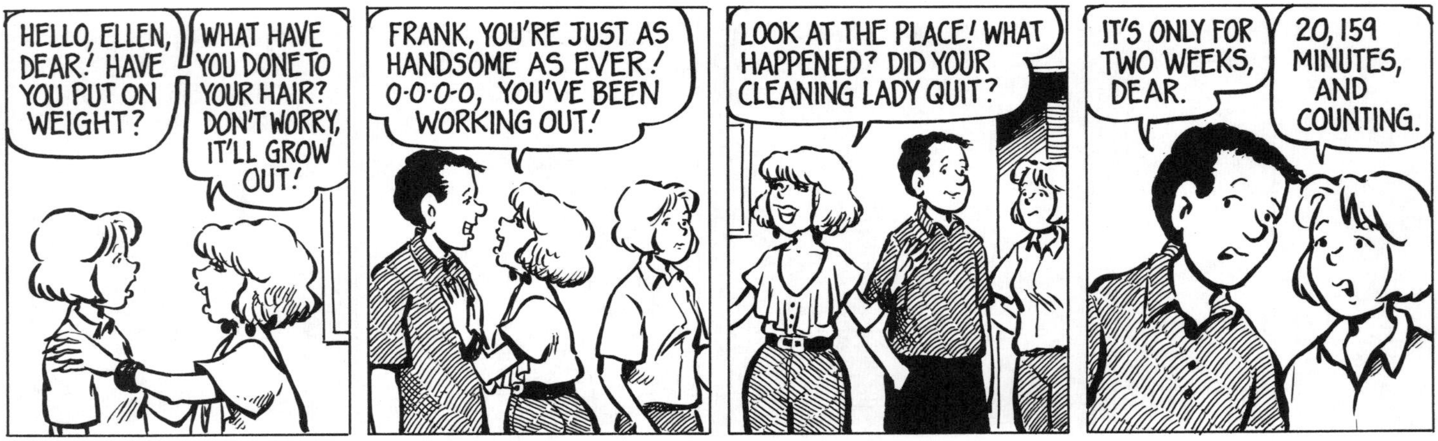
HELLO, ELLEN, DEAR! HAVE YOU PUT ON WEIGHT?
WHAT HAVE YOU DONE TO YOUR HAIR? DON'T WORRY, IT'LL GROW OUT!
FRANK, YOU'RE JUST AS HANDSOME AS EVER! O-O-O-O, YOU'VE BEEN WORKING OUT!
LOOK AT THE PLACE! WHAT HAPPENED? DID YOUR CLEANING LADY QUIT?
IT'S ONLY FOR TWO WEEKS, DEAR.
20,159 MINUTES, AND COUNTING.

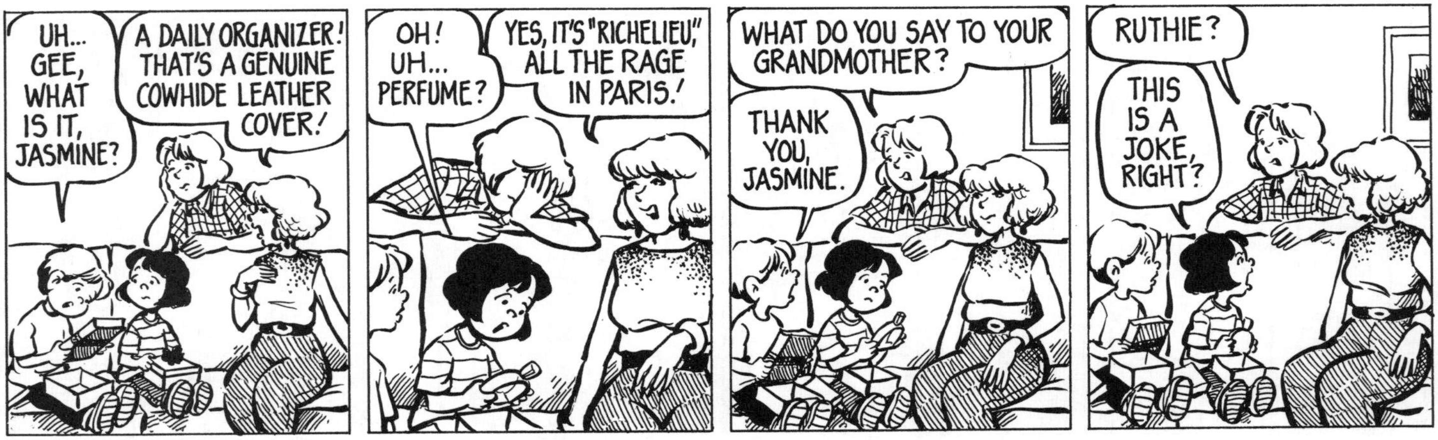
UH... GEE, WHAT IS IT, JASMINE?
A DAILY ORGANIZER! THAT'S A GENUINE COWHIDE LEATHER COVER!
OH! UH... PERFUME?
YES, IT'S "RICHELIEU," ALL THE RAGE IN PARIS!
WHAT DO YOU SAY TO YOUR GRANDMOTHER?
THANK YOU, JASMINE.
RUTHIE?
THIS IS A JOKE, RIGHT?

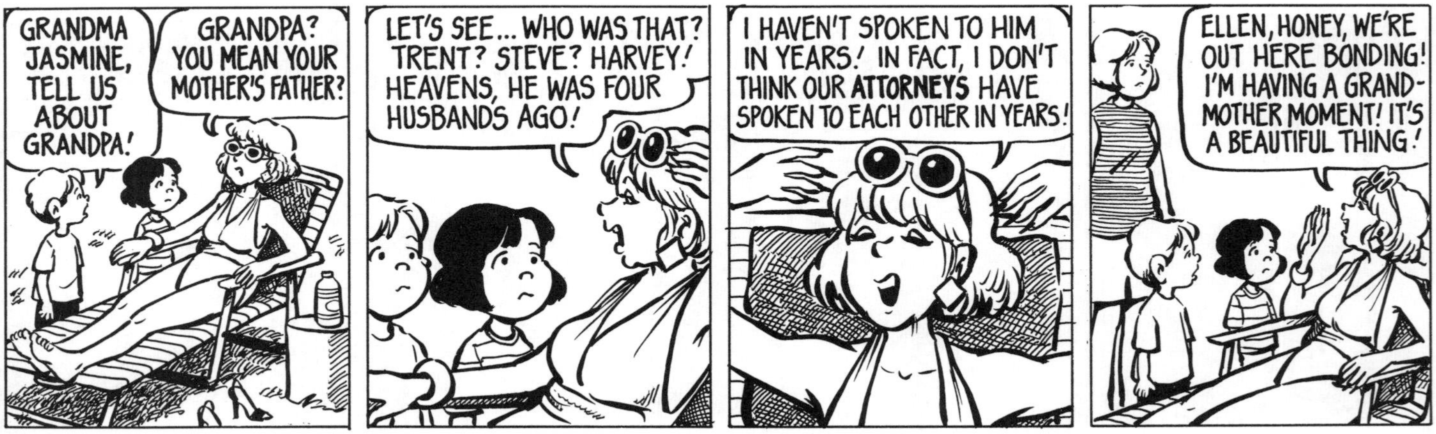
GRANDMA JASMINE, TELL US ABOUT GRANDPA!
GRANDPA? YOU MEAN YOUR MOTHER'S FATHER?
LET'S SEE... WHO WAS THAT? TRENT? STEVE? HARVEY! HEAVENS, HE WAS FOUR HUSBANDS AGO!
I HAVEN'T SPOKEN TO HIM IN YEARS! IN FACT, I DON'T THINK OUR ATTORNEYS HAVE SPOKEN TO EACH OTHER IN YEARS!
ELLEN, HONEY, WE'RE OUT HERE BONDING! I'M HAVING A GRAND-MOTHER MOMENT! IT'S A BEAUTIFUL THING!

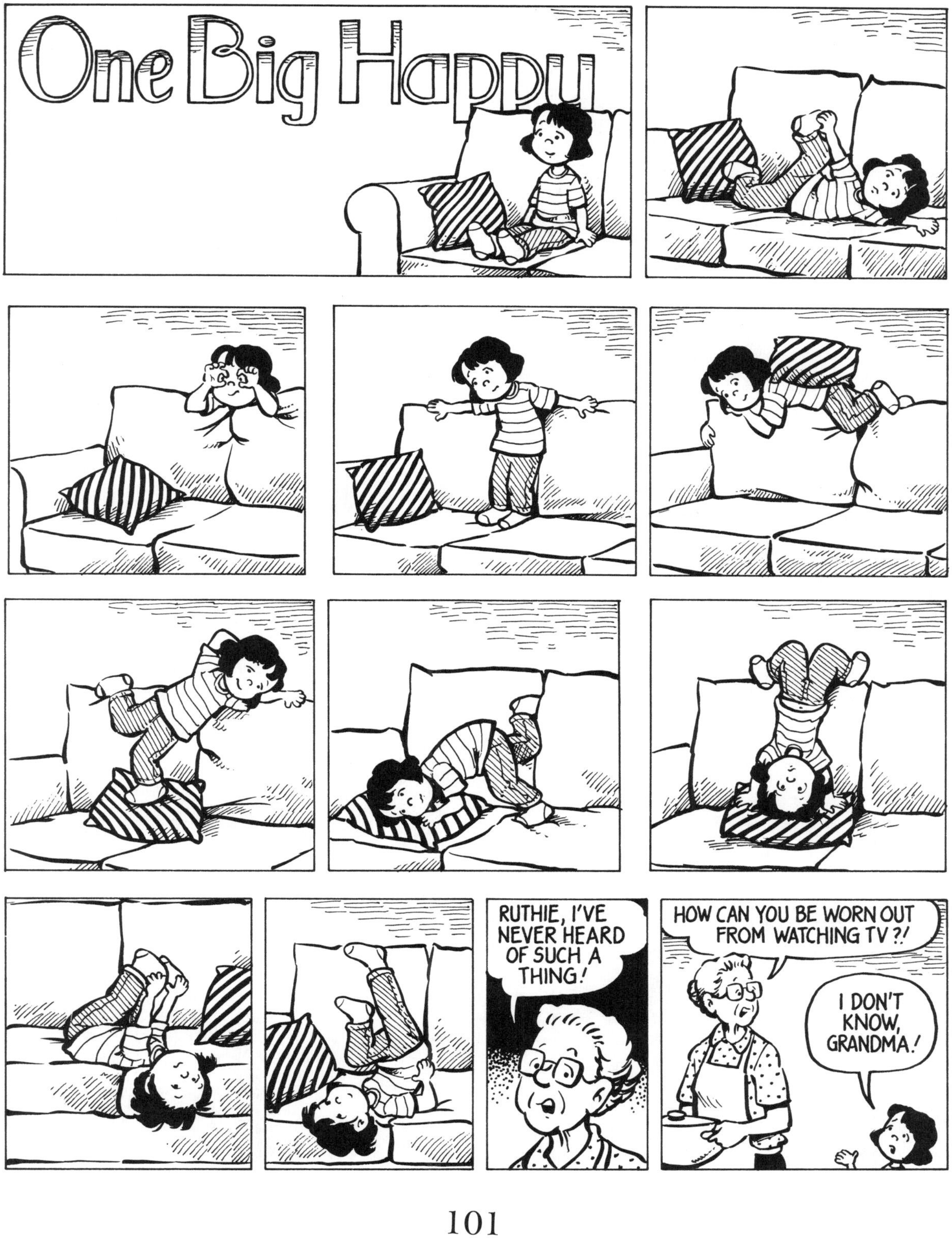
One Big Happy
RUTHIE, I'VE NEVER HEARD OF SUCH A THING!
HOW CAN YOU BE WORN OUT FROM WATCHING TV?!
I DON'T KNOW, GRANDMA!

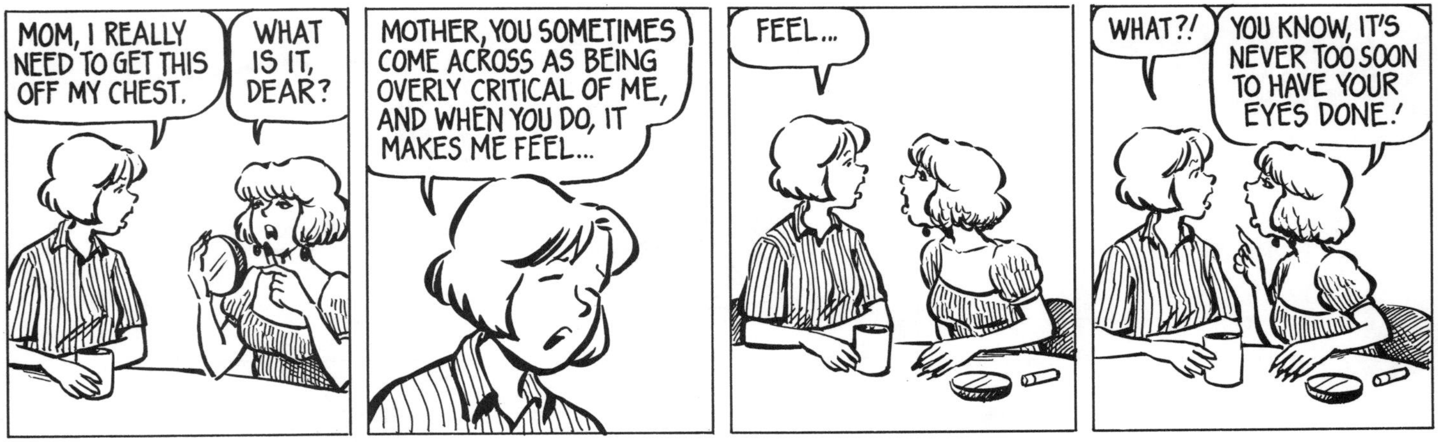
MOM, I REALLY NEED TO GET THIS OFF MY CHEST.
WHAT IS IT, DEAR?
MOTHER, YOU SOMETIMES COME ACROSS AS BEING OVERLY CRITICAL OF ME, AND WHEN YOU DO, IT MAKES ME FEEL...
FEEL...
WHAT?!
YOU KNOW, IT'S NEVER TOO SOON TO HAVE YOUR EYES DONE!

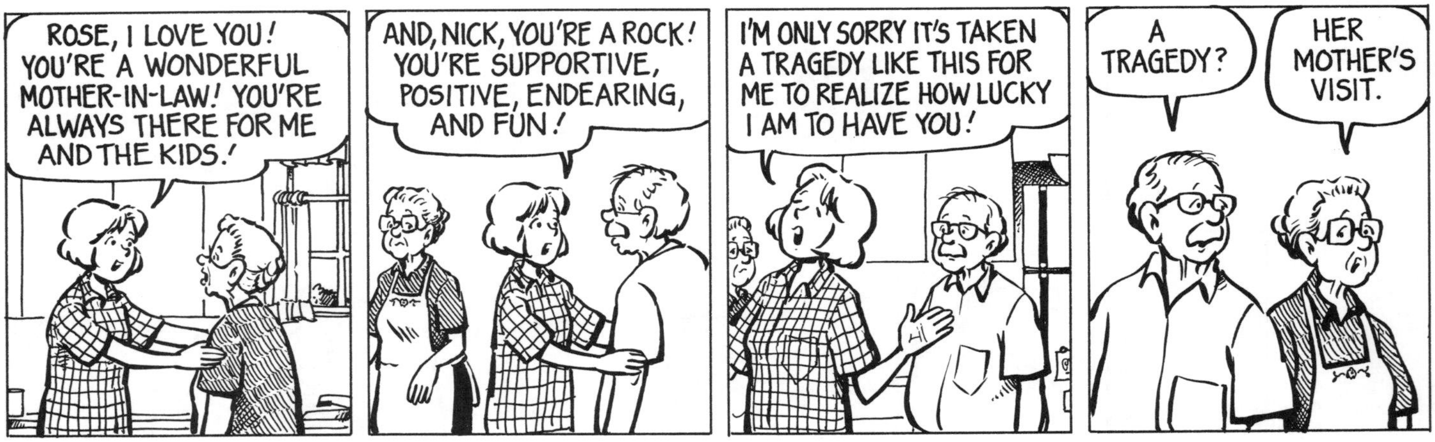
ROSE, I LOVE YOU! YOU'RE A WONDERFUL MOTHER-IN-LAW! YOU'RE ALWAYS THERE FOR ME AND THE KIDS!
AND, NICK, YOU'RE A ROCK! YOU'RE SUPPORTIVE, POSITIVE, ENDEARING, AND FUN!
I'M ONLY SORRY IT'S TAKEN A TRAGEDY LIKE THIS FOR ME TO REALIZE HOW LUCKY I AM TO HAVE YOU!
A TRAGEDY?
HER MOTHER'S VISIT.

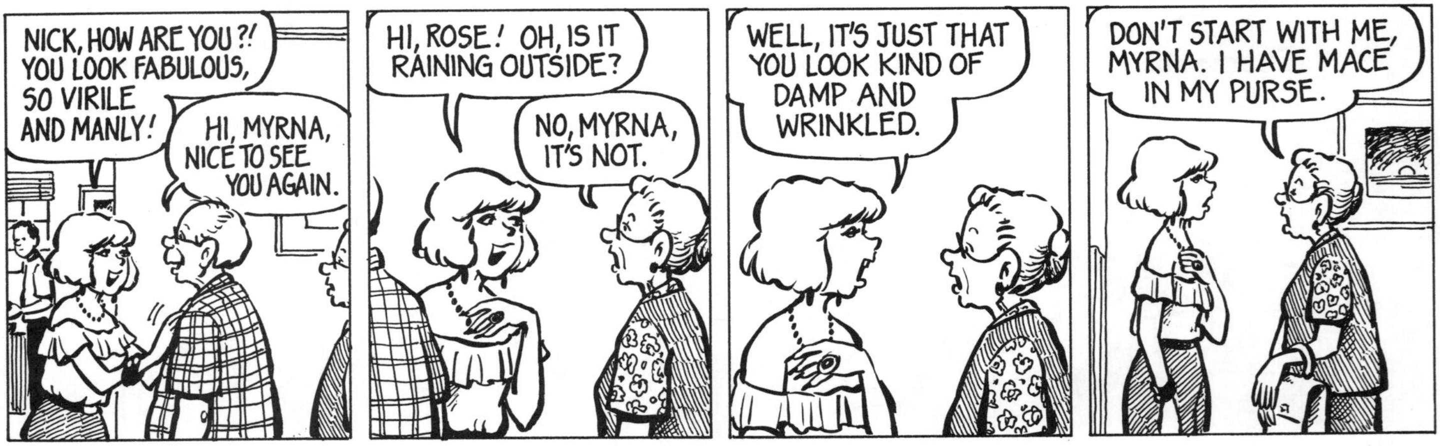
NICK, HOW ARE YOU?! YOU LOOK FABULOUS, SO VIRILE AND MANLY!
HI, MYRNA, NICE TO SEE YOU AGAIN.
HI, ROSE! OH, IS IT RAINING OUTSIDE?
NO, MYRNA, IT'S NOT.
WELL, IT'S JUST THAT YOU LOOK KIND OF DAMP AND WRINKLED.
DON'T START WITH ME, MYRNA. I HAVE MACE IN MY PURSE.

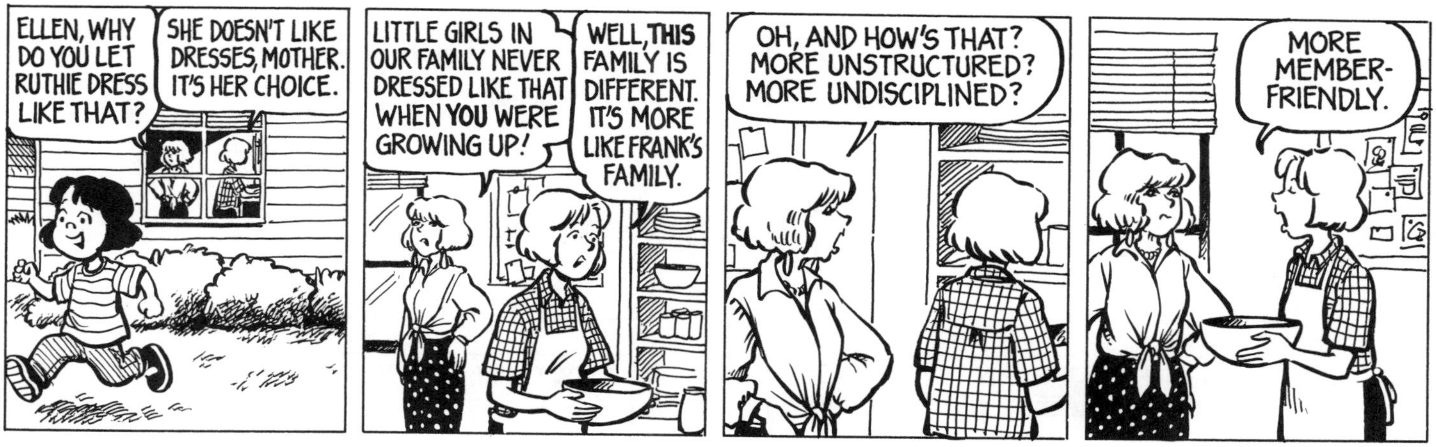
ELLEN, WHY DO YOU LET RUTHIE DRESS LIKE THAT?
SHE DOESN'T LIKE DRESSES, MOTHER. IT'S HER CHOICE.
LITTLE GIRLS IN OUR FAMILY NEVER DRESSED LIKE THAT WHEN **YOU** WERE GROWING UP!
WELL, **THIS** FAMILY IS DIFFERENT. IT'S MORE LIKE FRANK'S FAMILY.
OH, AND HOW'S THAT? MORE UNSTRUCTURED? MORE UNDISCIPLINED?
MORE MEMBER-FRIENDLY.

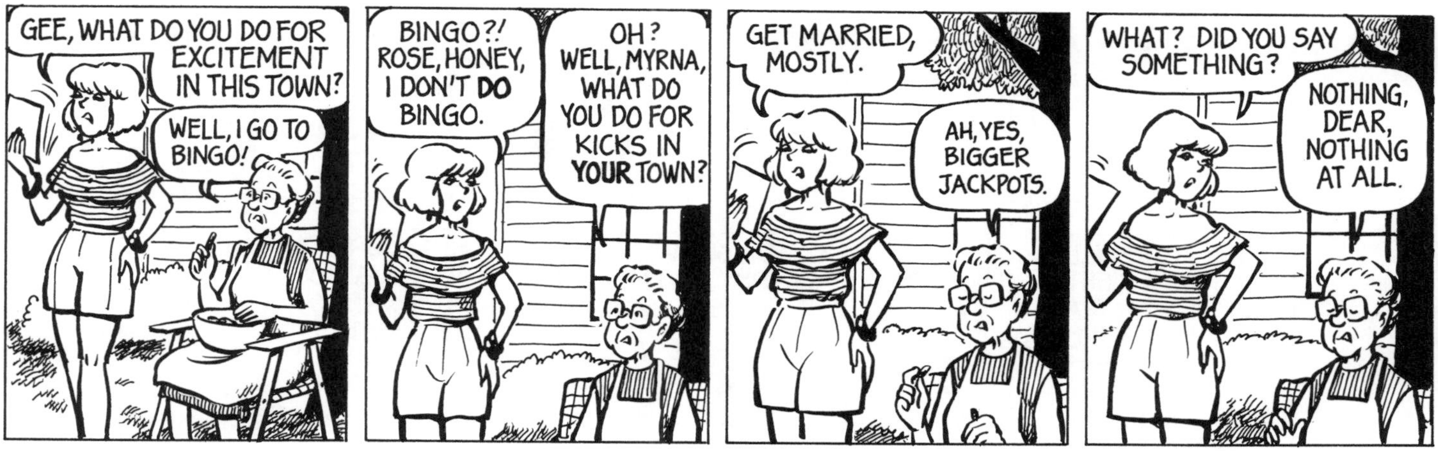
GEE, WHAT DO YOU DO FOR EXCITEMENT IN THIS TOWN?
WELL, I GO TO BINGO!
BINGO?! ROSE, HONEY, I DON'T **DO** BINGO.
OH? WELL, MYRNA, WHAT DO YOU DO FOR KICKS IN **YOUR** TOWN?
GET MARRIED, MOSTLY.
AH, YES, BIGGER JACKPOTS.
WHAT? DID YOU SAY SOMETHING?
NOTHING, DEAR, NOTHING AT ALL.

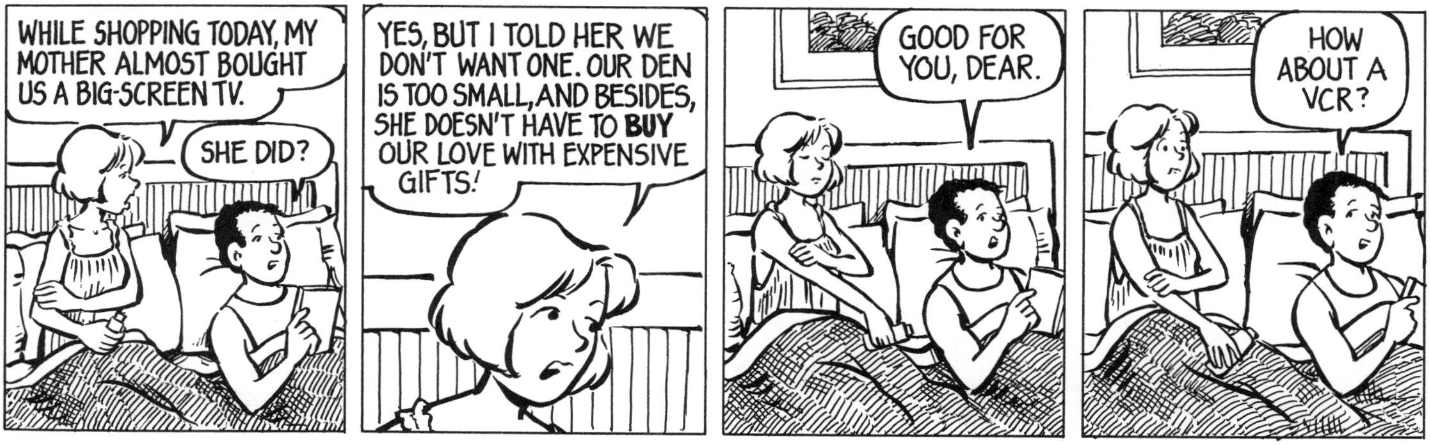
WHILE SHOPPING TODAY, MY MOTHER ALMOST BOUGHT US A BIG-SCREEN TV.
SHE DID?
YES, BUT I TOLD HER WE DON'T WANT ONE. OUR DEN IS TOO SMALL, AND BESIDES, SHE DOESN'T HAVE TO **BUY** OUR LOVE WITH EXPENSIVE GIFTS!
GOOD FOR YOU, DEAR.
HOW ABOUT A VCR?

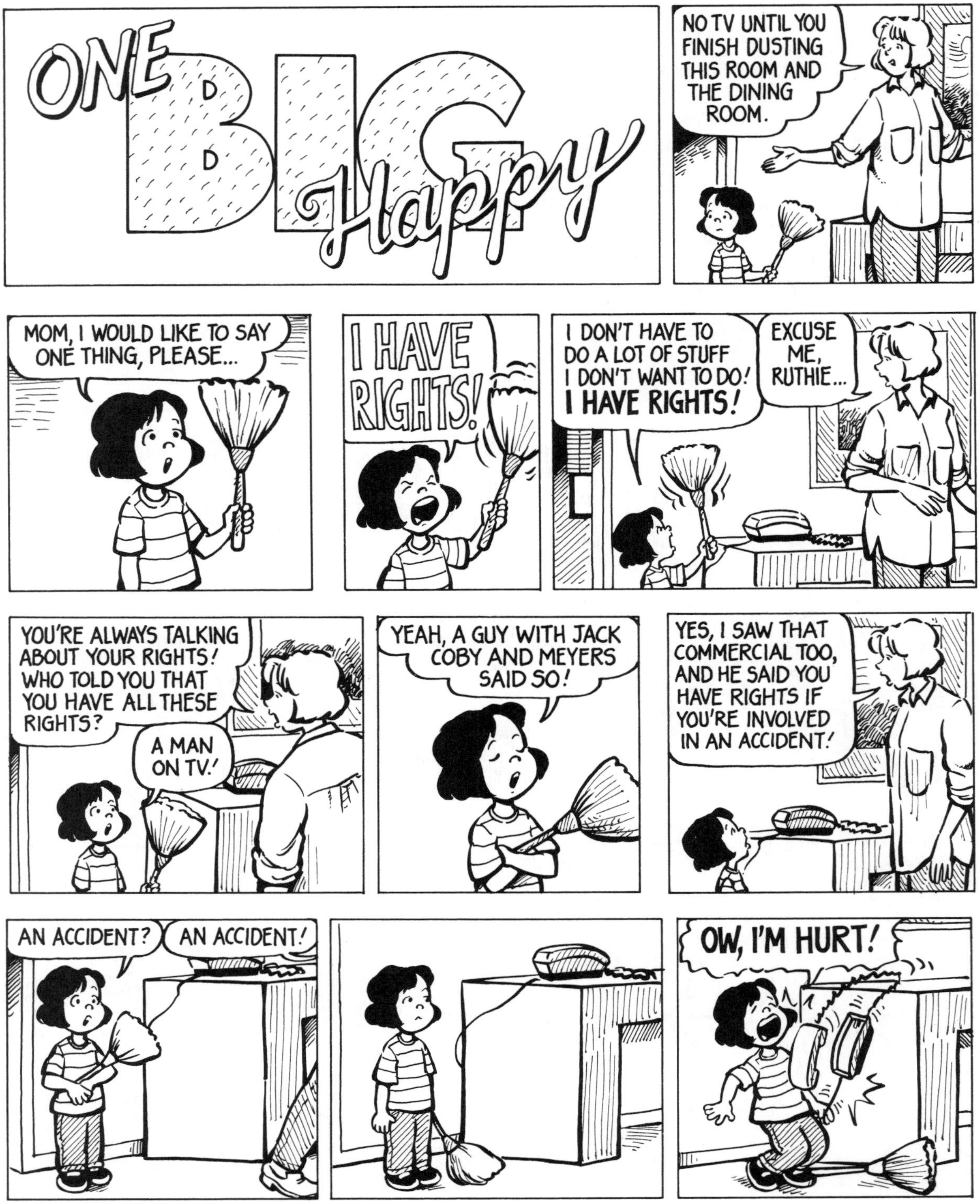
ONE BIG Happy
NO TV UNTIL YOU FINISH DUSTING THIS ROOM AND THE DINING ROOM.
MOM, I WOULD LIKE TO SAY ONE THING, PLEASE...
I HAVE RIGHTS!
I DON'T HAVE TO DO A LOT OF STUFF I DON'T WANT TO DO! I HAVE RIGHTS!
EXCUSE ME, RUTHIE...
YOU'RE ALWAYS TALKING ABOUT YOUR RIGHTS! WHO TOLD YOU THAT YOU HAVE ALL THESE RIGHTS?
A MAN ON TV!
YEAH, A GUY WITH JACK COBY AND MEYERS SAID SO!
YES, I SAW THAT COMMERCIAL TOO, AND HE SAID YOU HAVE RIGHTS IF YOU'RE INVOLVED IN AN ACCIDENT!
AN ACCIDENT?
AN ACCIDENT!
OW, I'M HURT!

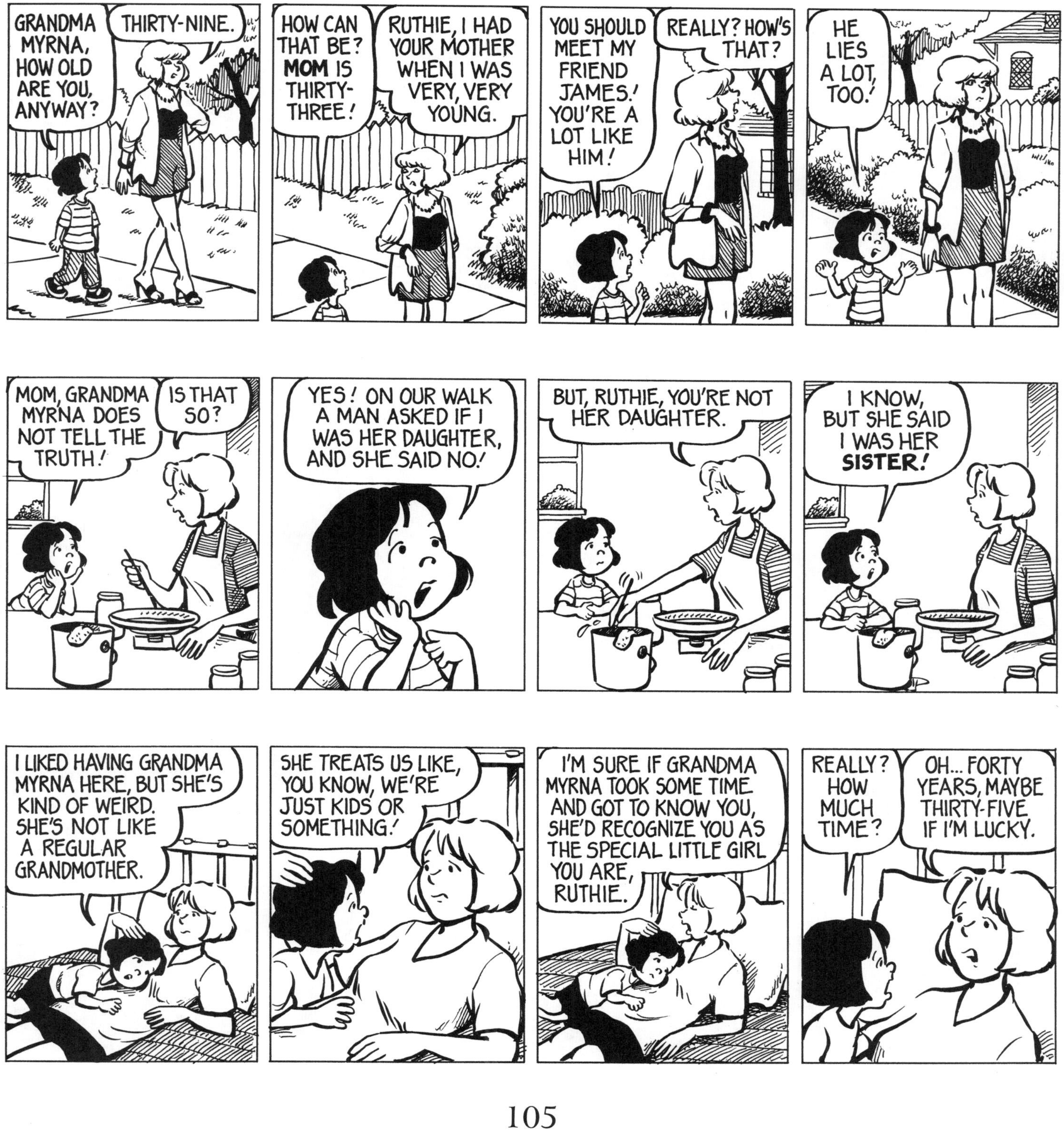
GRANDMA MYRNA, HOW OLD ARE YOU, ANYWAY?
THIRTY-NINE.
HOW CAN THAT BE? **MOM** IS THIRTY-THREE!
RUTHIE, I HAD YOUR MOTHER WHEN I WAS VERY, VERY YOUNG.
YOU SHOULD MEET MY FRIEND JAMES! YOU'RE A LOT LIKE HIM!
REALLY? HOW'S THAT?
HE LIES A LOT, TOO!
MOM, GRANDMA MYRNA DOES NOT TELL THE TRUTH!
IS THAT SO?
YES! ON OUR WALK A MAN ASKED IF I WAS HER DAUGHTER, AND SHE SAID NO!
BUT, RUTHIE, YOU'RE NOT HER DAUGHTER.
I KNOW, BUT SHE SAID I WAS HER **SISTER!**
I LIKED HAVING GRANDMA MYRNA HERE, BUT SHE'S KIND OF WEIRD. SHE'S NOT LIKE A REGULAR GRANDMOTHER.
SHE TREATS US LIKE, YOU KNOW, WE'RE JUST KIDS OR SOMETHING!
I'M SURE IF GRANDMA MYRNA TOOK SOME TIME AND GOT TO KNOW YOU, SHE'D RECOGNIZE YOU AS THE SPECIAL LITTLE GIRL YOU ARE, RUTHIE.
REALLY? HOW MUCH TIME?
OH... FORTY YEARS, MAYBE THIRTY-FIVE IF I'M LUCKY.

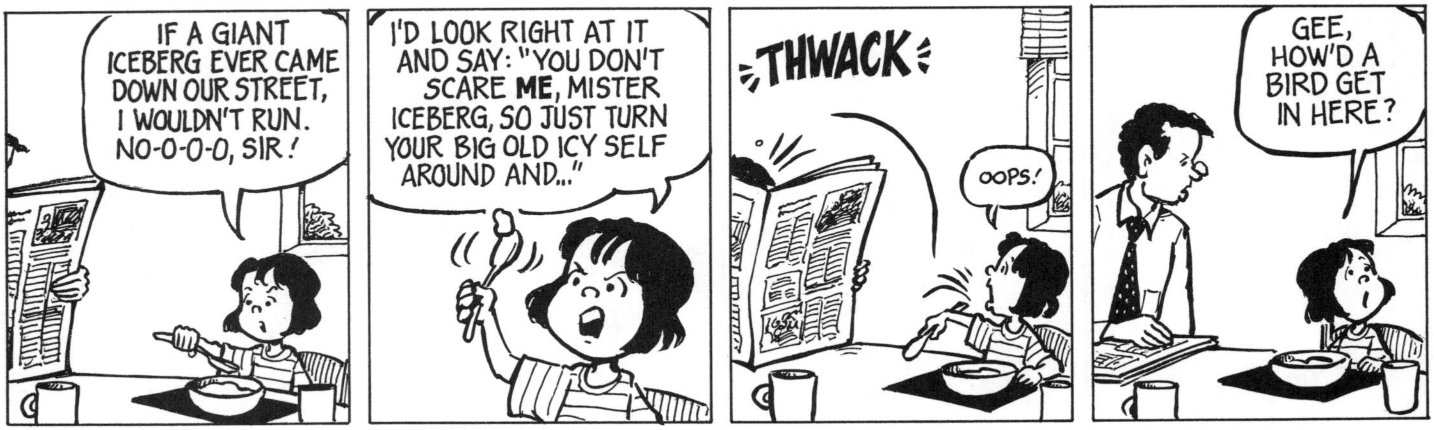
IF A GIANT ICEBERG EVER CAME DOWN OUR STREET, I WOULDN'T RUN. NO-O-O-O, SIR!
I'D LOOK RIGHT AT IT AND SAY: "YOU DON'T SCARE ME, MISTER ICEBERG, SO JUST TURN YOUR BIG OLD ICY SELF AROUND AND..."
THWACK
OOPS!
GEE, HOW'D A BIRD GET IN HERE?

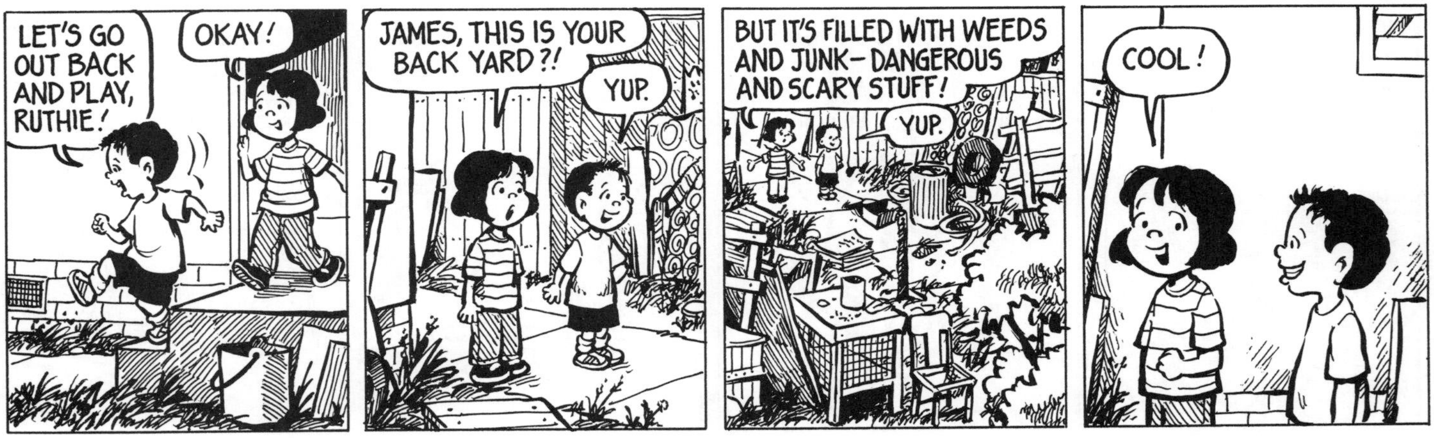
LET'S GO OUT BACK AND PLAY, RUTHIE!
OKAY!
JAMES, THIS IS YOUR BACK YARD?!
YUP.
BUT IT'S FILLED WITH WEEDS AND JUNK– DANGEROUS AND SCARY STUFF!
YUP.
COOL!

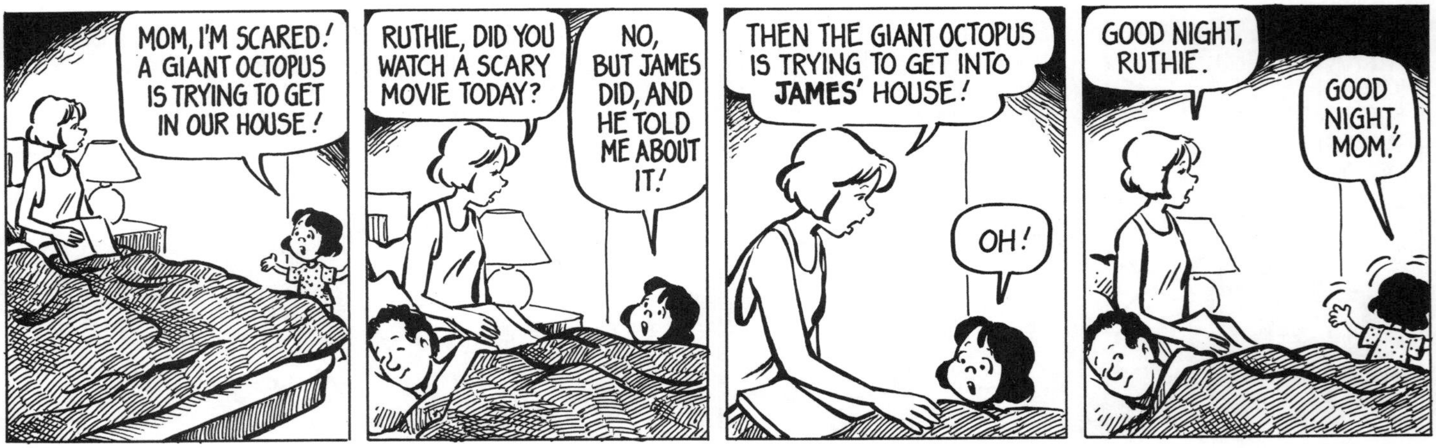
MOM, I'M SCARED! A GIANT OCTOPUS IS TRYING TO GET IN OUR HOUSE!
RUTHIE, DID YOU WATCH A SCARY MOVIE TODAY?
NO, BUT JAMES DID, AND HE TOLD ME ABOUT IT!
THEN THE GIANT OCTOPUS IS TRYING TO GET INTO JAMES' HOUSE!
OH!
GOOD NIGHT, RUTHIE.
GOOD NIGHT, MOM!

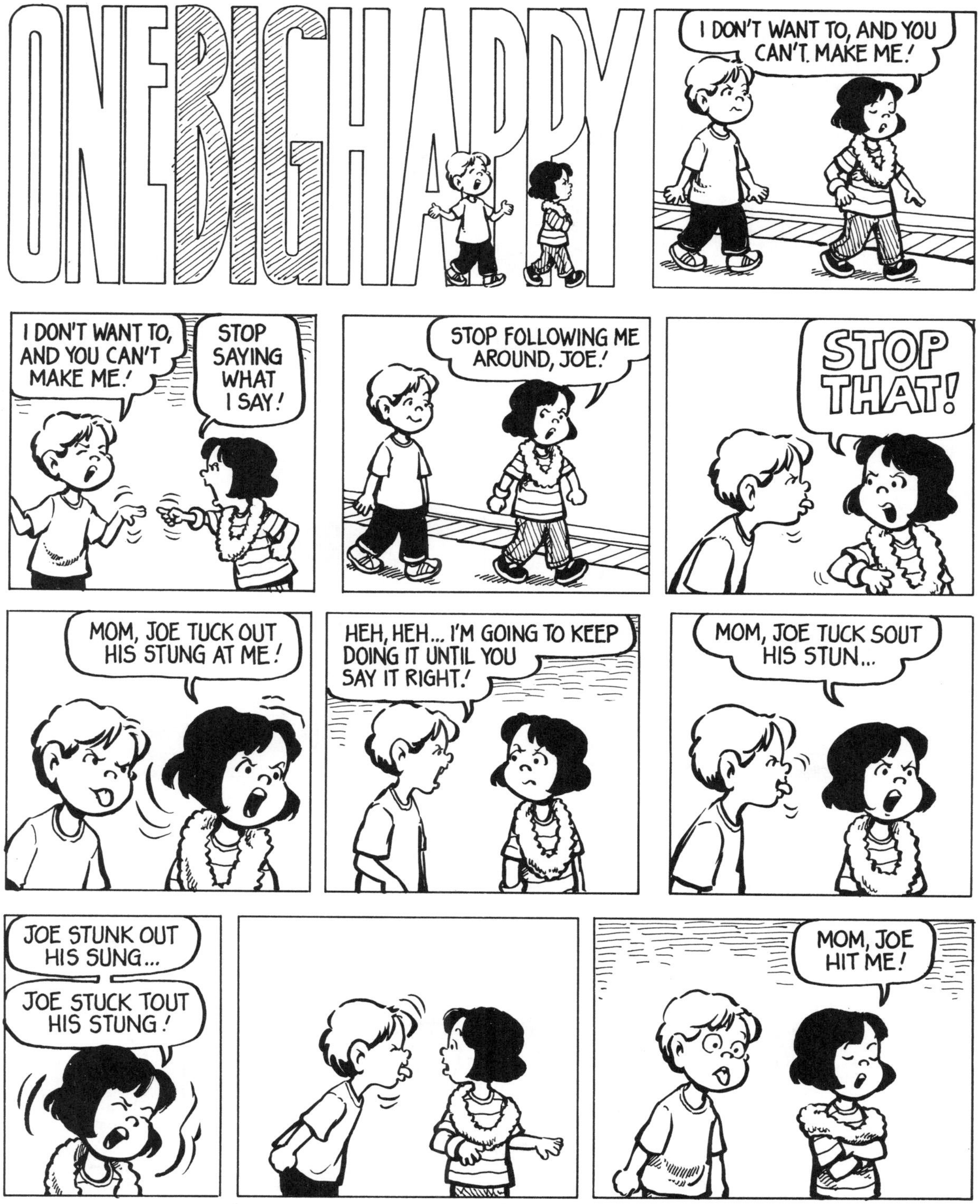
ONE BIG HAPPY
I DON'T WANT TO, AND YOU CAN'T. MAKE ME!
I DON'T WANT TO, AND YOU CAN'T MAKE ME!
STOP SAYING WHAT I SAY!
STOP FOLLOWING ME AROUND, JOE!
STOP THAT!
MOM, JOE TUCK OUT HIS STUNG AT ME!
HEH, HEH... I'M GOING TO KEEP DOING IT UNTIL YOU SAY IT RIGHT!
MOM, JOE TUCK SOUT HIS STUN...
JOE STUNK OUT HIS SUNG...
JOE STUCK TOUT HIS STUNG!
MOM, JOE HIT ME!

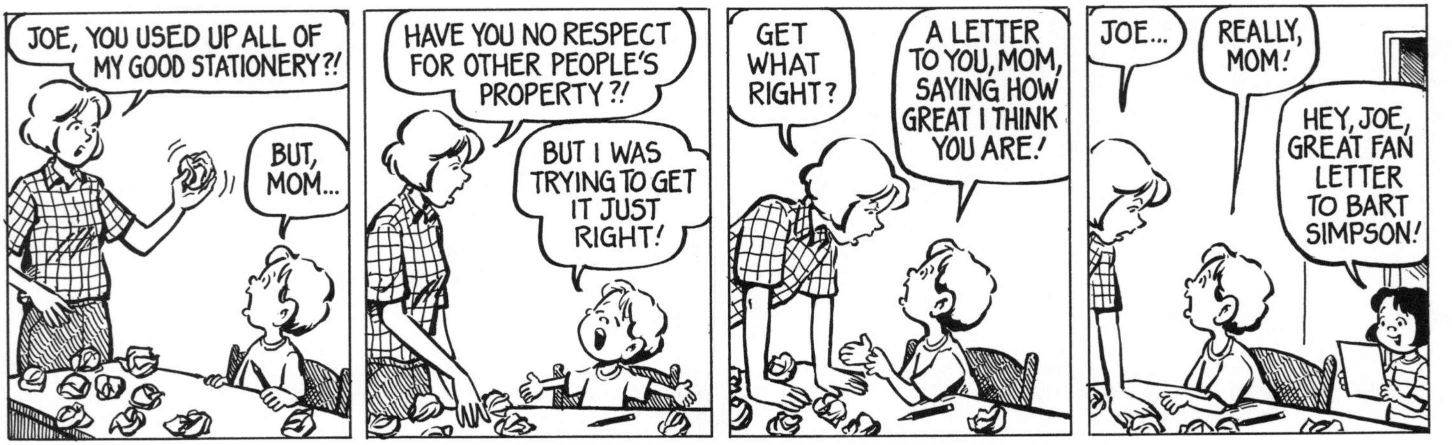
JOE, YOU USED UP ALL OF MY GOOD STATIONERY?!
BUT, MOM...
HAVE YOU NO RESPECT FOR OTHER PEOPLE'S PROPERTY?!
BUT I WAS TRYING TO GET IT JUST RIGHT!
GET WHAT RIGHT?
A LETTER TO YOU, MOM, SAYING HOW GREAT I THINK YOU ARE!
JOE...
REALLY, MOM!
HEY, JOE, GREAT FAN LETTER TO BART SIMPSON!

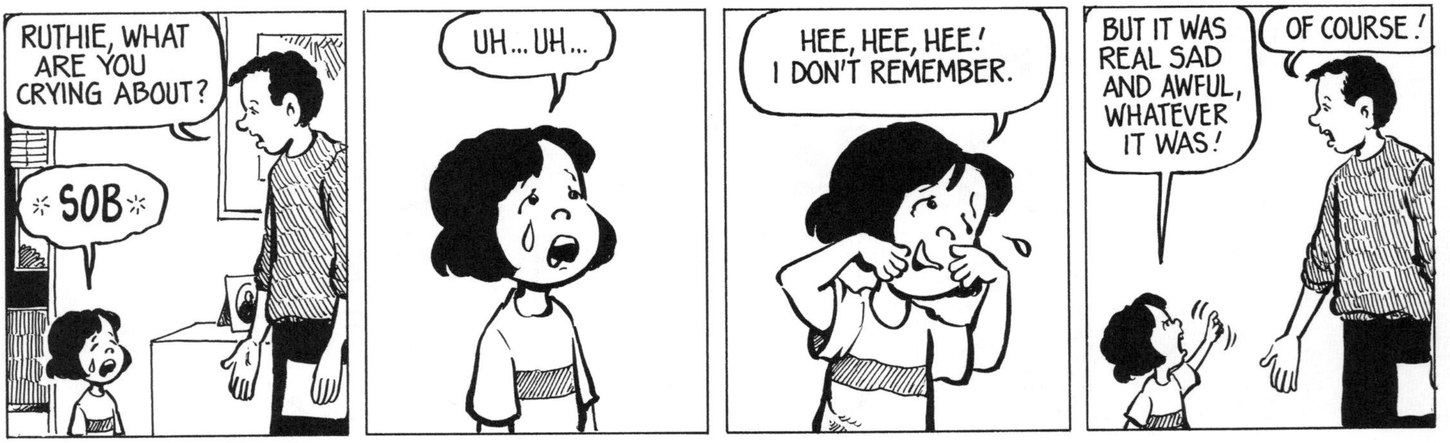
RUTHIE, WHAT ARE YOU CRYING ABOUT?
SOB
UH... UH...
HEE, HEE, HEE! I DON'T REMEMBER.
BUT IT WAS REAL SAD AND AWFUL, WHATEVER IT WAS!
OF COURSE!

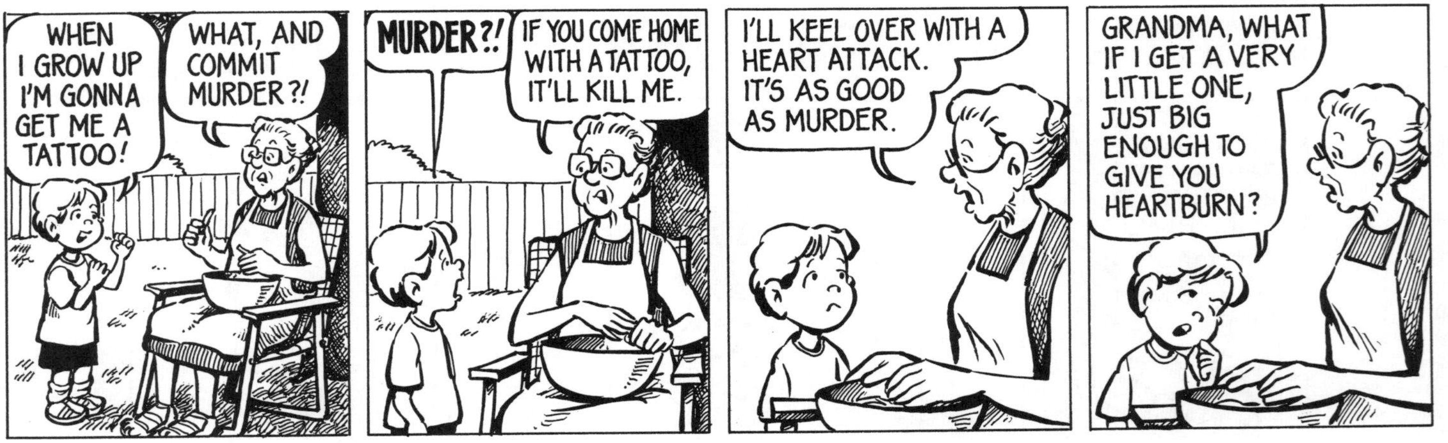
WHEN I GROW UP I'M GONNA GET ME A TATTOO!
WHAT, AND COMMIT MURDER?!
MURDER?!
IF YOU COME HOME WITH A TATTOO, IT'LL KILL ME.
I'LL KEEL OVER WITH A HEART ATTACK. IT'S AS GOOD AS MURDER.
GRANDMA, WHAT IF I GET A VERY LITTLE ONE, JUST BIG ENOUGH TO GIVE YOU HEARTBURN?

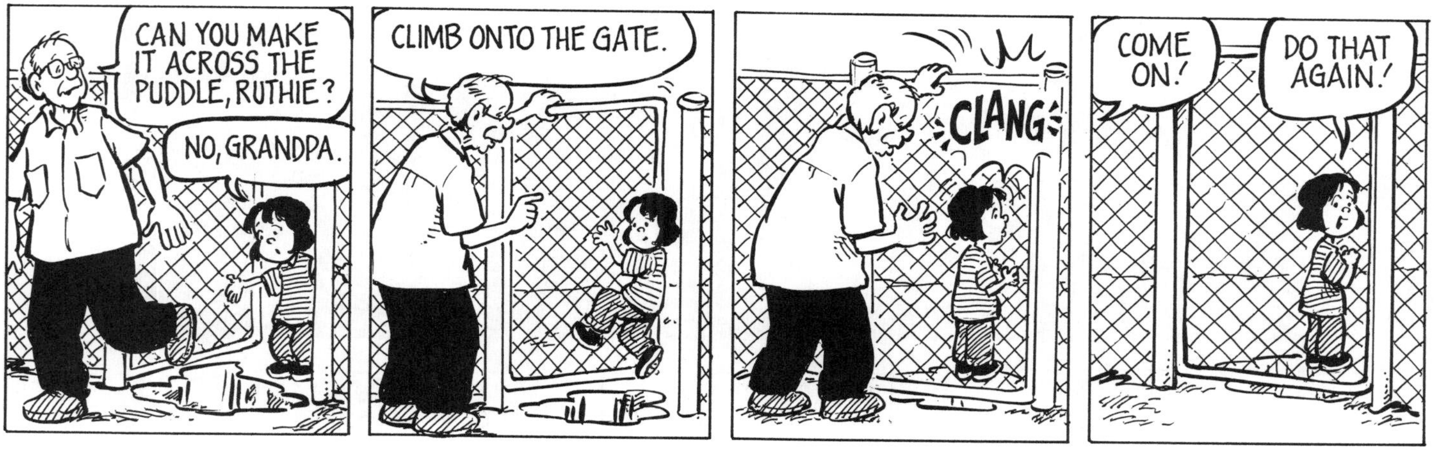
CAN YOU MAKE IT ACROSS THE PUDDLE, RUTHIE?
NO, GRANDPA.
CLIMB ONTO THE GATE.
CLANG
COME ON!
DO THAT AGAIN!

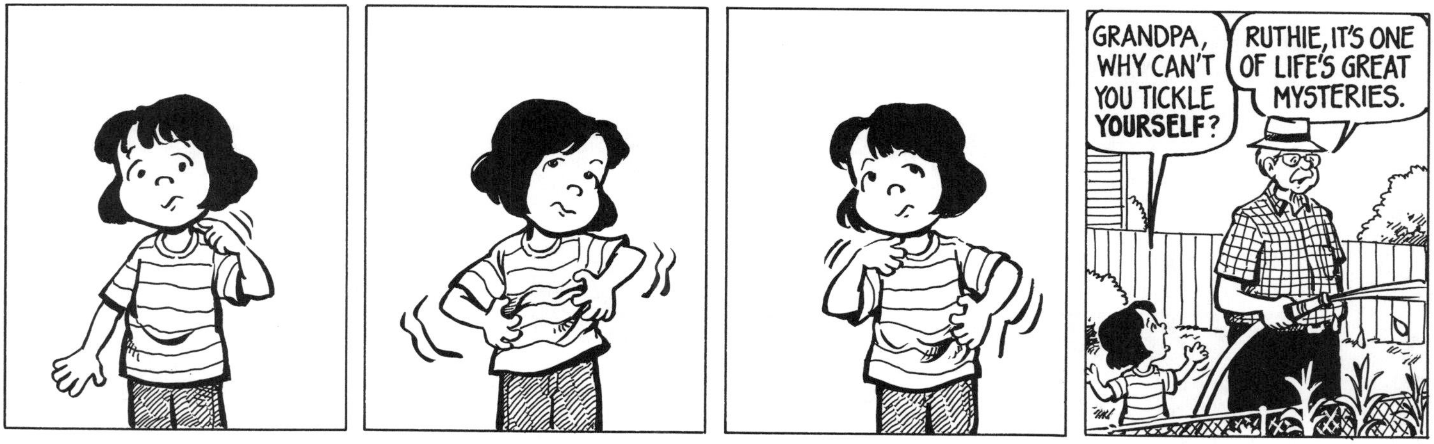
GRANDPA, WHY CAN'T YOU TICKLE **YOURSELF**?
RUTHIE, IT'S ONE OF LIFE'S GREAT MYSTERIES.

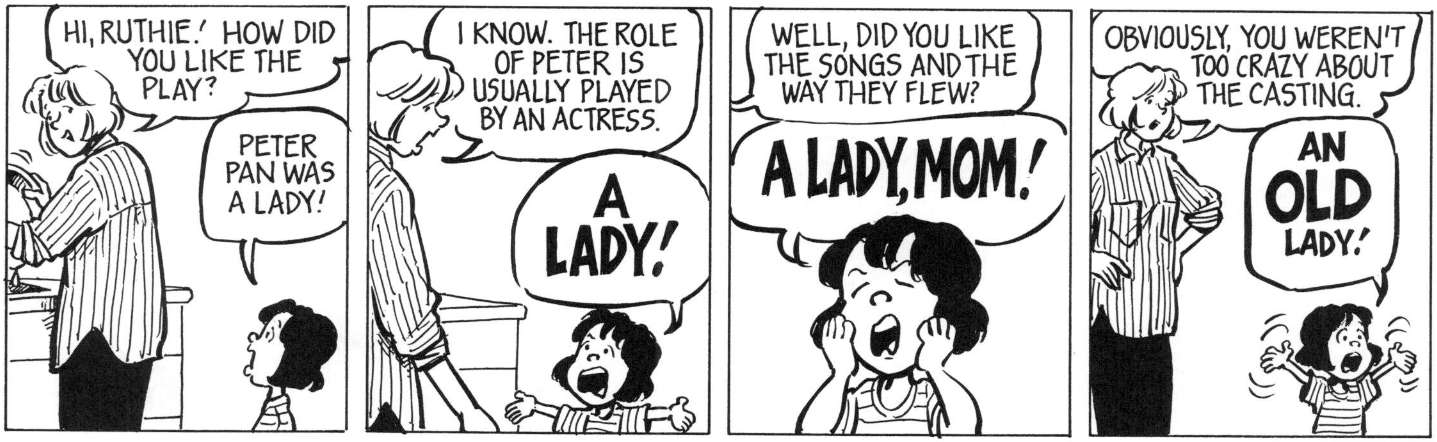
HI, RUTHIE! HOW DID YOU LIKE THE PLAY?
PETER PAN WAS A LADY!
I KNOW. THE ROLE OF PETER IS USUALLY PLAYED BY AN ACTRESS.
A LADY!
WELL, DID YOU LIKE THE SONGS AND THE WAY THEY FLEW?
A LADY, MOM!
OBVIOUSLY, YOU WEREN'T TOO CRAZY ABOUT THE CASTING.
AN OLD LADY!

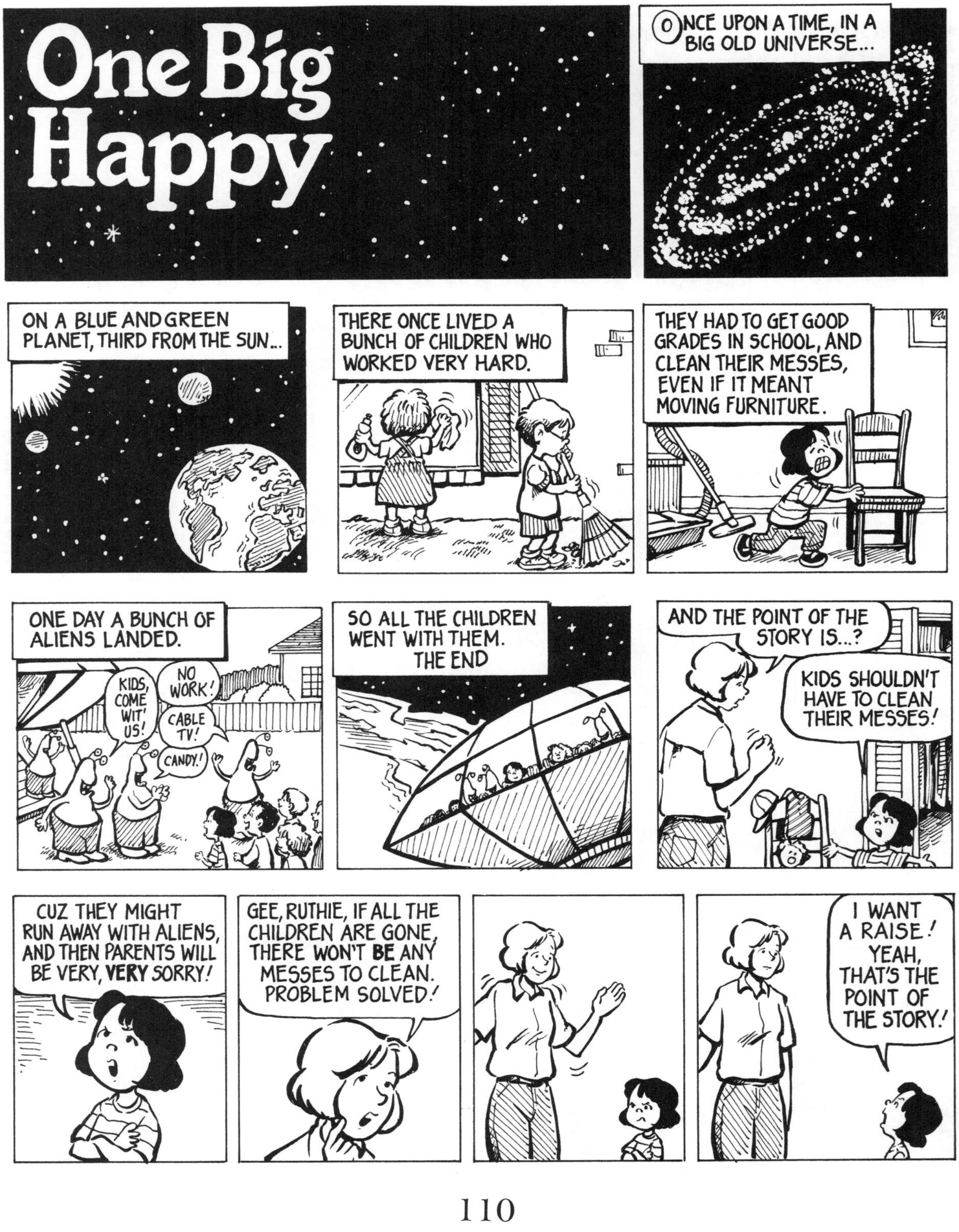
One Big Happy
ONCE UPON A TIME, IN A BIG OLD UNIVERSE...
ON A BLUE AND GREEN PLANET, THIRD FROM THE SUN...
THERE ONCE LIVED A BUNCH OF CHILDREN WHO WORKED VERY HARD.
THEY HAD TO GET GOOD GRADES IN SCHOOL, AND CLEAN THEIR MESSES, EVEN IF IT MEANT MOVING FURNITURE.
ONE DAY A BUNCH OF ALIENS LANDED.
KIDS, COME WIT' US!
NO WORK!
CABLE TV!
CANDY!
SO ALL THE CHILDREN WENT WITH THEM. THE END
AND THE POINT OF THE STORY IS...?
KIDS SHOULDN'T HAVE TO CLEAN THEIR MESSES!
CUZ THEY MIGHT RUN AWAY WITH ALIENS, AND THEN PARENTS WILL BE VERY, **VERY** SORRY!
GEE, RUTHIE, IF ALL THE CHILDREN ARE GONE, THERE WON'T **BE** ANY MESSES TO CLEAN. PROBLEM SOLVED!
I WANT A RAISE!
YEAH, THAT'S THE POINT OF THE STORY!

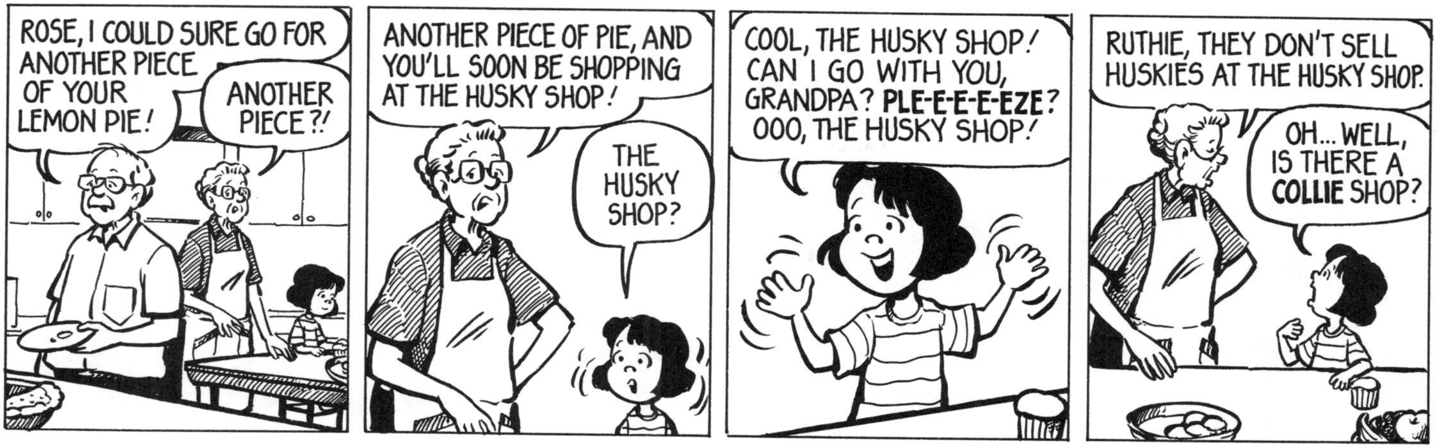
ROSE, I COULD SURE GO FOR ANOTHER PIECE OF YOUR LEMON PIE!
ANOTHER PIECE?!
ANOTHER PIECE OF PIE, AND YOU'LL SOON BE SHOPPING AT THE HUSKY SHOP!
THE HUSKY SHOP?
COOL, THE HUSKY SHOP! CAN I GO WITH YOU, GRANDPA? PLE-E-E-E-EZE? OOO, THE HUSKY SHOP!
RUTHIE, THEY DON'T SELL HUSKIES AT THE HUSKY SHOP.
OH... WELL, IS THERE A COLLIE SHOP?

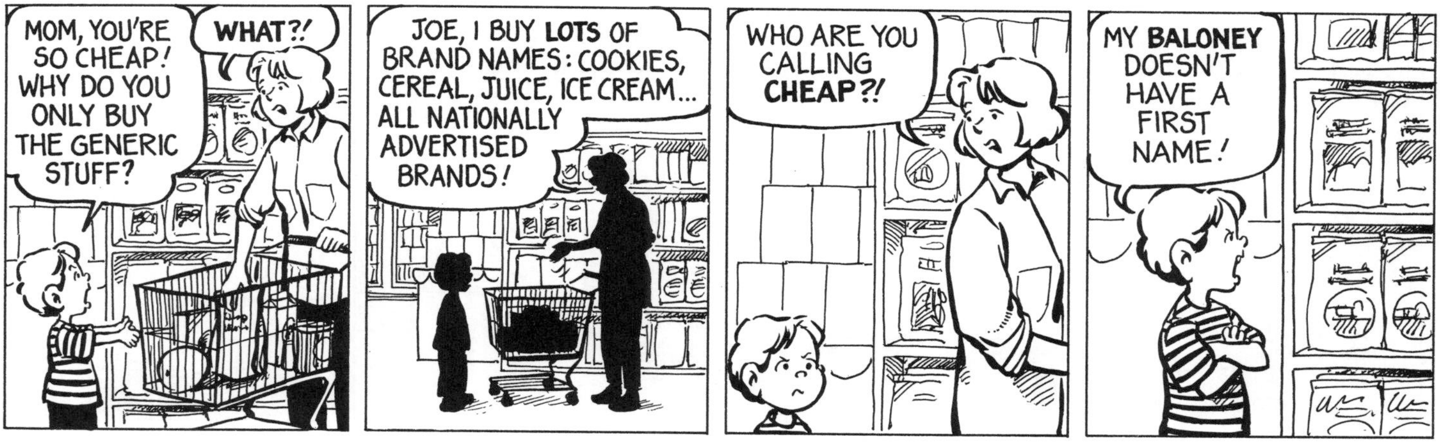
MOM, YOU'RE SO CHEAP! WHY DO YOU ONLY BUY THE GENERIC STUFF?
WHAT?!
JOE, I BUY LOTS OF BRAND NAMES: COOKIES, CEREAL, JUICE, ICE CREAM... ALL NATIONALLY ADVERTISED BRANDS!
WHO ARE YOU CALLING CHEAP?!
MY BALONEY DOESN'T HAVE A FIRST NAME!

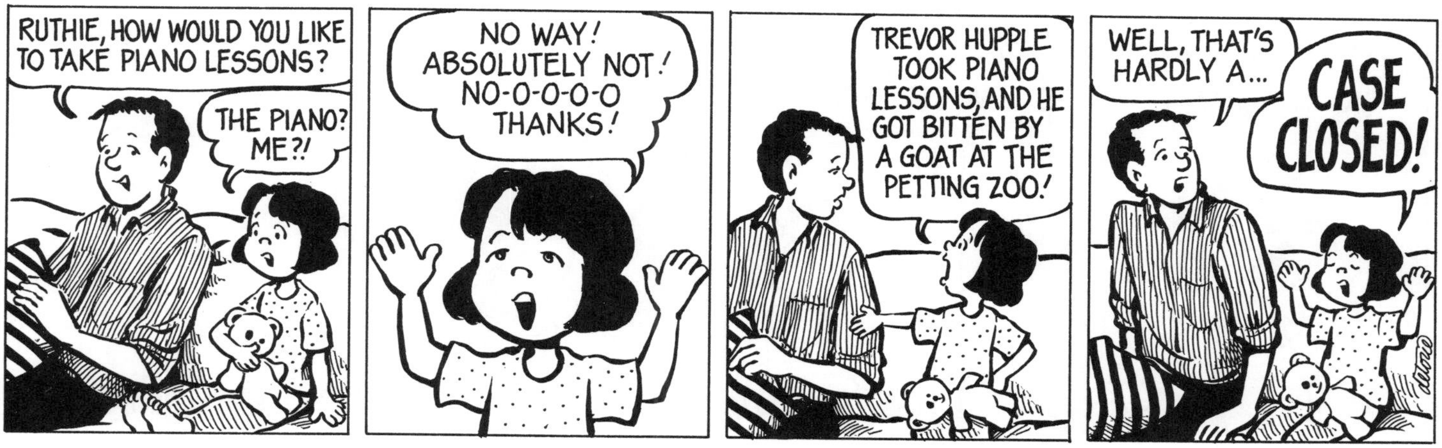
RUTHIE, HOW WOULD YOU LIKE TO TAKE PIANO LESSONS?
THE PIANO? ME?!
NO WAY! ABSOLUTELY NOT! NO-O-O-O-O THANKS!
TREVOR HUPPLE TOOK PIANO LESSONS, AND HE GOT BITTEN BY A GOAT AT THE PETTING ZOO!
WELL, THAT'S HARDLY A...
CASE CLOSED!

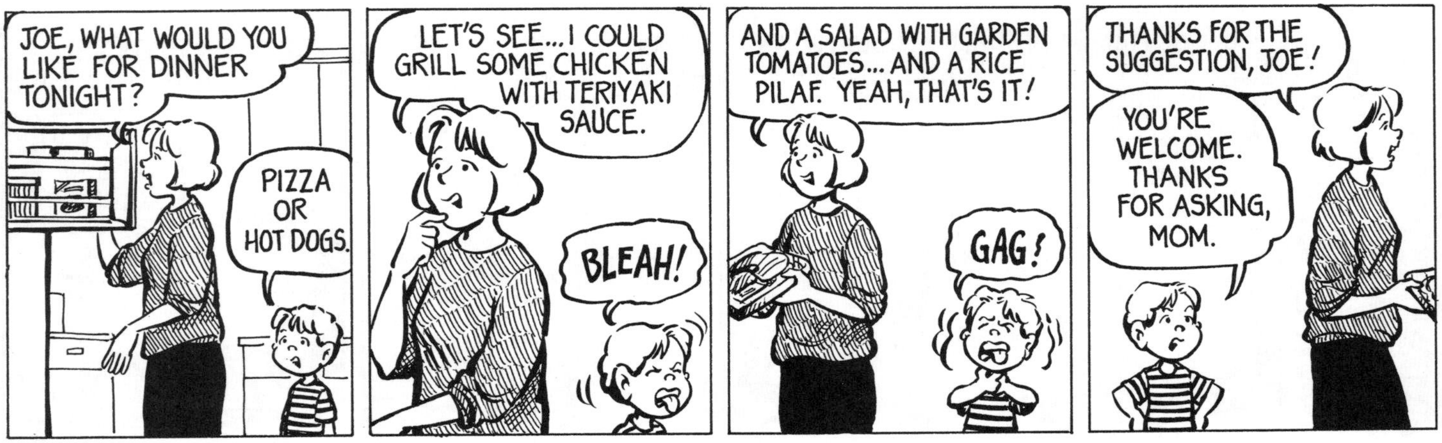
JOE, WHAT WOULD YOU LIKE FOR DINNER TONIGHT?
PIZZA OR HOT DOGS.
LET'S SEE... I COULD GRILL SOME CHICKEN WITH TERIYAKI SAUCE.
BLEAH!
AND A SALAD WITH GARDEN TOMATOES... AND A RICE PILAF. YEAH, THAT'S IT!
GAG!
THANKS FOR THE SUGGESTION, JOE!
YOU'RE WELCOME. THANKS FOR ASKING, MOM.

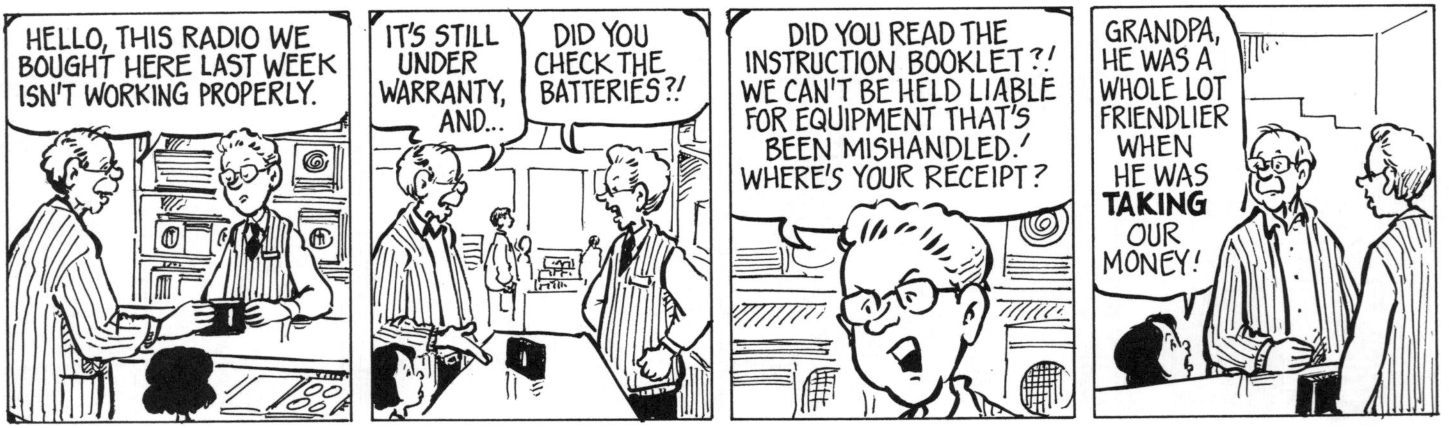
HELLO, THIS RADIO WE BOUGHT HERE LAST WEEK ISN'T WORKING PROPERLY.
IT'S STILL UNDER WARRANTY, AND...
DID YOU CHECK THE BATTERIES?!
DID YOU READ THE INSTRUCTION BOOKLET?! WE CAN'T BE HELD LIABLE FOR EQUIPMENT THAT'S BEEN MISHANDLED! WHERE'S YOUR RECEIPT?
GRANDPA, HE WAS A WHOLE LOT FRIENDLIER WHEN HE WAS **TAKING** OUR MONEY!

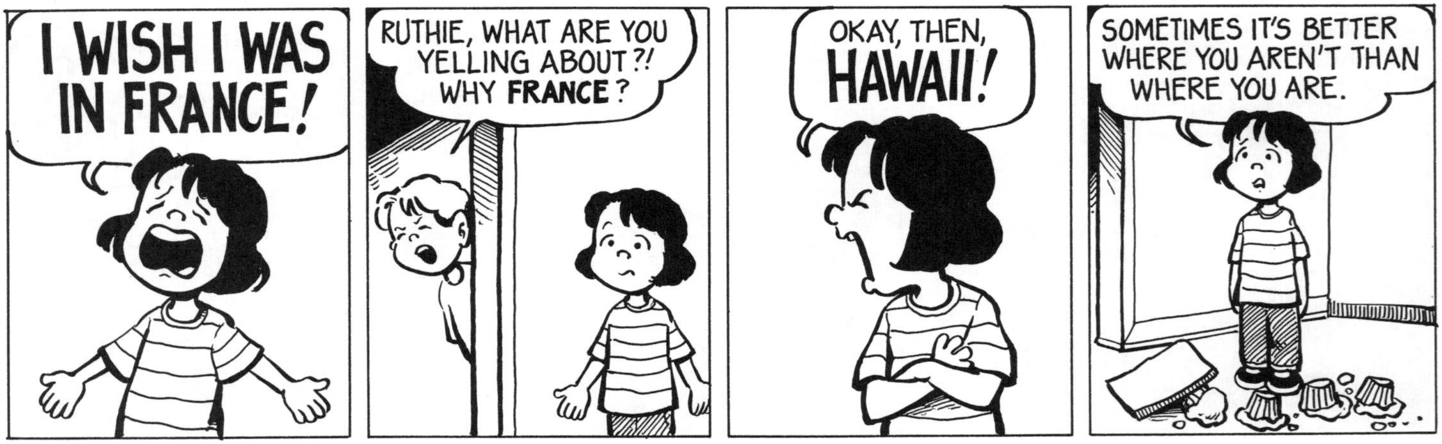
I WISH I WAS IN FRANCE!
RUTHIE, WHAT ARE YOU YELLING ABOUT?! WHY **FRANCE**?
OKAY, THEN, HAWAII!
SOMETIMES IT'S BETTER WHERE YOU AREN'T THAN WHERE YOU ARE.

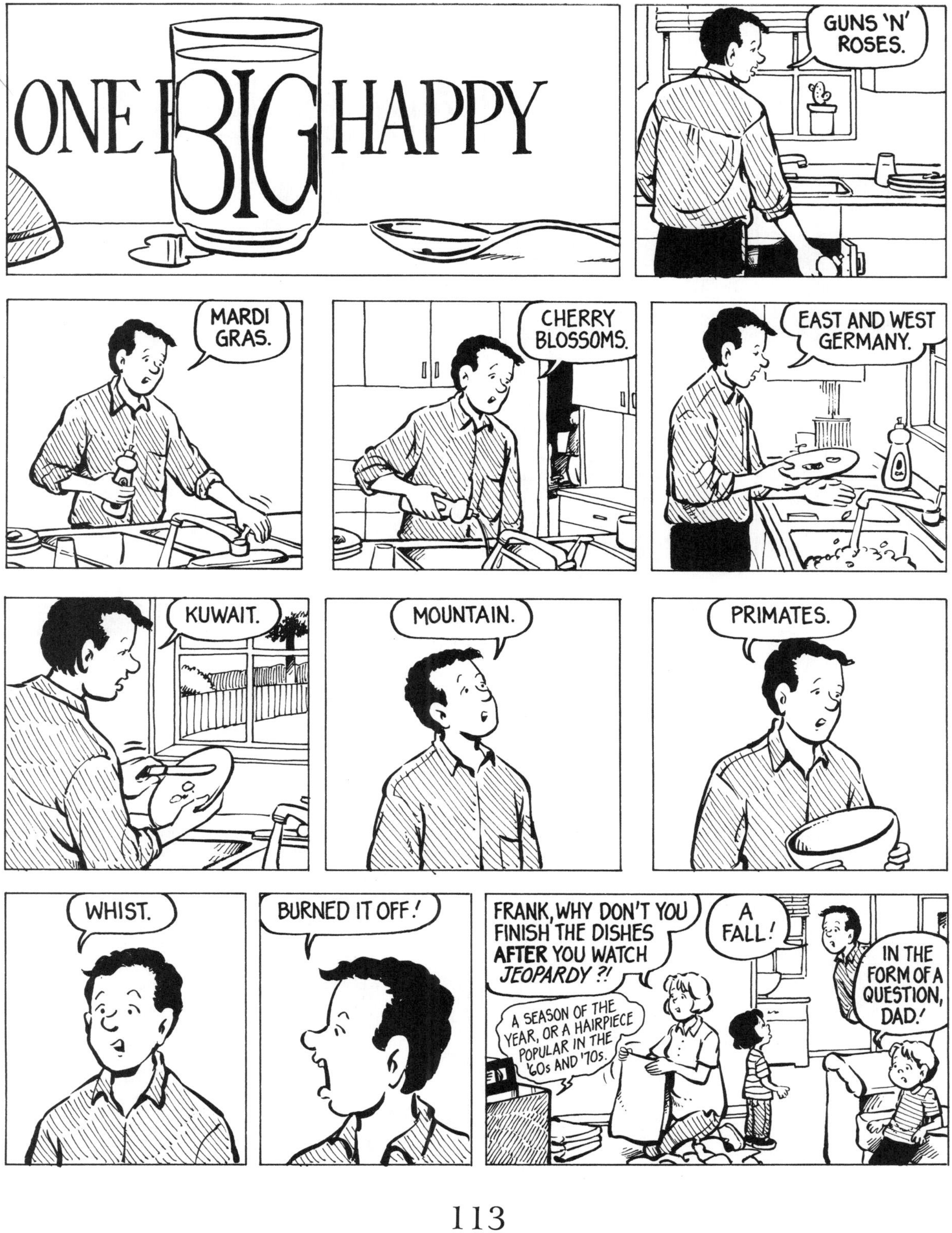
ONE BIG HAPPY
GUNS 'N' ROSES.
MARDI GRAS.
CHERRY BLOSSOMS.
EAST AND WEST GERMANY.
KUWAIT.
MOUNTAIN.
PRIMATES.
WHIST.
BURNED IT OFF!
FRANK, WHY DON'T YOU FINISH THE DISHES AFTER YOU WATCH JEOPARDY?!
A SEASON OF THE YEAR, OR A HAIRPIECE POPULAR IN THE '60s AND '70s.
A FALL!
IN THE FORM OF A QUESTION, DAD!

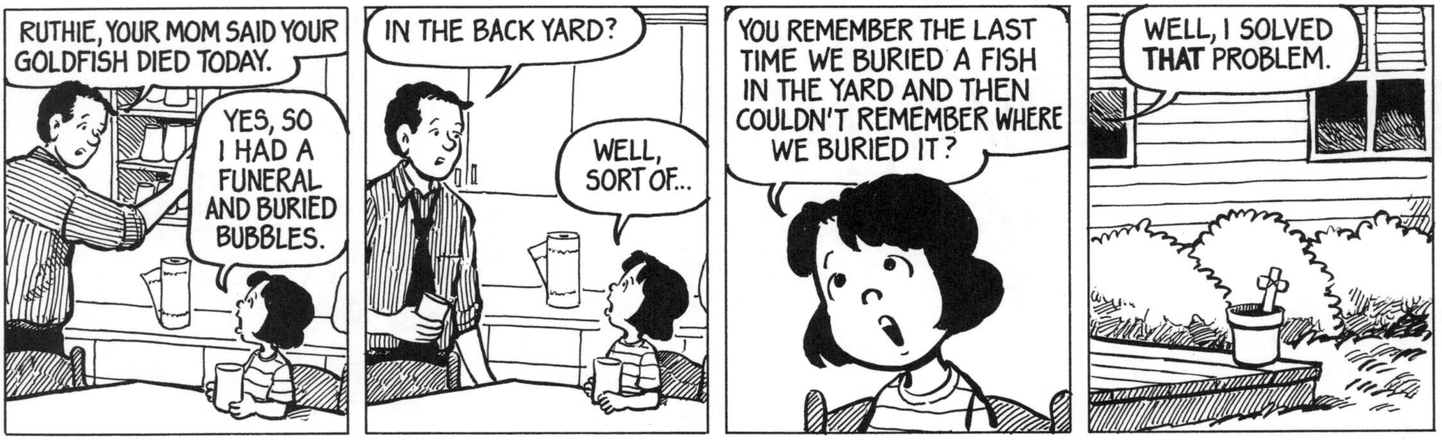
RUTHIE, YOUR MOM SAID YOUR GOLDFISH DIED TODAY.
YES, SO I HAD A FUNERAL AND BURIED BUBBLES.
IN THE BACK YARD?
WELL, SORT OF...
YOU REMEMBER THE LAST TIME WE BURIED A FISH IN THE YARD AND THEN COULDN'T REMEMBER WHERE WE BURIED IT?
WELL, I SOLVED THAT PROBLEM.

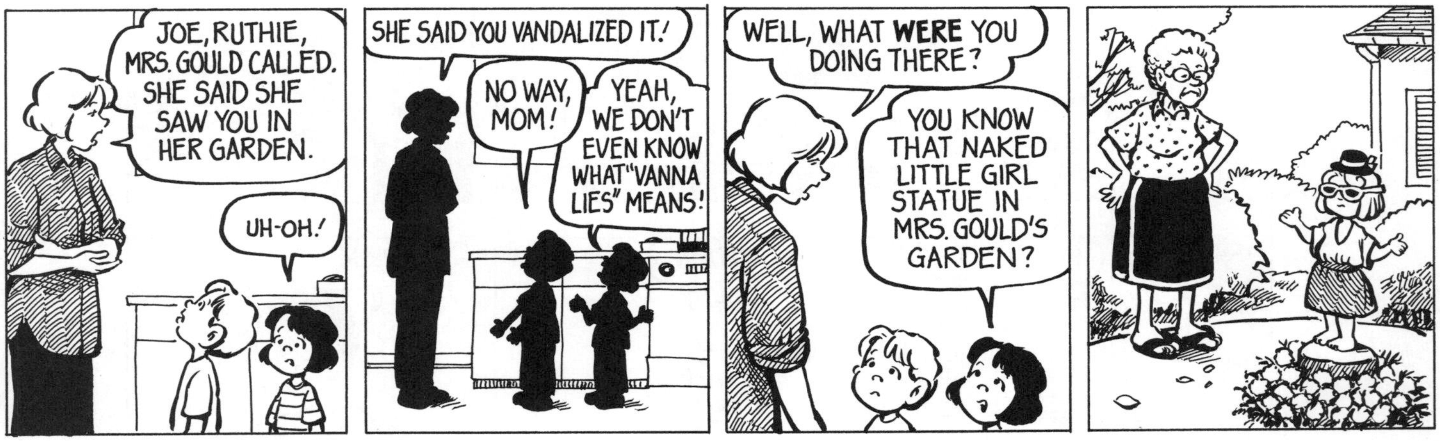
JOE, RUTHIE, MRS. GOULD CALLED. SHE SAID SHE SAW YOU IN HER GARDEN.
UH-OH!
SHE SAID YOU VANDALIZED IT!
NO WAY, MOM!
YEAH, WE DON'T EVEN KNOW WHAT "VANNA LIES" MEANS!
WELL, WHAT WERE YOU DOING THERE?
YOU KNOW THAT NAKED LITTLE GIRL STATUE IN MRS. GOULD'S GARDEN?

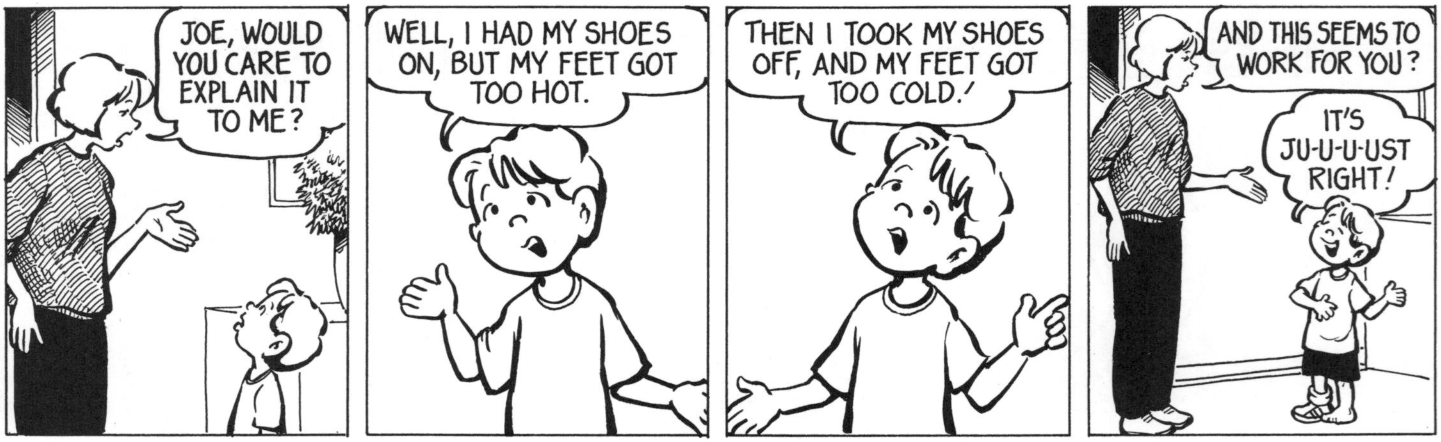
JOE, WOULD YOU CARE TO EXPLAIN IT TO ME?
WELL, I HAD MY SHOES ON, BUT MY FEET GOT TOO HOT.
THEN I TOOK MY SHOES OFF, AND MY FEET GOT TOO COLD!
AND THIS SEEMS TO WORK FOR YOU?
IT'S JU-U-U-UST RIGHT!

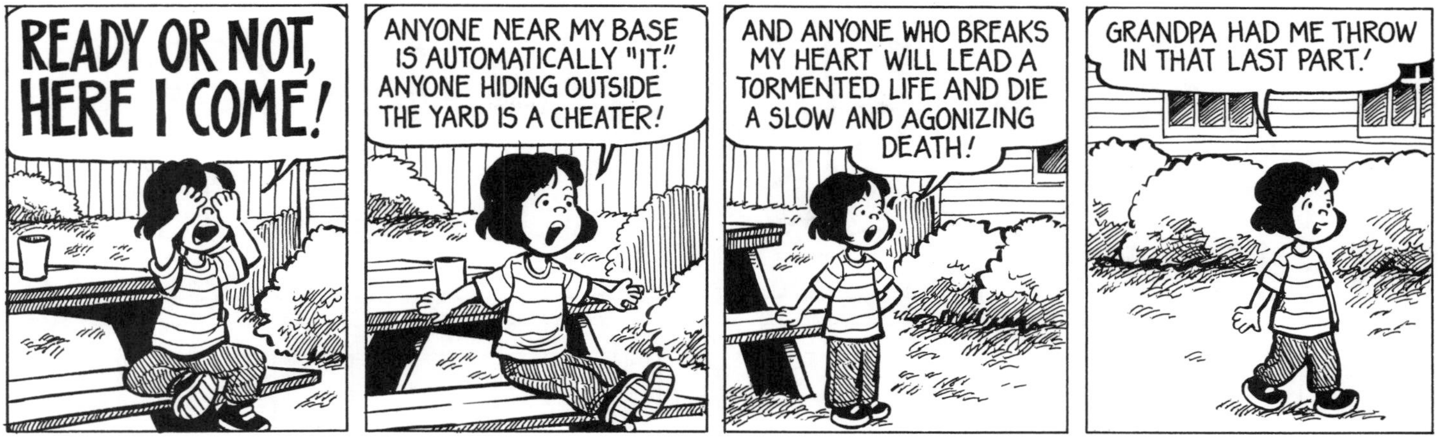
READY OR NOT, HERE I COME!
ANYONE NEAR MY BASE IS AUTOMATICALLY "IT." ANYONE HIDING OUTSIDE THE YARD IS A CHEATER!
AND ANYONE WHO BREAKS MY HEART WILL LEAD A TORMENTED LIFE AND DIE A SLOW AND AGONIZING DEATH!
GRANDPA HAD ME THROW IN THAT LAST PART!

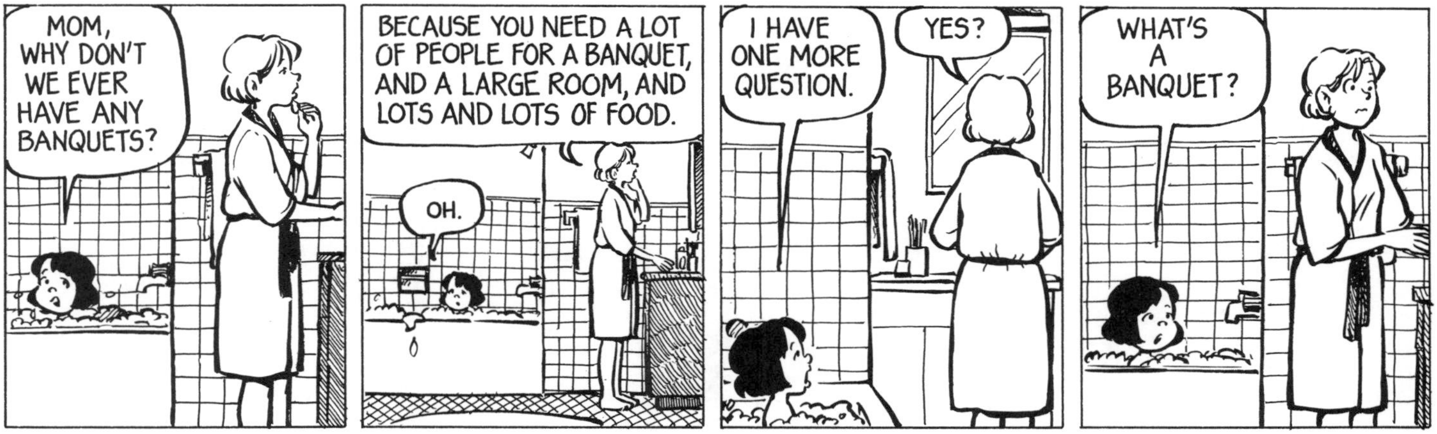
MOM, WHY DON'T WE EVER HAVE ANY BANQUETS?
BECAUSE YOU NEED A LOT OF PEOPLE FOR A BANQUET, AND A LARGE ROOM, AND LOTS AND LOTS OF FOOD.
OH.
I HAVE ONE MORE QUESTION.
YES?
WHAT'S A BANQUET?

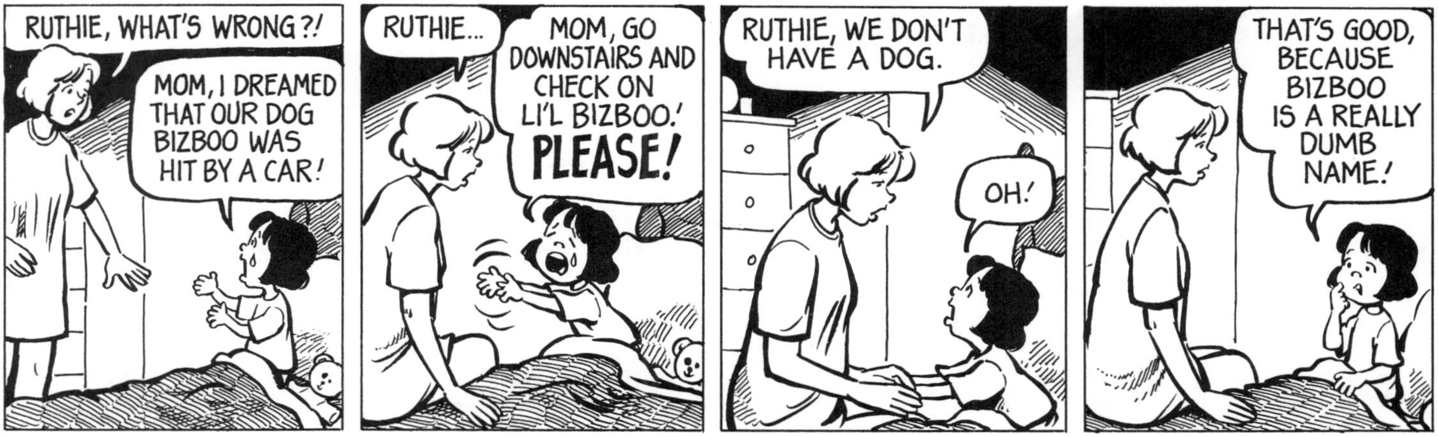
RUTHIE, WHAT'S WRONG?!
MOM, I DREAMED THAT OUR DOG BIZBOO WAS HIT BY A CAR!
RUTHIE...
MOM, GO DOWNSTAIRS AND CHECK ON LI'L BIZBOO! PLEASE!
RUTHIE, WE DON'T HAVE A DOG.
OH!
THAT'S GOOD, BECAUSE BIZBOO IS A REALLY DUMB NAME!

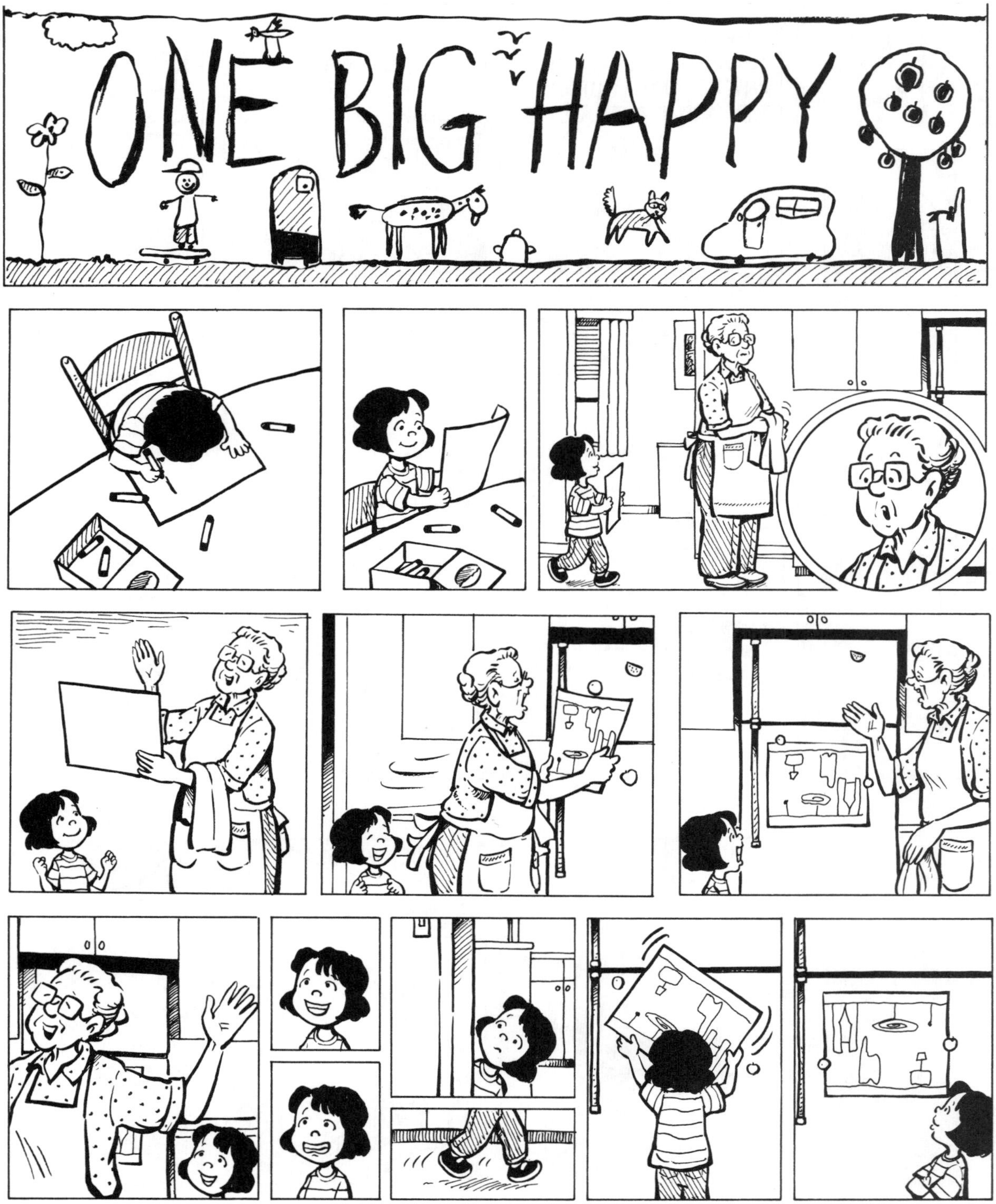
ONE BIG HAPPY

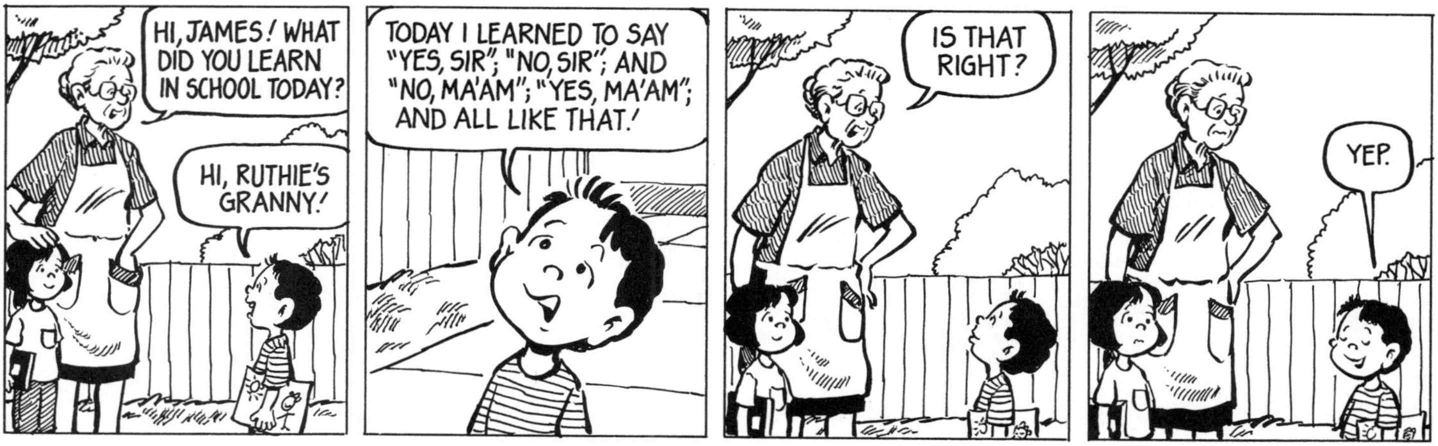
HI, JAMES! WHAT DID YOU LEARN IN SCHOOL TODAY?
HI, RUTHIE'S GRANNY!
TODAY I LEARNED TO SAY "YES, SIR"; "NO, SIR"; AND "NO, MA'AM"; "YES, MA'AM"; AND ALL LIKE THAT!
IS THAT RIGHT?
YEP.

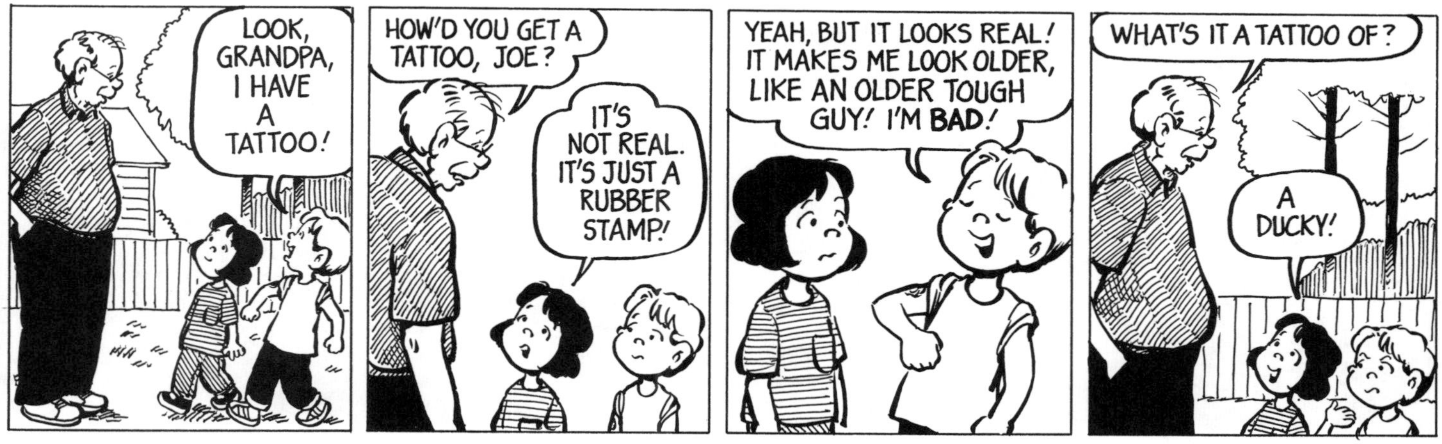
LOOK, GRANDPA, I HAVE A TATTOO!
HOW'D YOU GET A TATTOO, JOE?
IT'S NOT REAL. IT'S JUST A RUBBER STAMP!
YEAH, BUT IT LOOKS REAL! IT MAKES ME LOOK OLDER, LIKE AN OLDER TOUGH GUY! I'M BAD!
WHAT'S IT A TATTOO OF?
A DUCKY!

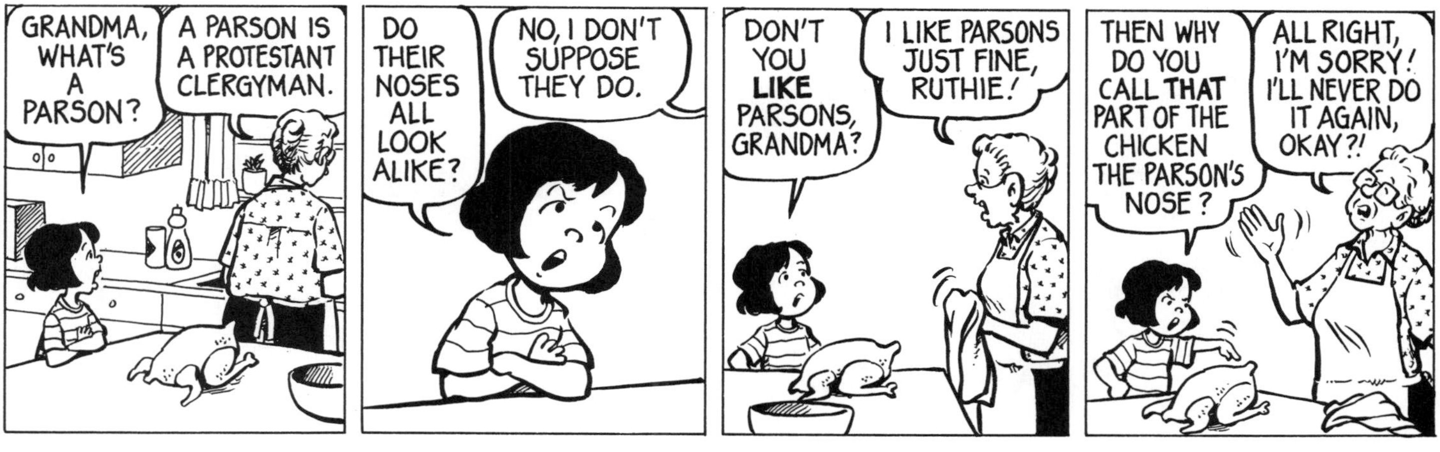
GRANDMA, WHAT'S A PARSON?
A PARSON IS A PROTESTANT CLERGYMAN.
DO THEIR NOSES ALL LOOK ALIKE?
NO, I DON'T SUPPOSE THEY DO.
DON'T YOU LIKE PARSONS, GRANDMA?
I LIKE PARSONS JUST FINE, RUTHIE!
THEN WHY DO YOU CALL THAT PART OF THE CHICKEN THE PARSON'S NOSE?
ALL RIGHT, I'M SORRY! I'LL NEVER DO IT AGAIN, OKAY?!

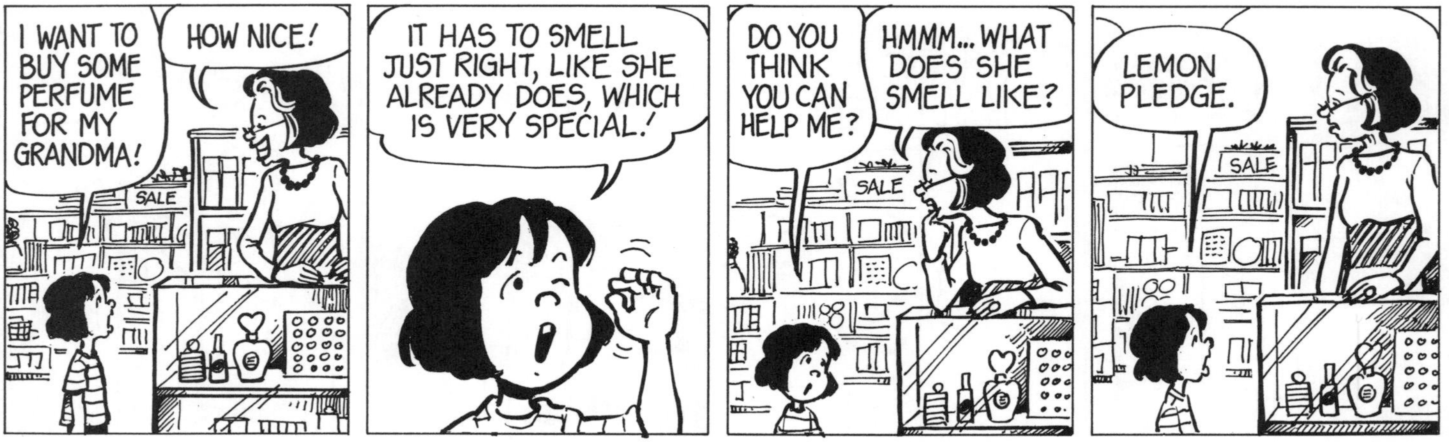
I WANT TO BUY SOME PERFUME FOR MY GRANDMA!
HOW NICE!
SALE
IT HAS TO SMELL JUST RIGHT, LIKE SHE ALREADY DOES, WHICH IS VERY SPECIAL!
DO YOU THINK YOU CAN HELP ME?
HMMM... WHAT DOES SHE SMELL LIKE?
SALE
LEMON PLEDGE.
SALE

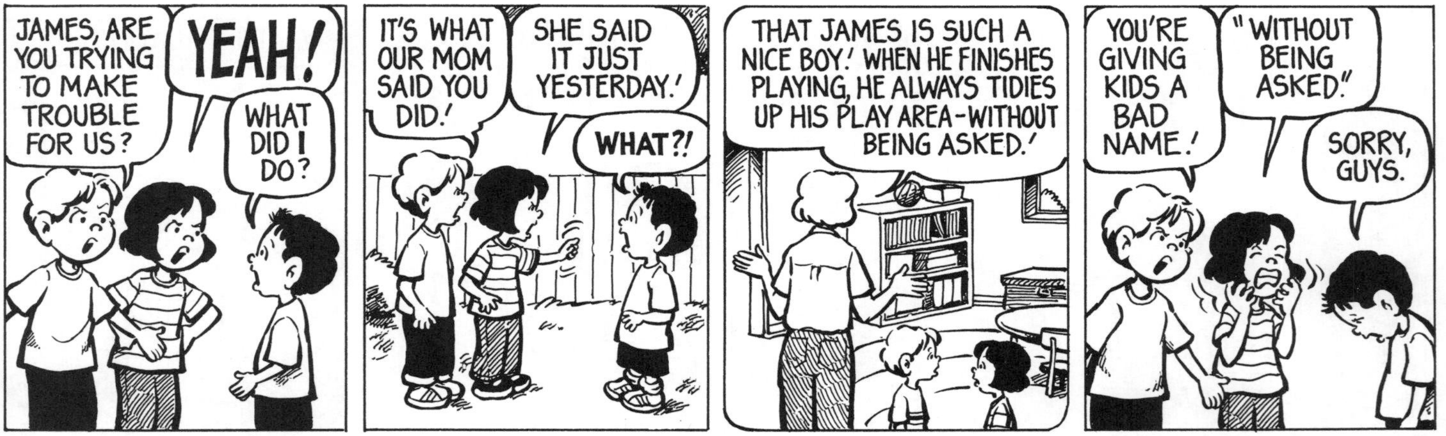
JAMES, ARE YOU TRYING TO MAKE TROUBLE FOR US?
YEAH!
WHAT DID I DO?
IT'S WHAT OUR MOM SAID YOU DID!
SHE SAID IT JUST YESTERDAY!
WHAT?!
THAT JAMES IS SUCH A NICE BOY! WHEN HE FINISHES PLAYING, HE ALWAYS TIDIES UP HIS PLAY AREA-WITHOUT BEING ASKED!
YOU'RE GIVING KIDS A BAD NAME!
"WITHOUT BEING ASKED!"
SORRY, GUYS.

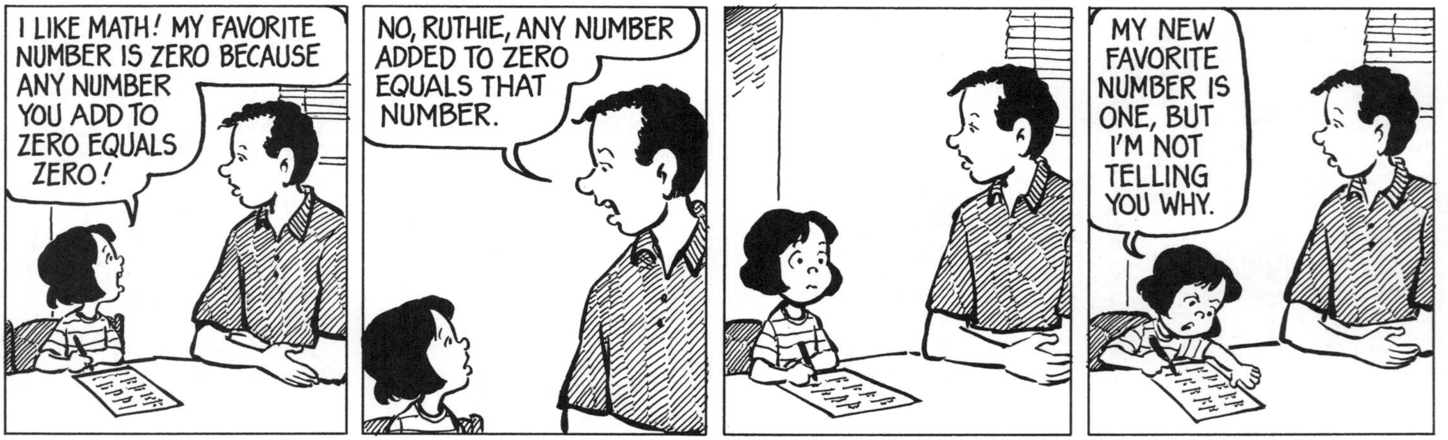
I LIKE MATH! MY FAVORITE NUMBER IS ZERO BECAUSE ANY NUMBER YOU ADD TO ZERO EQUALS ZERO!
NO, RUTHIE, ANY NUMBER ADDED TO ZERO EQUALS THAT NUMBER.
MY NEW FAVORITE NUMBER IS ONE, BUT I'M NOT TELLING YOU WHY.

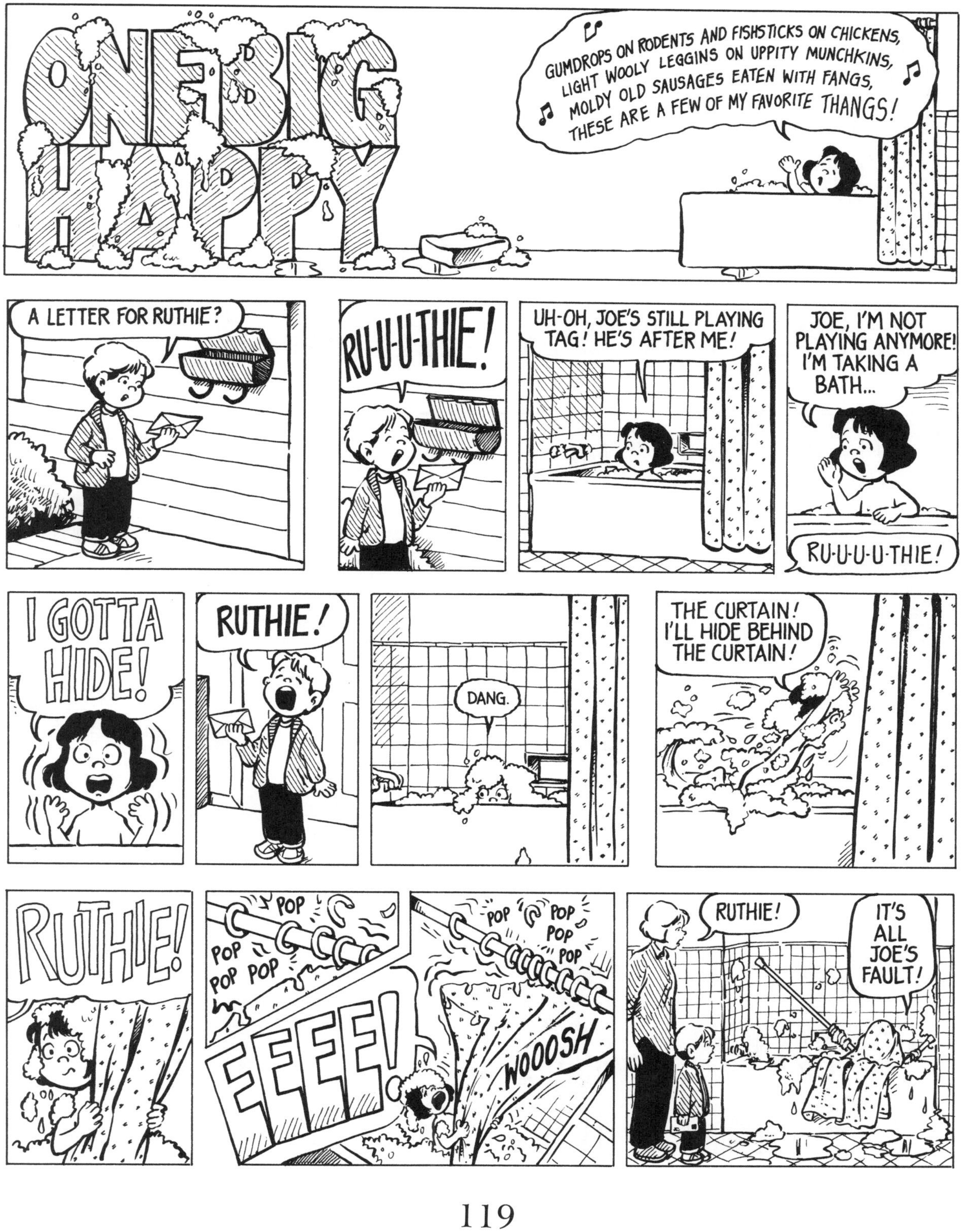
ONE BIG HAPPY
GUMDROPS ON RODENTS AND FISHSTICKS ON CHICKENS, LIGHT WOOLY LEGGINS ON UPPITY MUNCHKINS, MOLDY OLD SAUSAGES EATEN WITH FANGS, THESE ARE A FEW OF MY FAVORITE THANGS!
A LETTER FOR RUTHIE?
RU-U-U-THIE!
UH-OH, JOE'S STILL PLAYING TAG! HE'S AFTER ME!
JOE, I'M NOT PLAYING ANYMORE! I'M TAKING A BATH...
RU-U-U-U-THIE!
I GOTTA HIDE!
RUTHIE!
DANG.
THE CURTAIN! I'LL HIDE BEHIND THE CURTAIN!
RUTHIE!
POP
POP POP POP
EEEE!
POP POP POP POP
WOOOSH
RUTHIE!
IT'S ALL JOE'S FAULT!

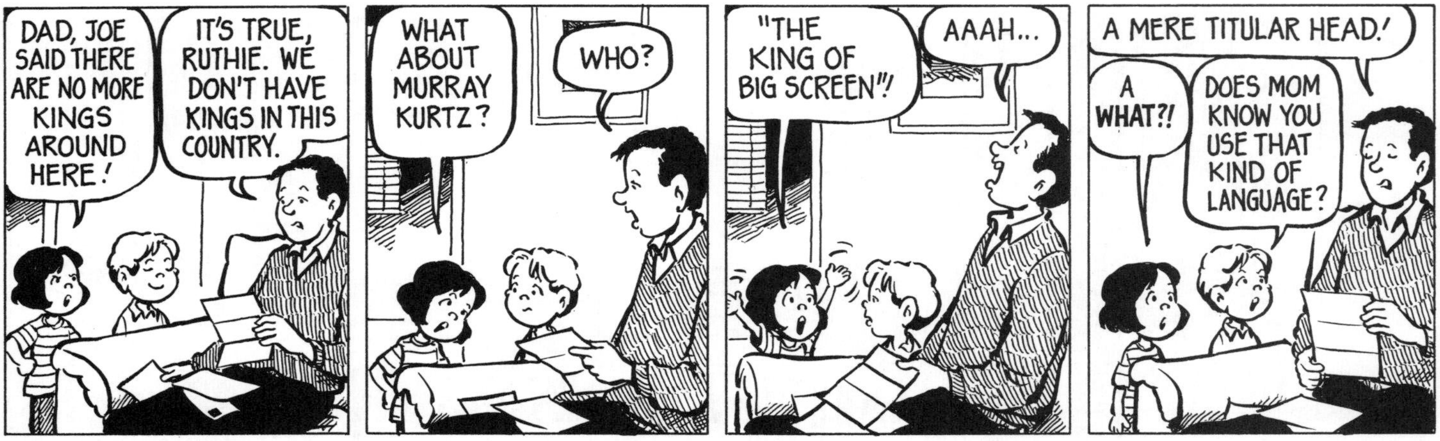
DAD, JOE SAID THERE ARE NO MORE KINGS AROUND HERE!
IT'S TRUE, RUTHIE. WE DON'T HAVE KINGS IN THIS COUNTRY.
WHAT ABOUT MURRAY KURTZ?
WHO?
"THE KING OF BIG SCREEN"!
AAAH...
A MERE TITULAR HEAD!
A WHAT?!
DOES MOM KNOW YOU USE THAT KIND OF LANGUAGE?

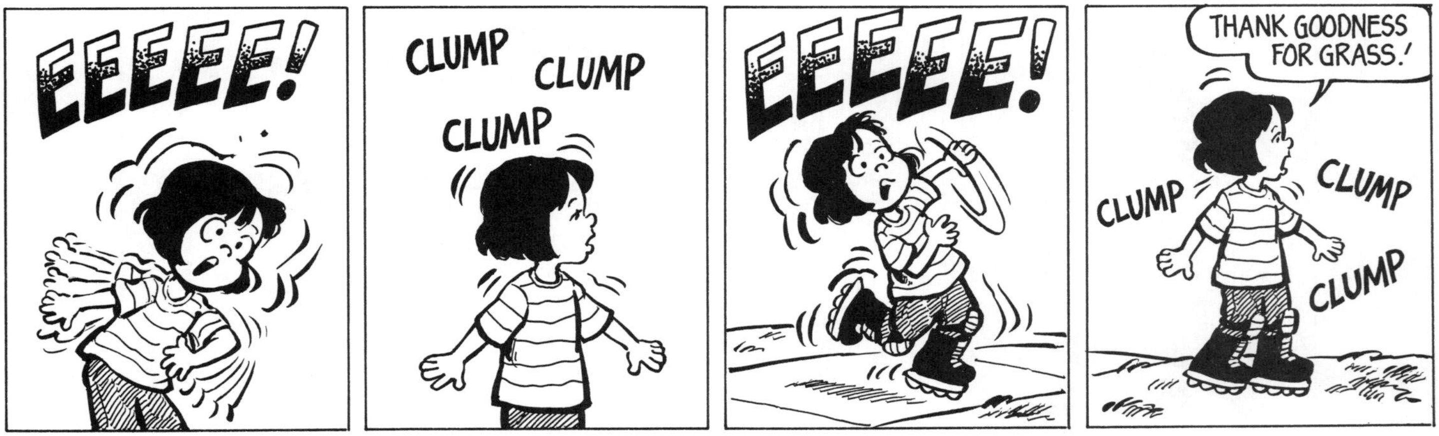
EEEEE!
CLUMP
CLUMP
CLUMP
EEEEE!
THANK GOODNESS FOR GRASS!
CLUMP
CLUMP
CLUMP

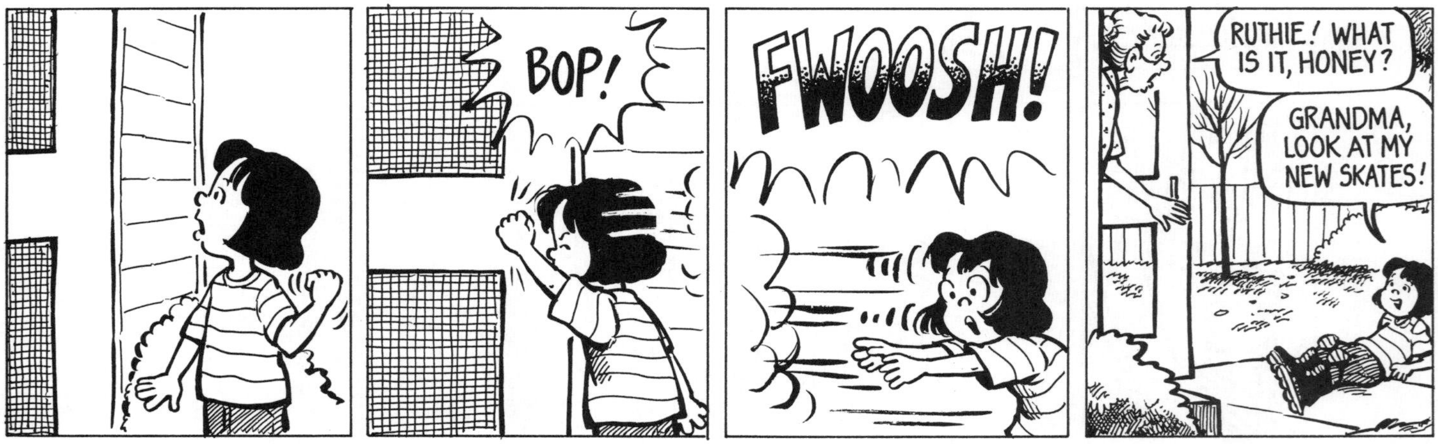
BOP!
FWOOSH!
RUTHIE! WHAT IS IT, HONEY?
GRANDMA, LOOK AT MY NEW SKATES!

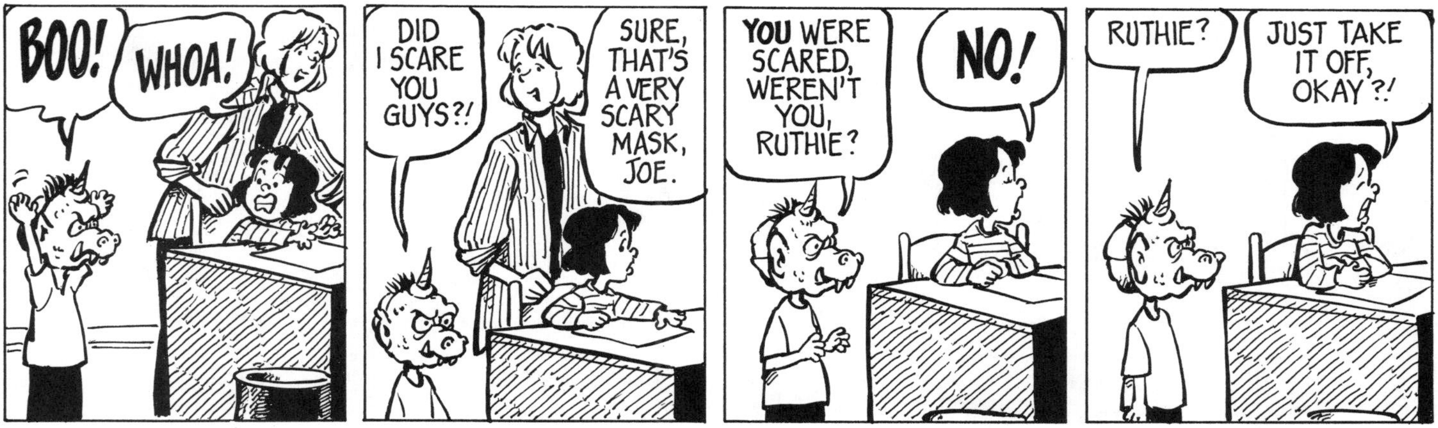
BOO!
WHOA!
DID I SCARE YOU GUYS?!
SURE, THAT'S A VERY SCARY MASK, JOE.
YOU WERE SCARED, WEREN'T YOU, RUTHIE?
NO!
RUTHIE?
JUST TAKE IT OFF, OKAY?!

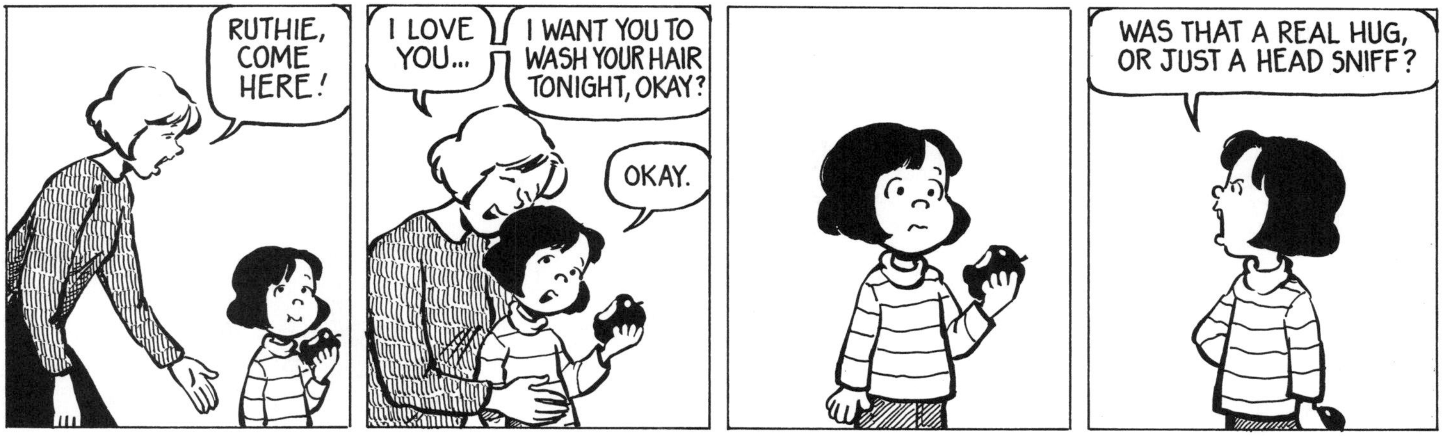
RUTHIE, COME HERE!
I LOVE YOU...
I WANT YOU TO WASH YOUR HAIR TONIGHT, OKAY?
OKAY.
WAS THAT A REAL HUG, OR JUST A HEAD SNIFF?

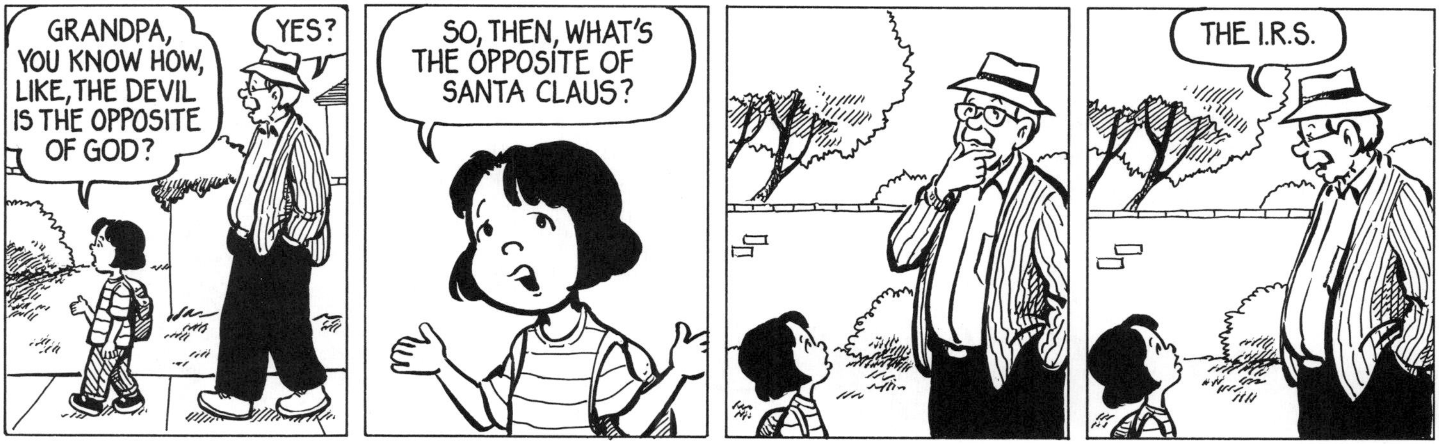
GRANDPA, YOU KNOW HOW, LIKE, THE DEVIL IS THE OPPOSITE OF GOD?
YES?
SO, THEN, WHAT'S THE OPPOSITE OF SANTA CLAUS?
THE I.R.S.

ONE BIG HAPPY

THIS IS PUTTING ME TO SLEEP! I CAN'T KEEP MY EYES OPEN! I'M FALLING A...

HEY, WAIT A MINUTE!

CHICKENS
(A very important REPORT)
by
JOE
(the great)!!!

People have been eating chickens since way back when.

The ancient Romans ate chickens. They also ate peacocks, parrots, larks, + flamingos.

(But that's another whole story)

In this country, chickens didn't become real popular until the 1930's when scientists found a way to make chickens fatter faster.

EAT!

Normally a hen will lay about 20 eggs a month.

But a chicken in New Zealand laid 361 eggs in a year!

Hey, quit shoving! You quit shoving! I'm telling on you! Move over! Boo! Yeah, like I care! Like, where?! Stop that! ..: Tickle, tickle!

Most eggs contain one yolk, but many contain two or more. The record is NINE from a hen in New York state.

The largest chicken on record was from California. Her name was "Weirdo", and she weighed 22 lbs.

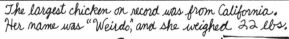

Weirdo killed a rooster and two cats, and beat up a dog and a grown man. Really!

VERY GOOD REPORT, JOE! AND YOU THOUGHT RESEARCHING A TOPIC WAS BORING!

IT WAS BORING, DAD, UNTIL I GOT TO THE KILLER CHICKEN PART!

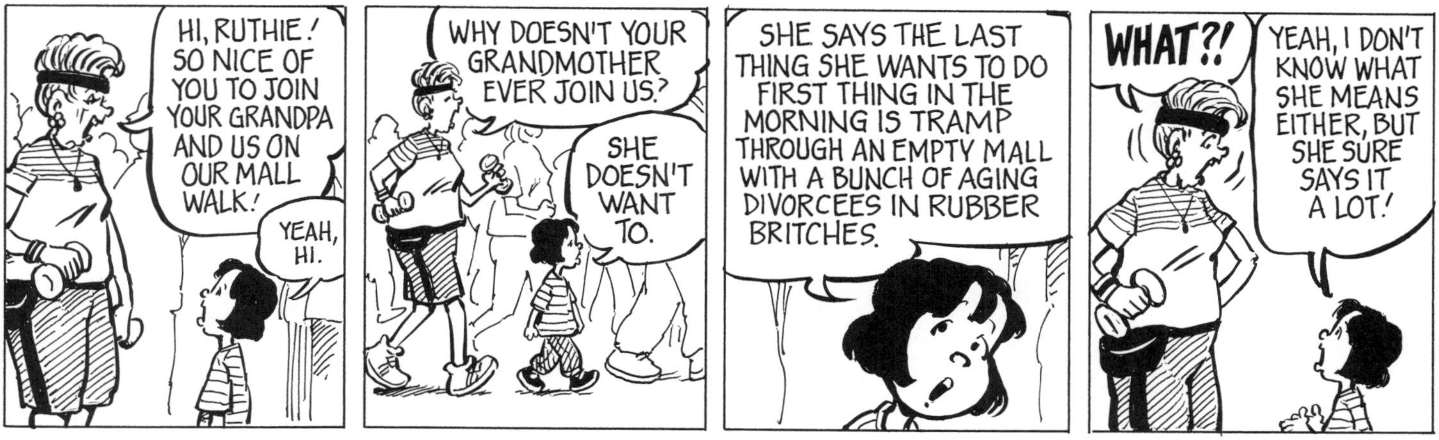
HI, RUTHIE! SO NICE OF YOU TO JOIN YOUR GRANDPA AND US ON OUR MALL WALK!
YEAH, HI.
WHY DOESN'T YOUR GRANDMOTHER EVER JOIN US?
SHE DOESN'T WANT TO.
SHE SAYS THE LAST THING SHE WANTS TO DO FIRST THING IN THE MORNING IS TRAMP THROUGH AN EMPTY MALL WITH A BUNCH OF AGING DIVORCEES IN RUBBER BRITCHES.
WHAT?!
YEAH, I DON'T KNOW WHAT SHE MEANS EITHER, BUT SHE SURE SAYS IT A LOT!

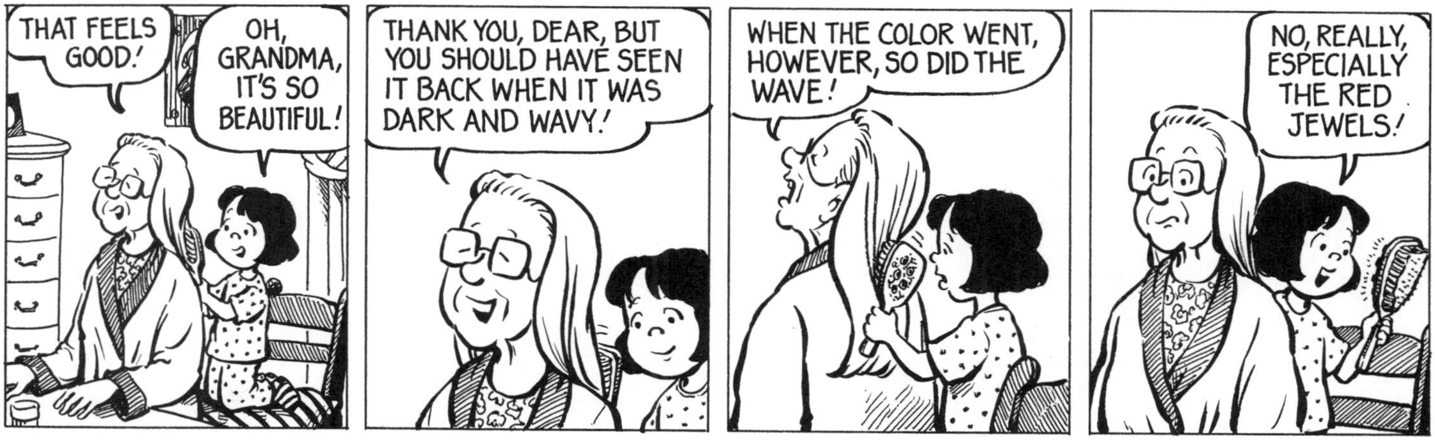
THAT FEELS GOOD!
OH, GRANDMA, IT'S SO BEAUTIFUL!
THANK YOU, DEAR, BUT YOU SHOULD HAVE SEEN IT BACK WHEN IT WAS DARK AND WAVY!
WHEN THE COLOR WENT, HOWEVER, SO DID THE WAVE!
NO, REALLY, ESPECIALLY THE RED JEWELS!

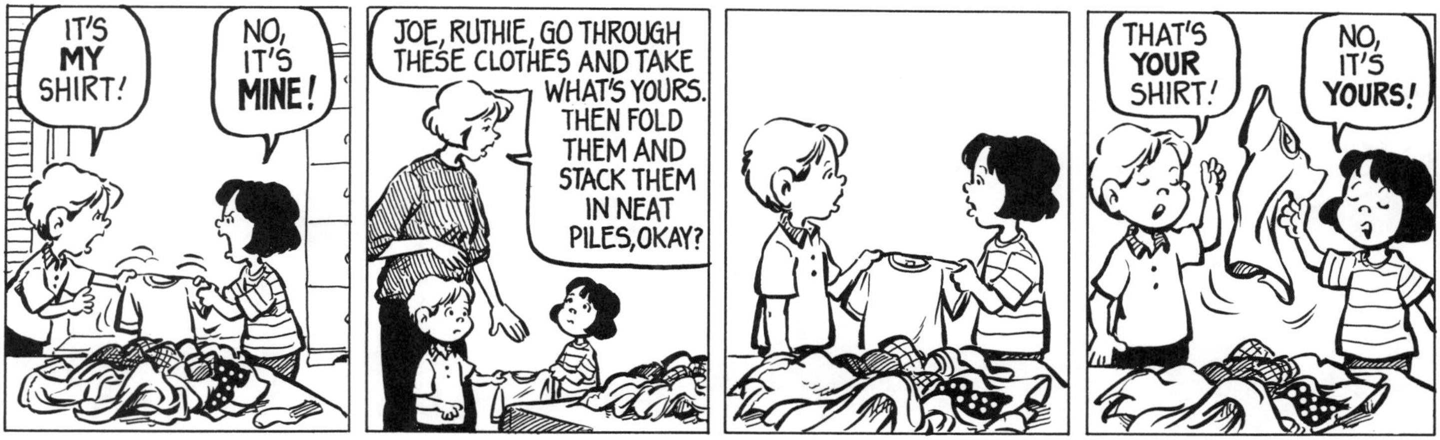
IT'S **MY** SHIRT!
NO, IT'S **MINE**!
JOE, RUTHIE, GO THROUGH THESE CLOTHES AND TAKE WHAT'S YOURS. THEN FOLD THEM AND STACK THEM IN NEAT PILES, OKAY?
THAT'S **YOUR** SHIRT!
NO, IT'S **YOURS**!

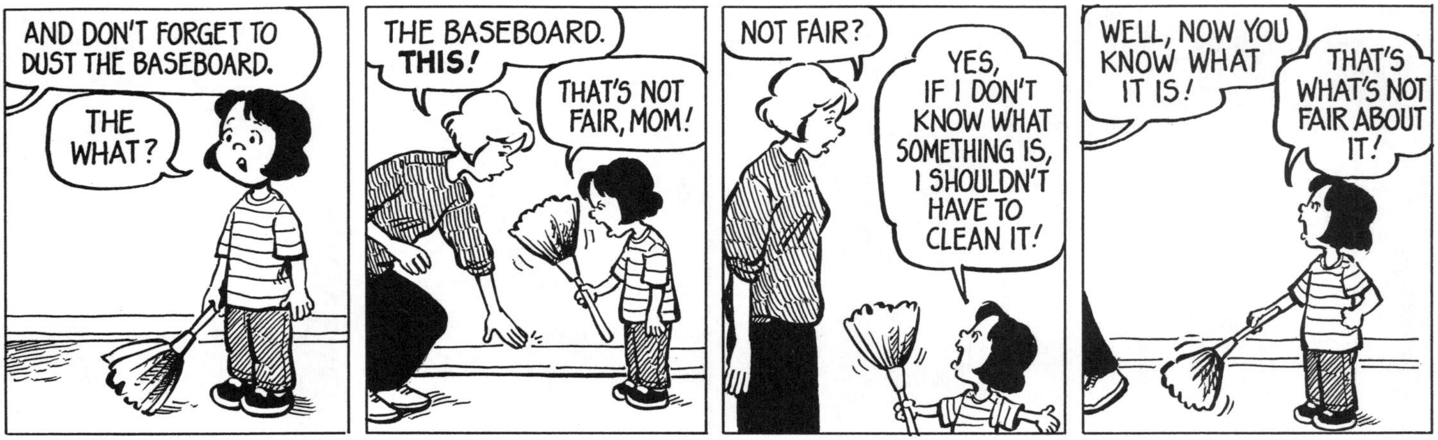
AND DON'T FORGET TO DUST THE BASEBOARD.
THE WHAT?
THE BASEBOARD. **THIS!**
THAT'S NOT FAIR, MOM!
NOT FAIR?
YES, IF I DON'T KNOW WHAT SOMETHING IS, I SHOULDN'T HAVE TO CLEAN IT!
WELL, NOW YOU KNOW WHAT IT IS!
THAT'S WHAT'S NOT FAIR ABOUT IT!

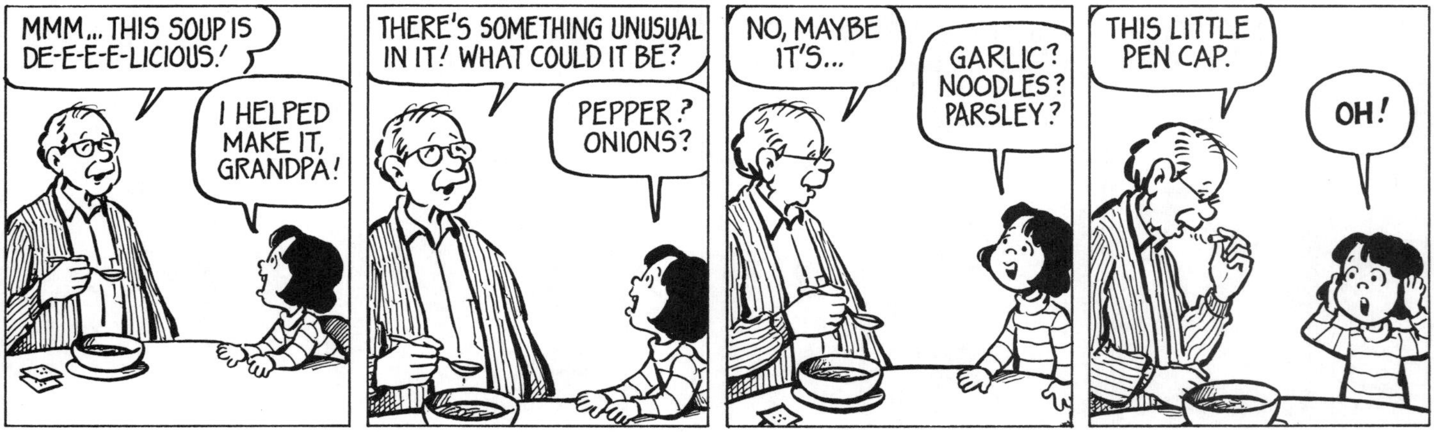
MMM... THIS SOUP IS DE-E-E-E-LICIOUS!
I HELPED MAKE IT, GRANDPA!
THERE'S SOMETHING UNUSUAL IN IT! WHAT COULD IT BE?
PEPPER? ONIONS?
NO, MAYBE IT'S...
GARLIC? NOODLES? PARSLEY?
THIS LITTLE PEN CAP.
OH!

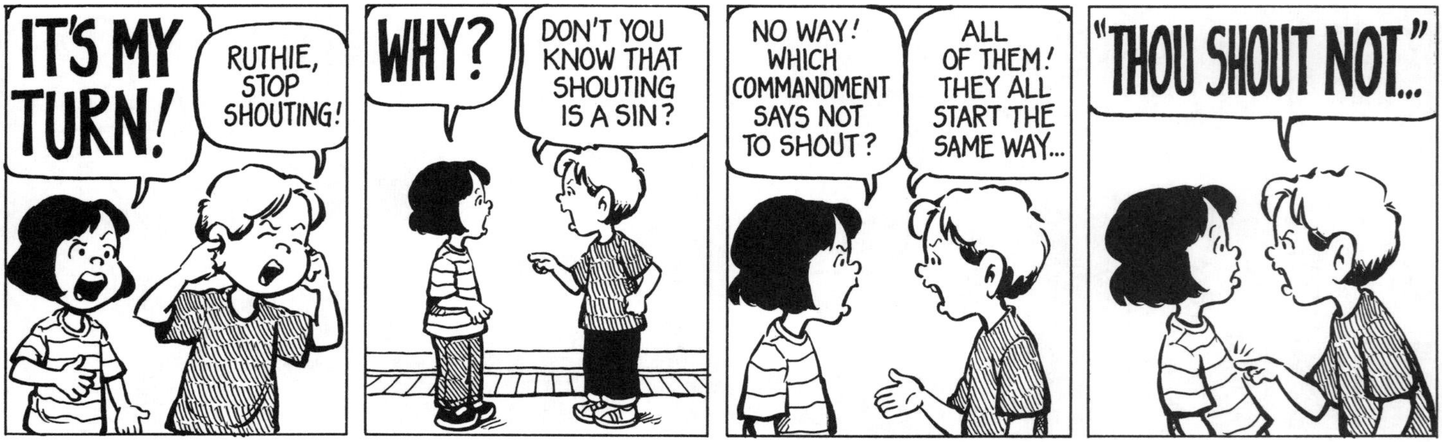
IT'S MY TURN!
RUTHIE, STOP SHOUTING!
WHY?
DON'T YOU KNOW THAT SHOUTING IS A SIN?
NO WAY! WHICH COMMANDMENT SAYS NOT TO SHOUT?
ALL OF THEM! THEY ALL START THE SAME WAY...
"THOU SHOUT NOT"...

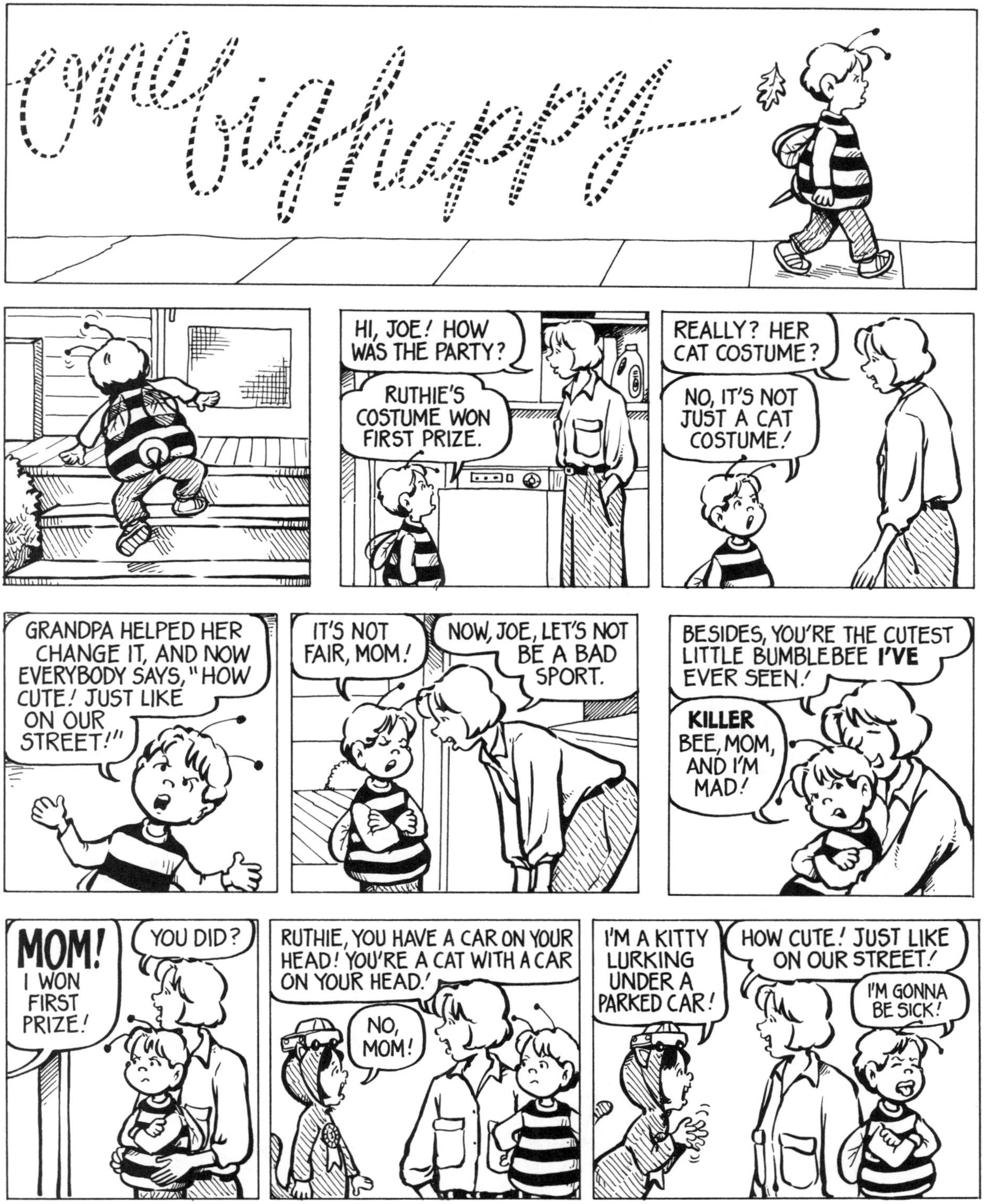
one big happy
HI, JOE! HOW WAS THE PARTY?
RUTHIE'S COSTUME WON FIRST PRIZE.
REALLY? HER CAT COSTUME?
NO, IT'S NOT JUST A CAT COSTUME!
GRANDPA HELPED HER CHANGE IT, AND NOW EVERYBODY SAYS, "HOW CUTE! JUST LIKE ON OUR STREET!"
IT'S NOT FAIR, MOM!
NOW, JOE, LET'S NOT BE A BAD SPORT.
BESIDES, YOU'RE THE CUTEST LITTLE BUMBLEBEE I'VE EVER SEEN!
KILLER BEE, MOM, AND I'M MAD!
MOM! I WON FIRST PRIZE!
YOU DID?
RUTHIE, YOU HAVE A CAR ON YOUR HEAD! YOU'RE A CAT WITH A CAR ON YOUR HEAD!
NO, MOM!
I'M A KITTY LURKING UNDER A PARKED CAR!
HOW CUTE! JUST LIKE ON OUR STREET!
I'M GONNA BE SICK!

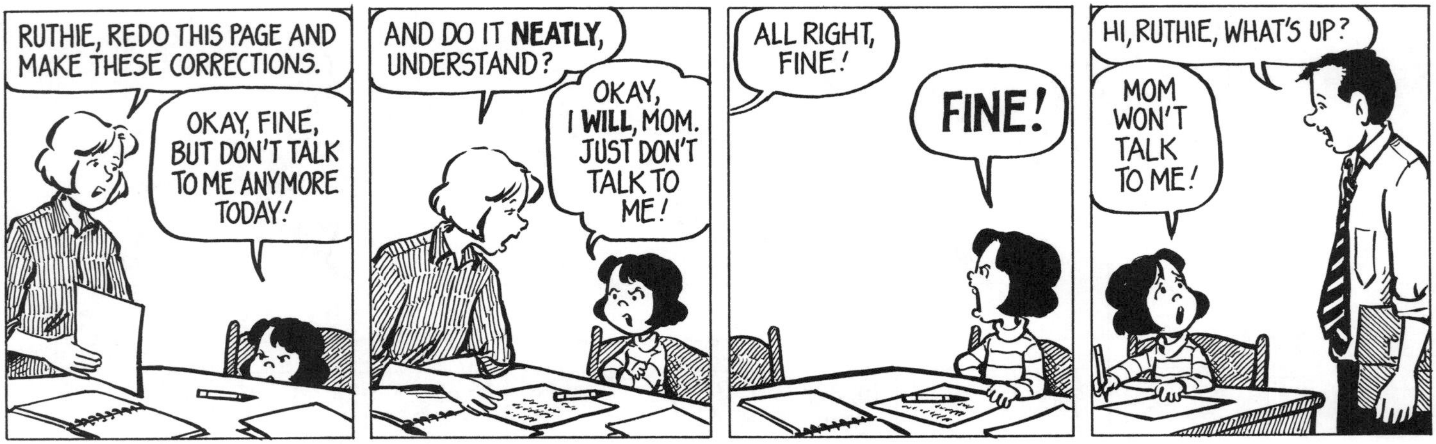
RUTHIE, REDO THIS PAGE AND MAKE THESE CORRECTIONS.
OKAY, FINE, BUT DON'T TALK TO ME ANYMORE TODAY!
AND DO IT **NEATLY**, UNDERSTAND?
OKAY, I **WILL**, MOM. JUST DON'T TALK TO ME!
ALL RIGHT, FINE!
FINE!
HI, RUTHIE, WHAT'S UP?
MOM WON'T TALK TO ME!

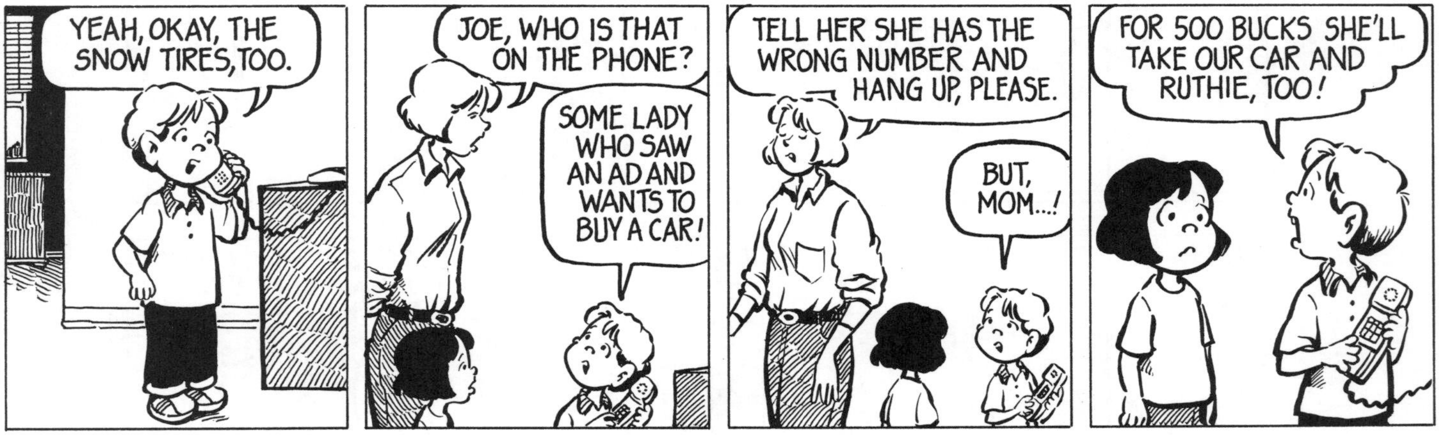
YEAH, OKAY, THE SNOW TIRES, TOO.
JOE, WHO IS THAT ON THE PHONE?
SOME LADY WHO SAW AN AD AND WANTS TO BUY A CAR!
TELL HER SHE HAS THE WRONG NUMBER AND HANG UP, PLEASE.
BUT, MOM...!
FOR 500 BUCKS SHE'LL TAKE OUR CAR AND RUTHIE, TOO!

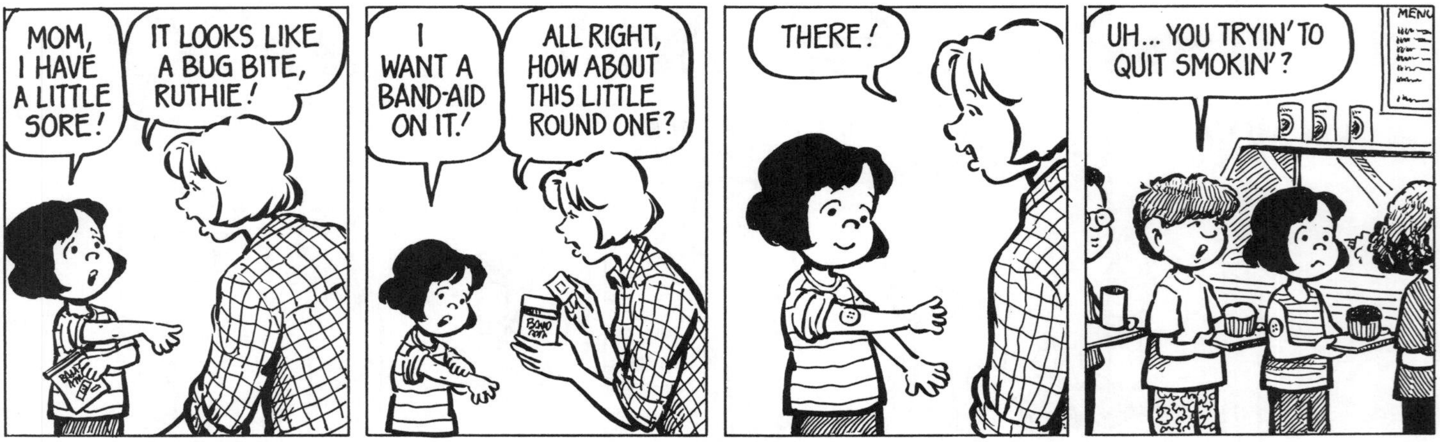
MOM, I HAVE A LITTLE SORE!
IT LOOKS LIKE A BUG BITE, RUTHIE!
I WANT A BAND-AID ON IT!
ALL RIGHT, HOW ABOUT THIS LITTLE ROUND ONE?
THERE!
MENU
UH... YOU TRYIN' TO QUIT SMOKIN'?

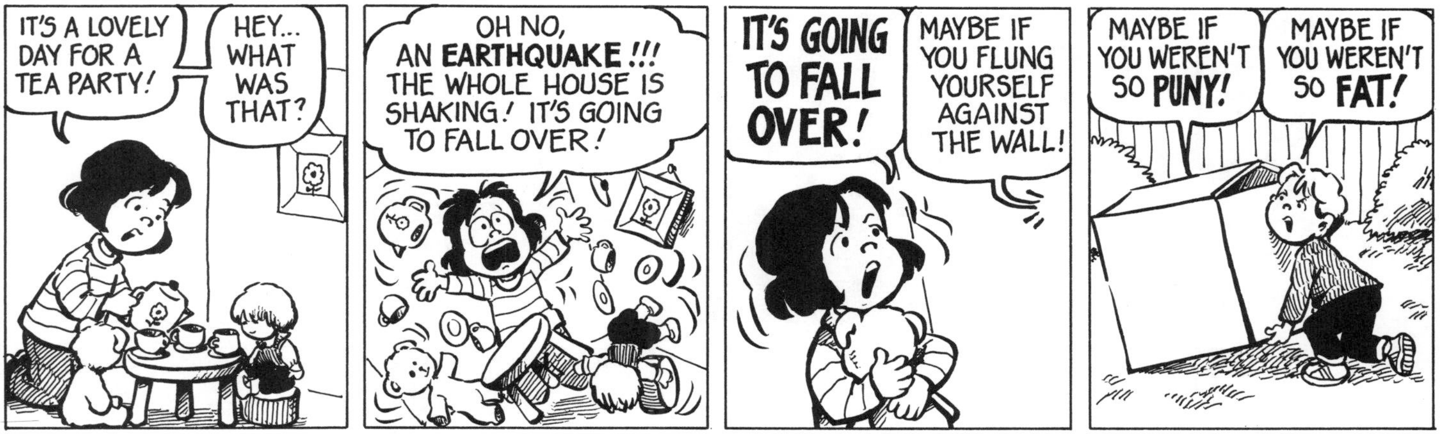
IT'S A LOVELY DAY FOR A TEA PARTY!
HEY... WHAT WAS THAT?
OH NO, AN **EARTHQUAKE**!!! THE WHOLE HOUSE IS SHAKING! IT'S GOING TO FALL OVER!
IT'S GOING TO FALL OVER!
MAYBE IF YOU FLUNG YOURSELF AGAINST THE WALL!
MAYBE IF YOU WEREN'T SO **PUNY!**
MAYBE IF YOU WEREN'T SO **FAT!**

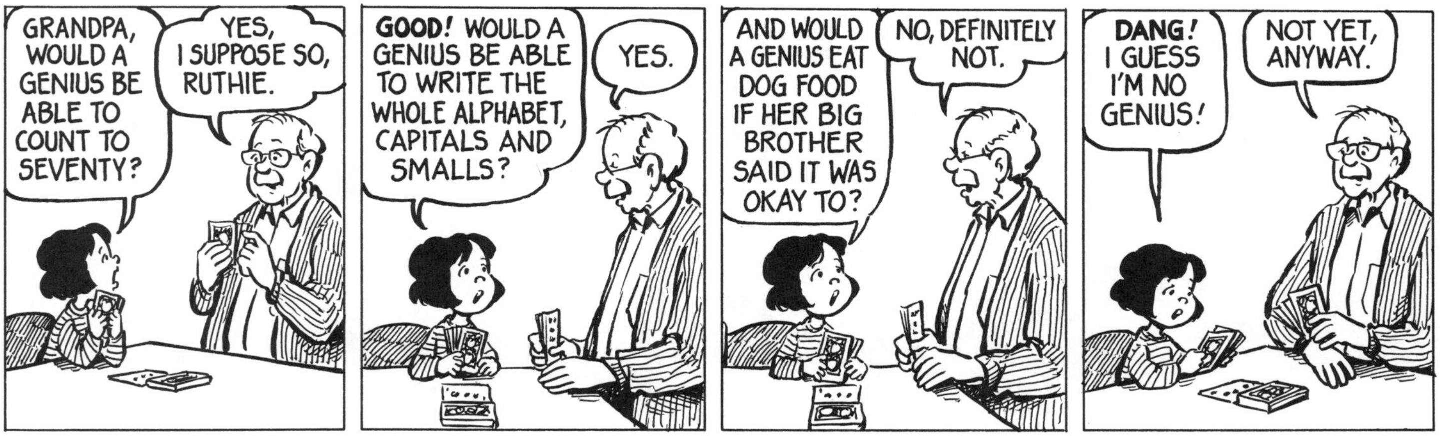
GRANDPA, WOULD A GENIUS BE ABLE TO COUNT TO SEVENTY?
YES, I SUPPOSE SO, RUTHIE.
GOOD! WOULD A GENIUS BE ABLE TO WRITE THE WHOLE ALPHABET, CAPITALS AND SMALLS?
YES.
AND WOULD A GENIUS EAT DOG FOOD IF HER BIG BROTHER SAID IT WAS OKAY TO?
NO, DEFINITELY NOT.
DANG! I GUESS I'M NO GENIUS!
NOT YET, ANYWAY.

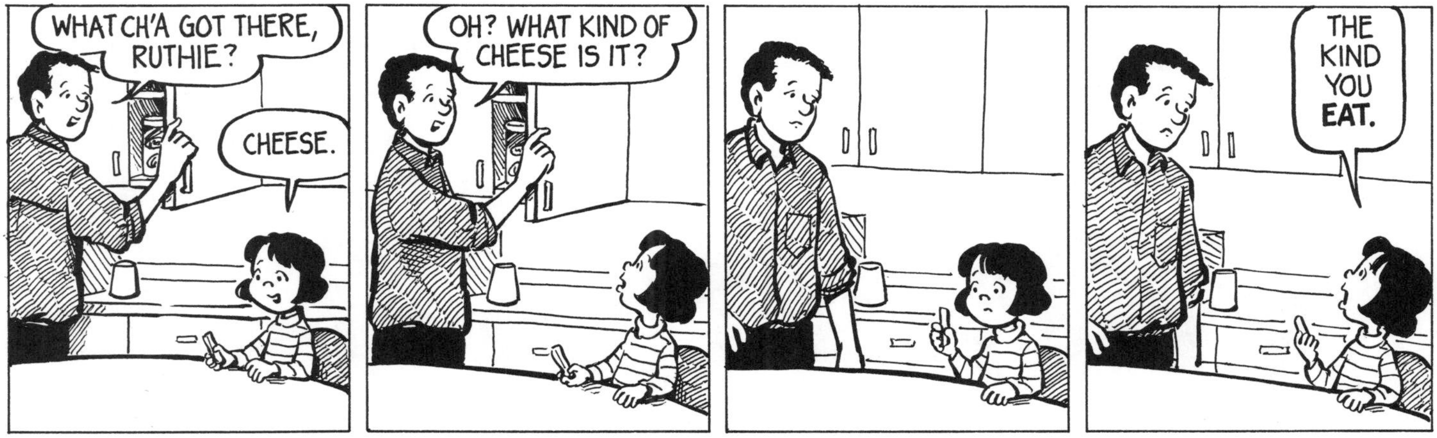
WHATCH'A GOT THERE, RUTHIE?
CHEESE.
OH? WHAT KIND OF CHEESE IS IT?
THE KIND YOU **EAT.**

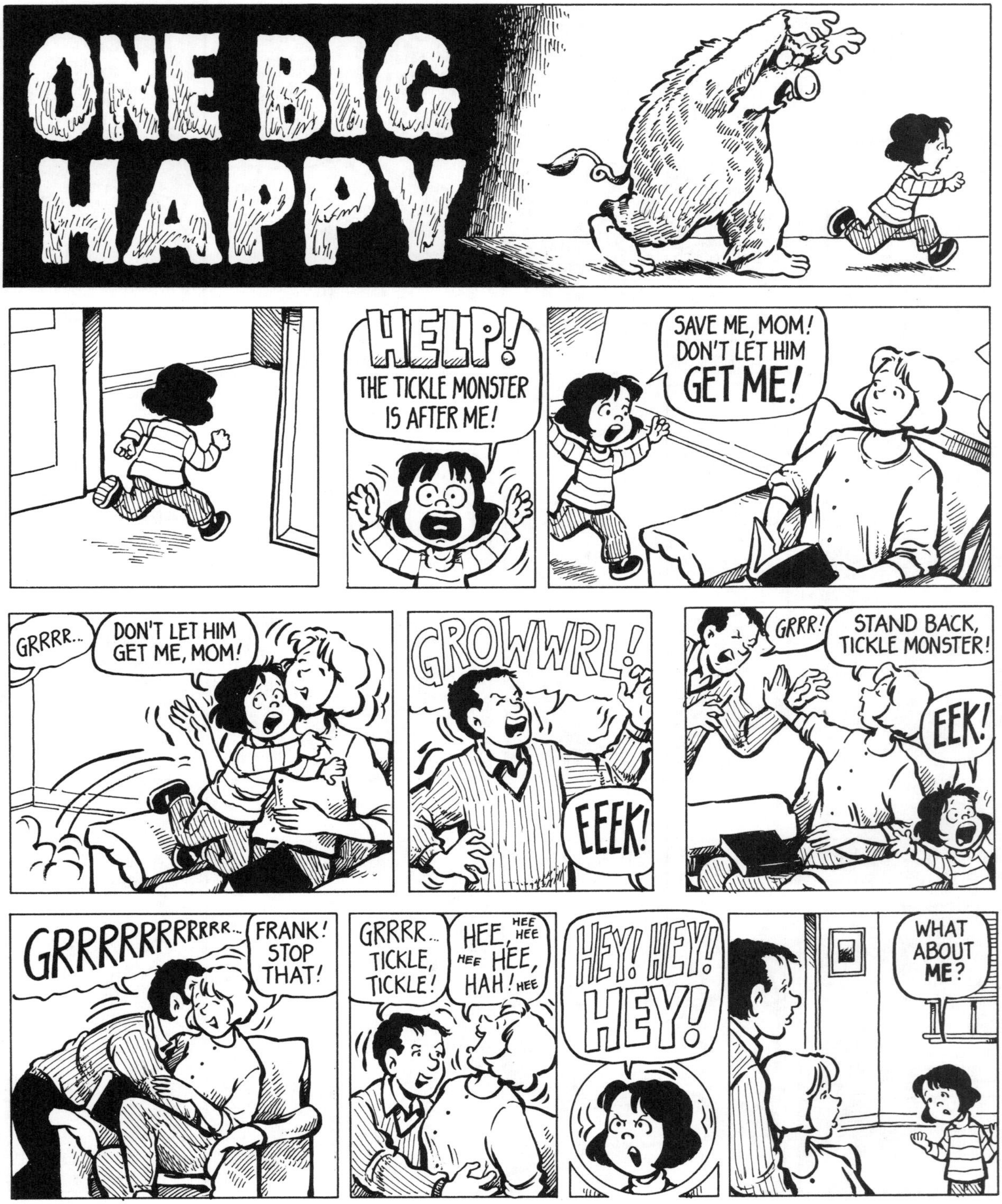
ONE BIG HAPPY
HELP! THE TICKLE MONSTER IS AFTER ME!
SAVE ME, MOM! DON'T LET HIM GET ME!
GRRRR...
DON'T LET HIM GET ME, MOM!
GROWWRL!
EEEK!
GRRR!
STAND BACK, TICKLE MONSTER!
EEK!
GRRRRRRRRRR...
FRANK! STOP THAT!
GRRRR... TICKLE, TICKLE!
HEE, HEE HEE HEE HEE, HAH! HEE
HEY! HEY! HEY!
WHAT ABOUT ME?